Local Legitimacy and International Peacebuilding

Local Legitimacy and International Peacebuilding

Edited by
OLIVER P. RICHMOND AND
ROGER MAC GINTY

EDINBURGH
University Press

Edinburgh University Press is one of the leading university presses in the UK. We publish academic books and journals in our selected subject areas across the humanities and social sciences, combining cutting-edge scholarship with high editorial and production values to produce academic works of lasting importance. For more information visit our website: edinburghuniversitypress.com

Edinburgh University Press Ltd
The Tun – Holyrood Road, 12(2f) Jackson's Entry, Edinburgh EH8 8PJ

First published in hardback by Edinburgh University Press 2020

Typeset in 10/13 Giovanni by
IDSUK (DataConnection) Ltd

A CIP record for this book is available from the British Library

ISBN 978 1 4744 6626 4 (hardback)
ISBN 978 1 4744 6627 1 (paperback)
ISBN 978 1 4744 6628 8 (webready PDF)
ISBN 978 1 4744 6629 5 (epub)

CONTENTS

CONTRIBUTORS

Dr Volker Boege is a peace researcher and historian. Senior Research Fellow at the Toda Peace Institute, Tokyo, Japan; Honorary Research Fellow at the School of Political Science and International Studies (POLSIS) at The University of Queensland, Brisbane, Australia (UQ); Co-director of Peace & Conflict Studies Institute Australia (PaCSIA). Fields of work: post-conflict peacebuilding and state formation; non-Western approaches to conflict transformation; environmental degradation and conflict. Main regional area of expertise: Oceania. Over the last few years, Volker has worked on research projects which address peacebuilding and state formation in Pacific Island Countries and West Africa. He currently is involved in peacebuilding projects in Bougainville (Papua New Guinea) with PaCSIA, and a project on 'climate change and conflict in the Pacific' with the Toda Peace Institute.

Marco Donati works at the United Nations Department for Peace Operations and has served with peacekeeping since 2000, when he joined the UN mission in Kosovo (UNMIK), where he served as a Local Community Officer. He later worked for the UN mission in the Democratic Republic of Congo (MONUC), where he supported humanitarian operations and the implementation of protection of civilians strategies in Ituri and Katanga, before joining the UN Mission in Haiti (MINUSTAH) in 2008, where he worked on strengthening local governance. In June 2011, he joined the Policy and Best Practice Service in New York where he leads the Civil Affairs team providing policy and guidance support to civil affairs components in peacekeeping operations, with a specific focus on improving approaches to address local conflict; support protection of civilians strategies; engage with local communities and actors; enhance situational awareness; and promote effective governance in conflict affected situations.

Dr Allard Duursma is a senior researcher at the Center for Security Studies (CSS) at ETH Zurich. His research interests include international mediation, the termination of proxy conflicts, local peacemaking efforts in the context of peacekeeping missions, and early warning and conflict prevention. He uses both qualitative and quantitative research methods. He completed his PhD in International Relations at the University of Oxford in 2015. His dissertation focused on international mediation efforts in civil wars in Africa. His research has been awarded with several prizes, including the Lord Bryce Prize for best dissertation in International Relations/Comparative Studies in Great Britain.

Dr Lisa Ekman (née Karlborg) has written extensively on local legitimacy with a focus on the relationship between external military forces and local host populations, largely based on fieldwork in the United States and Afghanistan. She is Assistant Professor of War Studies at the Swedish Defence University (Stockholm), and her current research mainly focuses on military professionalism and civil–military relations in the context of international military operations.

Dr Toufic Haddad is the Director of the Kenyon Institute, the Jerusalem-based affiliate of the Council for British Research in the Levant. He is the author of *Palestine Ltd.: Neoliberalism and Nationalism in the Occupied Territories* (2016) and co-editor of *Between the Lines: Readings on Israel, the Palestinians and the US War on Terror* (2007). Haddad holds a PhD in Development Studies from the School for Oriental and African Studies (SOAS) in London.

Dr Sara Hellmüller is Senior Researcher and SNSF PRIMA Project Leader at the Graduate Institute of International and Development Studies. Until 2019, she worked as a senior researcher at swisspeace and as a lecturer at the University of Basel. Moreover, between 2017 and 2019, she was a post-doctoral fellow at the University of Montreal. Sara obtained her PhD in Political Science from the University of Basel. During her doctoral studies, she was a researcher and research coordinator at swisspeace, a visiting scholar at Columbia University in New York, and an affiliated researcher at the University of Bunia in DR Congo. Sara has (co-)led several multi-annual research projects, such as on the role of norms in mediation (2015–2019, funded by the SNSF), civil society inclusion in mediation (2018–2020, funded by the United States Institute of Peace), and most recently on how changing world politics influence UN peace operations (2020–2024, funded by the SNSF). She has also obtained funding for shorter-term projects implemented in cooperation with partners in Lebanon, Norway, Syria, Turkey and the United States. Her research has been published in English, French and German and she is the author of the book *Partners for Peace* (2018). In the framework of her employment at swisspeace, Sara has built up their Syria program (including direct support to the UN office of the Special Envoy for Syria from 2016 to 2018) and has been involved in several peace processes, such as in Guinea-Conakry, Guinea-Bissau, Libya and Darfur.

Dr Stefanie Kappler is Associate Professor in Conflict Resolution and Peacebuilding at Durham University. She holds a PhD from the University of St Andrews and has conducted fieldwork in Bosnia-Herzegovina, South Africa, Cyprus and Northern Ireland, among others. Stefanie is currently working on a range of externally funded projects that investigate the politics of memory in relation to peacebuilding, the cultural heritage of conflict, as well as the role of the arts in peace formation processes. Her recent publications include a co-authored monograph on *Peacebuilding and Spatial Transformation: Peace, Space and Place* (2017) as well as a number of journal articles that investigate the spatial manifestations of memory politics in post-conflict scenarios, the contested nature of 'post-conflict curating' and arts-based approaches to peacebuilding.

Dr Florian Krampe is a Senior Researcher in SIPRI's Climate Change and Risk Programme, specializing in peace and conflict research, environmental and climate security, and international security. His primary academic interest is the foundations of peace and security, especially the processes of building peace after armed conflict. He is currently focusing on climate security and the post-conflict management of natural resources, with a specific interest in the ecological foundations for a socially, economically and politically resilient peace. Dr Krampe is Affiliated Researcher at the Research School for International Water Cooperation at the Department of Peace and Conflict Research at Uppsala University.

Roger Mac Ginty is Professor in the School of Government and International Affairs, and Director of the Durham Global Security Institute, both at Durham University. He edits the journal *Peacebuilding* (with Oliver Richmond) and the Palgrave book series, *Rethinking Political Violence*. He co-directs the Everyday Peace Indicator programme with Pamina Frichow.

Dr Yoshito Nakagawa holds a PhD in Humanitarianism and Conflict Response from the University of Manchester. His research focuses on political order in East Timor and Somaliland. Yoshito has long-standing experience as a development consultant in several war-affected countries across sub-Saharan African and Latin America.

Borja Paladini Adell is peacebuilding and dialogue practitioner. He has worked in Colombia for 15 years contributing to the peace process in different capacities. As UNDP official, he supported local organizations and institutions in developing strategic approaches to peace connecting humanitarian, development, governance and peacebuilding dynamics. As the Kroc Institute for International Peace Studies Director in Colombia, Borja co-designed and led the Barometer Initiative, an engaging and inclusive methodology to monitor and support the verification of the 2016 peace agreement between the Government and the FARC guerrillas. He has also advised the Government of Colombia and different UN agencies in mainstreaming peacebuilding in their policies. A lecturer in Peacebuilding Practice in different Colombian Universities, Borja is at present Practitioner in Residence Fellow at the Peace Research Institute of Oslo.

Oliver P. Richmond is a Research Professor in IR, Peace and Conflict Studies at the University of Manchester, UK. He is also International Professor at Dublin City University. His publications include *Peace Formation and Political Order* (2016), *Failed Statebuilding* (2014), *A Very Short Introduction to Peace* (2014) and *A Post Liberal Peace* (2011). He is editor of the Palgrave book series, *Rethinking Peace and Conflict Studies*, and co-editor of the journal *Peacebuilding*.

James Tanis is a Bougainville peacebuilder. He studied at the Papua New Guinea University of Technology in Lae. His studies were interrupted by the start of the crisis in Bougainville. He returned home and joined the Bougainville Revolutionary Army (BRA). He became a BRA commander and later a minister in the secessionist Bougainville Interim Government (BIG). In the first phase of the peace process, he participated in numerous rounds of high-level negotiations. He was one of the Chief Negotiators of the Bougainville Peace Agreement of August 2001 (BPA). In the following years, he was Vice President of the Bougainville People's Congress. In 2008, he was elected President of the Autonomous Region of Bougainville and held this position until 2010. In 2012–2013 he studied at the Australian National University in Canberra and obtained a Masters in International Affairs. After his return to Bougainville, he continued work in peacebuilding, in recent years as Secretary of the Department of Peace Agreement Implementation of the Autonomous Bougainville Government (ABG). In 2018 and 2019, he was deeply involved in the preparations of the Bougainville independence referendum in advisory positions to the ABG and the government of Papua New Guinea. He has published reports, book chapters and journal articles and participated in several research projects on Bougainville peacebuilding.

Kristina Tschunkert is a PhD researcher at the Humanitarian and Conflict Response Institute at the University of Manchester. Her research focuses on everyday economics of humanitarian aid interventions and its interrelatedness with peace and conflict in the context of host–refugee relations in Lebanon. She has consultancy experience with NGOs in Iraq and Lebanon, predominantly concerning livelihoods and cash and voucher assistance programmes.

Dr Gëzim Visoka is Associate Professor of Peace and Conflict Studies at Dublin City University, Ireland. His research focuses on post-conflict peacebuilding and statebuilding, transitional justice, global governance, foreign policy, and diplomatic recognition. He is Associate Editor of *Peacebuilding* journal and Editor-in-Chief of *The Palgrave Encyclopedia of Peace and Conflict Studies*. Dr Visoka has authored and edited numerous books, including: *The Oxford Handbook of Peacebuilding, Statebuilding, and Peace Formation* (with Oliver P. Richmond, 2020); *Routledge Handbook of State Recognition* (with John Doyle and Edward Newman, 2019); *Normalisation in World Politics* (with Nicolas Lemay-Hébert, 2020), *Acting Like a State: Kosovo and the Everyday Making of Statehood* (2018); *Shaping Peace in Kosovo: The Politics of Peacebuilding and Statehood* (2017). Dr Visoka has published his work in leading outlets, such as: the *Journal of Common Market Studies*, *Review of International Studies*, *Foreign Policy Analysis*, *International Studies Review*, *International Peacekeeping*, *Civil Wars* and *Journal of Human Rights Practice*, among others.

Florian Zollmann is Lecturer in Journalism at Newcastle University. He researches the intersections of modern warfare, propaganda and the media. With Richard Lance Keeble and John Tulloch, he jointly edited *Peace Journalism, War and Conflict Resolution* (2010). His latest book, titled *Media, Propaganda and the Politics of Intervention* (2017) assesses US, UK and German media reporting of human rights violations in Kosovo, Iraq, Libya, Syria and Egypt.

Marco Donati

The Riddle of Legitimacy

I landed my first job with the UN in 2000, working for the UN Mission in Kosovo at a time when UN peacekeeping was still at its peak with 18 field missions spread over four continents. Back then, UN peacekeeping was embarking on some of its most ambitious tasks and my experience in Kosovo was very much at the heart of it: rebuilding functioning institutions for a multi-ethnic society that would share and benefit from those institutions.

While grasping the complexity of the Kosovar conflict and appreciating the thin line that divides just from right and right from wrong, I came to understand that the international legitimacy of the Mission, derived from the firm political will of the international community expressed through the Security Council, was not the only source of justification for our presence. Rather, further legitimacy could be found in the smiles of ordinary people – and most of all the children – raising their fingers in a sign of victory whenever a UN vehicle passed by. It had to be proof that I was on the right side of history!

However, as I spent my time working with the ostracized and isolated Kosovo-Serb communities, that picture became murkier and much harder to comprehend. The legitimate aspirations of the two communities did not add up to the same vision of peace and security. As the mission strived to build a multi-ethnic society in Kosovo, working to develop inclusive institutions and mechanisms, those same ordinary people – and most of all those once-smiling children – started giving dirty looks to passing UN vehicles. Our blue flag no longer made us righteous in the eyes of one community, while the other had always been resentful or mistrustful of the peace we were meant to build. The international legitimacy of the intervention seemed quickly at odds with the notion of state legitimacy (for example, the government in Belgrade versus the authorities in Pristina) and even more so at the community level, with different aspirations, concerns and priorities even within the same ethnical groups.

My first brush with the riddle of legitimacy quickly showed that there was not one single source of legitimacy that could be relied upon to generate consensus among people. What legitimacy meant in the stratosphere of international law and conventions, solidly anchored to the inscrutable notion of sovereign state legitimacy, looked quite different on the surface in the face of political agendas and power struggles. The situation became even more complex and hard to grasp when drilling below the surface, where diverging notions of what legitimate power and authority meant emerged based on social and cultural conventions deeply rooted in history and traditions.

Kosovo may have provided my first opportunity to question what legitimacy and whose legitimacy mattered in the case of UN peace interventions, but it was not the last. As I tried to make sense of reality in Eastern Democratic Republic of Congo, questions multiplied while answers became more elusive: some armed groups could not be simply discarded as bearing no legitimacy whatsoever because there were communities that saw them as the only ones defending their interests. This quickly became attached to the process of marginalization and exclusion of communities whose aspirations were perceived as not being legitimate on the simple ground that they did not belong to the 'polis'.

When I worked in Haiti a few years later, the riddle of legitimacy once again took on different forms: no longer easily discernible on the surface because of the lack of ethnic and tribal distinctions, the Haitian socioeconomic dynamics demonstrated that there is never a shortage of reasons to cast someone out of the 'polis' and to lay a claim to legitimate power and authority. Efforts by the mission and other UN and non-UN actors to 'extend state authority' and promote good and democratic governance all focused very much on institution building, capacity development and mechanisms underpinning an ideal, functioning state. Such efforts did not incorporate a real and deep understanding of what that implied for the people, and their multiple stratified identities, in terms of exercising authority, managing power and resources and trifling with the levers of exclusion and marginalization.

I was first associated with this book in 2016 at a time when my office was finalizing a report reviewing the role of peacekeeping operations in implementing mandates in support of what, in UN jargon, is defined as 'restoration and extension of state authority'. The report echoed what many had been saying for some time in the development arena – most notably with the emphasis placed by the 2011 World Development Report on the importance of legitimate institutions for sustainable peace – but also by the 2015 report by the High-level Independent Panel on Peace Operations (HIPPO) with its strong pitch for more people-centred and field-oriented peace operations. In other words, the conclusions were that the presence of state institutions and even their capacity to deliver services is not sufficient to sustain peace unless these institutions are perceived as legitimate.

The term legitimacy comes with a somewhat reassuring sense that all things done in its name are just and right. The word evokes the idea of a universal agreement on what the undisputed foundations of our society are and therefore an accepted justification of how power and authority are articulated and exerted for the higher common good. Legitimacy should be unequivocal and intuitively simple to interpret but, as this book skilfully articulates, it is entirely the opposite. There is persisting tension between the axiom that peaceful societies require a social contract, which aligns popular expectations with the interests of the elites and international norms, and the reality that the political agenda and the vested interest of both sides are often at odds with each other.

There is ample research suggesting that legitimacy and sustaining peace are intimately connected and that one cannot be pursued independently of the other, but what does that look like in the murkier world of competing forms and sources of legitimacy? What does this mean for the UN peacekeeping operation enjoying the international legitimacy bestowed on them by Security Council resolutions, but then expected to maintain that legitimacy to operate in the host country by maintaining the consent of the host government, who may or may not be pursuing domestic legitimacy according to the democratic canon? Moreover, how can the legitimacy of the intervention be reconciled with that of the solution that is being offered when there are obvious gaps in reaching an inclusive political settlement? How do we reconcile the often-antithetic legitimate aspirations of different communities and groups in order to devise a solution that effectively sustains peace in the long term?

While this book does not have all the answers, it does raise plenty of good questions and formulates hypotheses that are helpful in navigating the meanders of what the implications of using the notion of legitimacy to sustain peace entail. For instance, the idea that legitimacy cannot be framed only as a political construct and that socio-cultural, identity-related and economic issues equally contribute to shape different understandings and contexts for what legitimacy is about is a useful way of enlarging our perspective and our analytical imperatives.

The call for improved analysis, including from an anthropological perspective, in peacekeeping contexts has existed for some time, but resource scarcity and certain rigidity within the system to accept new ways of doing business have prevented this from being mainstreamed through analysis and planning processes. Nevertheless, a new emphasis on people-centred approaches and community engagement has helped nuance the understanding UN peacekeeping missions have of what is required and who needs to be involved to bring the peace process home, so to speak, including through the lenses of perceived legitimacy.

Interesting prospects also stem from the hypothesized fallacy of there being one possible single system aligning international, state and local-level strands of legitimacy which would then require all efforts to focus on achieving this convergence. Accepting instead the fluidity offered by multiple levels of legitimacy, which can overlap but can also be irrevocably juxtaposed, allows to avoid the risk of putting all of your eggs in one basket. Instead of focusing on a static end-state characterized by a somewhat idealized reconciliation of intents around a 'new' social contract, there could be a stronger emphasis on dynamics solutions and a variable-geometry approach to sustaining peace that takes stock of the different kinds of legitimacy focusing on what offers the smaller risk of relapse into conflict in a specific given context. It would not even be a question of cynically seeking a 'legitimate enough' quantum, but rather finding ways of reducing the friction between different kinds of legitimacy that can foster synergy.

This, in turn, raises questions about whether there is any room in the realm of international politics for an approach that, instead of focusing its efforts on sustaining peace by 'stabilization' and institution-building, would privilege notions of 'state formation' that prioritize political processes that will not necessarily result in reconciling these different levels and sources of legitimacy, but could possibly create space for a 'peaceful resolution' of their differences and allows viable hybrid formulas where these may be the best answer to local contexts and realities. If all of this sounds confusing, it's because it is.

It feels as if, having navigated the troubled seas of human societies and conflict, we now realize the compass we were using is not necessarily leading to the magnetic north and that there is instead a multiplicity of magnetic poles with no definite destination ahead, but rather a range of options. This may not simplify the navigation but contributes to clarify its parameters and revisiting expectations: there is a method in this madness if one can only contemplate the multiple, often contradictory, layers, perspectives and contexts that determine what the notion of legitimacy can contribute to efforts of sustaining peace and addressing conflicts.

It has been said that the United Nations was not created in order to bring us to heaven, but to save us from hell. SG Dag Hammarskjold (1954)

Marco Donati, Civil Affairs Officer, UN-DPO, New York

Legitimacy and Peace in the Age of Intervention

Oliver P. Richmond and Roger Mac Ginty

Context and Introduction

Political theorists and philosophers have long been interested in the question of the legitimacy of political authority, where it comes from and how it may be maintained or improved, from both instrumental and ethical perspectives.[1,2] Normally, such debates were focused upon the state and the fulcrum of power, legitimacy and authority. They then extended to the development of international institutions and law to cement the architectures of legitimacy at the state level.

Legitimacy within the state is generally taken to refer to the justification for rule, which has normative and sociological dimensions, the first pointing to the importance of standards and, the second, to beliefs.[3] In an ideal situation, standards and beliefs are mutually reinforcing and populations consent to those who claim authority over them. At the international level, legitimacy rests on the general consent of states, international law and the capacity of any agreement, organisation or treaty to deliver its objectives.[4] Both levels are concerned with inducing a 'constitutional moment' at national and international levels (the latter emerging through the UN system, different types of international law, and regional organisations such as the European Union or, alternatively, African Union). Security actors are closely connected to this evolution, such as NATO, along with the development of supranational forms of foreign policy. Connecting both perspectives has long been thought to represent a virtuous circle for an otherwise opaque and imprecise concept.[5] Likewise, policymakers and scholars from around the world have recently become more interested in these matters, especially in the light of various interventions in the post-Cold War world, to bring about peace, development, and to build better states.

However, legitimacy is far from being vague or imprecise and it can be disaggregated across scales and issues with some precision according to normative conceptions of historical, distributive, and social justice in and between societies. Contradictions creep in when these various scales are connected into a united whole at state level, or a universal framework at international level, distorted by power relations. This radically re-orients traditional conceptions of state legitimacy and state–society relations in the mould of Hobbes, Rousseau or Locke, or efficiency, or even international law. It points to the very significant limitations of a nationalist, bureau-cratic or technocratic focus on efficiency or power as the basis for legiti-macy, which overlooks both norms and social consensus and their relation to leadership in a social contract. Yet, much of the evidence shows that, in the short to medium term, power-relations define the course of conflict, and powerful third parties determine the course of peace; both often run counter to the claims of progressive civil society actors, instead drawing on ethno-nationalist, tribal, religious, or populist loyalties, or in the case of external actors, seeing their normative standards tempered by geopolitics, the lack of resources and political will.

The UN's Capstone Doctrine[6] pointed to how legitimacy for a peace operation should be present in the eyes of local populations if such a mis-sion is to succeed and various documents, culminating in the Sustainable Development Goals of 2015 have built upon this assumption. The EU, OECD-DAC donors, the IFIs and, to a point, the US and UK militaries have followed suit. It has made the complex peace operations of the 1990s, or the later state and nation-building operations, very hard to repeat, however, as can be seen in the cases of Syria and Libya. How can one know the mind of a conflict-affected subject? How can a democratic decision be arrived at before such institutions exist, or where conflict, the state, and armed groups deny political freedom? This is especially the case in complex intervention sites like Afghanistan and Libya where the state is a highly artificial con-fection with weak centrifugal forces. Furthermore, when one looks at the situations in Timor Leste, Kosovo, or Bosnia, for example, one can see the complexities of legitimacy and the long-term effect of building states which to various degrees do not or cannot relate to the full range of local systems of legitimate authority. Sections of society are excluded from peace, power structures are not fully mitigated, and the progressive aspects of liberal peacebuilding are blocked to varying degrees. Yet, connecting legitimacy to a mission's success is seen by some as too ambitious for both legitimacy and the objectives of any peace intervention, because it connects state–soci-ety relations to international norms and law. This is seen as either a practi-cal or a normative over-extension, and possibly both.

'Stabilisation' is the latest policy buzzword to describe intervention in conflict environments predicated on not leading to 'mission creep' or risking a clash of values, raising fresh questions about legitimacy for intervention and for what type of state or peace intervention aims to create.[7] A common view is that external actors can only ever have limited legitimacy, drawn mainly from international institutions and law, which is distant. Some legitimacy can be drawn from a peace agreement, especially if that agreement has democratic validation, and some may be drawn from international law and human rights, but there may be complex tensions with local identities, interests, and norms, which obscure any agreement. This is so even if they are saving lives and building a state, and so they should restrict themselves to limited security goals and public goods, because only local systems of legitimacy can produce viable government, according to others. Thus, legitimacy is an essentially contested concept, so far only narrowly understood mainly in terms of authoritarian or democratic political authority inside a state, resting on identity, power and effectiveness, and international law and power at the international level, resting on the various conventions and UN Charter, in line with economic and military hegemony.[8] Despite academic work on readily apparent hybrid political orders, much of the policy world seems coy on judging where precisely legitimacy might lie on a democratic–authoritarian axis. Enforcement has been weak at the domestic level, meaning that intervention has often collaborated with authoritarian forms of political authority (as in Cambodia), and even weaker at the international level, where rights, justice and welfare (the functions of the liberal state) are rarely upheld. This means that the legitimate authority of international actors is often weaker than national and local leaders, and yet the latter are often involved in the conflict itself (as was clear after the Dayton Agreement in Bosnia and Herzegovina (BiH)).

Consequently, recent academic and policy calls have been made for a clearer understanding of the way in which peace processes are legitimated in society, their relationship with state level and international processes, how local ownership and participation can be promoted, and how the structural causes of violence can be internally mitigated.[9] There has also been an interrogation, in some academic debates at least, of the temporalities of peace, conflict and intervention. Linear understandings of time that may seek to identify 'moments' in which authority is legitimised deserve unpacking to take account of complex temporalities and dynamics. This Introduction engages with the relationships that are built up during peace-building processes in terms of experiences so far. It takes stock of the emerging empirical evidence about local peace formation praxes in the context of scalar approaches to power-sharing, institutional building, rule of law programming, security reforms, and development and the state level, and its tensions with international legitimacy and relational political authority. It explores the development of legitimate institutions and reforms designed to engage with the causal factors of conflict in situ, drawing on a wide range of networks in order maximise the legitimate authority of the process. Finally, it identifies the obstacles common to projects from local to global and discusses the types of legitimate political authority that appear to exist, as well as their characteristics.

First, the Introduction provides a short theoretical review on the classical problem of legitimate authority across a range of disciplines. It then combines this with an institutional and local-focused interrogation of peace processes (for example, peacebuilding and peace formation) in order to differentiate the inclusive and trans-scalar legitimacy these produce as opposed to nationalist, sectarian, or power/profit driven versions. This is designed to produce an enhanced understanding of the complex tensions in the peacebuilding field through an inter-regional dialogue aimed at critically evaluating a range of comparative cases. This provides the basis for a preliminary but global dialogue between social claims, political interests, law and institutions, and global actors encompassed by a peace process. This may require a kind of 'listening project'[10] in order to understand the complexities of legitimate political authority and its formation. The methods and knowledge are available to both interrogate our existing forms of legitimacy and the new possibilities. This all points to multiple forms of legitimate authority and the existence of complex relationality, which need to be taken into account in modern peace settlements.

Central Issues

Having introduced the often contested and multi-scalar issues at play, the central issues in the relationship between classical notions of peace and legitimacy are identified as:

1. how might legitimate authority be amassed, maintained and exercised to create security and peace for development in view of people's often oppositional claims, and to build a state;

2. how is legitimacy locally perceived and constructed among different groups in society (state formation versus peace formation groups), and with what differences to international norms, and

3. most controversially, when (if ever), and how can external models, levels of coercion or even interventionary force be used legitimately for these goals according to local perspectives?

4. how can local and state legitimacy build or support global legitimacy?

This points to complex dynamics of horizontal and vertical forms of legitimacy, across society, and from international to local scales, in normative, institutional, and efficiency frameworks. It also points to a fifth possibility:

5. Multiple forms of legitimate political authority exist in peace processes, spanning local, regional and global scales, pointing to the interconnectivity of the dynamics of war and the need for a rethinking of the nature of contemporary peaceful political order. Relationality, affectivity, networks, hybrid and complex systems of legitimate political authority need to be considered.

Exploring these questions may help us understand why the international liberal peacebuilding paradigm has been increasingly questioned on theoretical grounds and on the basis of empirical research during the unsettled period since the end of the Cold War. It might also help us understand why foregrounding systems of local legitimacy also points to entrenched and obstructive power structures, which tend to block equality, relationality and sustainability. Indeed, these power structures are strengthened by inequality and uncertainty. This carries us along a traditional path towards international law, organisations and trusteeship as the unified solution, which has also shown itself to be very unsatisfactory in the search for more positive forms of peace in the context of real world alterity, beyond liberal forms of quasi-trusteeship, and Eurocentric notions of limited human rights. There is a sense in the contemporary era that many international actors who were convinced of the righteousness of their roadmap to political legitimacy in sites of intervention are now at a loss to rationalise intervention. There has been a noticeable shift from the quite extensive intellectual scaffolding used to justify international intervention in the late 1990s and early 2000s to very shallow forms of legitimisation. Intervention to lead to democracy and human rights has largely been replaced by minimal narrations of the legitimacy of intervention and favoured regimes using the language of security and stabilisation.

One of the main areas of contestation regards the nature of relationships between those who 'make' peace and those on whose behalf peace is being made. This relational dynamic points to the problem of how top-down and Weberian notions of legitimacy carried forward by intervention tend to be in conflict with bottom-up, Foucauldian versions, often focused upon autonomy and self-determination, sometimes cosmopolitan versions of these. External and local views understand political legitimacy differently, though rights, democracy, and prosperity can be taken as a generally agreed shorthand. The devil is in the detail however: who has rights, which rights, where is the middle ground for democratic institutions and who controls the resources? Are systems of domination and self-interest, legitimate authority, international law, a modern state, or localised social practices and conventions the basis for legitimacy in conflict-affected environments? What do the networked, scalar, and hybrid nature of aspects of contemporary international relations (IR) do to political authority, and what does this mean for peace settlements?

In this latter context, who has the moral right to govern in such states (and how to connect this right with actual material capacity): international actors, political elites, or societal actors? And how to bridge their many differences in order to enable coherent and stable governance? In cases of war endings, it might be that international actors need to govern in a system of trusteeship, at least briefly, as in Afghanistan, Iraq, Bosnia, Kosovo or Timor Leste, whereas in cases of low level violence, or the implementation of peace agreements, or for development purposes, national elites may rule through power-sharing deals. Where this is difficult local people often organise their own systems of government where they can, as most recently in Syria, where in some areas local governance is the only way of organising facilities and some security in the absence of a widely accepted form of state authority.[11] Local governance is often informally connected to global networks, however.

The legitimacy of governance in either set of local or external cases is clearly connected to its norms, identity, historical resonance, and effectiveness, and yet little research has been carried out on how legitimacy is shifting in recent times. Nevertheless, legitimate political authority is needed for any peace process to work, and the evidence indicates that UN authority is short-term and only sporadically effective, state level power-sharing authority is longer term, powerful but polarising and potentially autocratic, and local authority tends to be networked, subterranean and lack significant agency, and widely vary between anachronistic and progressive positions on peace and order.

The question of who governs legitimately in contemporary IR points to the need to disaggregate scales and networks of authority, and the different normative aspects of rights and duties that exist in societies, the state, and at the international level. Political legitimacy is not solely determined by a neat hierarchy of institutions, each governing the one beneath it. This has always been an imaginary, yet it has been an imaginary with considerable traction. This disaggregation highlights a disjuncture regarding local, state and international spaces and systems, international norms and human rights, and the instrumental and procedural legitimacy that peacekeeping and peacebuilding strategies enjoy,[12] which tend to be fixed through states. It also highlights their limited and fleeting nature. It also points to tensions between, on one level, international actors and national elites, and, on another level, between national elites and sub-national communities over the nature of the state and its legitimate authority and the increasing levels of critical and mobile agency citizens can deploy. Indeed, it may point to the need for new – rather than old – forms of polity to emerge through peace processes and peacebuilding. Social practices, shared goals, institutions and political, military and economic power remain in an uncomfortable relationship in conflict-affected societies, from the Pacific to Sub-Saharan Africa, from the Middle East and Timor Leste to Kosovo. There has been an inevitable trade-off between the legitimacy and the effectiveness of peace-building and statebuilding rather than a close and intimate relationship between legitimacy and capacity. The broad legitimacy of peacebuilding strategies and institutions, however, are an essential precondition of a sus-tainable peace. It has long been recognised that there is probably a causal link between the political claims of the subaltern and society, legitimacy and good government, which is increasingly linked to the ability of global governance in political or economic form to give rise to global justice (in distributive and historical terms).

The project of the twentieth century was to extend some sort of political and social contract from the subaltern to the international, and back again. This has not yet failed, but it looks unlikely to succeed in the medium term at least. Meanwhile, the nature of politics across local to international scales is changing, meaning peace processes and peacebuilding aimed at legiti-macy needs to adapt also. Mobility, scale jumping, expanded rights claims, the blurring of consensus and types of political legitimacy and authority, as well as the rise of digital technologies, have become very significant. Crucial in all of this has been the move away from this imaginary of a neat hier-archy of institutions, with the upper-most institutions receiving legitimacy and fealty from the bottom-most. Instead, it is more accurate to conceive of a messy assemblage of claims to legitimacy and the *de facto* exercise of legitimate authority.

Different Approaches to Legitimacy

The experience of the last twenty-five years indicates that, contrary to Seymour Lipset's standard argument, state performance for immobile and territorialised national citizens is far from the only source of political legitimacy.[13] This has been reinforced by recent examples of populism and anti-incumbency that often challenges narratives favoured by established elites. In conflict-affected societies, as well as in settled states, many of these assumptions have now broken down. Such argumentation may have made sense in an era of centralised, industrial scale authority, especially when compared to the previous, customary, religious and small-scale order. Nor can legitimacy be said to emanate fully from the monopoly of the use of force, from leadership, law, expertise or dominant norms in the international system or state.[14] Neither can it be merely drawn from communitarian and localised political community and its identity or religious institutions. Of course, all of these factors are crucial, but empirical evidence suggests the contemporary formation of legitimacy is very complex because it is also both historical and social. It is also multiple, and networked, mobile, normally not aligned and so contains contradictions when viewed in the round rather than merely from the top-down.

Yet, legitimacy includes the acknowledgement of local agency in the establishment of peace, whether it is traditionalist, nationalist or progressive; and local ownership of the peace process and its outcomes. Indeed, the 'local turn' in peacebuilding has perhaps been one of the most significant trends in peace implementation over the past decade and a half, a trend reinforced by the localisation agenda of the SDGs. This means that it also emanates from historical political community and its consent building practices (including various forms of oppositional and consensual and democratic governance), which is often a localised, but overlapping, affair. It also points to the importance of equality and justice. It also relates to knowledge and rights claims, however, and access to networks, mobility and new technologies.

In classical liberal thinking such political community validates state and international forms of legitimacy, producing government, governance and, hence, peaceful order within these limits. This is very much an 'analogue' framework of industrial and state-centric modernity, determined by power, citizen-state or civil-society, state, and international contracts and relationality. Peace in this view is largely a trickle-down concept. National and international elites construct a peace that the subnational and local can benefit from. In a sense, the munificence of peace trickles down from a peace accord, constitution and the stability brought about by statebuilding. This top-down and bottom-up framework for political order has now been surpassed in many ways.

We argue that legitimacy emerges through entanglements in transnational, transversal and trans-scalar networks, rather than merely engaged in horizontal or vertical power-relations. Such social and politically networked forms of legitimate authority cannot be captured in Weberian categories, nor are they solely derived from process or efficiency.[15] Perhaps they cannot be aligned. They are likely to be messy, dynamic and difficult for any single discipline or research methodology to capture with accuracy. Crucial to our understanding of the complexity of legitimacy is the need to free ourselves from the notion of legitimacy as purely a political construct. It has socio-cultural, identity-related and economic sources as well. It does not necessarily regard the institutions of the state as having very much to do with legitimacy in this broader sense. It is not difficult to conceive of areas in conflict-affected areas in which the state is barely, if at all, present. In such cases, the natural unit of authority may be the family, kin-group or another sub-state grouping that may have transnational dimensions. Affiliation to such a group might be influenced by ethnic group or some other identity marker that is naturalised and expected. It is worth considering how in such circumstances the state, or an intervening coalition of states, might be considered alien – especially if they have no track record of providing security or other public goods. This vantage point offers a direct challenge to IR and other statist perspectives: how can such perspectives take seriously the familial and immaterial? It is not clear, as of yet, that IR is prepared for such sociological perspectives.

In the orthodox view, legitimacy includes legality at national and international levels, as well as various forms of the social contract in which the state plays a facilitative or negative role as the provider of security and public goods, effective and efficient. However, local legitimacy also connects to social and subjective dynamics such as belief systems, norms and identity, which help shape institutions, customs and law. They may be predicated on equality or a stable system of stratification. Such institutions must thus be flexible or fluid even, rather than eternally motionless, given the constant shift in conditions. This more comprehensive and accurate perspective on legitimacy modifies the usual Weberian understandings of traditional and customary societal sources of authority, charisma of leaders or of rational-legal understandings within the context of the modern state, which may be evaluated according to its procedural and effective qualities.

This raises the long-standing concern about how far we can generate a peaceful social contract within existing frameworks of political and economic institutions and approaches of fixed rather than networked and mobile categories? If power-relations over legitimate authority are multi-dimensional, then any progressive contract that outlaws violence and deals with justice broadly defined has to reflect the reality of modern day political and everyday life on local, state, and global stages, simultaneously. It must be multiple, local, transversal and transnational, allowing for scale jumping in order to maintain justice and accountability: this is perhaps the basis for a system of checks and balances for a global and digital age, where it is becoming clear that the expansion of rights that gained momentum under liberal peacebuilding points toward conceptions of peace related to global justice (incorporating distributive, historical, gender and environmental elements).

Thus, legitimacy emanating from local, state and international sites tends not to be aligned in the way that liberal peace thinking imagines. Neither does it align with geopolitical assumptions about the centrality of power. This is a core problem for UN peacekeeping and peacebuilding, which expects Security Council and Charter authorisation to eventually align with host states and local societies, or at least with global power and norms.[16] This points to the need to think about fluid and networked forms of legitimacy, agonistically misaligned, which operate from multiple sites of local authority (social, cultural, identity, elites and so on), connecting to state agencies and institutions, and onwards to the institutions of global governance despite normative and practical differences.

Legitimacy is networked over and around the three main levels (local/state/international), seen horizontally or vertically, and can thus be understood in negative/narrow and positive/broad forms: negative legitimacy points to procedure, effects and a superficial connection with a social base and their claims. It might also point to the problematic legitimacy of ethno-nationalism or other forms of discrimination. It may also emanate from socially distant entities such as the state and the international community. Positive forms point to a deeper understanding of legitimacy, connected to positioned justice claims in a society and a global and networked society, as well as questions of inequality. These approaches rest upon multiple sites of legitimate authority, across networks and scales. They are relational, entwined, often in tension, but also are accommodated.

Furthermore, it seems inescapable that Rawls was right that legal and material inequalities, which are difficult (though not impossible) to justify, are conflict inducing, and that the role of government and law, from the local to the international level is to redress them.[17] To achieve this, subaltern claims must be clearly represented and responded to by institutions of political and social authority, including at the community level, as well as in constitution and international law. Their authorisation of legitimacy as an inclusive framework, and their adjudication of freedom and liberty is normally limited by boundaries and relations, however. These are tensions that need to be relieved in practice. Despite such tensions, their 'performance' may not just be 'on paper' but in practice and history; a track record of legitimate performance is necessary across local to global scales to avoid internal contradictions in overlapping political architectures (such as with human rights at the global level, but political interests or exclusion at the regional and domestic levels, seen most viscerally in the case of the Palestinians or the current waves of migration to Europe from conflict zones).

Legitimacy is thus also produced through social practices, discourses, and performances. Legitimacy in this more complex form points to the power of attraction of the overall peace architecture: whether the form of state and economy on offer can create and maintain a society-, state- and region-wide proscription against violence in direct forms and also offer a way out of more subtle, indirect forms of violence. Both the League of Nations and the UN, subsequent human rights and humanitarian law, the liberal peace, global capital, and so forth, have in modernity presented attractive, broadly consensually framed systems of legitimisation, especially where they have actively redistributed material resources (mainly in social democracies, increasingly now undermined by neoliberalism). In an increasingly networked and participatory global environment in which north and south are entangled and fluid, rights and equality, democracy and mobility are more in demand in various modified forms in all aspects of local, national and global life, even though they are producing contradictory dynamics and expectations. Political, economic, social and cultural models must be even more consensual and attractive to the majority, in the various complex ways that majorities are now self-constructed (across territories, cultures, religions, classes, ideologies, regions and globally). It can be assumed that there will be significant tensions between local, state and global approaches to legitimacy, pitting claims for expanded rights against identity, the transcendence of territorial boundaries, as well as tensions between capital and global justice.

There is a certain delay in international accounts of legitimacy as compared to this emerging sense. The UN and international donors tend to take liberal international law as the standard for legitimacy, creating a rational–ethical amalgam.[18] They have built a framework of expertise projecting this through state reform, hoping for a 'norm cascade' or an 'extension of state authority' into conflict-affected societies in which civil society also simultaneously produces accountability vis-à-vis state elites.[19] National actors tend to set the primacy of national interests over international law, but also claim to represent their population through the state's constitution and within global governance institutions. This points to public, power and identity forms of legitimacy rather than rational-legal notions of legitimacy, in instrumental terms, which controls the means of violence as its base, builds a social state upon related institutions, and contributes to an international architecture. It also points to processes and performances of institutions, states and policies as important deciders of the depth of legitimacy.

Local peace formation actors (as opposed to nationalists or sectarians), whether in broader society or in civil society tend to place international law first but connect to a large degree with more contextual forms of social agency and power often related to so-called traditional or nationalist forms of authority. They are often less likely to accept external expert knowledge as automatically legitimate but point instead to more complex and multi-level deliberations. Indeed, sometimes they see external or national forms of legitimacy as based upon coercion and disrespectful of their social order. Their version of legitimacy may well be historicised, relational and networked, pointing to the quality of transactions between citizens and institutions or elites as well as the interfaces that mediate such transactions, which ultimately point to the establishment of legitimate authority.[20] However, the latter may be established on the basis of good and benign leadership following expert knowledge, or solely on the claims of citizens and social movements, or a mixture and balance of both citizen claims and expert knowledge. What we have seen more recently, however, is that local forms of peace agency tend to be opposed to hierarchical power arrangements and to territorial configurations of power, and yet have little in the way of material capacity. This means that though local peace formation legitimacy may be crucial in forming a stable social contract, it tends not to be able to scale up against state power, as seen in the so-called Arab Revolts from Syria to Egypt. It is also often not legible to international actors or seems secondary to their conceptions of legitimacy.

Ultimately, this means that there are a range of forms of political legitimacy and authority, and war means the state's claim to have unified or mediated them has failed. International intervention is an attempt to try again, this time led by liberal institutions and human rights law. This prioritised the legal-rational dimension of legitimacy over its special historical, social, normative, structural, spiritual and organic qualities. It highlights the insights of Weber, Kant and Locke and later iterations of the liberal peace as important principles for the state and the international community, ignoring the contextual weight of existing legitimate authorities (in plural). However, a focus on the broad range of legitimacies also point to the insights of Gramsci and Marx relating to how society forms its politics and why it mobilises against unjust political and economic power, including anti- and post-colonial dimensions.

Legitimacy can be viewed in top-down or bottom-up, informal or formal, vertical or horizontal ways, although it is not organised according to strict binaries. It is connected to the international, the state, the social, contractual, constitutional or identity frameworks. It connects a whole range of economic, political, social and cultural systems, based on both cooperation and consensus or competition and conflict. However, these are entangled in fluid, relational, oppositional, participatory or trust based systems. In practice, legitimacy connected to grass-roots contexts and actors is networked, relational[21] and hybrid as a consequence.

Yet, political legitimacy is now widely understood to relate to legitimate authority solely in the states-system, mainly determined by law, with the function of controlling the means of violence and representing the political interests of citizens and states. Political legitimacy allows for norms, identity and interests to be mediated through institutions that organise power and politics, whilst avoiding violence in direct form. This indicates that, simultaneously, it denotes respect for local institutions, customs, law and identity, as well as consideration of local needs; considerations related to state law, constitutions and sovereignty; and international law, human rights law and humanitarian law. In other words, political legitimacy and related authority is also connected to navigating around the problem of structural cultural violence in social contexts, not merely direct violence between or within states. There are clear tensions, however, in these different facets and demands, which are little understood so far.

Structure of the Book

This book is organised around a series of case studies that allow for the in-depth consideration of legitimacy (its sources, manifestations and complications). Some of the fieldwork behind the chapters, and some of the face-to-face discussions by the editors and authors, have been funded by the British Academy under their 'Tackling the UK's International Challenges' programme. The international challenge in this case is that many of the 'rules' surrounding legitimate political authority seem to have changed. More precisely, many of the assumptions that underpinned what became known as 'the liberal peace', or the preferred forms of peacemaking for leading states, international organisations and international financial institutions (IFIs), have fallen away. In the 1990s and early 2000s, legitimate political authority was discussed in terms of democracy and the extension of rights. Now, with the hubris of the liberal peace shattered by the bloody and inconclusive outcomes in Afghanistan, Iraq, Libya and elsewhere, there is an emphasis on security and stabilisation. There is an understanding among many (though not all) in the policy world that inclusion and social cohesion are important to achieve and maintain forms of peace, but much less consensus on how that might be achieved. This book is an attempt to capture a very dynamic picture. In particular, the chapters take seriously local and bottom-up perspectives on legitimacy, what it is, and how it might be achieved and justified. At the heart of all of this is power, and the tensions between 'power over' (or top-down forms of power) with other forms of power that might be horizontal or bottom-up. Many of the chapters in this book examine forms of legitimacy that might be described as 'non-standard'. That is, they do not easily fit within the rubrics offered by political science and its models of legitimate political authority.

In Chapter 1, Volker Boege and James Tanis examine what they describe as the hybridization of legitimacy through processes of peace formation in Bougainville. In doing so, they open up the concept of 'hybrid legitimacy' as both a challenge and an extension of liberal forms of legitimacy. This arises at the interface of the state/non-state and local/international fault lines, establishing relational processes of engagement between what might be seen to be opposed to 'traditional' and 'modern' authority structures. The authors argue that there is a wide gap between rational-legal legitimacy and non-rational-legal, hybrid forms of legitimacy. External support for peace-building has to bridge this gap, as might be seen in the case of peace formation in Bougainville.

In Chapter 2, Gezim Visoka examines relationality and its implications for intervention and legitimacy in Kosovo. He argues for the fluid nature of the legitimacy of peacebuilding in terms of institutional and everyday metrics which validate or resist peacebuilding. In practice, institutional and everyday metrics of legitimacy evolve and open up the possibility of generating new peace-enabling approaches to post-conflict societies.

Chapter 3, by Borja Paladini Adell, examines the concept of territorial peace through a legitimacy-building lens. The chapter's main thesis is as follows: in order to achieve a higher quality peace in Colombia, and to overcome the deep division and polarization that the armed conflict generated—and which has been maintained throughout the peace process—'territorial peace' needs to pay special attention to the legitimacy of the state in the territories most affected by the armed conflict, as well as drug trafficking and illicit economy dynamics. In this sense, legitimacy is not something that is automatically derived from Colombia's status as a well-integrated democratic state within the international political order. Rather, it is something that must be built and developed through direct interaction with the communities that suffer the violence and pressure of the illegal armed actors and the historical absence of the state. The concept of territorial peace assumes that for peace to be successful it has to be based in the regions where disputants are expected to coexist.

In Chapter 4, Toufic Haddad analyses the complexities and contradictions of legitimacy in the Occupied Palestinian Territory during the Oslo peace process. Efforts were made to ensure it was perceived to be legitimate both locally and internationally. However, international legitimacy in many senses undermined local legitimacy, while local attempts to maintain a distinct set of legitimate political aspirations could not be reconciled easily with international legitimacy, undermining Palestinian national aspirations and welfare. In turn, this undermined Palestinian support for the Oslo process. Haddad argues that international actors resorted to rent provision, elite formation and social engineering as a substitute, leading to complete stalemate, and finally the seeming collapse of concern about legitimacy on both sides, the hijack and diversion of the political process.

In Chapter 5, Stefanie Kappler analyses the 'illusion of legitimacy through participation' in Bosnia and Herzegovina, and discusses the fraught question of whether there is a peacebuilding authority from below emerging, how it might be constituted and to what effect. Kappler argues that external peacebuilding actors have tended to resort to participatory techniques to co-opt the subjects of peacebuilding into a system of governmentality. Legitimacy excludes the possibility of resistance, but this undermines the democratic process, leading existing power-structures to stay unreformed. For this reason, peacebuilding and society have not aligned in Bosnia, and the forces of nationalism, militarism and capitalism continue to hold sway to some degree.

Florian Zollmann examines the tensions between legality and legitimacy relating to the intervention in Iraq in Chapter 6. He argues that the reconstruction of Iraqi society after the 2003 Iraq War failed because the US-coalition dismantled the nationalised economy and imposed neoliberalism. Recession, corruption, sectarianism and resistance were the results. Thus the 'peace intervention' had legitimacy at the stage of intervention, if not legality, but lost legitimacy in the transitional stages that followed. This chapter examines if and how international reconstruction efforts might have won a higher degree of legitimacy vis-à-vis the Iraqi population, and how the population came to constitute legitimacy over the transitional period.

In Chapter 7, Sara Hellmüller examines the dynamics of local legitimacy in relation to the UN mediation in Syria. She argues that while civil society inclusion has become a prominently mentioned source of legitimacy in mediation, a peace process also has to perform to be considered legitimate by the broader population. Yet, authors often pit inclusion and performance against each other arguing that the participation of civil society reduces the efficiency of a mediation process by increasing the number of actors present. Analyzing the strategic decisions of three UN Special Envoys on Syria, the chapter provides a necessary corrective to this narrative by showing that both inclusion and performance are sources of legitimacy and not necessarily at odds with each other.

Yoshito Nakagawa examines the relationship between democratisation and legitimacy in a hybrid polity such as Somaliland in Chapter 8. He argues that societal forces have legitimised politics, incorporated the societal council of elders into the state, and so have established a hybrid polity. Home-grown democratisation of clan-based re-legitimised politics led to winners and losers across the hybrid polity, also pointing to dynamics of de-legitimised politics.

In Chapter 9, Allard Duursma examines the place of legitimacy in international mediation, with reference to the case of Sudan. His chapter is critical of the use of power mediation in civil wars, which overlooks important ideational factors, which help contribute to success. He argues that legitimacy may pull the conflict parties towards compliance with a mediator or it may maintain the mediation process over time. This chapter examines these dynamics in the context of the Intergovernmental Authority on Development's mediation between the Government of Sudan and the Sudan People's Liberation Movement.

Chapter 10, written by Florian Krampe and Lisa Ekman, examines questions of legitimacy and reciprocity in state–society relationships in Afghanistan and Nepal. They argue that legitimacy is an indicator of social and political stability. A post-conflict structural-normative framework for state–society relations emerges through the *interactions* of domestic state and non-state actors, often with the involvement of external actors, and requires social support to establish legitimacy. The stability of this new setup depends on society perceiving it as legitimate, and indicates the complex entanglement of elements peacebuilding demands.

In the final chapter, Roger Mac Ginty and Kristina Tschunkert examine the complex system of legitimate authorities in Lebanon. Here the plurality of legitimate political authority becomes apparent. Important in this case is the ambivalence that many actors have towards the state of Lebanon and how they seek legitimacy through other routes such as kinship networks and political dynasties. The chapter also addresses the legitimacy of international actors such as international non-governmental organisations (INGOs): from where do they gain their legitimacy? While some legitimacy is derived from actions inside Lebanon (such as performance on humanitarian tasks) much legitimacy is derived from outside of Lebanon (such as adherence to international legal statutes). This again comes back to the issue of power.

Notes

1. This study was partly funded by a University of Manchester seedcorn grant and by a British Academy Global Challenges grant entitled, 'Local Political Authority and Mobility', British Academy.

2. Franck, Thomas M., *The Power of Legitimacy Among Nations* (New York and Oxford: Oxford University Press, 1990); Applebaum, Arthur I., 'Legitimacy without the duty to obey', *Philosophy & Public Affairs*, 2010, 38: 3, pp. 215–39; Beetham, David, *The Legitimation of Power* (London: Macmillan Education, 1991); Hurd, I., 'Legitimacy and authority in international politics', *International Organization*, 1999, 53: 2, pp. 379–408; Rawls, John, *A Theory of Justice* (Cambridge, MA: Harvard University Press, 1971).

3. Weber, Max, *Economy and Society*, (Berkeley: University of California Press, [1922] 1980).

4. Caney, Simon, 'Cosmopolitan Justice and Institutional Design', *Social Theory and Practice*, 2006, 32: 4, p. 748.

5. Schmelzle, Cord, 'Effectiveness and legitimacy in areas of limited statehood', *SFB-Governance*, Working Paper Series 26, November 2011, p. 5.

6. UN Department of Peacekeeping Operations, *Capstone Doctrine: Peacekeeping Operations: Principles and Guidelines* (New York: DPKO, 2008).

7. *UK Approach and Principles of Stabilisation*, Stabilisation Unit, 2014, <https://assets.publishing.service.gov.uk/government/uploads/system/uploads/attachment_data/file/784002/Chapter_1_The_UK_Government_s_Approach_to_Stabilisation__incl._exec_sum_.pdf>

8. Schmelzle, 'Effectiveness and legitimacy in areas of limited statehood', p. 17.

9. For example, see the UN's Sustaining Peace Agenda, 'High-level meeting on efforts undertaken and opportunities to strengthen the United Nations' work on peacebuilding and sustaining peace', 24–25 April 2016: General Assembly Resolution, A/RES/70/262; Security Council Resolution S/RES/2282 (2016).

10. Anderson, Mary B., Dayna Brown and Isabella Jean, *Time to Listen: Hearing People on the Receiving End of International Aid* (Cambridge, MA: CDA, 2012).

11. Khalaf, Rana, 'Governance without government in Syria: civil society and state building during conflict', *Syria Studies*, 2015, 7: No 3.

12. See, for example, UN, *Presence, Capacity, and Legitimacy: Implementing the extension of state authority mandates in peacekeeping* (New York: UNDPKO, 2017), p. 4.

13. Lipset, Seymour, *Political Man* (New York: Doubleday, 1960), pp. 77–83.

14. Weber, Max, *On Charisma and Institution Building: Selected Papers*, S. N. Eisendtadt (ed.) (Chicago: The University of Chicago Press, 1960); Weber, Max, *Economy and Society. An outline of interpretive sociology*, G. Roth and C. Wittich (eds), (Berkeley, Los Angeles and London: University of California Press, 1978); Weber, Max, *From Max Weber: Essays in Sociology*, H. H. Gerth and C. Wright Mills (eds), (London: Routledge, 1991); Cook, D., 'Legitimacy and Political Violence: A Habermasian Perspective', *Social Justice*, 2003, 30: 3, pp. 108–26.

15. Boege, Volker, 'Legitimacy in hybrid political orders – an underestimated dimension of peacebuilding and state formation'. *Conference paper presented at the European Consortium of Political Research conference*, Potsdam, Germany, 10–12 September 2009.
16. Focus Group, UNDPKO, UN HQ, New York, 3 May 2018.
17. Rawls, John, *A Theory of Justice* (Cambridge, MA: Harvard University Press, 1971), p. 302.
18. Buchanan, A. and R. Keohane, 'The legitimacy of global governance institutions', *Ethics and International Affairs*, 2006, 20: 4, pp. 405–37.
19. Finnemore, M. and K. Sikkink, 'International norm dynamics and political Change', *International Organization* 1998, 52: 4, pp. 887–917; Sunstein, Cass R., 'Social norms and social roles', *Columbia Law Review*, May 1996, 6: 4, pp. 903–68.
20. Boege, 'Legitimacy in hybrid political orders'.
21. Qin, Y., *A Relational Theory of World Politics* (Cambridge: Cambridge University Press, 2018).

ONE

The Hybridization of Legitimacy in Processes of Peace Formation: the Bougainville Case

Volker Boege and James Tanis

Introduction

For almost a decade (1989–1998), the South Pacific island of Bougainville was the theatre of a violent conflict which cost thousands of lives and led to the large-scale destruction of livelihoods, infrastructure, the economy, political institutions and social structures and relations. It was the longest and bloodiest violent conflict in the South Pacific after the end of the Second World War. After a cease-fire came into effect in April 1998, long-term processes of peace formation and state formation commenced, which continue today.[1]

A host of actors and institutions at the local societal level, the regional and national political level, as well as the international level, have been involved in these processes. They all lay claim to legitimacy, and they all – more or less – enjoy legitimacy in the eyes of the people on the ground. Multiple legitimacies are grounded in different normative frameworks though. Hence, empirical legitimacy as it is emerging in the course of peace formation and state formation, and as it is shaping peace formation and state formation, is hybrid legitimacy, with contradictory and seemingly mutually exclusive sources and forms of legitimacy intertwining and blending.

In the following, we'll explore this uneasy co-existence, interaction and mutual permeation of different sources and types of legitimate authority in Bougainville peace and state formation, arguing that the hybridisation of legitimacy as an ongoing process is an essential characteristic of the emerging peace and state, which emerge as hybrid themselves, and arguing that this hybridity of legitimacy, rather than being an obstacle and hindrance, is the foundation of sustainable peace and resilient political community. This has far-reaching implications for international peace-building actors; they have to acknowledge the limitations of their own liberal understandings of legitimacy and constructively engage with the hybridization of legitimacy.

With Max Weber, we understand legitimacy in an empirical sense, as the belief in the right to govern (or to build peace), and the belief in the right-fulness of certain acts of governance (or acts of peacebuilding).[2] It is this empirical legitimacy in the domestic realm that matters in peace and state formation, not so much international normative legitimacy.[3]

With Max Weber, we use the differentiation of three ideal types of legiti-macy – rational-legal, traditional and charismatic – as a starting point for our analysis,[4] at the same time, taking his point that these ideal types can-not be found in 'pure' form in empirical cases, acknowledging that 'the great majority of empirical cases represent a combination or a state of tran-sition among several such pure types'.[5]

We do not follow Max Weber's assertion that rational-legal legitimacy will trump the other types in the course of history and will become dominant (albeit contaminated by remnants of traditional and charismatic aspects).[6] Rather, we take his remarks about 'combinations' or 'transitions' further to conceptualize hybridisation of legitimacy as the dominant and permanent feature of legitimate political authority in the context of peace and state formation. Hybrid legitimacy is thus not another – static – ideal type of legitimate authority, but must instead be seen in a processual and relational mode. We shall elaborate on this relational and processual understanding of hybrid legitimacy by exploring the legitimacy of actors and institutions of peace and state formation in contemporary Bougainville. Before we do so, we'll give a very brief overview over violent conflict and peacebuilding on the island so as to provide some background and context for our analysis of hybridization of legitimate authority. And once we have gone through the Bougainville case, we'll end the chapter with some brief reflections on what this case can tell us about legitimacy in peace and state formation in more general terms.

Violent conflict and peacebuilding on Bougainville

The main cause of the decade-long war on Bougainville was the opera-tion of an enormous gold and copper mine, the Panguna mine in the mountains of central Bougainville, which, in the 1970s and 1980s, was one of the biggest open-pit mines in the world. The benefits and costs of mine-induced 'development' were perceived by many Bougainvilleans as extremely unevenly divided, with the bulk of the mining revenues flowing to outsiders (the Australian mining company which was the majority owner and operator of the mine, and the Papua New Guinea (PNG) central government in the far-away capital city of Port Moresby) and the local communities left with the negative environmental and social effects.

The people in the mine area demanded meaningful environmental protection measures, compensation for environmental damage and a larger share of the revenues generated. The mining company and the PNG government rejected these demands and, as a consequence, members of local clans brought the mine to a standstill by acts of sabotage in late 1988 and established the Bougainville Revolutionary Army (BRA). Fighting between the BRA and the security forces of the PNG government soon spread across the whole island. The BRA adopted a secessionist stance and called for independence for Bougainville.

After almost ten years of privation and bloodshed, the people on Bougainville were war-weary and exhausted and there was a widespread desire for a return to normalcy and peace. A stalemate had developed in which neither side believed there was anything to be gained by continuing the war. Hence, a window for initiating a peace process opened. New Zealand facilitated a first round of peace talks in 1997, and in April 1998 a permanent cease-fire came into effect. From then on, a comprehensive peace process developed, with the signing of a political settlement, the Bougainville Peace Agreement (BPA) in 2001, the adoption of a constitution for the Autonomous Region of Bougainville (AROB) in 2004 and elections to an Autonomous Bougainville Government (ABG) in 2005 as crucial milestones at the political level.[7]

Peacebuilding on Bougainville is still ongoing today, and it can be argued that it will only come to a close with the conduct of a referendum on the future political status of the region and the implementation of referendum results. Such a referendum is provided for by the BPA (Bougainville Peace Agreement 2001). According to the BPA, the referendum has to comprise the option of full independence for Bougainville, and it has to be carried out ten to fifteen years after the first ABG elections, that means sometime between June 2015 and June 2020. In May 2016, the ABG and the government of PNG agreed on 15 June 2019 as the target date for the referendum. It had to be postponed, however, and actually took place on 23 November 2019. A vast majority of Bougainvilleans opted for independence, and currently Bougainville is transitioning towards independence. This transition process most probably will take years.

Traditional Legitimate Authority

The time of war was a time of statelessness on Bougainville. The institutions of the PNG state withdrew from Bougainville; the PNG government was unable to maintain a monopoly over the legitimate use of force. On the other hand, the secessionist movement was unable to establish such a monopoly and the accompanying state institutions. The ensuing vacuum was filled to a large extent by customary institutions and forms of traditional governance.[8] This resurgence of non-state local customary institutions and traditional leadership during the war paved the way for traditional authorities playing a prominent role in Bougainville peace and state formation today.

During the war, traditional authorities such as elders and chiefs once more became responsible for regulating conflicts and organizing community life. In doing so, they referred to longstanding customary norms and ways of operating – according to most accounts, to the satisfaction of the members of their communities.[9] In fact, in some areas, the war led to the emergence of new forms of 'traditional' leadership, for example, new types of chiefs.[10] Traditional authorities were entrusted with an important role in dealing with violent conflicts in the local context. They organised reconciliations at the intra- and inter-communal level, utilising customary methods of conflict resolution. And post-conflict traditional authorities and the customary ways of dispute resolution, reconciliation and restoration of social order pursued by them provided the grassroots basis for successful peace formation.[11]

Building on these positive experiences, currently traditional authorities and customary institutions are seen as a backbone of state formation, as well. A widely held view on Bougainville is: what has worked in ancestral times and what has worked in peacebuilding now also should be utilized for the functioning of the state system.[12]

In its final report, the Bougainville Constitutional Commission acknowledged that the 'majority of our people in rural communities live under traditional rather than the formal system of government'.[13] The Bougainville Constitution makes comprehensive reference to customary forms of leadership and formally recognises traditional systems of government and the role of chiefs and other 'traditional' leaders.[14] Of course, this reference to *kastom* should not be confused with a re-orientation towards 'pure' pre-colonial custom.[15]

Today's traditional authorities are bestowed with legitimacy rooted in the customs and culture of their communities, be it as (hereditary) chiefs, be it as spiritual leaders (with strong connections to the invisible world) or be it as elders who enjoy the respect of community members due to certain personal qualities and deeds. At the same time, 'modern' factors come into play for legitimising their leadership roles today: a good formal education, business success in the cash economy, positions in government or public service, in the church or in civil society organisations can enhance legitimacy in the customary local sphere.[16] This legitimacy might still be called 'traditional', although some sources of this legitimacy are not, leading to actual hybridisation of legitimacy.

The inclusion of traditional leaders and governance into the state system is vividly debated. It poses a legitimacy dilemma. There are those who prefer to keep the chiefs and other traditional authorities outside the state, because they cannot be put under the rules of an alien (western) system and because there is the danger that they get entangled in 'politics', and as a consequence lose respect and legitimacy. There are others, however, who would prefer to have them included in the state system as they are the 'real' local level government anyway.

The debate about the pros and cons of the establishment of an Advisory Body of 'traditional authorities' in the government structure of Bougainville, complementing the ABG, is an expression of this dilemma. The provision for an Advisory Body in the Bougainville Constitution is the result of a debate during the Constitution-making process about the idea of an Upper House (of chiefs and other traditional authorities). There was support for the idea of such an Upper House 'as a place where the traditional chiefs could play a major role',[17] in particular as custodians of custom and culture. The opposing view was 'that it would not be appropriate to have chiefs and other traditional leaders actually sitting in formal political and governmental roles (. . .). The roles of chiefs are at the local level, with the community, where they exercise authority because of stature, not law. It would be potentially demeaning to chiefs and the chiefly system of power, to bring them into the formal system of government in such a direct way'.[18]

Finally, the decision was taken against an Upper House, and in favour of the establishment of an Advisory Body of chiefs and other traditional leaders. Even this Advisory Body, however, has not been established yet. The main reason given is the high costs of such an additional constitutional body, but the contradictory views on its desirability are another reason. Interestingly, the most articulated opposition against an advisory body of traditional authorities comes from explicitly 'modernist' forces on the one pole (those who do not want a political role for traditional authorities in a modern democratic state at all) and intransigent 'traditionalist' forces on the other pole (those who do not want 'traditional' authority being tainted by 'modern' alien influences).

At present, 'traditional' authorities are still widely recognized by the vast majority of 'ordinary people' and the political elite alike as significant legitimate actors who have important roles to play in local governance, peacebuilding and maintenance of political community, and there is no doubt that they will remain legitimate actors in the future.[19]

Legitimacy of State Institutions

Bougainville has a well-established and functioning political system, grounded in the principles of liberal democracy. The formal state system is based on the BPA and on the Bougainville Constitution. The BPA paved the way for the establishment of the AROB (within the state of PNG), with its own constitution and government, the ABG. Elections of a Bougainville parliament and president were first held in 2005, and again in 2010 and 2015. Election campaigns and the elections themselves ran smoothly on all three occasions, assessed as free and fair by international observers. ABG ministers are selected from within the parliament by the president as head of the ABG.

Members of the ABG and the Bougainville House of Representatives present themselves as legitimised through formal democratic process, notably elections which are the legally proscribed way of deciding on legitimate political leadership. The electorate, the people on the ground, appreciate the right to vote, make use of this right in numbers that are comparable to well established democracies and recognize the elected members of the ABG and House of Representatives as their legitimate leaders.[20]

However, there is more to the legitimacy of these leaders than just this rational-legal dimension. This can be illustrated by the following story:

In October 2012, the Regional Member for Bougainville in the national parliament of PNG, Joe Lera, was initiated as a paramount chief in his home district in Bougainville after his election to parliament earlier in 2012.

> The people of Tokunotui in the Haisi area of Siwai district, South Bougainville, elevated themselves during a historical ceremony at the Haisi Catholic Mission Station to support their son, the newly elected Regional MP for Bougainville, Joe Lera, in his five years of politics in the 9th PNG Parliament. The ceremony began from Chief Lera's birthplace at Sumikatume village, where prayer warriors bestowed him God's Blessing, then his mother's relatives led him in a procession to the Haisi Catholic Parish and handed him over to the father's relatives who initiated him as paramount Chief. Clan Chief Aloysius Luku performed the initiation ceremony and presented the Hon. Chief Joseph Lera to the people of Bougainville. He said the people of

Haisi had pride in their victory and pledged to support Joe Lera in providing leadership in the Autonomous Region of Bougainville and Papua New
Guinea as a whole.[21]

In another news report, more details are given:

> The procession started from the village and went to the parish area where the
> community witnessed the traditional ceremony in which he had to climb the
> traditional platform (lauku) for him to be ordained by the chief Aloysius.
> The ceremony included traditional singing and dancing. At the end of the
> 30 minutes procession, students of Haisi Primary School sang the national
> and Bougainville anthems as the two community policemen present raised
> the flags.[22]

The fact that Lera won the elections and thus was bestowed with rational-
legal legitimacy was obviously not enough; he needed further legitimation
in his new role by way of becoming a customary chief. He needed to be initiated because he had to demonstrate that he was rooted in kastom. At the
same time, he had to demonstrate that he was an educated man, educated
in white man's knowledge, because he had been elected to an educated
man's position. In the initiation ceremony, various legitimising narratives
come together: the traditional (the role of family members from mother's
and father's side, the climbing of the traditional platform, the initiation by
another chief), the Christian (the event took place at a Catholic Mission
Station, 'prayer warriors' (themselves traditional/Christian hybrids) gave
God's blessing), and the modern state (singing of anthems, flag raising).
Lera is a legitimate leader not only because he is an elected parliamentar-
ian, but also because he is a chief, and the elements of his legitimacy are
inextricably interwoven: he is not only chief for his local people, but his
people bestow him with chieftaincy to serve the whole of Bougainville (and
PNG), and what he does in this wider 'political' context is legitimised by his
chiefly status; and he only became chief because he was elected to parliament before, and what he does in the local context is legitimised not only
by his chiefly status, but also by his status as Member of Parliament. His
legitimacy is thus hybrid legitimacy.

In a similar way, members of the ABG also refer to sources of legitimacy beyond the rational-legal realm. Bougainville's current President was
elected to this position in free and fair elections, but at the same time he is
a 'Paramount Chief'. In public, he is regularly referred to as President Chief
John Momis. His status as Paramount Chief[23] enhances his legitimacy. So
although John Momis is an elected president bestowed with rational-legal

legitimacy, for the people there is more to his legitimacy than just that – and Momis is well aware of this, and he makes use of it whenever he sees it as convenient, manoeuvring with different registers of legitimacy. His legitimacy is also hybrid.

Me'ekamui – Another Type of Legitimate Authority Altogether

Besides the ABG and its state institutions there is another political organisation which lays claim to pan-Bougainville ('national') legitimate authority and indeed enjoys empirical legitimacy with sections of the Bougainville populace. This is the Me'ekamui movement (Me'ekamui means 'Holy Land' in one of the local languages).[24] In 1998, an intransigent faction split from the BRA and established the Me'ekamui Defence Force (MDF) at the beginning of the peacebuilding phase. The Me'ekamuis did not join the weapons disposal process and the overall peace process. On the other hand, they never disturbed or undermined that process and tacitly adhered to the ceasefire provisions.[25]

Various Me'ekamui factions are in control of the area around the Panguna mine in central Bougainville and pockets of territory in the south. Me'ekamui territory was declared a 'no-go zone' for outsiders, in particular representatives of the state of PNG (and initially also of the ABG). The Me'ekamui people have their own structures of governance in the no-go zone; they control access to that zone by means of roadblocks and reject any interference of PNG institutions within their area of control. The 'border' between the no-go zone and the rest of Bougainville is rather porous, and there is considerable exchange. People from the no-go zone participated in the elections for the Bougainville parliament, Me'ekamui combatants provided security for the elections in the no-go zone, and Me'ekamui representatives even ran as candidates, and some indeed are members of the current Bougainville House of Representatives.

A special state of shared sovereignty has developed with regard to the Me'ekamui region. On the one hand, it is covered by the general provisions of the peacebuilding and state-building processes: the PNG and ABG authorities claim that those provisions apply to the whole of Bougainville, but these provisions are only implemented partially. On the other hand, Me'ekamui is a 'state' – or rather a very specific political entity – of its own. Over the last years, Me'ekamui authorities gradually have intensified cooperation with the ABG, especially with regard to the maintenance of order and the delivery of basic social services. Me'ekamui representatives are in permanent communication with ABG authorities, and they have demonstrated their interest in becoming official parties to the peace process, but they still insist on their 'independence'. The exchange between the no-go zone and the rest of Bougainville is increasing constantly, and institutions of the ABG have established themselves in the no-go zone. Some kind of formal 'reunification' of ABG and Me'ekamui in the future is becoming more and more probable.

On Me'ekamui territory *kastom* is strong and highly appreciated. Traditional authorities are held in high esteem, and the 'holiness' of Bougainville culture forms the core element of Me'ekamui ideology. But although the Me'ekamui movement understands and presents itself as traditional, embodying the customs of the people that have guided their lives since time immemorial, the reality is far from that. Among the Me'ekamui leadership, a considerable number of people can be found who cannot refer to traditional legitimacy (for example, as chiefs) in their communities. These people have attained leadership roles in the context of the secessionist movement, the BRA and Me'ekamui. They wrap themselves in the cloak of tradition, but their legitimacy is more of the charismatic kind, built on their performance during the war (as outstanding military commanders with charismatic authority) and/or during the establishment of an indigenous realm of governance after the war. This legitimacy is shaky, exactly because it is not – as proclaimed by them – deeply rooted in the customs of the olden days.

As a consequence, Me'ekamui also borrows from 'alien' legitimising concepts: Me'ekamui has its own 'state' institutions, a 'government' with its own prime minister, a 'House of Lords', and a 'general' of its Defence Forces. In fact, Meekamui mimicks the 'modern' state. Hence, Me'ekamui is not a territory where pre-colonial customary ways have been re-established. Rather, a mixture and amalgamation of introduced and customary local institutions can be found.

Me'ekamui utilizes kastom as an ideology in order to shape and strengthen a distinct Bougainville 'national' identity. This strongly resonates with many Bougainvilleans. It is built on a clear demarcation of 'us', the original inhabitants, and 'them', the foreigners: The clan that owns the Me'ekamui is called osikaiang, meaning the original inhabitants. This term originally refers to the first settler clan in a given territory, whereas newcomers are referred to as taborangku, meaning foreigners.[26] Today, taborangku is used for all foreigners (white people, Chinese people and so on), while all Bougainvilleans in relation to these foreigners are osikaiang. The terms Me'ekamui and osikaiang hence lay claim to legitimacy and contest the legitimacy of the foreigners who have come to Bougainville later.[27] These terms are not fixed, though. The fact that all Bougainvilleans are osikaiang in relation to foreigners does not eradicate the fact that there are

Bougainville clans which are osikaiang and others which are taborangku. Once the foreigners will have left, this inner-Bougainville delineation will come to the fore again.

Finally, Christianity comes into the legitimising mix. Me'ekamui – Holy Land – does not only refer to the sacred places of the ancestors, but also alludes to Christianity, and this combination is presented as being special to Bougainvilleans and serves as the means of distinction between them and their Holy Land on the one hand and all outside forces on the other.[28] Thus, the Me'ekamui movement is legitimised through 'a combination of custom, Christianity and nationalism',[29] with nationalism to be understood as pointing to indigeneity (place of origin, place of birth, connectedness to the land).[30]

Me'ekamui legitimacy is in constant flux and composed of various elements. It is hybrid legitimacy, mixing and blending rational-legal, traditional and charismatic sources of legitimacy.

The result of this enmeshment and blending of sources of legitimacy might look rather odd for external observers. However, it clearly appeals to a lot of people on the ground. Hence, although this state of shared sovereignty with two overlapping political entities – the Autonomous Region of Bougainville and the Independent Republic of Me'ekamui – covering the same territory and people, is far from what conventional wisdom wants a 'proper' state to look like, this arrangement works. One has to acknowledge that some sections of the population do not recognise the ABG as the (only) rightful and legitimate government.

The situation is further complicated due to splits in the Me'ekamui movement, with some armed groups in southern Bougainville claiming to be Me'ekamui, but not recognised as such by the Me'ekamui in central Bougainville. The most influential faction leader in the south of Bougainville is Noah Musingku, who commands a group of well-armed militants left over from the prior violent conflict. In his area of influence he has established a 'kingdom' – The Kingdom of Papaala – declaring himself King David Peii II and installing a 'royal government'. Originally a prophetical type of charismatic leader grounded in Melanesian 'cargo-cult' traditions, he tried to transform charismatic legitimacy by establishing this 'kingdom' and declaring himself 'king'. This can be seen as an example of the routinization of inherently unstable charismatic legitimacy. His coronation was attended by thousands of his followers, which is evidence of some empirical domestic legitimacy. He also lays claim to international legitimacy, positing that his kingdom and government has the recognition of the UN, International Monetary Fund (IMF) and other international organisations as well as a couple of similar 'kingdoms' all over the world.[31]

Other warlords in the south have formed shifting and contemporary alliances with Musingku or Me'ekamui factions in central Bougainville, or the ABG, for that matter. Just as the leaders of the MDF in central Bougainville, they enjoy charismatic legitimacy based on their status and deeds as commanders during the war.[32]

Legitimacy of Internationals

How do international peace- and state-builders fit into all this? How do they engage with this variety of legitimate authorities and how legitimate are they?

External actors played a positive role in the transition from war to peace and in early peacebuilding on Bougainville, and they still play a role today. The regional Truce Monitoring Group/Peace Monitoring Group and a United Nations (UN) Observer Mission, which were deployed to Bougainville for a couple of years after the ceasefire (until 2003 and 2005, respectively), are widely seen as exceptionally successful. This view is held both in the international discourse about peacebuilding and locally on Bougainville.[33]

After the stabilisation of the security situation on the ground, a considerable number of foreign development agencies, international non-governmental organisations (NGOs) and United Nations programmes and institutions became active in Bougainville. Australia is by far the largest bilateral donor and has the most visible presence on the ground, followed by New Zealand, the European Union and Japan. The United Nations Development Programme (UNDP) has a permanent office on Bougainville and is the most active and visible UN agency on Bougainville. Other UN agencies like UNICEF, UN Women, UN High Commissioner for Refugees (UNHCR) are also present, as well as the Asian Development Bank and the World Bank. A considerable number of Australian and other foreign NGOs run programmes on Bougainville in areas like literacy, food security, agriculture, health, water and sanitation (for example, Save the Children, World Vision and Oxfam).

External actors bring with them their own norms and values, their own ideas and concepts of 'proper' (that is Western liberal) peacebuilding, state-building, capacity-building, accountability and transparency, good (enough) governance, development, human rights, democracy, effectiveness and so on, accompanied by their own programmes and procedures of implementation. Talk of locals' 'empowerment', 'participation' and 'ownership' often remains superficial, constrained by the notion that the locals should be empowered to do and to own what the internationals think is best for them, namely the implementation of the internationals' norms and values, ideas and concepts according to the internationals' programmes and operational procedures. This way of thinking is based on the assumption that these norms, values and procedures and their protagonists are per se legitimate. But local understandings of legitimacy might differ. So far, however, external actors have not paid much attention to reflecting on differing understandings of legitimacy or scrutinizing their own legitimacy.[34]

The internationals legitimise their presence and activities with reference to international standards and agendas of peacebuilding, development assistance and state-building and with reference to their invitation by and collaboration with state institutions. They refer to legal negotiated arrangements as the basis of their presence and legitimise their operations by reference to laws, treaties and agreements endorsed by the relevant state authorities of PNG and Bougainville. In other words, they refer to international rational-legal legitimacy, which by them is seen as a 'natural' given. They do not have a proper grasp of the difference between international and local legitimacy.[35] The internationals' presence and activities might be perfectly legal, but this does not automatically translate into local empirical legitimacy. The fact that these outsiders are bestowed with international and rational-legal legitimacy does not necessarily matter for the locals.[36] What counts for them is whether internationals really make a contribution to peacebuilding, and whether their commitment to supporting Bougainvilleans in state-building and development really translates into tangible benefits for the locals. Only if this is the case can they enjoy legitimacy: they have to build their legitimacy on performance.

It is their abundant resources which make them influential players on the domestic scene, as these resources enable them to gain legitimacy through performance and make them much sought after partners for civil society and state institutions. The ABG and large sections of civil society more or less depend on the collaboration with external actors. Access to much- needed resources, finances, expertise and know-how can bolster the ABG's local empirical legitimacy, because it allows improvement of performance. Moreover, in large quarters of the populace, certain external actors like the UN, the EU or New Zealand have a good reputation, and are capable of demonstrating that collaborating with these important players enhances one's legitimacy.[37] On the other hand, local actors can (threaten to) challenge the legitimacy of internationals from the position of domestic empirical legitimacy whenever they deem this useful in the pursuit of their own political interests.

The internationals have to work with the host government (the ABG and the PNG government) and cooperate with state institutions on the basis of legal state-to-state arrangements; acknowledgement of the legitimacy of state institutions is a prerequisite of their presence and activities. At the same time, they also feel most comfortable in liaising and collaborating with state institutions because they think that they share the same understanding of legitimacy with them (which, as has been shown, can be a misunderstanding). Internationals are thus doubly constrained regarding their interactions with local legitimate authority – they are legally bound to work with and work through their state counterparts in the host country and recognise their legitimacy, and there is an attitudinal bias in favour of collaborating with these state counterparts (they are perceived as being from the same flesh, so to speak).

Apart from state institutions, internationals also feel quite comfortable in engaging with actors from civil society. They look familiar (local civil society built in the image of Western civil society) and internationals know how those actors operate (or at least they think they know, but again, this can be a misunderstanding). In fact, local Bougainvillean NGOs have received a considerable amount of external funding over the last few years; some NGOs would not be viable without that funding. Such external support can enhance the local civil society actors' empirical legitimacy as it allows them to improve their own performance and they can profit from the international partner's reputation and international networks. But it can also lead to legitimacy problems if local NGOs are seen as being over-dependent on external sources and dominated by alien interests. International NGOs' local legitimacy, on the other hand, depends on good relationships with their local partner organisations and the local reputation of those organisations.

Engaging with 'unfamiliar' local legitimate authorities is most challenging for internationals. They have problems seeing, understanding and acknowledging the legitimacy of actors like chiefs, elders, prophets or warriors. But they have learned to accept them as domestically legitimate. The fact that chiefs or the Me'ekamui are legitimate governance actors can hardly be overlooked. After all, Bougainville is a relatively small place, and even the internationals based in the main urban centres of Buka or Arawa cannot avoid contact with the patchwork of 'alien' local actors. And when the internationals go out 'into the field' they are confronted with the everyday reality of non-rational-legal legitimacy upfront.

Consequently, for example, it is normal procedure today that the UNDP representative attends traditional reconciliation ceremonies and mingles with chiefs and Me'ekamuis. And the community policing program of the New Zealand police, which provides training for Bougainville Community Auxiliary Police (CAPs), would not be possible without closely liaising with the chiefs of the CAPs' home areas. Although the program is under the auspices of the ABG and can be defined as a 'state' program, New Zealand police officers who run the CAP training program acknowledge the de facto legitimacy of 'non-state' chiefs and contribute to their legitimation as they pursue a hybrid-sensitive approach of engagement.

Hybridisation of Legitimacy

Everybody on Bougainville today is aware of the existence of different types of legitimate authority, and people believe in the legitimacy of different types of actors at the same time. As a consequence, people one day can happily vote in general elections for an ABG president, the other day attend the coronation of that strange self-proclaimed 'King David Peii II', and all other days follow their local chiefs. They do not have problems with bestowing these different actors with legitimacy in parallel. The sources and processes of legitimation of these various actors might look contradictory from the outside: an elected president, a self-proclaimed king and a hereditary chief refer to very different, and seemingly mutually exclusive, types of legitimacy – but what is mutually exclusive from an outsider's viewpoint can go together perfectly well in the people's everyday understanding of legitimate authority; that is, various forms of legitimacy co-exist and intertwine, leading to a situation of multiple legitimacies, and legitimacies stemming from multiple sources. Only very few on Bougainville today suggest that one type of legitimate authority should supersede the other (for example, political leaders to supersede customary leaders or vice versa). There are differences in the assessment of the legitimacy of different kinds of leadership, with some seeing traditional authorities or charismatic leaders as more legitimate, and others seeing legal-rational authority in the context of state functions and positions as more legitimate. In general, however, multiple legitimacies and the hybridization of legitimacy characterise governance structures and political leadership on Bougainville today. Different actors acknowledge the validity of the sources of and claims to legitimacy of other actors. Chiefs do not question the legitimacy of elected political leaders, and vice versa. Leaders who ground their legitimacy in kastom do not question the legitimacy of leaders who refer to elections and other democratic procedures as sources of their legitimacy, and vice versa.

Moreover, different legitimate authorities are prepared to actively contribute to the legitimation of other authorities. Chiefs, for example, bestow elected political leaders with additional 'traditional' legitimacy. The initiation of the Regional Member for Bougainville Joe Lera as a chief and the declaration of ABG President John Momis as Paramount Chief are telling illustrations of this mechanism. On the other hand, this also confirms and enhances the legitimacy of the chiefs. The willingness (and, in fact, eager-ness) of the elected political leaders to give themselves into the hands of the chiefs for such ceremonies and to become chiefs themselves is a clear indi-cation of the legitimacy of traditional authority. Furthermore, elected lead-ers and state institutions also actively confirm the legitimacy of traditional authorities both on an everyday basis (acknowledging their roles in local governance and dispute resolution) and in official declaratory politics (see, for example, the significance given to traditional authorities in the Bougain-ville Constitution). (Most) Chiefs, on the other hand, actively encourage their people to participate in state affairs (go to elections, attend meetings organised by state officials and so on) and to respect elected leaders and public servants as legitimate authorities. However, the different legitimate authorities are cautious not to claim exclusive legitimacy, because this could backfire on their own legitimacy. The ABG is willing to collaborate with the 'illegal' and 'illegitimate' Me'ekamui, and the Me'ekamuis are happy to acknowledge the ABG president (who is at the same time a paramount chief), and even the self-proclaimed king presents himself as king alongside the ABG president and a Me'ekamui prime minister.

All these actors are empirically legitimate stakeholders in peace and state formation, with their legitimacy and its components constantly re-nego-tiated and re-articulated. Seemingly contradictory and mutually exclusive forms of legitimacy intertwine and blend, and consequently legitimacy is hybridised; this means that the people's belief in these actors' right to gov-ern/to build peace, as well as the actors' justification of the right to govern/to build peace, combine elements that stem from genuinely different but confluent societal and cultural sources.[38]

Hybridity is not only the main feature of the legitimacy of all the actors on Bougainville, but also of the overall ensemble of legitimate governance. The interface and mutual permeation of different sources and types of legit-imacy is the most fascinating and most significant aspect of peace and state formation on Bougainville today. Legitimation as an ongoing process and the hybridisation of legitimacy rather than distinct static types of legitimate authorities characterise Bougainville peace and state formation. Hybrid legitimacy is thus not another – static – ideal type of legitimate authority, rather, it has to be thought of in the process and relational mode.

Conclusion

An environment of hybrid legitimate authority is not per se conducive to sustainable peace formation and formation of peaceful political commu-nity. Hybrid legitimacy should not be romanticised (nor should 'building' hybrid legitimate authority be a strategy and an aim of peace and state formation).[39] But a case can be made for engaging with it – as it cannot be made to go away by wishful thinking or enforcement or awareness building or any other method in the Western liberal peacebuilding and state-building toolbox.

For internationals, this means first and foremost to acknowledge that understandings of legitimacy of internationals and locals can differ widely and, consequently, there can be a wide gulf between what people on the ground deem to be legitimate authority and what proponents of the Western peacebuilding and state-building agenda think they should deem to be legitimate authority. Internationals have a tendency to use their influence in favour of their local counterparts in state and civil society. This is 'natural' – given that these actors are seen as being committed to the ideals of liberal peace and state-building – but not necessarily prudent in terms of peace formation and formation of political community. Overstretching support for specific types of legitimate authority at the expense of or to the detriment of other types can alienate those actors who miss out and drive them to take on hardened anti-foreigner attitudes, and it can even be counterproductive for the legitimacy of those actors who were to be supported. If the ABG, for example, is seen as being too close to Australian support (or perhaps even as being dependent on such support, or Chinese support, for that matter) this impacts negatively on its local empirical legitimacy (even if it might add to its international legitimacy).

On Bougainville, it was only in the everyday exchange with the locals that the internationals learned that, for the locals, not only (and not even primarily) rational-legal legitimacy of the formal institutions of the state counts, but also other types of legitimate authority, with the locals' concept of legitimacy reaching beyond rational-legal legitimacy in the sphere of anthropocentric governance – spirits, totem animals, and God can play legitimizing roles, too. This is the other-worldly dimension of legitimation, which is often ignored or underestimated by outsiders.

However, the internationals' presence and activities impact on legitimate authority in the local context. Locals' understanding of legitimacy is not fixed. It changes due to the interaction with outsiders who have a different understanding. The ongoing presence of internationals on Bougainville during the long period of peace and state formation has led to a myriad of everyday contacts between many locals and internationals, and this interaction has an impact on how the locals see themselves and their authorities. In this context, understandings of legitimacy change.[40]

The Bougainville experience clearly demonstrates that external peacebuilders need to understand the processes of negotiation and hybridisation of legitimacy in the local context and the difference between international and local legitimacy. They have to overcome their focus on rational-legal legitimacy which leads them to ignore, under-value or reject non-rational-legal forms of legitimacy. They have to acknowledge the legitimacy of different types of authorities and have to work with them in hybrid-sensitive peace formation.[41] In other words: they have to reach beyond the comfort zone of 'state' and 'civil society'. Finally, and perhaps most importantly, external peacebuilders and state-builders have to reflect on their own legitimacy and be open to question it.

Post Scriptum: The Referendum and Legitimacy

It may well be that Bougainville will become an independent state in the not too distant future. The referendum on independence was held on 23 November 2019, and a majority opted for independence. Hence, Bougainville is currently at the beginning of a new stage of state formation. Over the last few years, the focus of political activities was on getting Bougainville 'referendum-ready'. Traditional authorities like chiefs and elders, as well as the Me'ekamuis, have joined in referendum preparations and have declared their support for the conduct of the referendum. In fact, the collaboration of all the legitimate authorities on Bougainville, as well as a legitimate referendum process, was to be crucial for the future of peace and political order on the island. For assessing the legitimacy of the referendum, both the domestic and the international dimension had to be taken into account. People on the ground had to believe that they were able to make a free and informed decision so as to accept the outcome of the referendum as legitimate, and the 'international community' – the UN and its member states, as well as international civil society – had to be convinced that a free and fair referendum according to internationally accepted standards has taken place; in this context, it is important to note that international observers had been invited for the referendum. Based on a domestically and internationally legitimate referendum, the governments of PNG and Bougainville will have to negotiate the implementation of the referendum result. This means that the two governments will have to agree on the conditions for the transition towards independence.

The vote for independence in the referendum also means that the people and the political elite in Bougainville will have to build a new nation-state as a legitimate member of the international community of states, and as a legitimate polity domestically. While in the international realm, the new Bougainville will have to become a 'state' in the image of internationally accepted statehood and will have to comply with international norms of legitimacy;[42] in the domestic realm Bougainville might emerge as a home-grown variety of political community which will be considerably different from the model Weberian state, but nevertheless enjoy legitimacy in the eyes of its people, exactly because of this difference. The features of this home-grown legitimate polity are evolving right now under our eyes, in current peace and state formation, grounded in hybridized legitimate authority, and with 'peace' understood 'as the emergence of legitimate political order'.[43]

Notes

1. For the difference between peacebuilding and peace formation see Richmond, 'Failed statebuilding versus peace formation', pp. 130–40. Talking about peace-building or state-building suggests a planned, technical, linear and predictable endeavour. Peace formation and state formation by contrast hint at messy, contradictory, non-linear and complex long-term processes which involve a wide and diverse range of actors and institutions, be they state, para-state or 'non-stat e'/'customary'/'traditional'. Peacebuilding and state-building are (at best) only part of such complex peace and state formation.
2. Weber, *Economy and Society: An outline of interpretive sociology*, pp. 212–13.
3. If states and governments are seen as legitimate by their peers in the international system of states, they enjoy international legitimacy. They are recognized as sovereign equal members of the international community of states. This international legitimacy makes it possible for states to engage in international relations, become members of international organizations, establish diplomatic ties to other states, negotiate international treaties, participate in activities of the international community of states and not least secure international assistance, most notably, for developing countries, in the form of official development assistance (which, in turn, can bolster empirical legitimacy in the domestic realm). States which enjoy international legitimacy can be fragile (if they lack domestic empirical legitimacy), and states which lack international legitimacy can nevertheless be stable if the citizens of the state hold a firm belief in their legitimacy (that is, they enjoy domestic empirical legitimacy).
4. These are legitimacy based on (1) Rational grounds – 'resting on a belief in the "legality" of patterns of normative rules and the right of those elevated to authority under such rules to issue commands (legal authority). (2) Traditional grounds – resting on an established belief in the sanctity of immemorial traditions and the legitimacy of the status of those exercising authority under them (traditional authority); or finally (3) Charismatic grounds – resting on devotion to the specific and exceptional sanctity, heroism or exemplary character of an individual person, and of the normative patterns or order revealed or ordained by him (charismatic authority)'. Weber, *On Charisma and Institution Building: Selected Papers*, (Chicago: University of Chicago Press, 1968), p. 46.
5. Weber, *From Max Weber: Essays in Sociology*, pp. 299–300.

6. The notion of the supremacy of rational-legal legitimacy and of the final historical triumph of this type of legitimacy is a cornerstone of all kinds of modernisation theories and implicitly (and sometimes also more or less explicitly) underpins today's liberal developmental, peacebuilding and state-building interventions of (more or less) benevolent international (Western) actors from the Global North. It is a main mental impediment to engaging with the realities of hybridisation of legitimacy in the Global South.

7. Carl and Garasu, *Weaving consensus – The Papua New Guinea – Bougainville peace process*; Regan, *Light Intervention: Lessons from Bougainville*.

8 We use the terms 'traditional' and 'customary' interchangeably here. Today's 'customary institutions' or 'traditional authorities' are *not* the institutions of the pre-contact and pre-colonial past. Today's 'chiefs' and 'elders', for example, although called 'traditional leaders' are rather 'modern' social categories which emerged in the course of interaction between local indigenous societies and external actors, with different types of 'chiefs' evolving, and these types overlapped and mixed over time. The terms 'customary' and 'traditional' are used here to conceptualize the 'other' in relation to 'western' or 'modern' political, societal and cultural structures and practices. This follows the terminology used by people and leaders in Bougainville themselves (in official documents, public political speech and everyday conversations). However, as we'll show in the following, the social institutions these terms refer to are hybrids, there are no clear-cut boundaries between the realm of the exogenous 'modern' and the endogenous 'customary/traditional'. Rumsey, 'The articulation of indigenous and exogenous orders in highland new guinea and beyond', pp. 47–69.

9. Regan, '"Traditional" leaders and conflict resolution in Bougainville: reforming the present by re-writing the past?', pp. 290–304; Tanis, 'Reconciliation: my side of the island', pp. 58–61.

10. Connell, 'Holding on to modernity? Siwai, Bougainville, Papua New Guinea', pp. 127–46: 141.

11. Boege, 'Hybrid forms of peace and order on a south sea island: Experiences from Bougainville (Papua New Guinea)', pp. 88–106; Boege and Garasu, 'Bougainville: A Source of Inspiration for Conflict Resolution', pp. 163–82; Boege and Garasu, 'Papua New Guinea: A success story of post-conflict peacebuilding in Bougainville', pp. 564–80.

12. Sagir, *Traditional leadership and the state in Bougainville: A Background Paper*; Tombot, 'A marriage of custom and introduced skills: restorative justice Bougainville style', pp. 255–64.

13. BCC, *Report of the Bougainville Constitutional Commission*, p. 202.

14. *The Constitution of the Autonomous Region of Bougainville*. Adopted by the Bougainville Constituent Assembly at Buin on 12 November 2004, clauses 11–39.

15. *Kastom* is a Pidgin derivative of 'custom'. Moore, *Happy Isles in Crisis. The historical causes for a failing state in Solomon Islands, 1998-2004*, p. 27. *Kastom* has developed since the times of first contact and colonisation, incorporating exogenous

influences into pre-colonial custom and adapting custom to those influences. *Kastom* is nowadays often referred to by both politicians and 'grassroots' people in Melanesia in order to stress their cultural heritage and the distinctiveness of their own ways from introduced ways, often depicting *kastom* as rooted in ancient pre-colonial traditions.

16. Tanis, 'Nagovisi villages as a window on Bougainville in 1988', pp. 447–72.
17. BCC, *Report of the Bougainville Constitutional Commission*, p. 172.
18. Ibid, p. 172.
19. Boege, 'Hybrid forms of peace and order on a south sea island: Experiences from Bougainville (Papua New Guinea)', pp. 88–106; Boege, 'How to maintain peace and security in a post-conflict hybrid political order – the case of Bougainville. pp. 330–52.
20. The instrument of 'recall of members' gives voters additional control over their elected representatives. It comprises "the capacity of the voters of a particular constituency to recall their member if in their view he or she is not doing their job as the people wish. This procedure effectively allows the voters to sack their sitting member and replace him or her with another between elections. This provides a level of participation unheard of in most other democracies" (BCC, 2004: 217). The instrument of 'recall of members' echoes the position of traditional leaders in a customary context. They have to prove their leadership capabilities on a daily basis, and their leadership role is accepted by the people only if and as long as they provide genuine leadership. Hence the status and legitimacy of a leader can never be taken for granted, it can be challenged at any time.
21. *New Dawn on Bougainville*, 10 October 2012.
22. *New Dawn on Bougainville* 7 October 2012.
23. The institution of 'Paramount Chief' itself is not traditional (there were no paramount chiefs in pre-contact and pre-colonial Bougainville communities), but a modern hybrid, combining local customary notions of leadership and introduced notions of hierarchy.
24. Me'ekamui is a term used both in Kieta and Nagovis languages to refer to sacred areas or a tabooed location. In Sikolewa village in Bolave Constituency there is an actual piece of land called Me'ekamui, and, to this day, no one eats betel nut that grows there. It is an historical site for the clan because their clan domesticated a wild spirit and cared for it. When this clan claims legitimate ownership to that land and all other adjacent land, the clan members use their identity of lineage so as to demonstrate before other clans that they are legitimate owners of the land there.
25. Regan, *Light Intervention: Lessons from Bougainville*.
26. Original inhabitants can transfer legitimacy to the taborangku if the taborangku make the osikaiang indebted to them by helping them in hosting feasts and fighting.
27. The 'modern' ideological use of the terms goes back to 1969 when Damien Dameng, an influential 'cargo cult' leader, established a group called Me'ekamui Pontoku Onoring. He contested the legitimacy of the miners, missionaries and

kiaps who had come in from the outside by using the terms that are used in custom to identify indigenous inhabitants. His intention was to demonstrate that the colonial government, the Christian missions, miners and planters were taborangku (foreigners) and had no legitimate authority over Bougainville. In 1988, at the beginning of the war, this line of thought was taken up by Francis Ona, the leader of the secessionists, who by this move was able to win Damien Dameng's group over (most of them current Me'ekamui). In 1989, however, the secessionists decided to go with the terms Bougainville Revolutionary Army and Republic of Bougainville (instead of Me'ekamui). When Francis Ona decided not to join the peace process and to disassociate himself from BRA that joined the peace process he reactivated his earlier attempt to follow Dameng's course by renaming A Company of the Bougainville Revolutionary Army as Me'ekamui Defense Force.

28. Hermkens, 'Circulating matters of belief: Engendering Marian movements during the Bougainville crisis', p. 166.

29. Hermkens, 'Religion in war and peace: Unravelling Mary's intervention in the Bougainville crisis', p. 278.

30. Regan, 'Identities among Bougainvilleans', pp. 418–46.

31. Cox, *Financing the End-Time Harvest: Pyramid Schemes and Prosperity Gospels in Papua New Guinea.*

32. While many former commanders of the armed groups on Bougainville have either given up (or lost) their leadership positions, others have transformed themselves into legitimate leaders in the state context – as politicians, ministers of the ABG, members of parliament – or have become businessmen, at the same time maintaining the charismatic warrior legitimacy they obtained as outstanding warriors during the war. Although they have 'retired' into civilian life, they are tacitly acknowledged as leaders by their former fighters and, based on their charismatic legitimacy, can easily mobilise their 'boys' if the necessity arises. Although these leaders have aligned themselves with political institutions and leaders (either the ABG or the Me'ekamui), they enjoy legitimacy in their own right and therefore have to be taken into account as a specific type of legitimate authority in post-conflict Bougainville.

33. Adams, *Peace on Bougainville – Truce Monitoring Group. Gudpela Nius Bilong Peace*; Wehner and Denoon, *Without a Gun. Australians' Experiences Monitoring Peace in Bougainville, 1997–2001.*

34. Sending, Ole Jacob, *Why Peacebuilders Fail to Secure Ownership and be Sensitive to Context*, NUPI Working Paper 755 (Oslo: NUPI, 2009), p. 17. Sending criticises the assumption 'that the international (liberal) standards that peace operations, and peacebuilding efforts, adhere to are what *really* provides them with legitimacy. This amounts to invoking a *normative* definition of legitimacy where legitimacy is linked to general concepts of right and good (i.e. human rights), and it is thus possible that some actors "perceive" of this legitimacy in the wrong way – that they have misperceptions about what is and what is not legitimate in a normative sense. (. . .) In an *empirical* reading of legitimacy, by

contrast – one following from Weber's discussion of the matter – to talk about "perceived legitimacy" is nonsensical since legitimacy is, by definition, established and maintained through the perceptions, or beliefs, people may have regardless of their normative content'.

35. Ibid. p.15. '(I)n essence, peacebuilders tend to assume that the internationally established legitimacy of the liberal principles that they advance will automatically translate into domestic legitimacy of the state as viewed by the local population. (. . .) it is an open question whether different domestic groups see such principles as legitimate – especially when these are effectively being imposed from the outside rather than being developed through negotiations and debate domestically'.

36. Tadjbakhsh, 'Introduction: liberal peace in dispute', p. 2. 'While practitioners tend to think that legitimacy comes from the international consensus around liberal peace and the normative power of international institutions, such as the United Nations, local actors see legitimacy in their own consent'.

37. On the other hand, there are also (smaller) sections of the populace that do not approve of the collaboration with those foreigners. In particular, the Me'ekamuis and those with sympathy for the Me'ekamuis, as well as 'traditionalists' and 'nationalists' in remote areas, question the legitimacy of the internationals' presence in principle. Hence, the ABG's legitimacy can suffer if the ABG is seen as being too close to alien forces or even as being a 'puppet on the string' of those forces. The ABG therefore has to perform a balancing act in its relations with external actors. This became very obvious when the current government under President Momis tried to forge closer ties with China. The Chinese influence on Bougainville is seen with deep suspicion by many Bougainvilleans, and too close a relationship with Chinese business and political interests definitely would have a negative effect on the legitimacy of the ABG.

38. Some actors might 'officially' lay claim to a specific type of legitimacy, be it rational-legal or traditional or other. But this 'official' claim must not be confused with the empirical reality, as 'tacitly' other sources of legitimacy come into play as well.

39. Not to forget that the co-existence and contestation of different types and sources of legitimacy can also lead to a situation in which they undermine and subvert each other, with de-legitimation as the consequence.

40. Boege, Rinck and Debiel, *Local–International Relations and the Recalibration of Peacebuilding Interventions. Insights from the 'Laboratory' of Bougainville and Beyond.*

41. Richmond, *A Post-Liberal Peace.*; Mac Ginty, *International Peacebuilding and Local Resistance: Hybrid Forms of Peace.*

42. There is no other choice than becoming such a state. If Bougainvilleans want to secede from the state they are currently part of (PNG), they have to establish their own state (or join another state): the current international system does not allow for 'stateless' spaces. Territories inhabited by people have to belong to one state or another. Bougainvilleans do not mind being citizens of a state; in fact, they want to have their own state and to be citizens. But they want a home-grown variety of 'state', and keep their socio-cultural identities.

43. Heathershaw, *Post-Conflict Tajikistan: The Politics of Peacebuilding and the Emergence of Legitimate Order*, p. 173.

References

Adams, Rebecca (ed.), *Peace on Bougainville – Truce Monitoring Group, Gudpela Nius Bilong Peace* (Wellington: Victoria University Press, 2001).

BCC, *Report of the Bougainville Constitutional Commission*, Report on the third and final draft of the Bougainville Constitution, prepared by the Bougainville Constitutional Commission, Arawa and Buka, 2004.

Boege, Volker, 'How to maintain peace and security in a post-conflict hybrid political order – the case of Bougainville', *Journal of International Peacekeeping*, 2010, 14: 3–4, pp. 330–52.

Boege, Volker, 'Hybrid forms of peace and order on a south sea island: Experiences from Bougainville (Papua New Guinea),' in Audra Mitchell and Oliver P. Richmond (eds), *Hybrid Forms of Peace: From Everyday Agency to Post-Liberalism*. New York: Palgrave Macmillan, pp. 88–106.

Boege, Volker and Lorraine Garasu, 'Papua New Guinea: A success story of post-conflict peacebuilding in Bougainville', in Annelies Heijmans, Nicola Simmonds and Hans van de Veen (eds), *Searching for Peace in Asia Pacific: An Overview of Conflict Prevention and Peacebuilding Activities* (Boulder and London: Lynne Rienner, 2004), pp. 564–80.

Boege, Volker and Lorraine Garasu, 'Bougainville: A source of inspiration for conflict resolution', in Roland Bleiker and Morgan Brigg (eds), *Mediating Across Difference: Oceanic and Asian approaches to conflict resolution* (Honolulu: University of Hawaii Press, 2011), pp. 163–82.

Boege, Volker, Patricia Rinck and Tobias Debiel, *Local–International Relations and the Recalibration of Peacebuilding Interventions. Insights from the 'Laboratory' of Bougainville and Beyond*, INEF-Report 112/2017 (Duisburg: Universitaet Duisburg-Essen, 2017).

Bougainville Peace Agreement, 30 August 2001, in Andy Carl and Lorraine Garasu (eds), *Weaving Consensus – The Papua New Guinea–Bougainville peace process* (Conciliation Resources Accord Issue 12/2002) (London: Conciliation Resources, 2001), pp. 67–85.

Braithwaite, John, Hilary Charlesworth, Peter Reddy and Leah Dunn, *Reconciliation and Architectures of Commitment: Sequencing peace in Bougainville* (Canberra: ANU ePress, 2010).

Carl, Andy and Lorraine Garasu (eds), *Weaving consensus – The Papua New Guinea–Bougainville peace process* (Conciliation Resources Accord Issue 12/2002) (London: Conciliation Resources, 2002).

Connell, John (2007), 'Holding on to modernity? Siwai, Bougainville, Papua New Guinea', in John Connell and Eric Waddell (eds), *Environment, Development and Change in Rural Asia-Pacific: Between local and global* (London and New York: Routledge), pp. 127-46.

The Constitution of the Autonomous Region of Bougainville, Adopted by the Bougainville Constituent Assembly at Buin on 12 November 2004.

Cox, John, *Financing the End-time Harvest: Pyramid Schemes and Prosperity Gospels in Papua New Guinea.* State, Society and Governance in Melanesia Discussion Paper 2009/5 (Canberra: Australian National University, 2009).

Heathershaw, John, *Post-Conflict Tajikistan: The Politics of Peacebuilding and the Emergence of Legitimate Order* (London and New York: Routledge, 2009).

Hermkens, Anna-Karina, 'Religion in war and peace: Unravelling Mary's intervention in the Bougainville crisis', *Culture and Religion,* 2007, 8: 3, pp. 271–89.

Hermkens, Anna-Karina, 'Circulating Matters of Belief: Engendering Marian Movements during the Bougainville Crisis', in Lenore Manderson, Wendy Smith and Matt Tomlinson (eds), *Flows of Faith: Religious Reach and Community* (New York: Springer, 2012), pp. 161–81.

Mac Ginty, Roger, *International Peacebuilding and Local Resistance: Hybrid Forms of Peace* (Hampshire and New York: Palgrave Macmillan, 2011).

Moore, Clive, *Happy Isles in Crisis: The historical causes for a failing state in Solomon Islands, 1998-2004* (Canberra: Asia Pacific Press, 2004).

Regan, Anthony J., '"Traditional" leaders and conflict resolution in Bougainville: reforming the present by re-writing the past?' in Sinclair Dinnen and Allison Ley (eds), *Reflections on Violence in Melanesia* (Annandale–Canberra: Hawkins Press–Asia Pacific Press, 2000), pp. 290–304.

Regan, Anthony J., 'Identities among Bougainvilleans', in Anthony J. Regan and Helga M. Griffin (eds), *Bougainville before the Conflict* (Canberra: Pandanus Books, 2005), pp. 418-46.

Regan, Anthony J., *Light Intervention: Lessons from Bougainville* (Washington, DC: United States Institute of Peace, 2010).

Regan, Anthony J. and Helga M. Griffin (eds), *Bougainville before the conflict* (Canberra: Pandanus Books, 2005).

Richmond, Oliver, *A Post-Liberal Peace.* (London and New York: Routledge, 2011).

Richmond, Oliver P., 'Failed statebuilding versus peace formation', in David Chandler and Timothy Sisk (eds), *Routledge Handbook of International Statebuilding.* (London and New York: Routledge, 2013), pp. 130–40.

Rumsey, Alan, 'The articulation of indigenous and exogenous orders in highland new guinea and beyond', *The Australian Journal of Anthropology,* 2006, 17: 1, pp. 47–69.

Sagir, Bill, *Traditional leadership and the state in Bougainville: A Background Paper.* Isabel Tok Stori, Dialogue on Traditional Leadership, Buala, Santa Isabel Province, Solomon Islands, 19–21 July 2005.

Tadjbakhsh, Shahrbanou, 'Introduction: liberal peace in dispute', in Shahrbanou Tadjbakhsh (ed.), *Rethinking the Liberal Peace: External models and local alternatives,* (London and New York: Routledge, 2011), pp. 1–15.

Tanis, James, 'Reconciliation: my side of the island', in Andy Carl and Lorraine Garasu (eds), *Weaving consensus – The Papua New Guinea–Bougainville peace process* (Conciliation Resources Accord Issue 12/2002) (London: Conciliation Resources, 2002), pp. 58–61.

Tanis, James, 'Nagovisi villages as a window on Bougainville in 1988', in Anthony J. Regan and Helga M. Griffin (eds), *Bougainville before the Conflict* (Canberra: Pandanus Books, 2005), pp. 447–72.

Tombot, John, 'A marriage of custom and introduced skills: restorative justice Bougainville style', in Sinclair Dinnen (ed.), *A Kind of Mending: Restorative Justice in the Pacific Islands.* (Canberra: Pandanus Books, 2003), pp. 255–64.

Weber, Max, *On Charisma and Institution Building: Selected Papers*, S. N. Eisendtadt (ed.) (Chicago: The University of Chicago Press, 1968).

Weber, Max, *Economy and Society: An outline of interpretive sociology*, Guenther Roth and Claus Wittich (eds), (Berkeley: University of California Press, [1922] 1980).

Weber, Max, *From Max Weber: Essays in Sociology.* H. H. Gerth and C. Wright Mills (eds), (Abingdon: Routledge, 1991).

Wehner, Monica and Donald Denoon (eds), *Without a Gun: Australians' Experiences Monitoring Peace in Bougainville, 1997-2001* (Canberra: Pandanus Books, 2001).

TWO

International Intervention and Relational Legitimacy

Gëzim Visoka

Introduction

Legitimacy continues to dominate a wide range of political and social debates. In peacebuilding and statebuilding studies, securing local legitimacy is considered crucial for the success of peacebuilding interventions. Across scholarly and policy community, the legitimacy of peacebuilding interventions is measured based on static frameworks, which consist of three major layers: the quality of good intentions; the successful performance in practice; and the perceived positive impact in overcoming conflict legacies and preventing the recurrence of violence. However, evidence from conflict-affected societies experiencing international intervention show that peacebuilding efforts have not managed to reach their desired goals, have not performed as expected, and often have contributed to adverse outcomes.[1] If peacebuilding interventions are not managing to achieve their desired goals, how do they sustain their political legitimacy and justify their rule? To make sense of this condition of governing through failure, we must rethink the politics of legitimation in the context of peacebuilding and understand the social and political dynamics that underpin this mode of ruling. This chapter argues that legitimation is deeply relational and dialectical process. Contrary to many claims, legitimacy is not normative; rather, it is deeply anti-foundational. This, though, does not exclude the possibility that norms and values are used for the legitimation purpose. At best, legitimacy is a circular process of relational validation, acceptance and refusal. Relations are the source of agential empowerment and disempowerment. They are the essence of legitimation and delegitimation. Thus, only when conceiving legitimacy as relational, we can account for the complex and multi-dimensional dynamics of political acceptance, legitimation, validation, resistance and rejections in the context of peace interventions. This perspective contributes to and complements the concept of hybrid legitimacy put forward in the introduction of this volume to offer both conceptual nuances and empirical examples.

The international, the state and post-conflict subjects are all relational entities by nature. They are interdependent and constantly legitimise and delegitimise one another intentionally and unintentionally. Their meaning and identity derives from their relationships and the quality of relationships dictates their actions. Legitimacy in the context of post-conflict societies is essentially about balancing political dependency among competing power sources. Local legitimacy and consent is considered as important to foreign interveners because they justify interventions on the grounds of protecting local subjects in the aftermath of the conflict. Failure to do so would undermine their global credibility and local effectiveness. But they also need to secure legitimacy from local elites to reduce domestic political contestation, as well as reduce the costs of deliberative and democratic politics. Though they need the consent of local population to counterweigh their reliance on elite legitimation. In other words, legitimacy served as a tactical approach to preserve international acceptance of the norm of intervention in societies affected by conflict. On the other hand, local elites and governance structures in conflict-affected societies need popular and democratic legitimacy to reduce dependency from the international community, and consolidate their political power. However, they need external legitimation to compensate for their domestic contestation and poor governance performance. In this context, the legitimation of state institutions and local political elite takes place through an assemblage of past, present and future oriented narratives, and hybridisation of internal and external practices and strategies of legitimation. Finally, a relational understanding of legitimacy reveals that every act of legitimation is also an act of self-legitimation. In post-conflict societies, local subjects need to legitimise certain political actors and institutions to ensure that they fulfil their political obligations, realise their specific needs and protect their political and material interests. Citizens legitimise themselves and others through simultaneous political activism and passivism, participation and resistance.

In examining the relational nature of legitimacy, this chapter explores the distinct figuration of legitimation practices in a post-conflict context. It uses Kosovo as an illustrative case study. The first part of this chapter situates relational legitimation within existing perspectives on legitimacy to offer a conceptual embeddedness to the empirical examination of legitimacy in post-conflict societies. The second and main part explores the politics of relational legitimation in Kosovo between the international peacebuilding missions, local political elite and the ordinary citizens. The third and final part discusses the implications of the multi-directional nature of legitimacy for peacebuilding in the era of fluid and remote interventionism. Accordingly, the chapter seeks to open the conceptual scope for studying relational legitimacy in conflict-affected societies and contribute to emerging debates in hybrid forms of legitimacy.

Legitimacy, legitimation and relationality

Legitimacy continues to remain highly debatable in political theory and international relations (IR). Normative perspectives relate legitimacy with political claims of who has the right to govern. They consider that for rulers to enjoy legitimacy, their 'core principles need to be justifiable on the basis of shared goals and values'.[2] At the heart of this conception of legitimacy lies the sense of political obligations to represent a political community, and the same political community to obey the authority. Max Weber defined legitimacy as 'the prestige of being considered exemplary or binding'.[3] In this sense, popular support obliges rulers to 'behave in certain ways or try and live up to particular norms in the absence of coercion'.[4] This understanding of legitimacy entails 'the transfer of consent by subjects to rulers, often in some form of regularly renewed democratic contract'.[5] Undergoing this democratic deliberation process gives meaning to legitimacy grounded on the 'perception that an institution is right, fair and appropriate within a particular normative context'.[6] This perspective portrays legitimacy as a burden on rulers to deliver on the expectation of their subjects. Common sources of legitimacy are considered practices of consensus-building, and the extent to which governing authorities promote and practice transparency and accountability, as well as participatory and dialogical governance.[7] Legitimacy also entails the perception that the governing authorities operated based on rules and principles of procedural justice, fairness and equality, entailing thus elements of legality and morality.[8] In a nutshell, legitimacy makes governability more democratic.[9] Democratic theories of legitimacy are embedded on static ontologies and normative epistemologies, thus lacking conceptual fluidity to capture the dynamic and relational nature of legitimacy. What these existing claims on legitimacy lack is a relational conceptualisation of legitimation. They tend to remove the fluidity and reciprocity at the heart of human relations and social dynamics that underpin any form of social and governmentality.

Relationality is different from foundational ontologies. It embraces fragility, contingency and difference. Anya Topolski argues that relationality 'provides us with a sense of meaning by making us aware of how interdependent we are, how interrelated our lives are and our potential, together with others, to change and co-create others and the shared world'.[10] Social identities and roles are shaped by social relations. Social reality is the totality of relations between things, persons and events. Relational views of legitimation blur the binaries between the rulers and the ruled and enables accounting for informal political affiliations beyond the solid binaries: state and citizens. A relational notion of legitimation helps explain constant interaction between the rulers and its subjects beyond electoral cycles and occasional deliberations, as well as accounts for other everyday forms of legitimation beyond institutions. In this context, practices of legitimacy are social constructs which entail 'the political negotiation amongst the members . . . [which] seek out an accommodation between those seemingly absolute values, and attempt to reconcile them with a working consensus to which all can feel bound'.[11] Furthermore, Topolski argues that 'relationality does not believe people are meant to be managed or ruled, but rather that they are born to surprise, create and transform the world'.[12]

Relational legitimacy underlines processes of legitimation constituted by flows of social and political actions which shape the political authority and enable governmentality. Governing from the perspective of relationality requires everyday legitimation, which recognises the power of the powerless, the mutual constitution of legitimacy, as well as the responsibility of such a shared understanding of relations. In democratic theory, elections are the most fundamental form of bottom-up legitimation. There is a general perception that 'legitimation is about rulers, and once the citizens have made their contribution, and that contribution has been assessed, they can be put temporarily to one side of the account'.[13] Challenging this view, Rodney Baker argues that 'subjects also legitimise themselves, as citizens. They do so most obviously by voting, but also by party and group activities, by demonstrations, strikes and public campaigns'.[14] Relational politics of legitimation entail everyday performativity which requires material and discursive transactions in the form of public goods, political promises and legal preaching. For instance, the delivery of public goods gives 'content to the social contract between ruler and ruled'.[15]

While the process of legitimation involves legitimising the other, it can also entail using others as means for self-identification and self-legitimation. From this perspective, legitimation entails tactics upon which political authority is 'claimed, sustained and recognised'.[16] Or, as Barker argues, '[l]egitimation is not a condition of the success of rulers so much as a characteristic of the phenomenon of being a ruler'.[17] Politicians and government officials spend a great deal of time performing self-legitimation. Ruling is

intimately connected with self-legitimation. Barker argues that 'identification is the key to understanding legitimation, and legitimation is one of
the principal functions of identification".[18] Hence, as much as practices of
legitimation are about securing the compliance of subjects, they are directly
linked to convincing themselves about their identity as rulers. Public rites of
legitimation entail talking to and hearing from the ordinary subjects of government. Listening for democracy is often nothing less than a performance
in service of legitimation and not a genuine effort of democratic representation.[19] However, even in public spheres and deliberations, 'the principal
actor, the most consistently engaged performer, is still not the subject, but
the ruler'.[20]

A relational view of legitimacy permits the examination of reversal processes. Parallel to legitimacy, it is crucial to look at delegitimation practices
which are embedded on other discourses, enacted by different actors, and
through different practices. Legitimation of one's actual or projected rule
signifies delegitimation of the opponents. In this sense, legitimacy is inherently exclusionary. While 'legitimacy can sustain subjection'[21] it can also
lead to liberation. Whereas for the rulers, legitimation might be seen subjection, the ruled subjects legitimise themselves from the very act of granting
or withholding legitimacy. Critical voices consider legitimacy as a hegemonic attempt of rulers to secure compliance of subjects without coercion.
However, by the same token, resistance movements can easily be labelled as
counter-hegemonic attempts which often do not seek change of governance
but change of government. For every act of legitimation, there is simultaneous delegitimation of existing or prior rulers or government institutions.
Techniques of legitimation in fact are observable only through discursive
or affirmative delegitimation practices. We know legitimacy only when it
is eroded or when it is absent. Barker claims that only 'by discovering what
destroys legitimacy, it may be possible to speculate on what may sustain
it'.[22] Central role in delegitimation plays attribution of blame for failing
to deliver on popular expectations, as well as discredit on the grounds of
actors' identity, past histories and ideological affiliation.

How can these relational predicaments of legitimacy help explain the
dynamics and politics of legitimation in a peacebuilding context? First, from
a relational point of view, the figuration of peace is a product of the relations between different interdependent actors which by default engages in
legitimation and delegitimation activities.[23] While democratic principles of
legitimacy are common to understand the politics of legitimation, the like-
lihood to capture complex nature of legitimacy is higher when the analyses
are displaced to study context-specific and patterned practices. Similarly,
Jeni Whalan argues that how 'legitimacy is evaluated will differ between

cases and across time, and it is therefore unfeasible to derive general criteria of local legitimacy'.[24] She further maintains that 'while this control model of legitimation operates through a direct link between procedures and outcomes, the relational model emphasises the nature of interactions between the powerful and those subject to that power'.[25] Each political community develops distinct codes of legitimation. Institutionalised metrics of legitimacy often include the election turnout, public opinion polls of government support, compliance with government policies and the level of informality, and public participation in decision-making. However, legitimacy can be captured only when we account comprehensively for the processes, actors and discourses of legitimation and delegitimation, as well as disentangle relations of power and identification.[26]

In this sense, relationality is well-suited to explain a world affected by perpetual crisis where security, democracy, peace and justice can no longer be grounded on absolute foundations. It can also offer useful grounds for exploring local agency in post-conflict societies and their forms of legitimation. To understand the relational legitimation, it is necessary to explore new forms of knowing that go beyond the institutional understanding of legitimacy. As argued by Stefanie Kappler, 'legitimacy in terms of who is trusted to be a legitimate promoter of social change is constantly renegotiated by a variety of actors'.[27] Similarly, Paul D. Williams claims that 'it literally makes no sense to talk about the meaning of legitimacy outside of a particular set of historical structures and conventions'.[28] The remainder of this chapter explores the relational legitimation in peacebuilding context to offer some key insights on the politics of legitimacy after international intervention in conflict-affected societies.

Legitimising the Local and the Local Legitimacy

The international interventions in the past two decades are widely contested on legal and moral grounds. This is precisely because the involvement of foreign countries and international organisations to stop violence and build peace in intrastate conflicts has not only challenged conventional rules of sovereignty and non-interference, but also has brought about new practices of legitimation. In peacebuilding interventions, legitimacy is about exercising power with external validation and internal acceptance. As Whalan argues, legitimacy 'makes the exercise of power easier, less costly, more effective and more resilient'.[29] From the early days, proponents of liberal peace and interventionism have recognised that legitimacy is crucial for effective peacebuilding. For example, UN's Capstone doctrine maintains that the 'high degree of international legitimacy' gives multi-dimensional peace operations 'considerable leverage over the parties'.[30] In contrast to governments which derive legitimacy internally from democratic elections, international administrations are legitimised externally. According to the UN, 'the international legitimacy of a United Nations peacekeeping operation is derived from the fact that it is established after obtaining a mandate from the United Nations Security Council, which has primary responsibility for the maintenance of international peace and security'.[31] Across the board, international interventions legitimise their full exercise of sovereignty by invoking the consent of the international community and by emphasising their good intentions to restore peace and order, rebuild political institutions, reconstruct the economy and create the conditions for durable peace.[32]

During the initial period of intervention, the United Nations (UN) peace operations have not based their legitimacy on the consent, compliance and support of local subjects, but on external authority granted by the UN Security Council and reproduced through the technologies of power, donations and norm and knowledge transfers. International missions generate local legitimacy by building 'legitimate political authority'.[33] Dominik Zaum argues that 'an institution is legitimate if its power is justified in terms of moral and other socially embedded beliefs, and if those subject to its rule recognise that it should be obeyed'.[34] As byproducts of reconstructing legitimacy are incorporated, the re-establishing of the rule of law, rebuilding institutions, holding elections, promoting constitutional reforms and civil society develop.[35] However, as much as building local institutions is a means to building peace, such endeavours have created local sources and institutional structures necessary to legitimise the international rule. For example, international missions in Kosovo have ruled with no direct democratic legitimation, while enjoying legal, political, cultural and intellectual supremacy over local subjects. As with all other peace operations, local subjects in Kosovo were not consulted and asked about the mandate and character of international intervention.[36] On the contrary, local subjects were disempowered from the outset on the grounds of being incapable of governing themselves due to unresolved political status –dependent subjects in need of external support for becoming peaceful and liberal subjects. This disempowerment has taken place through a complex technology of discourses, practices and events. Local subjects were treated as residents and not empowered citizens – users of Kosovar habitus without political rights to shape it the way they want. The scope of democratic rights was limited by denying the right to referendum, whereas elite-driven and top-down initiatives suffocated free political choices, and the right to protest and resist was sanctioned through a political, security, cultural and economic apparatus of conditionality. Local subjects were denied the right to seek justice and appeal misconduct of foreign personnel. Ultimately, international missions did not enjoy full local support because they failed to identify with local subjects and were not trying to legitimise their actions to them but were primarily focused on exogenous legitimation from the headquarters, sponsoring states and great powers.[37] In service of this outward looking dynamic, the UN established a governance system in Kosovo which made local elite seek external legitimacy and not primarily rule based on popular legitimacy.[38]

Aware that the legitimacy of UN peacebuilding operations 'may erode over time',[39] sustaining the local legitimacy of international peace interventions has emerged as a political necessity to control local expectations, reduce local resentment and, above all, save liberal peacebuilding and prolong foreign rule over conflict-affected societies. Overtime, across many post-conflict societies, it became obvious that interventions operating based on external legitimacy, legal validity and acceptance among great powers and international bodies is not sufficient for the success of peacebuilding interventions. Suddenly, then the 'successful peacebuilding' started to be affiliated with 'reducing the possibilities for violent conflict and laying the foundations for a new social order that enjoys widespread legitimacy'.[40] The legitimacy gap represented odds between 'priorities and concerns of imported institutions' with 'priorities and needs of heterogeneous populations' everyday life'.[41] In peacebuilding literature, local legitimacy has come to signify a wide range of everyday and institutional attributes which signify the subject's acceptance of and support for local or international authorities based on individual or collective norms and values. Possessing local legitimacy reduces the cost of coercively exercising authority and reduces the bargaining process. Whalan defines local legitimacy as the 'evaluations by local actors about a peace operation's rightness, fairness, and appropriateness – that is, whether its practices rightfully cohere with the relevant framework of rules and values, are fair, and produce appropriate outcomes'.[42]

Across different conflict-affected societies, prolonged peacebuilding interventions resulted in the erosion of the legitimacy of the external forces. The increased dissatisfaction of local populations with failed peacebuilding efforts pushed the international community to adjust to more optimal forms of interventions. In Kosovo, for instance, the transfer of competences to local institutions occurred only when there was extensive pressure and criticism from local actors and on those circumstances when continuing to hold executive powers became problematic for the internal cohesion of UN's mission and wider international community.[43] To compensate lack of local legitimacy, the international missions have promoted a statebuilding agenda where they worked with a handful local interlocutors within the limited scope of ethnic power-sharing. To disguises their asymmetric power and maintain local legitimacy, international community started to promote the discourse of local or national ownership. Promoting 'local ownership' over political processes is increasingly viewed as means of providing internal legitimacy for international administrations.[44] Local ownership is understood as an internationally-managed process of the gradual transfer of externally-held power to legitimate and democratically-elected local representatives after consolidating local capacities and functioning institutions.[45] Similarly, Timothy Donias considers local ownership as crucial mechanism for enabling consensus-building between insider and outsider agents on how to build peace.[46]

On this point, Nicolas Lemay-Hérbert argues that 'cultural sensitivity, along with robust accountability mechanisms and a greater local ownership of the process, can help the mission garner a certain degree of legitimacy'.[47] Of similar opinion is David Roberts, who argues that 'emergent legitimacy derives from varying provision of locally determined basic needs by locally-originating (and sometimes externally-supported) informal institutions, rather than externally-imposed political agendas, in parallel with orthodox approaches, assured of their presence by the power of ideological hegemony.'[48] By placing local actors and institutions in the spotlight and 'responsibilising' them for the peacebuilding and statebuilding processes, international interventions hope to achieve their strategic goals and avoid friction with local societies. However, Donais is aware that 'local ownership is about convincing or cajoling local actors to accept the wisdom and utility of what remain externally defined policy prescriptions . . .'.[49] The discourse of local ownership thus signifies an attempt to reduce paternalistic forms of interventionism to more facilitative and consultative forms of engagement that respect local needs, dynamics and interests.

While local ownership and the establishment of local political institutions and the transfer of governance tasks to democratically elected representatives is a pedigree to preserving local legitimacy of international interventions, the fact that international missions retain executive powers does not resolve entirely the legitimacy deficit. For example, even though UN's Interim Administration Mission in Kosovo (UNMIK) established local policy-making and law-making institutions, they retained executive competences that could overrule any decision made by local democratically-elected institutions. Kosovo institutions ended up not being representatives of the Kosovo people but loyal representatives of the international community in Kosovo. The international missions expected that Kosovo institutions would not be sites where politics and democracy takes place, but bureaucratic and conformist sites for implementing international policy on Kosovo. This ultimately undermined the legitimacy of these institutions as every law they passed could not be enforced without the approval of the international administrators. Although UNMIK was responsible for governing Kosovo, the blame for any failures was attributed to Kosovo institutions. The policy of transferring competences and capacity-building to local institutions was not a process of enhancing the local ownership over the peacebuilding in Kosovo, but a mechanism to relocate the blame for failures to Kosovo's fledgling institutions. Another important segment that has undermined the legitimacy of international missions in Kosovo has been their unwillingness to be held accountable by the local population and offer transparency on the decisions that have fundamentally shaped the political and socio-economic life of Kosovar society.[50] They were less concerned with the substantive aspects of legitimacy, namely the appropriateness of their declared intentions with policy actions and their eventual intended and unintended outcomes.[51]

International peacebuilding missions do not operate in a spatial and relational vacuum. They need to relate and engage with the local interlocutors. To enjoy local legitimacy, the international missions must legitimise the local. As Donais maintains, 'local perceptions of the legitimacy of peacebuilding strategy and action can therefore be considered crucial to the success of any peace process'.[52] This relational dependency simultaneously represents the possibility for shaping peace and promoting reconciliation, as well as empowering peace-breaking structures and actors. While it is an inevitable entrapment, untangling the mechanisms of how this mutual legitimation takes place is key to understanding the post-conflict peacebuilding performance and outcomes. From a relational perspective, the legitimation of international missions in Kosovo was affected by the extent to which they responded to local demands for statehood and how sympathetic they were towards ethnic groups in Kosovo and their political leadership.[53] Legitimation is not prescribed only on locally-acceptable actions, but also on the relational histories of key actors. The degree of local acceptance and personal relations with local elites was essential for the political effectiveness of international missions. Similarly, the relationships between regional powers affect the relations between international missions and local actors. At the international level, the UN Security Council served as a platform to both legitimise and delegitimise Kosovo's quest for statehood, support and criticise peacebuilding agenda, and renew great power rivalry and antagonisms on Kosovo.[54] Supporters of UN's mission in Kosovo before independence became its opponents after independence, and vice versa. Before independence, the Russian Federation, together with

China and other non-permanent allies in the Council, have constantly tried to report on the problems and failures of UNMIK. On the other hand, the US, UK, France and other supporting non-permanent members in the Council have tried to portray a positive track-record of UNMIK's performance and impact in Kosovo. After independence, Russian Federation and Serbia became strong supporters of UNMIK's reconfigured mandate in Kosovo, whereas supporters of Kosovo independence demanded its downsizing and eventual closure. This signifies that international missions are sites for legitimising and delegitimising the foreign policies of dominant global and regional powers. The international, regional and local dynamics are deeply interrelated and mutually constitutive.

International interventions in post-conflict societies are exposed to multiple legitimation challenges, which significantly affect the peacebuilding process. Seeking external legitimacy at the expense of local legitimacy has been problematic as it has increased local resentment and non-compliance with external statebuilding and peacebuilding agenda. The more peacebuilding process enjoys international legitimacy, the more likely it is to suffer from the lack of local legitimacy as the priorities and needs are different. Under the disguises of local ownership, the international missions have consulted only certain political institutions and actors at the expense of bypassing wider population. This, in turn, has created custodian relations between international missions and local elites and excluded genuine processes of democratic accountability and legitimation. Most significantly, the need for legitimation has revealed the circular nature of power in post-conflict societies, whereby a local agency has played a far more significant role than often acknowledged in the literature.

State of Legitimation and the Legitimation of the State

Understanding relational legitimacy in the context of international interventions requires accounting for the legitimation practices of local actors, especially of the organised political and ethnic groups. The new state institutions emerging from the period of shared sovereignty with international community are not only expected to be accountable to local population but first and foremost serve foreign agendas. Hence, located between external forces and local constituencies, political elites in post-conflict societies have inevitably forced to come up with hybrid forms of self-legitimation. In the absence of state sovereignty and effective authority, political elites in Kosovo have legitimised their political conduct largely by recalling their past contribution in the struggle for freedom and statehood and have also justified their authority in implementing a social contract for making

Kosovo a modern, multi-ethnic democracy, fully integrated in the international society.[55] In doing this, they have exploited modern and traditional, formal and informal sites and methods of legitimation.

In democratic theory, elections are the most prominent form of legitimation. By holding democratic elections, the international missions have tried to establish a liberal political order where the political legitimacy of the new state derives from popular votes and institutional rules. Establishment of democratic institutions and regular elections first and foremost tended to legitimise the normative basis of intervention, and then control the emerging local political order. Jogo Salmon and Catherine Anderson hold that 'the normative standards through which the international community bestows legitimacy on the state often stand in contrast to the norms and rules of elite pacts and their expectant constituencies'.[56] This was precisely the case in Kosovo. Before independence, international observers largely overlooked election manipulation in Kosovo as they were interested in having a reliable government that would continue implementing international agenda on Kosovo. However, after independence, they observed large-scale irregularities during the national elections evident with breaching the secrecy of voting, collective voting of families and groups, intimidation of election observers and frauds during counting of ballots.[57] Political representatives in Kosovo have engaged in patronage politics to secure the popular vote often against constitutional and democratic rules.[58] Personal and place-based relations determined the politics of partisanship and who gained popular legitimacy. Political legitimacy was secured through modest bribes or the promise to secure jobs, scholarships and procurement contracts. It was a transactional process. In certain instances, legitimacy was secured through coercive measures, such as threatening public servants for losing jobs and community benefits if they would not vote for a particular political party or candidate. Manipulation of elections through patronage politics created false bases of legitimacy, which signifies why this 'fake consent' did not translate in everyday support for the laws and policies implemented by the government, and why people do not take political obligations and constantly resist and challenge the authority.

Beyond these contested democratic legitimation practices, political elites in post-conflict societies secure legitimation through other alternative methods. Timothy D. Sisk and David Chandler argue that a critical indicator of a state lacking legitimacy is 'the effort of ruling elites to legitimise their rule through fraudulent electoral processes, appeals to extreme nationalism or ideology, or the hegemonic exercise of power through narrow ethnic networks'.[59] Overwhelmingly, local elite legitimation was not based on the quality of their governance and democratic representation, but on the quality of past resistance and affiliation with certain historical figures.[60] The three main axes of legitimation among the Kosovo political elite included their participation in the liberation war; their role in the proclamation of independence and consolidation of statehood; and finally, their commitment for Euro-Atlantic integration. Often, politicians were not elected based on their political performance, but based on their personal and family relationship to political, nationalist and military figures. The closeness of politicians to certain political figures such as former President Ibrahim Rugova or Adem Jashari (one of the KLA military leaders) has granted them political legitimacy inside and outside electoral processes. In generating popular legitimacy, former armed and non-violent factions of the Kosovo political elite engaged in constructing public memory for certain war figures through erecting statues, monuments and nationalist symbols; annual commemoration through events, poetry, folk music and visual presentations; and naming public streets, objects, institutions and open spaces.[61] Such commemoration practices have benefited politicians affiliated with the region or family of the remembered and glorified combatants, which has been used to consolidate political power, gain material benefits, and control local and national political processes. Hence, the past was used to legitimise present rulers and commemoration facilitated legitimation.

Post-conflict states experiencing international intervention by default create custodian relations with external forces. Under these conditions, external legitimation appears to be more important than local legitimation. The local political elite in Kosovo needed legitimation not only from the citizens, but also from international community, namely acceptance by states and organisations that have supported Kosovo in its struggle for liberation and independence. Kosovo's dependency on external political, diplomatic, security and economic support has made democratic legitimacy insufficient for governing the fledgling state.[62] Hence, external legitimation has taken a central role in shaping political institutions, elite behaviour and the peace-building agenda. This legitimation process consisted of bilateral and multilateral meetings between Kosovar leadership and those of the United States and key EU member-states. Over the years, key figures of external legitimation involve presidents, prime ministers and distinguished personalities who have served in Western governments and have played a crucial role in Kosovo's recent history. In the aftermath of elections, Kosovar political parties were obliged to consult and discuss the government formation with foreign governments. These consecutive and intrusive acts of international intervention in political appointments meant that those political leaders would need to remain accountable to external actors more than Kosovo citizens, as well as prioritise external demands concerning institutional reforms over local needs for socio-economic development. Before independence, Kosovo leaders declared that they were accountable to the citizens of Kosovo but also to the international community. In practice, though, they were more accountable to the international actors than to the local population.[63] The local political factions in Kosovo have often misused the issue of international decision-making on Kosovo. In many occasions, local actors have articulated their own positions, while covering up with the justification that those positions are also those of the international community. Any time the local actors were not ready to take the responsibility for any actions and their eventual consequences, they have allocated the agency and responsibility to the international factors. This culture of evasion of political responsibility has been transcended and incorporated in Kosovo political institutions after independence.

In order to legitimise their rule in Kosovo, international missions have constantly engaged in delegitimation practices. The political agendas of international missions were never attached to the needs of local population in Kosovo, which explains why they have failed to change on their own terms the social and political order in Kosovo. To compensate lack of local legitimacy, the international community exerted pressure on a handful of authoritarian political elite who benefited from such externally-granted authority but also were held hostage through a complex technology of incentives and coercion. However, international missions have, by default, decided to distrust all local politicians in Kosovo aware of the sophisticated local institutional resistance and techniques of manipulation, which are seen to be more advanced than in many other more complex and protracted conflicts around the world. Disciplining and delegitimation of local elites was implemented through hybrid transitional justice processes and prosecution for corruption and organised crime. Contrary to what international actors might have intended, war crimes trials only generated more cohesion and unity among the Kosovo Albanian political elite, as well as boosted popular support and enabled nationalist discourses in expense of more moderate voices. The same dynamic has taken place among the Serb community in Kosovo. Allegations for war crime and abuse of power have only boosted the legitimacy of local leaders in the north of Kosovo. The local support against war crimes trials of key war proponents was also extended in cases where the very same protagonists were investigated for corruption and misuse of political office. Hence, the more ownership is transferred to local institutions, the more the legitimacy of the international peacebuilding agenda was contested and confronted. However, attempts to delegitimise the local institutions resulted in a backlash. Local actors have also proactively delegitimised international peacebuilding missions through hybrid methods deployed both within political institutions as well as outside institutions, combining conventional, legally acceptable political actions, and unlawful resistance practices.

The lack of universal recognition for Kosovo independence has raised questions regarding the international legitimacy of the fledgling state and its implications for domestic sovereignty and contested existence in the society of state.[64] The challenge remains for Kosovo how to pursue its unconventional quest for bilateral recognition outside the UN membership framework and overcome the contestation of the legitimacy of Kosovo's declaration of independence. Hence, the Kosovo government had to seek legitimation not only from its citizens and external forces, but also from the wider international community, namely individual states and international organisations. To secure international legitimation, Kosovo had to build an active diplomatic service, develop a strong narrative of why it deserves membership of international society and conduct a dynamic campaign for securing diplomatic recognition and joining regional and international bodies. Kosovo's everyday struggle for international legitimation shows that to become a sovereign state it is not sufficient only to have the classical attributes of statehood, such as territory, population, and government, but what it also requires a proactive discursively performative agency for securing international recognition and engagement in international relations. In turn, constitution of sovereignty through diplomatic recognition contributes to strengthening key domestic attributes of sovereign statehood. However, strengthening of Kosovo's international legitimation came at the expense of delegitimation of international missions in Kosovo. The more Kosovo claimed to gain internal and external sovereignty and respect for its constitutional and legal authority, the more it tried to reduce political dependency on international missions. Undoubtedly, external legitimation is a consequence of international administration of Kosovo, where the international community had a leading role in designing political institutions, granting powers to local actors and forming governments – all within and outside the democratic electoral processes. However, the continued attempt to seek external legitimation signifies that Kosovo continues to share its sovereignty with foreign forces and suffers from diplomatic dependency.

The fledgling political institutions in post-conflict societies are sourced with multiple modes of legitimation which paradoxically enables them to govern not based on their democratic performance but on exterior forces – resurrected either in the form of dependency on foreign entities or exploitation of collective past, ideology, and other local cultural and spatial affiliations. In Kosovo, relations have proven to be more powerful than democratic rules, norms and institutions. Perhaps the secret of effective peacebuilding and statebuilding does not lie only in building state institutions, but also in shaping the locus and networks of local relationships.

Subjects of Legitimation and the Legitimation of Subjects

Protagonists of post-conflict legitimation are not only international missions and the local political elite. Citizens are also subjects of legitimation. As David Roberts argues, '[t]he legitimacy of a polity, democratic or otherwise, rests in substantial part on its relevance to people and their needs'.[65] People's joint commitments, loyalty towards the laws, rules and institutions and the obligations are mutual, relational and contingent to the fulfilment of their basic and constitutive needs, entitlement of rights and freedoms, and development of agential capabilities. Hence, legitimising the state is a practice that citizens use to trade their loyalty in exchange of realising some of their needs, interests and rights. As much as politicians and institutions think they exploit citizens when seeking legitimation, so do citizens in relation to the government and politicians. In Kosovo, good relations with rulers in a perverse way empowered the ruled. Legitimising others simultaneously legitimises the self. Examples of such citizen self-legitimation include assembling and performing narratives of personal relations with the rules deriving from family connection, networks of friendship and place-based commonalities. Other examples include personal and family affiliation with common institutions, political parties and other social organisations. These relationships are often sourced with anecdotal and visual evidence of closeness to the rulers, which in turn provide agential capacities to citizens to achieve their everyday goals.

In post-conflict societies, networks of relations are more comprehendible for citizens than formalised, bureaucratic, and depoliticised institutional procedures. For example, formal institutions in Kosovo did not enjoy great popularity, not only because they failed to deliver on their promises and expectation, but also because there were other competing political and social forces which served as substitutes to institutions. It was the parapolitics, patronage politics and informal networks which served as a more tangible platform for relational legitimation. Parapolitics represent the hidden side of the multiplicity of governance regimes that each society has, which are driven by individual and collective desire for extraordinary power, legitimacy and resources outside the framework of contemporary regulatory states.[66] From this perspective, legitimation is not only about democratic performance or political identification, but also about the relationality of socio-economic and political figurations. In this sense, formal political institutions in Kosovo have ended up becoming instruments of genuine political entrepreneurs which operated both within and outside institutions through their network of loyal entities installed across all important governmental sectors. Real political decision-making took place outside formal institutions where those shadow structures were no longer parapolitical structures but well-consolidated networks of power.[67] Such non-institutional practices of legitimation explain why local political elites did not only rely on electoral turnout or public opinion polls to measure their political power. Rather, they trusted more relational networks and everyday indicators of legitimacy to rule with confidence, regardless of what external liberal democracy indicators predicated.

Rethinking the politics of how legitimacy is measured also reveals important trends in conflict-affected societies. Citizens' satisfaction is measured based on public opinion polls, their contribution to the state through paying taxes and protecting public goods, as well as mobilising in support or opposition of government. Trust is considered crucial for maintaining the government integrity and popular validity. Similarly, participation is seen as an essential feature of democracy, as a way of ensuring good government and as a way of enriching the social contract.[68] However, from a relational point of view, political trust and participation can essentially be conflictual. Citizens in their everyday realm have the capacity to find tactical solutions to fulfil their basic needs by exploiting informal networks, family and friendship structures and contacts within formal institutions. Undoubtedly, such subsistence reactions derive from the inconvenience, distrust and inability of people to cooperate with formal institutions, rules and formal requirements for economic and socio-political transactions, as well as the lack of regulation in the side of formal institutions. In addition, subsistence practice could be also supplementary and complementary responses to institutional vacuum or lack of regulatory and effective enforcement mechanisms. The more trustful the state is, the less political participation there will be and vice versa. Eric M. Uslander argues that 'people will be more likely to get involved in political life when they get mad and believe that some others, be they other people or political leaders, can't be trusted'.[69] This signifies that trust in government, taxation, as well as willingness to protest are not definitive indicators of the decline of democracy. For instance, Pierre Rosanvallon argues that distrust can be a reflection of citizens' desire 'to make sure that elected officials keep their promises and to find ways of maintaining pressure on the government to serve the common good'.[70] Effectively, social distrust is a tactic used by people to oblige the government to pay greater attention to social needs, improve democratic performance and invest in socially useful projects. From this perspective, passive citizenry does not mean that they do not engage in legitimation processes. Low level of political participation does not necessarily represent legitimacy crisis.[71] Political expression is manifested differently across different places and times.

Parallel to acts of (self)legitimation, subjects also engage in acts of delegitimation. The everyday is the space where delegitimation takes a freeride, where the truth and intrigues are produced and validated, where leaders are born and buried. Citizens can be unpolitical and thus with great degree of carelessness and irresponsibility attribute failures to government based on anecdotal evidence. The substance of citizen delegitimation represents the resentment and dissatisfaction towards a particular institution or politician on the premise of their unfulfilled needs or harmed interests. In Kosovo, delegitimation was embedded on three major discourses. The first discourse was based on identity politics, namely who is the politician, what is their background, and how are they perceived in public life. Hence, those that are affiliated with armed resistance and hard-core militarism in Kosovo considered pacifists as weak, traitors, and incapable of defending national interests. By the same token, more moderate voices considered ex-combatants as radical, uncivilised, and unintellectual and who govern through coercion, sabotage and corruption. The second discourse of delegitimation was based on the democratic performance of political leaders and institutions. Here the predominant focus was on corruption, nepotism and clan-based governance, as well as on social inequality and the rapid material wealth of political leaders. And finally, the third discourse of delegitimation was about the external relations of political leaders. Here the focus was on pointing out contested relations with former foes, or accusation for working for foreign governments and intelligent services. However, as much as these discourses of delegitimation are products of ordinary people, they also imitate speech acts of politicians, public opinion makers, civil society leaders, policy studies and media reports.

Conclusion: fluid interventionism and the future of legitimacy?

Legitimation of peacebuilding interventions has emerged as an important factor for sustaining peace in conflict-affected societies. Legitimacy is a political concept which facilitates the implementation of external agendas for building peace and restoring broken relations between groups in conflict. The international peacebuilding architecture in the past ten years has favoured a top-down, normative agenda based on universal blueprints of how to build peace and prevent conflicts. This has been a vertical conception of legitimacy privileging top-down forms of legitimation. In these instances, when we refer to local legitimacy, we simply mean the local acceptance of and compliance with external intervention. Local legitimacy is seen as legitimation of peacebuilding by representatives of the people, thus maintaining the distance between the external interveners and local genuine subjects. The analysis has complemented observations in the introductory chapter of this volume by highlighting the entangled, relational, and transversal nature of legitimacy. This chapter has provided a relational reading of legitimacy in the context of international interventions. Relations are central to understanding dynamics of peace formation and peacebreakage. Yet, mainstreaming relations and incorporating them into policy processes would be problematic for two major reasons.

First, a relational understanding of peacebuilding would require a different agenda for peace, not only focusing on building state institutions and changing political rules, but also developing a social agenda for addressing peoples' context-specific needs.[72] So far, international missions have aspired local legitimation not so much to achieve the normative goals and validate their peacebuilding agenda, but primarily to overcome local resistance and enable an uncontested and unrestrained rule. Seen from this perspective, legitimation has been more pragmatic than normative. In other words, listening to local actors has come into political consideration only when it was perceived by influential actors as beneficial for the expansion of their legitimacy base. Hence, embarking on a relational peacebuilding process would mean that relations with local people matter as much as investing in building institutions, establishing rule-based orders, and imposing economic reforms.

Second, the organisational design of peacebuilding missions would need to change, including the attitudes and skills of international personnel. Relational peacebuilding would require building a multi-layered infrastructure for peace; localised, hybrid, and indigenous forms of deliberative governance; local civil society-based peace formation initiatives; and adjustment to both rights-based and need-based development agendas. This would require working and living with communities, sharing spaces and recourses, building empathy and common identification. It would also entail abandoning current tendencies for cultural and material supremacy, as well as discharge from diplomatic privileges and immunities and being directly accountable to local subjects rather than only to external instances. Some of these predicaments are already discussed in the emerging literature on post-liberal forms of peacebuilding, yet more research is required to see the implications of hybrid and bottom-up forms of legitimacy.[73]

Notwithstanding the merits of this alternative possibility, a relational approach to legitimacy and peacebuilding would not necessarily promote comprehensive peace, justice, reconciliation and development as envisaged by the international community. Securing the legitimacy of one group through addressing their political, economic and social needs could take place at the expense of the other, undermining the claims of other ethnic and religious groups. Seeking a middle ground would also be perceived as overlooking structural and historical injustice and washing away the politics and power dynamics, which hold the key to peace more often than not. Furthermore, securing local legitimacy would entail some sort of permanent presence to ensure that trust between the citizens and international missions is established. This has double-edged implications. Short-term missions do not provide enough time to build relations with local subjects. Long-term interventions risk creating political dependency, trigger local resistance and promote neo-colonialism. For relational peacebuilding to work, heavy footprint interventionism would be required that is infiltrated beyond political institutions to reach out to most peripheral societal spaces. Arguably, all these alternative possibilities for generating local legitimacy run against the conclusions reached by critical scholars on the long-term, unintended negative impact of peace interventions.

These observations notwithstanding, as we are now entering the era of fluid and remote interventions, relational and local legitimacy, for instance, might no longer be a major concern for intervening powers. The history of peacebuilding in the recent decades has revealed both the limits of extensive and prolonged peacebuilding missions, as well as the consequences of short and light footprint operations. So far, external blueprints, imposition of political norms and economic systems, and faulty transitional international administrations have not been conducive and suitable to many conflict-affected societies. The longer the UN and other peacebuilding organizations stayed in post-conflict societies, local problems did not fade away and many normative and operational anomalies of UN peace operations came to the surface. The UN heavy footprint was criticised for being ineffective, for creating local dependency and for being undemocratic. At the global stage, the merging of peace-security-development nexus, launched after the War on Terror, revealed the mixed motives for intervention and weakened the case for the potential adverse outcomes and negative impact of such interventions. Most importantly, the fluid and unpredictable nature of post-conflict peace is increasingly alerting policy-makers to search for new forms of interventions. From direct and shared governance of these societies, the modes of interventionism are becoming more hidden, structural and liquid in nature. Because the foreign interveners know that they cannot build and keep peace in the shape they want, all they can do is influence it. Knowing the limits of past interventions evident with the prevalence of uncertainty and unlearning, external actors deploy what we may be call fluid interventions, which are rooted in precautionary logics, situational vigilance, and perpetual muddling through – in an attempt to avoid and mitigate the exposures of the past.[74] In the context of peacebuilding, fluid interventions operate as a remote and networked society of interveners spread across international organisations, diplomatic services of states, non-governmental and philanthropic communities and business consultancy.

While in the age of liberal interventionism securing local legitimacy was seen as a pragmatic move to reduce local contestation of interventions and facilitate smoother implementation of peacebuilding and statebuilding strategies, in the emerging age of fluid interventionism politics of legitimation take a different figuration.[75] The legitimacy of an operation is measured based on the pre-emptive engagement. To compensate for the impossibility of securing local legitimacy, we are now witnessing a shift towards post-interventionism manifested with fluid and remote engagements. Post-interventionism enables engagement without needing local legitimation as the operations are ad hoc, liquid and from proximity. Interventions have open-ended, short-term and fluid missions which do not require building solid relations with the local peoples, cultures and expectations. Means of remote interventions are: big data for early warning and conflict prevention, networking through media, surveillance from satellites, as well as using unmanned drones. These paradigmatic shifts are conceived by Colleen Bell and Brad Evans[76] as leading towards 'post-interventionary' engagements whereby conflict is tackled through non-military security technologies that seek to depoliticise local subjects and move away the key referent objects of conflict. Such remote interventions do not need local legitimacy as they are physically and normatively detached from the epicentres of interventions. More so, remote peacebuilding is a way to engage without needing legitimation.

Fluid interventions are outward-oriented in terms of political legitimation and moral validation. The norm of precision, precaution and prevention serve as self-legitimising mechanisms to preserve domestic democratic sanity, reduce international contestation and mitigate eventual backlash from the targeted societies. For this legitimation to take place, propagating global and domestic risk is crucial to offer an ontological reference to make any action tackling such risks politically acceptable and morally permissible. Hence, in the current transitional order, we are unwriting security, peace and development. In remote interventionism, sources of legitimacy and strategies of legitimation are fluid and adaptive. When governing authorities fail to perform and deliver results, they displace the responsibility to external factors. In the liberal and modern world, legitimacy has derived from providing stability and predictability. In a fluid world, legitimation is grounded in both preventive and pre-emptive measures, as well as post-event responses. Under these circumstances, the rulers are legitimised on their ability to empower subjects with resiliency which removes them from the responsibility for any consequences deriving from intervention in the first place. Under these conditions, legitimacy might not determine the normative grounds for intervention but certainly will influence the prospects for sustaining peace in conflict-affected societies.

Notes

1. Visoka, Gëzim, *Peace Figuration after International Intervention: Intentions, Events and Consequences of Liberal Peacebuilding* (London: Routledge, 2016).
2. Hurrell, Andrew 'Legitimacy and the use of force: Can the circle be squared?', *Review of International Studies*, 2005, 31, no. S1, p. 20.
3. Weber, Max, *Basic Concepts in Sociology* (New York: Citadel Press, 1962), p. 72.
4. Williams, Paul D. 'Regional and Global Legitimacy Dynamics: The United Nations and Regional Arrangements', in D. Zaum (ed.), *Legitimating International Organizations* (Oxford: Oxford University Press, 2013), p. 41.
5. Barker, Rodney, *Legitimating Identities: The Self-Presentations of Rulers and Subjects* (Cambridge: Cambridge University Press, 2004), p. 9.
6. Whalan, Jeni, *How Peace Operations Work: Power, Legitimacy, and Effectiveness* (Oxford: Oxford University Press, 2013), p. 51.
7. Call, Charles T. 'Beyond the "Failed State": Towards Conceptual Alternatives,' *European Journal of International Relations*, 2011, 17, no. 2, pp. 30–326; Papagianni, Katia, 'Participation and State Legitimation', in C. Call and V. Wyeth (eds.), *Building States to Build Peace* (Boulder, CO: Lynne Rienner, 2008), p. 52.
8. Clark, Ian, *Legitimacy in International Society* (Oxford: Oxford University Press, 2005), p. 20.
9. Coicaud, Jean-Marc, *Legitimacy and Politics: A Contribution to the Study of Political Right and Political Responsibility* (Cambridge: Cambridge University Press, 2014).
10. Topolski, Anya, *Arendt, Levinas and a Politics of Relationality* (London: Rowman & Littlefield, 2015), p. 224.
11. Clark, *Legitimacy in International Society*, pp. 29–30.
12. Topolski, *Arendt, Levinas and a Politics of Relationality*, p. 229.
13. Barker, *Legitimating Identities: The Self-Presentations of Rulers and Subjects*, p. 110.
14. Barker, *Legitimating Identities*, p. 111.
15. Rotberg, Robert, 'The Failure and Collapse of Nation-States: Breakdown, Prevention, and Repair', in R. Rotberg (ed.), *When States Fail: Causes and Consequences* (Princeton, NJ: Princeton University Press, 2004), pp. 2–3.
16. Zaum, Dominik, 'International Organizations, Legitimacy, and Legitimation,' in D. Zaum (ed.), *Legitimating International Organizations* (Oxford: Oxford University Press, 2013), p. 10.
17. Barker, *Legitimating Identities*, p. 20.

18. Barker, *Legitimating Identities*, p. 35.
19. Dobson, Andrew, *Listening for Democracy: Recognition, Representation, Reconciliation* (Oxford: Oxford University Press, 2014).
20. Barker, *Legitimating Identities*, p. 107.
21. Barker, Rodney, *Political Legitimacy and the State* (Oxford: Oxford University Press, 1990), p. 12.
22. Barker, *Political Legitimacy and the State*, p. 163.
23. Visoka, Gëzim, *Peace Figuration after International Intervention*.
24. Whalan, Jeni, *How Peace Operations Work: Power, Legitimacy, and Effectiveness* (Oxford: Oxford University Press, 2013), pp. 63–64.
25. Whalan, *How Peace Operations Work: Power, Legitimacy, and Effectiveness*, p. 73.
26. Visoka, *Peace Figuration after International Intervention*.
27. Kappler, Stefanie, 'Everyday Legitimacy in Post-Conflict Spaces: The Creation of Social Legitimacy in Bosnia-Herzegovina's Cultural Arenas', *Journal of Intervention and Statebuilding*, 2013, 7, no. 1, p. 24.
28. Williams, Paul D., 'Regional and Global Legitimacy Dynamics: The United Nations and Regional Arrangements', in D. Zaum (ed.), *Legitimating International Organizations* (Oxford: Oxford University Press, 2013), p. 44.
29. Whalan, *How Peace Operations Work: Power, Legitimacy, and Effectiveness*, p. 64.
30. UN, 'United Nations Peacekeeping Operations: Principles and Guidelines (Capstone Doctrine),' (New York: United Nations, 2008), p. 24. Available at <http://www.un.org/en/peacekeeping/documents/capstone_eng.pdf> (last accessed 22 May 2016).
31. UN, 'United Nations Peacekeeping Operations: Principles and Guidelines (Capstone Doctrine)', p. 36.
32. Zaum, Dominik, *Sovereignty Paradox: The Norms and Politics of International Statebuilding* (Oxford: Oxford University Press, 2007).
33. Kaldor, Mary, *New and Old Wars* (Cambridge: Polity, 2006), p. 132.
34. Zaum, 'International Organizations, Legitimacy, and Legitimation', p. 9.
35. Brinkerhoff, Derick W. (ed.), *Governance in Post-Conflict Societies: Rebuilding Fragile States* (London: Routledge, 2008), p. 6.
36. Visoka, Gëzim and Vjosa Musliu (eds), *Unravelling Liberal Internationalism: Local Critiques of Statebuilding in Kosovo* (London: Routledge, 2019).
37. Visoka, *Peace Figuration after International Intervention*.
38. Visoka, Gëzim and Oliver P. Richmond, 'After Liberal Peace? From Failed State-building to an Emancipatory Peace in Kosovo,' *International Studies Perspectives*, 2017, 18, no. 1, pp. 110–129.
39. UN, 'United Nations Peacekeeping Operations: Principles and Guidelines (Capstone Doctrine)', p. 37.
40. Donais, Timothy, *Peacebuilding and Local Ownership: Post-conflict consensus-building*, (London: Routledge, 2012), p. 71.
41. Lemay-Hébert, Nicolas, 'Everyday Legitimacy and International Administration: Global Governance and Local Legitimacy in Kosovo', *Journal of Intervention and Statebuilding*, 2012, 7, no. 1: 87.

42. Whalan, *How Peace Operations Work: Power, Legitimacy, and Effectiveness*, pp. 63–64.
43. Visoka, Gëzim, *Acting Like a State: Kosovo and the Everyday Making of Statehood*, (London: Routledge, 2018).
44. Caplan, Richard, *The International Governance of War-torn Territories: Rule and Reconstruction* (Oxford: Oxford University Press, 2005), p. 246.
45. Narten, Jen, 'Post-Conflict Peacebuilding and Local Ownership: Dynamics of External-Local Interaction in Kosovo under United Nations Administration', *Journal of Intervention and Statebuilding*, 2008, 2, no. 3, p. 369.
46. Donais, *Peacebuilding and Local Ownership: Post-conflict consensus-building*.
47. Lemay-Hébert, 'Everyday Legitimacy and International Administration: Global Governance and Local Legitimacy in Kosovo', p. 98.
48. Roberts, David, 'Everyday Legitimacy and Postconflict States: Introduction', *Journal of Intervention and Statebuilding*, 2013, 7, no. 1, p. 9.
49. Donais, *Peacebuilding and Local Ownership*, p. 4.
50. Visoka, Gëzim and John Doyle, 'Peacebuilding and International Responsibility', *International Peacekeeping*, 2014, 21, no. 5, pp. 673–92.
51. Visoka, *Peace Figuration after International Intervention*.
52. Donais, *Peacebuilding and Local Ownership*, p. 104.
53. Visoka, *Acting Like a State: Kosovo and the Everyday Making of Statehood*.
54. Visoka, Gëzim, *Shaping Peace in Kosovo: The Politics of Peacebuilding and Statehood* (Basingstoke: Palgrave Macmillan, 2017).
55. Visoka and Richmond, 'After Liberal Peace? From Failed Statebuilding to an Emancipatory Peace in Kosovo.'
56. Salmon, Jago and Catherine Anderson, 'Elites and Statebuilding', in D. Chandler and T. D. Sisk (eds.), *Routledge Handbook of International Statebuilding* (London: Routledge, 2010), p. 49.
57. ENEMO, 'Irregularities Affecting the Trust in the Democratic Process in Kosovo', Press Release, Prishtina, 12 January 2011.
58. Diezdzic, Michael (ed.), *Criminalized Power Structures: The Overlooked Enemies of Peace* (Lenham: Rowman and Littlefield, 2016).
59. Sisk, Timothy D. and David Chandler, 'Introduction: International Statebuilding in War-Turn Societies', in *Routledge Handbook of International Statebuilding*, D. Chandler and T. D. Sisk (eds.), (London: Routledge, 2010), p. xxi.
60. Visoka, Gëzim, 'Arrested Truth: Transitional Justice and the Politics of Remembrance in Kosovo,' *Journal of Human Rights Practice*, 2016, 8, no. 1, pp. 62-80.
61. Visoka, 'Arrested Truth: Transitional Justice and the Politics of Remembrance in Kosovo.'
62. Visoka, *Shaping Peace in Kosovo*.
63. Visoka, *Peace Figuration after International Intervention*.
64. Newman, Edward and Gëzim Visoka, 'The Foreign Policy of State Recognition: Kosovo's Diplomatic Strategy to Join International Society', *Foreign Policy Analysis*, 2018, 14, no. 3 pp. 367–387. See also: Visoka, Gëzim, John Doyle and Edward

Newman (eds), *Routledge Handbook of State Recognition* (London: Routledge, 2019).

65. Roberts, David, 'Hybrid Polities and Post-Conflict Policy', in D. Chandler and T. D. Sisk (eds), *Routledge Handbook of International Statebuilding* (London: Routledge, 2010), p. 101.

66. Visoka, *Shaping Peace in Kosovo*.

67. Diezdzic, Michael, Lauera Mercean and Elton Skendaj, 'Kosovo: The Kosovo Liberation Army', in M. Diezdzic (ed.), *Criminalized Power Structures: The Overlooked Enemies of Peace*, (Lenham: Rowman and Littlefield, 2016), pp. 155–201.

68. Chandhoke, Neera, 'What is the Relation between Participation and Representation?', in O. Tornquist, N. Webster and K. Stokke (eds), *Rethinking Popular Representation* (New York: Palgrave Macmillan, 2009), p. 28.

69. Uslander, Eric M. *The Moral Foundations of Trust* (Cambridge: Cambridge University Press, 2005), p. 193.

70. Rosanvallon, Pierre, *Counter-Democracy: Politics in an Age of Distrust*, Arthur Goldhammer (trans.), (Cambridge: Cambridge University Press, 2008), p. 8.

71. Rosanvallon, *Counter-Democracy: Politics in an Age of Distrust*, p. 18.

72. Richmond, Oliver P. *Failed Statebuilding: Intervention, the State and the Dynamics of Peace Formation* (New Haven, CT: Yale University Press, 2014).

73. Richmond, O. P., *Peace Formation and Political Order in Conflict Affected Societies* (Oxford: Oxford University Press, 2016).

74. Visoka, *Peace Figuration After International Intervention*.

75. Visoka, *Shaping Peace in Kosovo*.

76. Bell, Colleen and Brad Evans, 'From terrorism to insurgency: re-mapping the post-interventionary security terrain', *Journal of Intervention and Statebuilding*, 2010, 4, no.4, pp. 364–90.

THREE

From a Divisive Peace Agreement to a Legitimate Peace in Colombia

Borja Paladini Adell

Introduction

In December 2016, one of the world's longest and most damaging armed conflicts came to an end. More than eight million victims later,[1] the Government of Colombia and the FARC-EP guerrilla (Revolutionary Armed Forces of Colombia – People's Army) signed a peace agreement that was negotiated over five years in Havana, Cuba.[2] After three years of implementation, important progress has been made in the development of the agreed commitments, as observed by two of the independent institutions invited to support the verification and evaluation of the implementation: the Kroc Institute for International Peace Studies and the United Nations Political Mission.[3] In this period, the armed conflict between the Government of Colombia and the FARC ended, despite some significative splitting dissidences,[4] and the guerrilla has become a democratic political actor that competes in elections. Much of the agreement remains to be implemented, however, and many difficulties to be overcome still lie ahead.

In this paper, I explore the concept of territorial peace through a legitimacy-building lens. The article's main thesis is as follows: in order to achieve a higher quality peace in Colombia, and to overcome the deep division and polarisation that the armed conflict generated – and which has been maintained throughout the peace process – territorial peace needs to pay special attention to the legitimacy of the state in the territories most affected by the armed conflict, as well as drug trafficking and illicit economy dynamics. In this sense, legitimacy is not something that is automatically derived from Colombia's status as a well-integrated democratic state within the international political order. Rather, it is something that must be built and developed through direct interaction and dialogue with the communities that suffer the violence, the pressure of the illegal armed actors, and the historical absence of the state.

Throughout the paper and its conclusions, I present the peace agreement and its implementation process as the basis for a transformative peace in Colombia; a peace that may help the country to overcome the main causes of the armed conflict and consolidate state legitimacy across the national territory, and in the face of pressure from diverse networks of legal and illegal actors that compete with the state. These actors are often more effective at building political authority and popular following than the state. I believe that the recent peace agreement has created a unique opportunity to extend and deepen the democratic legitimacy of the state not only as a top-down process, but as constructive interaction between local legitimacies that derives from local social actors and the opportunities created by national and international normative frameworks embodied in the Colombian constitution and in the text of the 2016 peace agreement.

First, I present a brief theoretical framework on legitimacy, social order and territorial peacebuilding in Colombia, laying the theoretical and analytical foundations for the rest of the paper. Second, I present the concept of territorial peace, understood as the need to perceive peace not only as the end of the armed conflict with the FARC, but as a territorial transformation process that addresses the conflict root causes and, from the perspective of local population, the weak or lack of legitimacy of the state at the local level. In this section, the concept of territorial peace enters into dialogue with concepts of legitimacy and traditional peacebuilding. Third, we describe the Havana agreement as an opportunity to achieve a transformative peace and to consolidate the democratic legitimacy of the state throughout Colombian territory. Finally, we explore the main advances and difficulties in peace agreement implementation from a legitimacy and territorial peacebuilding perspective.

Much of the data supporting this paper is taken from the Kroc Institute for International Peace Studies' own work in Colombia, which I coordinated until June 2019. The Government of Colombia and the FARC-EP invited the Kroc Institute to design a methodology that would be able to identify progress in peace agreement implementation in real time, providing technical support through follow-up, verification and accompaniment of the peace agreement's Implementation Follow-up, Impulse and Verification Commission (CSIVI) and the International Verification Component

(CIV) through the publication of regular reports.[5] CSIVI and CIV are the two main peace agreement implementation verification bodies, staffed by representatives of the Colombian government and the FARC, as well as two respected experts and research institutions who provide implementation observation and analysis.

Comprehensive peace agreement implementation status reports (covering progress, difficulties, gaps, setbacks, implementation sequencing) are regularly presented to the CSIVI, the CIV, and public opinion in general.[6] Other shorter confidential reports are also prepared that include alerts, concerns or proposals about implementation prioritisation. Kroc Institute information also provides comparative international perspectives for the Colombian implementation process. The Kroc Peace Agreements Matrix Program (PAM) compares implementation progress in Colombia with that of thirty-four comprehensive peace agreements signed internationally over the last forty years.[7]

The data is drawn from a broad empirical database that includes more than 14,000 implementation events that are collected from primary and secondary sources, validated by the Kroc Institute team in Colombia, and registered in a database that is updated daily. The database facilitates a concrete and detailed follow-up of 578 implementation provisions (measurable and observable commitments extracted from the text of the peace agreement) from the beginning of its implementation on 1 December 2016 to date. These provisions are organised into eighteen themes and seventy subthemes. This detailed monitoring provides a very broad empirical basis for Kroc's quantitative and qualitative analysis of the status of the implementation.

The Kroc Institute is also monitoring the implementation of crosscutting territorial, gender and ethnic approaches included in the agreement. The seventy subthemes included in the monitoring matrix are analysed from these perspectives, including analysis of the implementation of 130 provisions related to gender, eighty related to ethnic communities, and 309 other measures that are stipulated in the agreement for implementation at a territorial level.

The qualitative analysis presented in this paper has also been drawn from dialogue and reflection between the Kroc Institute and more than 280 territorial, national and international actors with which it has carried out information exchange and joint analysis. This is then fed into its real-time agreement implementation-monitoring framework.

The article presents the peace process, and the implementation of the peace accord, as a moment of change in the competition for legitimacy between different actors. Our Colombia analysis is developed from three starting points:

1. The peace process increased the legitimacy of the Colombian state at the international level. Several facts confirm this idea. For example, the international community unanimously accompanied the peace process. Various countries (for example, the USA[8] and Germany[9]), the European Union[10] and the UN[11] appointed special delegates for the process. Others accepted the roles of guarantor, facilitator or accompanier: Cuba, Norway, Chile and Venezuela. The peace process and the comprehensive peace agreement received the unanimous support of the Security Council of the United Nations, which approved the deployment of two political missions to Colombia. Another factor that proves Colombia's increased international legitimacy is the country's recent entry to the Organisation for Economic Cooperation and Development (OECD),[12] or to NATO[13] as a 'global partner'. Another fact that appears anecdotal, but is important for the daily life of Colombians, is that since 2010 (coinciding with the start of peace agreement negotiations), Colombians can travel without a visa to seventy-six countries and fourteen non-state territories.[14] Before that, they could only travel without a visa to twenty-six countries and one non-state territory.

2. The signing of the peace agreement meant that the FARC stopped fighting for recognition as a political authority in the territories under their control. The peace agreement implicitly or explicitly implied several things: (1) Despite some splitting groups, the FARC-EP abandoned their weapons and, therefore, lost their coercive capacity and territorial control. (2) Within a year, the FARC became a political party that has competed in the Colombian election cycle. (3) The FARC accepted that the Colombian security forces were the main security providers and guarantors during the process of cantonment, disarmament and political, social and economic reincorporation from the first day of the bilateral and definitive ceasefire. The Government created a series of units within the security forces to fulfil this role, such as the UNIPEP – Special Police Peace Consolidation Unit.[15]

3. The implementation of the peace agreement is an opportunity to extend the democratic legitimacy of the Colombian state to territories where its presence has been token, the internal armed conflict at its most intense, and a diversity of actors – among them

the FARC – contested the political authority and legitimacy of the state. These actors developed effective forms of political authority and popular following through coercive means and the creation of a social order that served the purposes of the armed actor and of the local population.

Illegal Forms of Social Order, Armed Conflict and Legitimacy

My entry point for the notion of legitimacy for this article is the competitive, contextual nature of legitimacy. In countries with internal armed conflict, different actors, with diverse sources of legitimacy, compete in order to gain recognition as political authorities. These actors often achieve the respect, recognition and following that they need in order to govern over the local population. So, internal armed conflicts can be explained as competition for legitimacy between socio-political adversaries. In the Colombian case, it is a competition between the formal holders of legitimacy (the incumbent, the state and its institutions) and the insurgents (guerrillas, protestors, non-violent activists and charismatic leaders, amongst others).[16] These actors, in the framework of their strategic and/or military policies, compete for political recognition and authority from the local population, seeking their respect, support, following and/or submission, be it voluntary or forced.

Legitimacy through political authority is a rich concept and can be approached from different perspectives. According to Conciliation Resources there are different types of legitimacy: local and domestic legitimacy; organic legitimacy (grounded organic legitimacy); legitimacy based on processes or results-based legitimacy; international legitimacy; and constitutional legitimacy, amongst others.[17]

For the sake of clarity, I will focus on two main actors in this paper: the Colombian state and the FARC guerrilla. In some territories, other actors have sought to consolidate their power and claim political legitimacy through coercion. However, only the FARC, and to a lesser extent the ELN guerrilla, have tried to develop a military–political strategy by deliberately challenging the political authority and legitimacy of the state by subverting its power, territorial control and formal sovereignty. Other actors, such as the paramilitaries, which resulted from an alliance between large landowners and other de facto powers and agents of the state, responded illegally to the struggle against the guerrilla insurgency. The big drug cartels (Medellín, Cali, Clan del Golfo and others) on the other hand, have not sought to undermine the state, nor have they claimed to be a legitimate authority throughout Colombian territory. Their reach has been more local and focused – a strategy aimed at controlling territories, narco-trafficking routes and communities, as well as public officials through bribery and threats, in order to develop their criminal business without interference.

In addition to their coercive capacity, the state and the FARC have competed for the recognition, approval, obedience and support of the civilian population. The former did so through its formal status as an independent and sovereign republic, recognised by other states within the international political system. It defines itself as a social state under the rule of law, organised in the form of a unitary republic, decentralised, with autonomy for its territorial units, democratic, participatory and pluralistic, based on respect for human dignity, the work and solidarity of the individuals who belong to it, and the prevalence of the general interest.[18]

The latter defined itself as a legitimate organised armed response by Colombian campesinos (peasant farmers) who took up arms in 1964 as a revolutionary movement of a military political nature that set out to seize political power in the country given that legal, peaceful and democratic paths for political struggle were closed. According to the FARC, armed struggle was necessary to bring about structural reforms and transformations in Colombia that would democratise access to land and other productive assets and reopen legal, peaceful and democratic means of taking power.[19]

Regardless of the legal and foundational bases of each of the actors, the fifty-year clash for political authority between the two has had catastrophic consequences for Colombia. Both the state and the FARC were able to develop bases on which to build domestic or internal legitimacy in some territories. Despite the hegemonic views of the two sides, neither was able to consolidate its status as legitimate political authority throughout Colombian territory through war. Over the last fifty years, the relative legitimacy of the two actors has evolved and changed over time, in space (Colombian territory) and through the recognition of their peers (other states, other insurgent actors in the country and internationally).

Following intense guerrilla pressure during the 1980s and 1990s, the state has been consolidating its authority throughout Colombian territory via a combined strategy of coercion and extension of the social contract that underpins its legitimacy, and in so doing materialise the commitment to consolidate the rule of law. There are still territories, however, where this kind of social contract does not deliver effective rule of law governance. Various actors, including the FARC, had or still govern through coercion and the creation of parallel social arrangements[20] and governance mechanisms (shadow governance).[21]

In these territories not uniquely governed by the state, the guerrillas and other non-state armed actors have been able to exercise political authority and establish effective forms of control and order. Several studies have demonstrated how the arrival and supremacy of an armed group in a territory does not generate anarchy as might be thought. It is in the interest of the armed group, rather, to create governance mechanisms and establish behavioural standards that allow it to regulate social, economic and political relations in its territories.[22] These armed actors have been able to generate social order not only through subjugating the civilian population through coercion, but also through establishing a series of norms, governance mechanisms and benefits for the local population that promote obedience to, and acceptance of, the emerging authority and its consolidation. These social arrangements vary from region to region according to the armed group that is in control and the nature of its leadership. Sometimes the control that is exercised is minimal and only focused on certain elements of community life. Other times the social and political control is intense and exhaustive.[23]

The acceptance of the population, sometimes voluntary, sometimes forced, is the result of one or more reasons that are not always mutually exclusive. Firstly, for ideological reasons: the population simply accepts the military–political strategy of the insurgency. Secondly, for interest: the population benefits from certain social protection networks that are established by the insurgent actor and believe that this represents an opportunity to improve their lives. Three, for profit: the insurgent actor can provide personal benefits (favours, for example) and, above all, public goods that benefit the 'governed' communities. These include small infrastructure projects, expeditious and effective local judicial and conflict resolution mechanisms, security and protection in relation to other legal or illegal armed actors, norms that generate order and regulate private behaviour, and environmental protection, amongst others.[24] Four, for self-interested coexistence: the population is part of and benefits from the illegal economies that predominate in many of these regions (for example, drug trafficking, smuggling or illegal mining).[25] Five, amongst other reasons, passive resignation: the population is subjected to armed coercion and the overwhelming power of the actor.[26]

By way of example, Ana Arjona analysed in detail how the FARC played an important role as an environmental protection authority in several regions, protecting and regulating natural resource use such as logging, deforestation or the regulation of fishing rights. The FARC were also able to control violence within the civilian population in some territories and in so doing create a certain a degree of monopoly over the use of force and prevent local people from becoming state informants.[27] In several regions, the FARC were also able to control and regulate the private behaviour of people through, for example, the obligation to participate in political marches, strikes, roadblocks or other expressions of social protest. They also established rules around the buying and selling of property and land or restricting people's freedom of movement, amongst others. The FARC was also very effective at developing mechanisms for local micro-conflict management and the provision of community justice, including the resolution of conflicts over land boundaries, child support and inheritance disputes. Communities considered these local justice and conflict resolution mechanisms to be much more effective and faster than the judicial system's own procedures.[28]

Of course, the effectiveness of this kind of social and political control depends on the guerrilla being able to maintain a hegemonic territorial role that is not disputed by other armed actors, whether legal or illegal. Political authority is always fragile and subject to constant competitive pressure from state or non-state armed actors.

Peace Process, Territorial Peace and Legitimacy

The main thesis of this paper is as follows: in order to achieve a higher quality peace in Colombia, and to overcome the deep division and polarisation that the armed conflict generated, territorial peacebuilding must pay special attention to the legitimacy of the state, especially in the territories most affected by the armed conflict and drug trafficking and illicit economy dynamics. The implementation of the peace agreement is an opportunity to extend the democratic legitimacy of the Colombian state to those territories where its presence has been token, the internal armed conflict was suffered most intensely and a diversity of actors – among them the FARC – challenged its political authority.

The former government's High Commissioner for Peace, Sergio Jaramillo Caro, launched the concept of territorial peace during the peace negotiations. At the heart of the government's concern for the peace process in Colombia is that it would guarantee the human rights of Colombians living in the conflict-affected territories. For Jaramillo Caro, peacebuilding in Colombia had created a unique opportunity to overcome the state's failure to produce public goods, satisfy rights and ensure conditions for expressing political demands throughout the national territory. His thesis concentrates on the need to take advantage of the end of conflict with the FARC to develop state institutions in the war affected territories as a way of ensuring that all Colombians enjoy the same basic rights.[29] The main objective of the talks with the FARC according to this theoretical framework was to reach an agreement that would contribute to a stable and lasting peace in Colombia. Post-agreement peacebuilding, on the other hand, should be the responsibility of society as a whole.[30] Jaramillo Caro presented territorial peace as an explicit opportunity to leverage the change in Colombia what was not achieved by fifty years of war, in particular:

1. Generate rural development and close the huge gaps between urban and rural Colombia, thus eliminating the factors that allowed violence to flourish and take root in these territories in the first place – extreme poverty, lack of opportunities and the weakness of institutions in regulating public life.
2. Remove violence from politics and consolidate a solid, inclusive and participatory democracy that respects even the most radical social protest and opposition, including conditions of safety for those who wish to express day-to-day dissent.
3. Guarantee the human rights of all Colombians throughout the national territory, including victims' rights to truth, justice and reparation as guarantees that Colombia´s history of violence will not be repeated, and its negative effects will be addressed.

The government's position is not new. Many social actors have argued for a locally based peacebuilding process without explicitly mentioning the concept of territorial peace, a process that involves popular participation in alliance with state institutions and the international community. For example, several territorial development and peace programs (PDPs) have been implemented in Colombia over the last twenty-five years. These programs are expressions of territorial civil society alliances. They usually involve the participation of the Catholic Church, local universities, trade unions, civil society actors and national and international cooperation organisations. The PDPs are initiatives conceived, promoted and structured by civil society organisations and institutions that seek to agree and coordinate joint public, private and community peacebuilding initiatives at the local and regional level. In addition to promoting a culture of respect for human life, social integration and regional identity, they seek to generate wealth, improve quality of life and achieve a participatory democratic order.[31]

Although territorial peace is not a novel concept, it does have significant merits. For the first time within the framework of a peace process, the state has recognised that peace is not the exclusive responsibility of the armed actors. It recognises that peace should be built from the territorial level and through broad alliances between state institutions and grassroots organisations. The idea of the democratic legitimacy of the state is at the heart of the territorial peace concept. Another merit is that it encapsulates in only two words the commitment to build a transformational peace by integrating local and institutional efforts.

At the theoretical nexus between territorial peace, peacebuilding and legitimacy, I have identified a series of interesting analytical elements:

First, the territorial peace concept places the principal focus on developing state legitimacy by tackling the main causes of the armed conflict through the provision of public goods and services in alliance with the civilian population.

Second, territorial peace tries to find ways of making effective the most significant constitutional promises of the Republic of Colombia as an expression of the social rule of law. Particularly important is the eternally unfulfilled promise that the state will promote, protect and guarantee the human rights of Colombian men and women. Today, the state does not guarantee rights, particularly in those territories most affected by the armed conflict, direct and structural violence, and by social orders created by illegal armed actors.

Third, territorial peace focuses on peacebuilding means, not just the ends. The procedures employed to build peace are as important as the outcomes that are being sought. Participation, inclusion, oversight, social control, autonomy and community agency are not a mere rhetorical exercise, but the very essence of a process of mutual recognition and legitimisation between state and society – the concrete expression of the social contract that underpins the state itself as a political institution.

Fourth, territorial peace emphasises the need for the state and its institutions to become a regulating actor in public life. Peace requires strong, transparent institutions, oriented to public service (and not to the defence of private interests). It also needs to put in place practices and norms that can be universally accepted in order to promote coexistence and cooperation as mechanisms for collectively facing the country's background problems from the territories, combining the political, technical, economic, social and community resources of various public and private actors. This includes the agendas and proposals of the communities and social organisations in the processes of change, without waiting for 'those people from Bogotá', the centralised state, to solve their problems with their 'Power Point visits'.[32] These four elements are the foundations for building the democratic legitimacy of the state. The four pillars are fundamental if people are going to stop perceiving the state as something alien, but rather as a social and political construct for which they are also responsible. Within this logic, the state becomes legitimate when it ceases to be a strange, distant, cold and bureaucratic entity that only generates obstacles and problems for the population, and is seen rather as a joint venture, a meeting space between society and institution; an engine of change and guarantor for human rights.

These arguments resonate with Richmond and Mac Ginty's ideas on hybrid legitimacy presented in this book's introduction and conclusion.

Local peace formation as a bottom-up networked process and peace consolidation as a top-down state-induced dynamic can reinforce themselves producing a more accepted and legitimate political authority that reduce the opportunities violent actors have to fill the 'legitimacy gap'. A hybrid legitimacy approach may create a more transformative and sustainable peace.

Peace Agreement, Implementation and Domestic Legitimacy

The Colombian peace agreement is a vehicle for bringing about a transformative peace that will help the country to overcome the main causes of its armed conflict and consolidate state legitimacy throughout the national territory. The recent peace agreement has created a unique opportunity to widen and deepen the democratic legitimacy of the Colombian state. Following the FARC's decision to recognise the legitimacy of its political authority, the state must now focus on consolidating its internal legitimacy, especially in those territories where other illegal and/or insurgent actors are still challenging its authority.

According to the academic literature, the perception of state legitimacy can be achieved and maintained in two ways. One, legitimate authority is recognised because the state has assumed and maintained power through fair or appropriate procedures (process or procedural legitimacy). According to this logic, an institution that exercises and maintains its authority by respecting fair, transparent and inclusive procedures that create opportunities for dialogue and the meaningful participation of the governed in decision-making processes, achieves greater democratic legitimacy and acceptance than one that does not. Two, the authority is recognised as legitimate because it is capable of effectively generating collective benefits through the provision of public goods and services (outcome or performance legitimacy): everyday security, judicial and conflict resolution mechanisms, health services, education and services that provide social and economic welfare.[33]

The two ways are complementary. The quality of the processes through which power is accessed and public life is governed, and the effectiveness of government action for public benefit and interest, reinforce each other's legitimacy and strengthen the state's authority vis-à-vis other actors that compete for political authority in certain territories. Understanding this relationship is essential for improving peacebuilding processes and strengthening state legitimacy.[34]

In this article, we propose a third factor for understanding how states develop their legitimacy in contexts of armed conflict and peace processes. Legitimate authorities, in my opinion, do not only consolidate by combining fair processes and providing goods and services that cater to the general interest. They also strengthen their legitimacy because they are perceived as a neutral actor that regulates relationships of conflict and cooperation in society, without being a party to conflict with its own interests. In this respect, a state develops legitimacy when it ceases to be one of the conflict parties and plays the role of facilitator, bringing together different social actors interested in conflict management through non-violent transformation and the proactive regulation of social relationships.

From this perspective, legitimacy is strengthened when a political authority has the capacity to build bridges between different social actors and generate opportunities for them to meet and recognise each other and in so doing create constructive interactions within a context of polarisation and entrenched conflict. These opportunities should help to overcome social polarisation and fragmentation, generating instead a common ground where differences can be addressed through dialogue, cooperation and the constructive management of dissent. John Paul Lederach argues that this is the political capacity of individuals and institutions to mediate and facilitate constructive and strategic change processes in contexts of entrenched armed conflict and strong polarisation. This capacity must be aimed at developing quality relationships and interactions in the middle of deeply rooted conflicts in order to overcome the division. Relationships and interactions that are not defined by mutual recrimination, friend–foe logics and the reactionary dynamics associated with conflict escalation and chronification, but defined, rather, by the ability to generate trust-building spaces, constructive dialogue capable of promoting and sustaining interactions that over time promote peace, non-violent social change and conflict transformation.[35] Indeed, a political authority that manages to facilitate these processes is more legitimate than one that is perceived as part of the conflict, or interested in a particular outcome of the political process. A political authority that manages to facilitate these processes is more legitimate than one that is perceived as part of the conflict or interested in a particular outcome of the political process.

In conclusion, the combination of fair procedures, the provision of collective benefits through the act of governing, the ability to recognise the value of local agency, promote acts of mediation, facilitation and non-violent transformation of conflict and tension between different social actors, creates the basis for a stable and sustained exercise of democratic and legitimate political authority.

The implementation of the agreement is therefore an opportunity to extend the democratic legitimacy of the state for the following reasons. First, the peace agreement includes a wide range of measures to improve the state's capacity to provide goods and services, especially in those territories most affected by the armed conflict, illicit economies, the pressure from other illegal armed actors and institutional weakness. The peace agreement is full of specific provisions that seek to make the state the main provider of justice, protection, security, education, health and other elements that increase the quality of peace (welfare, economic development, basic social and economic infrastructure and other public goods). The table below summarises succinctly the six points of the peace agreement from the provision of goods and services perspective.

Table A Main components of the peace accord for the provision of goods and services

Point 1. Towards a new Colombian countryside. Integral Rural Reform.	• Land fund, other land distribution measures and the mass formalisation of small and medium properties. • Mechanisms for the resolution of conflicts over land ownership and use, new agrarian jurisdiction and the strengthening of food production. • Multipurpose land registration and improvement, territorial planning and environmental protection. • National Integral Rural Reform Plans: tertiary roads, irrigation, electrification and connectivity, rural education, health, housing and drinking water supply, productive development, labour formalisation and social protection, progressive guarantee to the right to food. • Participatory, whole-of-society, inclusive rural and territorial development plans for 170 most depressed and war-affected municipalities in Colombia (PDETs programs).
Point 2. Political Participation. Democratic opening to build peace.	• Security guarantees and protection for the political process and for social leadership and the defence of human rights. • Democratic and equitable access to the media within the framework of carrying out politics or political opposition and social mobilization.
Point 3. End of conflict and security and protection guarantees.	• Political, economic and social reincorporation for ex-combatants and youth. • Special investigation and dismantling of organised crime unit. • Integral security system for the political process. • Integral security and protection program for communities and organisations in the territories. • Integral action against landmines.
Point 4. Solution for the illicit drugs problem.	• National Crop Substitution Program – PNIS, connected to PEDTs program (see next table). • National Comprehensive Intervention Program against the Consumption of Illicit Drugs. • Strategy for effective prosecution in relation to the laundering of assets involved in drug trafficking and corruption associated with drug trafficking.

Continued

Point 5. Integral Truth, Justice and Reparation System.	• Comprehensive Truth System (Truth Commission, Missing Persons Search Unit), Justice (Special Jurisdiction for Peace) and Reparation (early acts of recognition of responsibility and reparation, collective and individual reparation, psychosocial rehabilitation, return of displaced people and land restitution).
Point 6. Implementation, verification and endorsement.	• International technical and financial accompaniment of the peace agreement. • Awareness raising and communication of the agreements.

Two, the peace agreement emphasises and proposes a series of participatory and inclusive peacebuilding and democratic opening mechanisms that focus on procedures for legitimising peacebuilding.

Table B Principal mechanisms for consolidating the end of conflict, peace-building and democratic opening

Point 1. Towards a new Colombian countryside. Integrated Rural Reform.	• Development Plans with a Territorial Approach (PDETs, as known in Colombia), through which the national state, local authorities, and social and community actors are expected to build participatory, inclusive, long-term plans from, with and for the territories, aimed at their transformation and national integration.
Point 2. Political Participation Democratic opening for peace-building.	• Statute of guarantees for exercising political opposition (Opposition Statute) • Guarantees and promotion of citizen participation for organisations and social movements, and for social mobilisation and protest. • Creation of National and Territorial Reconciliation and Coexistence Councils. • Citizen control and oversight of the peace-building process. • Measures to promote greater participation in national and local politics, in particular of the most vulnerable and excluded sectors (equal opportunities for access to democratic political competition, promotion of electoral participation and reform of the electoral system, quality of the electoral process and equality of conditions for access to it, promotion of the political representation of populations especially affected by the armed conflict, promotion of women's political and civic participation).

Point 3. End of conflict and security and protection guarantees.	• Verification and monitoring mechanisms to protect the bilateral and definitive cease-fire, facilitate the cantonment of troops, the abandonment of arms and the FARC political and socioeconomic reincorporation process under secure conditions (UN Political Mission). • National Commission for Security Guarantees. • Measures to prevent and fight against corruption.
Point 4. Solution for the illicit drugs problem.	• Participatory designing and development of integral community and municipal substitution and alternative development plans – PSID. • Fight against corruption associated with drug trafficking strategy.
Point 5. Integrated Truth, Justice and Reparation System.	• Promotion, prevention and protection of human rights and the strengthening of protection mechanisms for human rights defenders and their organisations.
Point 6. Implementation, verification and endorsement	• Follow-up, Promotion and Verification Commission for the implementation of peace agreements. • Measures to incorporate the agreements in the territorial and national planning and financing cycles of the Colombian state. • International Verification Component and mechanisms for international implementation accompaniment. • Comprehensive system for implementation transparency. • Agreement endorsement.

The agreement includes at least an additional sixty-seven citizen participation measures in the implementation of the six final points of the agreement: entities (twenty-six); community dialogue mechanisms (eleven); direct citizen participation in the design or implementation of plans and programs related to agreement implementation (twenty-five); and citizen oversight mechanisms (five).[36]

Implementation Evaluation from a Democratic Legitimacy and Territorial Peacebuilding Perspective

On paper, the peace agreement presents a broad set of commitments that can help increase the democratic legitimacy of the state through the provision of public goods, the improvement of democratic processes and citizen participation and the consolidation of the social contract as laid out in legal terms in the 1991 Constitution.

Following two-and-a-half years of implementation, what advances have there been from a democratic and domestic legitimacy of the state perspective? Has progress been made in the provision of goods and services? Have the procedures through which legitimacy is consolidated improved? What are the main challenges for peacebuilding at the national and local level?

The main qualitative and quantitative results according to Kroc Institute's evaluation are as follows:[37]

- As of 31 August 2019, that is almost three years after the start of implementation, 73 per cent of the 578 measures agreed between the government and the FARC are in the process of implementation: 25 per cent have been completed, 13 per cent have an intermediate level of progress, 35 per cent a minimal level of progress, and 27 per cent of the commitments have yet to be started. The implementation schedule has a fifteen-year horizon.
- The two most advanced points of the agreement are point three (end of the conflict) and point six (mechanisms for verification and monitoring of implementation).
- Despite some significant dissidences, the end of the armed conflict with the FARC has been achieved in record time. The United Nations has observed that only a couple of years after the signing of the peace agreement, a successful cease-fire between the parties has not only been maintained: the FARC have also voluntarily concentrated their troops, handed over their weapons and converted into a democratic political party. In addition, most of their 14,000 ex-combatants (between combatants, militiamen and prisoners) have received a set of initial benefits to help begin their reincorporation process into social and economic life (ex-combatant certification, monthly substance subsidy, training in educational skills and educational levelling and access to social protection mechanisms, amongst others)[38]. With the handing over of their arms and their conversion into a political party, the state's main competitor for political authority ceased to exist as an armed adversary and submitted to the protection of the state as its security guarantor.
- On the other hand, the implementation process has been very resilient to date: the various implementation mechanisms, mutual guarantees, safeguards and international accompaniment measures agreed between the government and the FARC in point six of the agreement are working. Together, the government and the FARC,

with strong international support, are committed to the agreement implementation process, have faced various crises and temporary obstacles through negotiation and dialogue, and have shown flexibility when the renegotiation of certain elements of the agreement were unclear, or underdeveloped in its provisions.

- Another important advance is related to the normative and institutional foundations for the implementation of the agreement. The government and congress have laid the foundations for implementation through various legal and regulatory instruments. In eighteen months, a broad set of regulatory adjustments have been developed: eleven new laws, including four specific constitutional amendments; at least ten additional laws are passing through Congress; the president of Colombia has issued thirty-five decrees with force of law and more than eighty presidential or ministerial ordinary decrees for the normative development of the peace agreement. It has also created or redesigned various institutions, programs, mechanisms, plans (dependent on the government or with autonomy) in charge of the implementation of the agreement, amongst other measures:

  - Point 1: Rural Development Agency, Agency for Territorial Renewal, National Land Agency, Land Fund. Sixteen national plans for integral rural reform (focused on the provision of rural public goods in prioritised territories: health and rural education, rural infrastructure and tertiary roads, connectivity and rural electrification and social protection in rural areas, amongst others).
  - Point 2: National Council for Peace, Reconciliation and Coexistence and Territorial Councils.
  - Point 3: United Nations Political Mission and the government – FARC – UN Tripartite Mechanism for ceasefire verification. National Plan (CONPES) for the Long Term Reintegration of Veterans. More than twenty political, strategic, operational and programmatic measures to improve post-agreement security and protection.
  - Point 4: Voluntary Substitution of Illicit Crops Program.
  - Point 5: Special Jurisdiction for Peace, Truth Commission (Commission for the Clarification of Truth, Coexistence and Non-Repetition), Special Unit for the Identification of Disappeared Persons in the context of, and caused by, the armed conflict.
  - Point 6: Final Agreement Follow-up, Promotion and Verification Commission, International Verification Commission.

The following are the main problems, red flags and criticisms:

- *First,* various contextual elements are turning implementation into a highly complex process. The main problem is the dynamic surrounding drug trafficking and illegal economies. This situation has led various armed groups to try to co-opt the vacuum left by the FARC in several territories. The territorial disputes and armed confrontation between criminal gangs, FARC dissidents, drug traffickers and the ELN guerrillas has exacerbated the violence in some regions. Faced with this complex reality, the broad set of political, strategic, operational and programmatic measures to improve security, guarantee the occupation of the territory by the state and protect social leaders in these territories have not yet become effective. This problem is being aggravated by state weakness and the quality of local political elites. Colombia is a very centralised and presidential country. The state tends to 'arrive' in the territories from Bogotá or Medellín, instead of building a consolidated presence throughout the national territory. Authority is exercised in many territories in a delegated manner. National elites delegate control of many parts of the country to regional elites in exchange for territorial support and votes in national elections.[39] These regional elites often encourage patron–client, corrupt practices – on many occasions in alliance with illegal armed actors.[40] This delegation creates a vacuum of state legitimacy and authority in the territories. Illegal armed actors and territorial elites take advantage of this vacuum to create their own undemocratic and patron–client social orders. In addition, the destructive and corrupting power of drug trafficking complicates the situation even further. The corruption of local public officials (security forces, prosecutor's office, mayor's offices) destroys the little confidence that citizens have in the local state authorities and the limited legitimacy that the state has been able to accumulate internally thanks to the peace process being lost.
- *Second,* and related to the previous point, is the security situation faced by social leaders and human rights defenders. The state has not yet effectively filled the vacuum left by the FARC in several territories with strong illegal economies. Various armed actors are trying to control those territories in order to control and exploit their illegal economies. Armed actors, old and new, are seeking to impose their authority through violence, often attacking social leaders that are committed to the implementation of the peace

agreement through its different instruments. In many territorial contexts, these leaders are now the spearhead of the peace process and the democratic legitimacy of the state. Authorities acting from various branches of the state, however, often stigmatise social leaders as guerrillas, criminals or collaborators of illegal armed actors. This kind of finger pointing has very perverse effects on peace. It not only limits citizen participation in territorial peace-building (one of the great promises of the agreement), but also prevents the state from being perceived as responsible for the protection and safety of these leaders. Social leaders often, therefore, see the state as the enemy instead of the guarantor for their rights.

- *Third*, there is concern about the limited progress made in implementing the points of the agreement that focus on transforming the root causes of the armed conflict – problems associated with land and the quality of the democratic and electoral system. These are the issues that lag the most in the Kroc Institute monitoring. The fact that there are no concrete impact results, yet in key indicators such as the structure of land ownership or the quality of democracy, citizen participation or guarantees for political opposition is normal. The implementation schedule is fifteen years. That said, progress in implementing the most transformative measures of the peace agreement is slow. The legislative agenda that will sustain these changes is blocked in the Congress. For example, the legal bases needed to facilitate the distribution and formalisation of land ownership, the new agrarian jurisdiction, or the measures to clarify territorial planning have not yet been approved. There are also doubts about the financial capacity of the state to implement the participatory programs for territorial transformation and the national plans for the provision of rural public goods and services. Without these measures, the great division between urban centres and the rural periphery plagued by poverty, illegal economies and undemocratic political elites cannot be overcome. Nor have the normative and political reforms been approved that improve the electoral system, guarantee and enrich citizen participation processes (including social protest), and broaden the participation and political representation of victims in decision-making forums such as the Congress of the Republic. A commitment that the Congress did not approve at the end of 2017 was the sixteen special electoral districts for victims in the most conflict-affected territories. The rejection of this commitment by the congress representatives has a lot to do with the stigmatisation of victims and social leaders in those territories, and the resistance of regional political elites to cede power.

- *Fourth*, it is worrying that the full potential of territorial peace, as originally conceived, is not being exploited. The peace agreement is very rich in terms of addressing the root causes of the armed conflict and in prioritising the territories most affected by the war, institutional weakness, drug trafficking, illegal economies and poverty. Also, for prioritising and including these territories' most excluded populations: small producers, women, indigenous people and afro-Colombian communities, amongst others. Equally, it is very rich in developing a wide range of mechanisms and measures that align the peacebuilding process with the goals that are being sought: mechanisms for participation, inclusion, accountability, transparency and dialogue, amongst others. Several voices are now claiming that the implementation of the agreement has become a 'hurried' exercise and 'from Bogotá'. A bureaucratic, formal process, a 'parading of institutional logos' focused on the fulfilment of institutional goals and not on building trust and constructive relationships between communities and the state.[41] The pressure created by the change of government has led to the acceleration of an agreement implementation that is not always sensitive to territorial realities, to local people's rhythms and their way of participating in public life. The bureaucratic logic that underpins the implementation process is affecting the quality of the peace that is being built and the potential for the state to play its mediator and regulator role for the construction of social and political relations. The rush to deliver results sometimes ignores the contribution of the communities, as expressed in their agendas, proposals, ideas and priorities that are not always considered. They feel invisible. The government's haste has also reduced the quality of participatory processes.[42] It may also be affecting the potential for peacebuilding processes to promote a form of territorial governance that is oriented towards peace – the democratic, political, social and technical capacity that allows alliances to be made, cooperate with others and reach consensus in the public and collective interest.

Conclusions

All these concerns put into question the potential for peace to bring about new relationships between state institutions, conflict-affected territories and their communities. A lot of thinking is done about the transformation of territories, but little about the transformation of institutions, their ways of working and their ways of relating to society. Together with the security problems we have analysed above, and the doubts surrounding the financial backing for the agreement agenda, these elements raise serious questions about the peace process's capacity to transform ordinary people's quality of life or develop the democratic legitimacy of the state.

Peace should be understood as a complex social process, a political construction through which the state and society must meet, develop trust and cooperate, and in so doing build a social contract that makes peace an irreversible process. In many Colombian regions, armed actors are still more effective at gaining popular following than the state. These actors exert their power through coercion but reinforce their authority through being more effective than the state in terms of day-to-day popular problem solving. In order to beat this perverse form of authority, the state needs to commit more to developing its authority and legitimacy with the civilian population. It needs to be quicker and more effective at providing public goods and services in the most violence and crime-affected territories, provide physical and human security, and generate inclusive, transparent, sustained and transformative peacebuilding processes. Policy-makers also need to understand that it is not just about taking the state to the territories, but about generating conditions for the development of the social contract that will sustain any state that emerges from the territorial level. As the Kroc Institute concludes in its Second Report on the Effective Status of the Implementation of the Peace Agreement, communities, organisations and local authorities are not mere recipients of goods and services. They can also influence public policy issues and help to shape government legitimacy. If Colombia is anything, it is a society that is organised and knows what it wants in relation to peace. The country could be seen as a 'world champion' of civil society involvement in peace issues. This locally organised desire for peace is an opportunity, not a threat. They are processes that have shaped peace at the territorial level in the face of state weakness or absence. It will therefore be essential to work with these local resources to strengthen state legitimacy at the territorial level. According to this logic, combining the exercise of political authority (providing security, protection) with the effective and transparent provision of public goods and services (infrastructure, local justice, conflict resolution mechanisms), the promotion of quality regional political and social participation processes (opportunities for dialogue, transparency and accountability) will allow the state to build peace with legitimacy, and in so doing eliminate the spaces for illegal armed actors. The commitment to inclusion and participation, the centrality of the victims, and the emphasis on territorial peace are fundamental for generating a quality peace process. Only in this way will it become a collective national project for rural reform, economic and social development, justice and a definitive end to the armed conflict. A legitimacy and peacebuilding approach is important if the country is to enjoy a lasting and sustainable peace.

Notes

1. Official Victims Register – Government of Colombia's Victims Unit, 1 September 2019, Registro Único de Víctimas, Unidad para las Víctimas, Gobierno de Colombia. Available at <https://www.unidadvictimas.gov.co/es/registro-unico-de-victimas-ruv/37394> (last accessed 18 February 2020).
2. Final Agreement to End the Armed Conflict and Build a Stable and Lasting peace, 22 November 2016. Available at <http://especiales.presidencia.gov.co/Documents/20170620-dejacion-armas/acuerdos/acuerdo-final-ingles.pdf> (last accessed 18 February 2020).
3. Kroc Institute for International Peace Studies, State of Implementation of the Colombian Final Accord, December 2016–April 2019. Available at <https://kroc.nd.edu/assets/333274/executive_summary_colombia_print_single_2_.pdf> (last accessed 18 February 2020). More information here: Peace Accords Matrix Colombia <http://kroc.nd.edu/research/peace-processes-accords/pam-colombia> (last accessed 18 February 2020); United Nations S/2019/530, 2019, United Nations Verification Mission in Colombia, Report of the Secretary-General, New York: United Nations. Available at <https://colombia.unmissions.org/sites/default/files/n1918521.pdf> (last accessed 18 February 2020); More information here: UN Verification Mission in Colombia <https://colombia.unmissions.org> (last accessed 18 February 2020).
4. Iván Márquez Rearming is a Wake-Up Call: Efforts to Fully Implement the Colombian Peace Accords Need to be Escalated, WOLA, 29 August 2019. Available at <https://www.wola.org/2019/08/ivan-marquez-farc-rearming-colombian-peace> (last accessed 18 February 2020).
5. Final Agreement to End the Armed Conflict and Build a Stable and Lasting peace, 22 November 2016, Bogotá: High Commissioner for Peace Office, pp. 2012. Available at <http://especiales.presidencia.gov.co/Documents/20170620-dejacion-armas/acuerdos/acuerdo-final-ingles.pdf> (last accessed 18 February 2020).
6. More information and documents are available at Kroc Institute for International Peace Studies, Peace Accords Matrix Colombia, <http://kroc.nd.edu/research/peace-processes-accords/pam-colombia/> (last accessed 18 February 2020).
7. More information is available at University of Notre Dame, Peace Accords Matrix, <https://peaceaccords.nd.edu> (last accessed 18 February 2020).
8. The New York Times, <https://www.nytimes.com/2016/02/06/world/americas/a-democratic-diplomat-at-ease-with-both-guerrillas-and-the-gop.html> (last accessed 18 February 2020).

9. Federal Foreign Office, <https://www.auswaertiges-amt.de/en/newsroom/news/150402-kolumbien-koenigs/270586> (last accessed 18 February 2020).
10. European Union External Action, <https://eeas.europa.eu/headquarters/head-quarters-homepage/2521/eu-will-support-peace-process-colombia-special-envoy-eamon-gilmore_en> (last accessed 18 February 2020).
11. UN Verification Mission in Colombia, <https://colombia.unmissions.org/en/leadership> (last accessed 18 February 2020).
12. The OECD, <https://www.oecd.org/latin-america/countries/colombia/#d.en.345234> (last accessed 18 February 2020).
13. North Atlantic Treaty Organization, <https://www.nato.int/cps/en/natohq/news_155030.htm> (last accessed 18 February 2020).
14. Oportunidades para viajar, <http://especiales.presidencia.gov.co/Documents/20180214-mas-oportunidades-para-conocer-mundo/especial-visas.html#el-pasaporte> (last accessed 18 February 2020).
15. Unidad Policial para la Edificación de la Paz – UNIPEP, <https://www.policia.gov.co/unidad/unipep> (last accessed 18 February 2020).
16. Mitchell, Christopher, 'By what right? Competing sources of legitimacy in intractable conflicts', in Landon E. Hancock and Christopher Mitchell (eds), *Local Peacebuilding and Legitimacy: Interactions between national and local levels* (New York: Routledge, 2018), p. 1.
17. Ramsbotham, Alexander and Achim Wennman (eds), *ACCORD: Legitimacy and Peace Processes – From Coercion to Consent.* (London: Conciliation Resources, 2014).
18. Constitution of Colombia (1991). In English: <https://www.constituteproject.org/constitution/Colombia_2005.pdf> (last accessed 18 February 2020).
    In Spanish: <http://www.corteconstitucional.gov.co/inicio/Constitucion%20politica%20de%20Colombia.pdf> (last accessed 18 February 2020).
19. FARC-EP, <http://www.farc-ep.co/nosotros.html> (last accessed 18 February 2020).
20. Arjona, A., N. Kasfir and Z. C. Mampilly, *Rebel Governance in Civil War* (Cambridge: Cambridge University Press, 2015).
21. Idler, Annette and J. F. F. Forest, 'Behavioural Patterns among (Violent) Non-State Actors: A Study of Complementary Governance', *Stability: International Journal of Security and Development*, 2015, p. 4.
    Idler, Annette, *Arrangements of Convenience: Violent Non-State Actor Relation-ships and Citizen Security in the Shared Borderlands of Colombia, Ecuador and Venezuela*, (Oxford: University of Oxford, 2014).
    Idler, Annette and Borja Paladini Adell, 'When Peace Implies Engaging the "Terrorist": Peacebuilding in Colombia through Transforming Political Violence and Terrorism', in Ioannis Tellidis and Harmonie Toros (eds), *Researching Terrorism, Peace and Conflict Studies Interaction, Synthesis and Opposition* (London: Routledge Critical Terrorist Studies, 2014).
22. Kalyvas, S., 'Promises and Pitfalls of an Emerging Research program: the micro-foundation of violence', in S. Kalyvas, I. Shapiro and T. Masoud (eds), *Order, Conflict, Violence* (New York: Cambridge University Press, 2008).

Wood, E. J. 'The social processes of civil war: the wartime transformation of social networks', in *Annual Review of Political Science*, 2008, No. 11, pp. 539–65. Idler and Forest, 'Behavioural Patterns among (Violent) Non-State Actors: A Study of Complementary Governance', p. 2.

Idler, *Arrangements of Convenience: Violent Non-state Actor Relationships and Citizen Security in the Shared Borderlands of Colombia, Ecuador and Venezuela*.

Duncan, Gustavo, *Los Señores de la Guerra. De Paramilitares, Mafiosos y Autodefensas en Colombia* (Bogotá: Editorial Planeta, 2006).

23. See Arjona et al., *Rebel Governance in Civil War*.

24. See, as an example, 'Manual de Convivencia para el Buen Funcionamiento de las Comunidades expedido por el Frente 32 Arturo Medina del Bloque Sur de las FARC EP, con incidencia en el departamento del Putumayo'. Available at <http://www.pares.com.co/grupos-armados-ilegales/farc/farc-dan-conocer-manual-de-convivencia-en-putumayo> (last accessed 18 February 2020).

25. Arjona, Ana, 'One national war, multiple local orders: an inquiry into the unit of analysis of war and post-war interventions', Forum for International Criminal and Humanitarian Law (FICHL) International, Peace Research Institute, Oslo (PRIO), 2009, Available at <http://www.anamarjona.net/docs/Arjona%20 PRIO.pdf> (last accessed 18 February 2020).

26. Ibid.

27. Arjona, Ana, *Rebelocracy: Social Order in the Colombian Civil War* (New York City: Cambridge University Press, 2016).

28. Avila, Ariel and Juan Diego Castro, *Los retos en convivencia, administración de justicia y seguridad rural en el posconflicto. Análisis FES* – Friedrich-Ebert-Stiftung, 2015. Available at <http://library.fes.de/pdf-files/bueros/kolumbien/11353. pdf> (last accessed 18 February 2020).

29. Jaramillo Caro, Sergio. *La paz territorial Bogotá: Oficina del Alto Comisionado para la Paz del Gobierno Colombiano*, 2014.

30. Gobierno de Colombia – FARC EP. Acuerdo General para la Terminación del Conflicto ya Construcción de una Paz Estable y Duradera, 2012.

31. Programas de Desarrollo y Paz Territorial. Available at <http://redprodepaz.org. co/que-es-un-pdp-2> (last accessed 18 February 2020).

32. Interview with social leader and former mayor of a municipality in Nariño, 2014.

33. Boege, Volker, Anne Brown, Louise Moe and Anna Nolan, 'Framing paper and final report of the Project Final Report Addressing Legitimacy Issues in Fragile Post-conflict Situations to Advance Conflict Transformation and Peacebuilding', The University of Queensland/Berghof Foundation, 2012. Available at <https:// www.berghof-foundation.org/nc/es/about-us/grants/supported-projects/ grant-2009-university-of-queensland> (last accessed 18 February 2020).

34. Ibid.

Tadjbakhsh, Shahrbanou. 'Conflicted Outcomes and Values: (Neo)Liberal Peace in Central Asia and Afganistan', *International Peacekeeping*, 2009, 16: 5, pp. 635–51.

35. Lederach, John Paul, 'Building Mediative Capacity in Deep-Rooted Conflict', *The Fletcher Forum of World Affairs*, 2002, 26: I Winter/Spring.
36. Fundación Ideas para la Paz, Participación Ciudadana en el Posconflicto, Recomendaciones para saldar una deuda histórica en Colombia, (Bogotá: FIP, 2017), Available at <http://www.ideaspaz.org/publications/posts/1542> (last accessed 18 February 2020).
37. Informe 2 sobre el Estado Efectivo de la Implementación, Instituto Kroc de Estudios Internacional de Paz, August 2018, more information available at <http://kroc.nd.edu/research/peace-processes-accords/pam-colombia> (last accessed 18 February 2020).
38. United Nations, Report of the Secretary-General on the United Nations Verification Mission in Colombia, S/2018/279, 2 April 2018.
39. Robinson, James and Daron Acemoglu, *Why Nations Fail: The Origins of Power, Prosperity and Poverty (New York: Crown Publishers*, 2012).
40. La Silla Vacía, *El dulce poder: así funciona la política en Colombia* (Bogotá: Aguilar, 2012).
41. Instituto Kroc/Pastoral Social/Universidad Javeriana, Memorias del Conversa-toria Enfoque Territorial en la Implementación del Acuerdo de Paz, Bogotá, August 2018.
42. Fundación Ideas para la Paz, Programas de Desarrollo con Enfoque Territorial: Cambiar el rumbo para evitar el naufragio, Nota Estratégica 05 (Bogota: FIP, 2018). Available at <http://ideaspaz.org/media/website/sirirPDET_Final.pdf> (last accessed 18 February 2020).

FOUR

Banners, Billy Clubs and Boomerangs: Leveraging and Counter-Leveraging Legitimacy in the Occupied Palestinian Territory

Toufic Haddad

Introduction

The convergence of Palestinian national conceptions of legitimacy with those introduced by international peace and statebuilders during the Israeli–Palestinian peace process was always a delicate and fractious affair.

While Western donor states and the United Nations (UN) tend to broadly assert that their global interventions defend and propagate 'international legitimacy' embodied in liberal humanist values, the implementation of international legal norms and resolutions, and respect for human rights conventions, the Palestinian case study strikingly contravenes these claims.[1]

Instead of propagating international legitimacy, the institutions and processes established by these actors in the Occupied Palestinian Territory (OPT) de facto came to manage the fallout generated by the *absence* of the application of these norms. This significant incongruence transformed the question of legitimacy into a struggle over which party in the Western-sponsored Israeli–Palestinian peace process was capable of instrumentalising and even leveraging legitimacy over the other.

While this approach was problematic in its own right, it also came in the context of a longer historical experience of internal Palestinian leveraging manoeuvres on behalf of Fateh, the main Palestinian partner to international peacemaking interventions. For years, Fateh engaged in exploiting its monopoly over legitimacy within the movement to steer the latter in the direction of accepting international legitimacy norms. This was undertaken upon the belief that this 'pragmatic' strategic direction could bear fruit in the balance of forces internationally and regionally, while averting serious confrontation with the movement's main Arab patrons. The decision nonetheless led to deep tensions within the Palestinian movement that were never truly resolved, but subsequently were given space to thrive after the failure of this process.

As the serious asymmetric power relations between Israel, Western donors and the Palestinians began to be exposed with the breakdown of July 2000 Camp David negotiations, Fateh's strategy to use international legitimacy norms to achieve Palestinian rights appeared to fail. A period of far more deadly political violence was soon ushered in, with the question of legitimacy openly instrumentalised by Israel and Western donors against their former Palestinian 'partner' in peacemaking. Israel and Western donor states would repeal diplomatic and financial support to the Palestinian Authority (PA), while Israel militarily destroyed PA institutions as a means to leverage different political concessions, including institutional reforms proposed by the World Bank and International Monetary Fund.

The continued leveraging of legitimacy by Western donor states to produce a subservient 'legitimate' PA, would ultimately generate dual efforts to reconstitute Palestinian legitimacy anew.

International peace- and statebuilders believed they could produce an entirely new set of legitimate Palestinian political practices and leaders through their powerful oversight of international aid and the political economic interventions this entailed.

Alternatively, oppositionist Palestinian actors embodied most significantly within the Islamic Resistance Movement – Hamas – saw the opportunity to capitalise upon the delegitimisation of the process overall, and indirectly that of Fateh's leadership and strategy. Hamas' decision to enter into the political arena and capture the very apparatus donors had paid Fateh to construct, de facto consolidated an intolerable situation of hybrid legitimacy for international donors. Hamas' success would in turn lead Israel and international statebuilders to promptly besiege and sanction the new endeavour. In doing so, donors exposed their own instrumentalisation of legitimacy norms, opposing in practice the liberal Weberian state model they nominally claimed to be supporting.

The Palestinian case study thus reveals valuable lessons regarding the limitations and consequences of those who effectively seek to monopolise, instrumentalise, produce and leverage legitimacy, be they international peacemaking practitioners or national elites. If held too tightly, the question of legitimacy transforms from a banner, into a billy club, and then into a boomerang, with all the unpredictability these instruments are known to embody when used by the self-assured. The ensuing negative, hybrid arrangement barely qualifies as peaceful or legitimate by all parties, perpetually reproducing more violence and instability as the context's new norm.

The Banner

Roots of Palestinian Legitimacy

The 1969 takeover of the Palestine Liberation Organisation (PLO) by Fateh together with other guerrilla groups that emerged upon the crest of Palestinian self-mobilisation efforts on the post-1967 scene marked the final assertion of Palestinian control over the Palestinian cause, away from the existing ideological, religious and political movements that attempted to claim the mantel of Palestine in the vibrant post 1948 political period – be these pan-Arab nationalists (Nasserist or Baathist), pan-Islamists (mainly the Muslim Brotherhood) or Communist currents.[2]

The takeover was seminal in Palestinian organising history as it marked the moment when a new set of Palestinian national actors emerged to definitively break from the movement's former ways and leaders, and the perceived interference of foreign states and agendas. These actors derived from different social classes than the traditional pre-1948, patrician-family based leadership, and were largely refugee in origin, with many educated from urban middle class backgrounds. They were equally influenced by the rise of Third World anti-colonial movements (particularly Algeria and Vietnam), while seeing themselves as independent Palestinian manifestations of the period's radical zeitgeist. The question of what was now considered 'legitimate' Palestinian political praxis needed to go through the newly constituted actors leading the movement and the institutions they controlled – namely the PLO and the Palestine National Council (PNC), its legislative body, and not the Arab states.

It is worth appreciating that the Palestinian movement's sensitivity to questions of legitimacy derived from the paternalistic approach of the Arab states over the Palestinian cause, despite their failures in the 1948 and 1967 wars. Moreover, Palestinian fears regarding the interference of 'external agendas' within their cause were further fuelled by having to organise their struggle from the objective conditions of dispersal, reliant upon the (not always existent) good will of host states. In fact, the desire for autonomy from external interference played a significant role in the PLO adapting its political agenda from maximalist sloganeering, towards the creation of an independent Palestinian state 'even on one square inch of Palestine', quoting Fateh co-founder Salah Khalaf.[3]

1974 would mark the seminal year in which two key issues related to the question of Palestinian legitimacy would be determined.

First was the introduction and passing of the 'Ten Point Program' at the Twelfth Session of the PNC in June.[4] This plan affirmed a stageist approach to Palestinian liberation, calling for the establishment of a Palestinian national authority 'over every part of Palestinian territory that is liberated' with the aim of 'completing the liberation of all Palestinian territory'.[5]

Second, October 1974 would mark the year when the Arab Summit in Rabat officially recognised the PLO as the 'sole and legitimate representative of the Palestinian people'. This recognition was considered important as it gave formal Arab acknowledgment to direct Palestinian leadership over their cause, while also pushing back Jordanian interests in asserting claims upon the West Bank, and which remained in place until 1988.

The near simultaneous occurrence of these events was not by chance. After the 1973 War, which witnessed the Arab–Israeli conflict increasingly enfolding within the calculus of Cold War dynamics, the Arab state backers of the PLO pressured the movement to adopt a clear, diplomatic and pragmatist agenda towards its cause – offering diplomatic, military and financial support for the Palestinian cause as long as its agenda did not endanger the hold on power of the conservative patrimonial and neo-patrimonial Arab regimes themselves.

Fateh thus became the faction of choice of most Arab governments, receiving the bulk of its financial and military endowments, including Egypt and the Gulf states. Fateh's non-ideological affinity to any greater revolutionary project (Islamist, pan-Arabist or leftist) together with its explicit eschewing of intervening in inter-Arab affairs and class struggle, assured these powers that the Palestinian movement under Fateh leadership could be contained and controlled, while not posing a threat to these powers' own seats of authority.[6]

The passing of the Ten Point Plan, while simultaneously anointing Fateh as the pre-eminent Palestinian institution to control the PLO and mediate Palestinian legitimacy, would align a set of institutions and interests within Palestinian politics, and between Palestinian and Arab politics that would inevitably structure the production of Palestinian legitimacy and its political agenda for years to come. It effectively created a Palestinian monopoly over legitimacy overseen by Fateh, indirectly regulated through Gulf capital and political interests, often at the expense of genuinely inclusive democratic debate and resources distribution.

The Billy Club

The Internal Leveraging of Fateh legitimacy

In the early years of this strategy, the maximalist legacy of the PLO's ultimate goal to liberate all of Palestine was able to coexist with the stageist/statist approach to liberation, as long as the PLO retained an active and credible military presence on the territorial borders of historical Palestine.

However, after the expulsion of the PLO from Lebanon in 1982 and the demise of a military option, the PLO would be forced to mobilise exclusively around its statist agenda, without an effective means of coercion. The movement would subsequently be forced to take explicit measures that would lead to political and institutional transformations for establishing a Palestinian state in the 1967 Occupied Territory (the West Bank, East Jerusalem and Gaza Strip) and all this entailed with respect to confronting currents and legacies within the movement that opposed these moves and still retained a 'total liberation' approach.

This would induce what pre-eminent Palestinian scholar Yezid Sayigh describes as the 'three interrelated patterns of internal change' of the mid-1980s, culminating in 'the end of an entire phase in the history of the contemporary Palestinian national movement' – rejecting the armed struggle approach and seeking the establishment of negotiations with Israel that would ultimately end with the Oslo process.[7]

First was the successful marginalisation of rejectionist groups opposed to Arafat, while co-opting the 'loyal' opposition (composed mainly of the leftist Popular and Democratic Fronts for the Liberation of Palestine – PFLP and DFLP – each 'critical of Arafat himself but loyal to the PLO'). Second was the assertion and 'confirmation of Arafat as the single most important national symbol and arbiter of Palestinian politics'. Third was the relocation of the focus of the Palestinian national struggle from the diaspora to the OPT. Behind these transformations were what Gilbert Achcar describes as a 'double degeneration' of Fateh – bureaucratic and bourgeois – whereby it was so integrated into the PLO that it 'became hard to tell the two apparatuses apart'.[8]

These three internal changes would facilitate the PLO's political and diplomatic turn towards accepting US conditions for holding official talks: the 'renunciation of terrorism'; 'acknowledging the right of Israel to live in peace and security', and the 'confirmation of UN Security Council Resolution 242'. The PLO believed that acceptance of international legitimacy norms harboured the genuine possibility of realising Palestinian rights. This manoeuvre was always seen as controversial within the Palestinian movement, however, given the historical legacy regarding the application of these norms – particularly the UN's 1947 Partition Plan for Palestine, which Palestinians viewed as unfairly legitimising the partition of Palestine, Zionist colonisation, and led to the mass expulsion of Palestinians from the future Jewish state soon after the resolution's passing, and later during the 1948 War.[9]

Even though the UN subsequently passed a series of resolutions in favour of Palestinian rights in the post-1948 period,[10] the organisation, its resolutions, and the legitimacy they claim to embody, remain sceptically viewed by the movement's main actors. Recall that the main UN resolution of the post-1967 period – UN resolution 242, passed unanimously by the UN Security Council after the 1967 war – was historically rejected by the Arab states and the PLO, as it implicitly accepted partition for the conflict's resolution; on the one hand proclaiming the 'inadmissibility of the acquisition of territory by war' while also calling for 'the need to work for a just and lasting peace in the Middle East in which every State in the area can live in security'. This de facto acceptance of the existence of Israel in its pre-1967 manifestation was rejected by the majority of Palestinian political factions, including Fateh who rejected partition and Zionist settler claims to Palestine from the beginning.

However, after repeated historical setbacks for the PLO, Fateh justified a strategic shift of direction for the PLO, heading toward accepting various UN resolutions, including 242. These internal changes to the agenda and strategy of the organisation were seen by Fateh as the necessary bitter pill the PLO needed to swallow to retain relevance and legitimacy in a shifting post-1973 international climate not in its favour. They represented a significant shift from the movement's earlier maximalist position, and the success of both international leveraging efforts against the movement (represented in repeated Israeli military aggression against the PLO combined with Western stiff-arming), and internal leveraging by Fateh and Arafat, over the PLO and Palestinian politics as a whole. In this regard, these manoeuvres were less the success of internal processes of convincing oppositionists, and more the product of historical setbacks the movement faced, together with Fateh exploiting its monopoly positioning.

Palestinian popular willingness to accept this change of tack by its leadership was always reserved, and conditioned by a need for this gambit to bear tangible fruit, where earlier strategies of liberation had failed. If this move was not to be seen as a political concession away from the movement's former goals, it needed to be justified as an alternative pragmatic path to incrementally realising Palestinian rights. By accepting the international 'rules of the game' – rejecting armed tactics against Israel, and accepting UN resolutions – the Fateh leadership argued that Palestinian rights could be protected and realised, as it was Israel that ultimately was the guilty party for violating international law.[11]

External Efforts to Leverage Legitimacy

With the financial and political straights the PLO was put through after the collapse of the Eastern Bloc and the 1990–1 Gulf war, the movement was so significantly weakened that it was willing to accept significant additional political and institutional compromises to its agenda to ensure the movement's survival. According to chief Palestinian negotiator at Oslo, Ahmed Qrei' (Abu Ala), the PLO had only two months left of finances to cover its expenses by the time the Oslo Accords were signed.[12] This significantly weak financial and political positioning on behalf of the PLO would in part justify why many Palestinians saw these Accords not as a victory for the historical movement, but as 'a Palestinian Versailles', emphasising the agreement as one of surrender.[13]

The PLO's signature to the Declaration of Principles (DOP, hereafter the Oslo Accord) and subsequent accords,[14] made the organisation a political partner to a highly problematic agreement that was a far cry from fulfilling minimal Palestinian national expectations in substance and deed. The word 'occupation' does not feature in the DOP's text. No Palestinian national rights are affirmed therein, with all major issues of the conflict – the question of borders, Jerusalem, settlements, refugees and water – delayed to final status negotiations. Israel was to redeploy from the centres of Palestinian residential areas, but the majority of the land in the OPT was to remain under direct Israeli control. Even areas under the jurisdiction of the PA could be entered into by the Israeli army in cases of 'hot pursuit'. Palestinians were to ensure Israeli security while Israel was to remain in charge of all international and internal 'border' crossings, effectively controlling Palestinian trade, labour flows and economy. There were also no guarantees that Israel would end settlement expansion.

These and other aspects of the DOP placed them in sharp contrast to the implementation of international legal norms pertaining to the rights of an occupied people, and the responsibilities of the occupying powers to assure them, embodied in the Fourth Geneva Convention of 1949. They equally were distant from the aspiration for Palestinian self-determination and the former positions of the movement, putting Fateh in direct confrontation with other Palestinian factions and the expectations they and international peacebuilders had constructed around the process.

These tensions would only deepen in light of Israel's *actual* implementation of the Oslo Accords, which demonstrated a close adherence to a different agenda entirely: those in conformity with its historical plans towards the OPT, broadly outlined in manifestations of what is known as the Allon plan.[15]

After the 1967 War, then-defence minister Yigal Allon outlined how to preserve Israel's strategic interests in the context of the contradictory predicament it found itself in arising from Israel's occupation of the OPT. The results of the war left Israel governing an additional one million Palestinians in the West Bank and Gaza, implicitly challenging how Israel could maintain itself as a 'Jewish democratic state.' The Allon plan promised to resolve this contradiction by recommending Israel establish autonomous self-governance zones in the most concentrated Palestinian residential areas, while maintaining control over key geostrategic, ideological and resource-rich areas throughout the OPT. The autonomous areas were to be administered through Jordan, as a way to get Palestinian civilian adminis-trative needs nominally beyond Israeli responsibility, and demographically off its books. Israel could thus continue colonisation of Palestinian land, integrating the 1967 conquests with those of 1948.

Later versions of this plan would prove more flexible in accepting other potential governance candidates for Palestinian administration. Menachim Begin attempted to establish his own legitimate Palestinian 'partners' through a network of local collaborators that became known as the 'village leagues'. Although this attempt would ultimately fail, Israel was savvy enough to con-sider the PLO as a potential candidate for this task as well, with Allon himself opining in 1977 that, 'Certainly, if the PLO ceased to be the PLO, we could cease to consider it as such. Or if the tiger transformed itself into a horse, we could mount it. At that moment, we would deserve some headlines in our favor'.[16]

In this respect, the establishment of the PA out of the weakened PLO was seen as an opportunity for Israel to leverage the Oslo Accords towards its larger historical agenda of the Allon plan. The Accords would reconfigure the architecture of Israel's control over OPT land and people, disengaging from the problems and costs associated with maintaining a direct presence in Palestinian towns, while nonetheless maintaining a firm grip overall stra-tegic levers of Palestinian life and economy, and continuing the process of Zionist colonisation through settlement expansion. All this was to be operationalised by leveraging the peace process and its rubric of interna-tional legitimacy against Palestinian national self-determination claims and institutions.

The Role of Western Aid

Engineering a context in which it was possible to market the accords domes-tically and internationally as a bona fide peace process, when two diametri-cally opposed agendas were attempting to actualise themselves within the same framework, and while forces were asymmetrically balanced, was only possible thanks to a set of key factors linked to how Western donor states approached the accords and their implementation.

The international community's backing of the US-led peace process, would prove instrumental in masking the incongruence between the realisation of Palestinian rights and the actual power provided to Pal-estinians through the DOP. The accords had what Israeli scholar Meron Benvenisti called a 'deliberate ambiguity' to them that preserved the semblance that the negotiations process could in principle realise Palestinian aspirations.[17] However, they contained no written guarantees that these negotiations were committed to realising these aspirations or that Israel was obliged to uphold its obligations under international law, including the withdrawal from occupied territory or the ending of settlement expansion. Furthermore, the accords stipulated that arbitration of disputes between Israel and the Palestinians was to be handed over to joint Israeli–Palestinian committees agreed on by both parties, or to Israel's main ally, the United States, thus reproducing the asymmetry between the parties in negotiations. In fact, chief Israeli negotiator Uri Savir explicitly stipulated that the framework for resolving disputes would not rely upon international legal norms,

> As to outside arbitration, you [the PLO] must decide whether we are to act as partners, and solve all our differences through dialogue, or request Security Council-like arbitration and end up with a pile of resolutions that will remain no more than numbers.[18]

More important than the DOP's precise wording was the role of Western donor state peacebuilding efforts designed to back the project economically and diplomatically. The 1994 granting of the Nobel Peace Prize to Rabin, Peres and Arafat acted as a quick rubberstamp from the international community towards the process, while resurrecting the PLO and Arafat as a legitimate 'partner' in that process. Accompanying this was the financial and political backing these states committed themselves to in terms of implementing a self-described 'Marshal Plan' for the peace process, which promised a series of major local and regional economic and development programs.[19] Most of these projects would never get off the ground, as Israel's closure regime would prevent the OPT being transformed into an attractive place for international or regional capital.

Donors, of course, were also instrumental to creating the institution of the PA itself, which had limited governance powers in the areas from which the Israeli army redeployed. The US, EU and Japan provided the lion's share of start-up costs and training, operating within a liberal peacebuilding paradigm that could ensure the democratic practice of the Palestinian government-to-be while preserving its liberal economic orientation towards Israel and regional markets.[20]

Here, a common interest emerged between Israel, Western donors and Fateh leaders intended to use the process of the PA's creation to fulfil a series of individual, yet divergent political agendas. The holding of Palestinian elections for presidency in 1995, and the Legislative Council (PLC) in

1996, served to produce a 'legitimate' Palestinian leadership that each set of actors saw as advancing its individual agenda.

For Israel, elections were seen as actualising crucial elements of the Allon plan (creating autonomous zones and self-governance bodies) while serving as a Palestinian referendum ratifying the peace agreements, and institutionalising the formal ties it would now have with the Palestinian people and leadership. As As'ad Ghanem notes,

> The elections were to enhance the status of the leadership with which Israel was negotiating. Moreover, it was important for Israel to give some permanent status to the geographical areas concerned in the negotiations, namely, the West Bank and the Gaza Strip. Holding elections within those areas would demarcate the boundaries of the autonomous regions, and contribute to separating those Palestinians within the boundaries from those outside them.[21]

Palestinian political commentator Ali Jirbawi has also noted that Western-backed elections also facilitated the formation of an elected body (the PLC) that would constitute an alternative to the Palestinian National Council (PNC) considered more radical and committed to the PLO's older agenda.[22]

Western donors were hence facilitating the creation of an alternative set of institutions which could produce a legitimacy of their own, despite only governing over a mish-mash of different 'autonomous' areas of the West Bank and Gaza (full civil and security control in Area A: 18 per cent of the West Bank; 65 per cent of Gaza; civil control in Area B: 42 per cent of the West Bank). This apparatus was also to be embodied in a substantial administrative bureaucracy (today numbering almost 170,000 civil and security employees – roughly 23 per cent of the total work force), with considerable influence over markets in these areas as well. In this respect, Western donor interventions were de facto creating a new institution, financially dependent on donors and the good will of Israel to enact policy. This set of institutions could produce its own legitimacy, while leveraging legitimacy away from the older PLO agenda and the institutions that produced the latter.

Alternatively, the PLO leadership saw in these elections and the establishment of the PA, an opportunity to renew its legitimacy mandate, aligning the movement behind Arafat and his path, both in negotiations and on the ground, now that the movement was back from exile and rooting itself in the OPT.[23]

Despite the far from ideal conditions in which they took place, voter turnout for the PLC elections was high, witnessing 86.8 per cent of registered voters in Gaza and 73.5 per cent in the West Bank.[24] Voters noted that the personal trait that most motivated them to vote for different candidates was linked to the candidate's 'participation in the struggle to end the Israeli occupation'.[25]

In the Shadow of Instrumentalised Legitimacy
Democracy Deterred

Less visible to the public spectacle behind the peace process, and the new framework of legitimacy it was promoting, was a series of underlying, compromising problems.

First was the fact that the new PA was almost entirely dependent on Western donor aid, and lacked sufficient financial resources to sustain itself and the cost of 'buy in', thanks to Israel's historical policy of de-developing the OPT.[26]

Second was the fact that the new Palestinian leadership needed to exert various forms of internal leverage and coercion against other Palestinians of its own to establish itself domestically. In many ways, this was written into the DOP in so far as the PA was to be responsible for protecting Israeli security. Direct policing of other Palestinians through political repression, and even cases of killing protesters, exemplified the policing role the PA was expected and indeed did play between 1994 and 2000.[27]

But in addition to the physically coercive means of leverage were institutional and political means that Fateh now possessed through its dominance of the PA, and strengthened through Western finance and training – both civilian and security.

In late 1995, Arafat took a decision to scrap the expected 1996 municipal elections, preferring to govern on the local level through appointed personnel, via the Ministry of Local Government. These personnel were invariably appointed based on patronage links with members of Fateh and large family clans. The PA's establishment and alignment with traditional patronage networks reversed the pluralistic political arrangements that had emerged during the 1987 intifada, and which had challenged the quiescent approach of traditional elites who had dominated OPT politics between 1967 and 1987. This reversal was the most significant socio-political transformation to take place in the OPT resulting from the establishment of the PA, and only could have taken place with the consent of Western donors who failed to protest this basic democratic violation of its Palestinian partner. Indeed, the latter had little problem with Arafat scrapping local elections knowing that they were likely to prove problematic to Oslo's implementation if opposition factions were able to advance their agendas through control of municipalities.

In this way, Fateh used Western donor financing to help auto-cascade international legitimacy locally, while consolidating itself on the ground through the purchase of patronage, and symbiotically advancing Israel, Western donor and Fateh interests.

Years later, former US ambassador to Israel Martin Indyk would note that 'the Israelis came to us [at the beginning of the Oslo process] and said basically, "Arafat's job is to clean up Gaza. It's going to be a difficult job. He needs walking-around money," because the assumption was he would use it to get control of all of these terrorists who'd been operating in these areas for decades'.[28]

The explicit acknowledgment that the construction of a neopatrimonial regime around Arafat required the use of off-budget accounts by the PA, is significant to underscore here, because soon after Arafat was to reject US and Israeli offers at the July 2000 Camp David summit, international accusations of corruption would begin to significantly emerge against Arafat and his leadership.[29] Arafat's international legitimacy was to be challenged by Western donors and Israel when he failed to deliver upon the expectations of these players, while his failure to deliver upon Palestinian expectations domestically (in regards to democratic praxis, or realising Palestinian rights through negotiations) would also undermine legitimacy domestically. This double erosion of legitimacy within Fateh's own hybridised legitimacy would be the movement's undoing as it created the basis for the movement to be seen as compromised on four separate fronts: upstream (with the internationals), downstream towards Palestinian society which looked to it for leadership; sidewise, with respect to other political factions and, finally, even within the movement itself.

The Political Opposition

In addition to this less visible set of contradictions to international peace-building was the question of how these policies marginalised the political opposition to Oslo. Fateh was attempting to leverage its control over the institutions of the PLO to push forward its strategic gambit on the Oslo process, both on the ground and through the PA. Alternatively, opposition factions insisted on rejecting the Accords and boycotted its institutions in the 1996 elections for the Palestinian Legislative Council (PLC).

When asked to explain his movement's position to boycott these elections, senior Hamas leader Mahmoud Zahhar noted,

The Palestinian Authority [. . .] was born of an agreement one of whose parties, Israel, is an occupying power. And it is this party that in fact dominates and controls the fate of our land. [. . .] Are we really independent? Can we really decide our policy in the shadow of Israeli domination? [. . .] In short, Israel wants to use these elections to lure us into the trap of the political game. Just as it succeeded in luring the PLO in the 1970s.[30]

Zahhar's statement was identifying that the 'legitimacy' that the peace process sought to produce was being effectively weaponised against those who were against the Oslo agenda. It became a tool to leverage Palestinian concessions and better control them in the *absence* of the implementation of international legal norms and human rights conventions.

Zahhar:

> The problem is that we always use as our starting point international acceptance of a power rather than the people's acceptance. What's the use of having a state that is accepted by the Arab and Western states if the people are against it? [. . .] Isn't the most important thing to be in harmony with one's people? What is the source of legitimacy – the general will of the people, or acceptance by America and the Western powers? I leave you to choose which is preferable.[31]

Hamas' refusal to participate in the 1996 PLC elections was 'categorical', as the movement saw these elections as 'a function of the autonomy status'. The movement was careful to also note, however, that it was not in opposition to Palestinian democracy, but was actually seeking ways to defend it. Zahhar would call instead for elections to the Palestinian National Council, seeking to assert this framework as the true source of Palestinian legitimacy, given it was the main legislative body of the PLO. Hamas was thus able to situate itself on a sophisticated political footing during the peace process years (1993–2000), basing itself on a political and strategic judgment about the nature of international peacemaking efforts, and the unlikely prospects for their success in the long term.

'Time is the remedy,' Zahhar would note. 'We know that the PLO's practice will inevitably lead to its downfall. There is no need therefore to bring this about through confrontation. It is enough to wait'.[32]

The Boomerang

Counter-Leveraging Legitimacy

The prescience of Hamas' position would become more apparent in the wake of the failure of the Camp David summit in the summer of 2000, when the final status negotiations revealed that Israel's 'best offer' failed to come close to meeting Palestinian expectations or international legal obligations.[33]

Israel demanded it maintain a significant Israeli military and settlement presence across the OPT in any final arrangement; that the Palestinian entity created would be demilitarised and effectively non-sovereign; very few refugees would be allowed to return to their homes and properties, while Israel would maintain sovereignty over East Jerusalem.

The lifting of the mask surrounding the peace process' 'deliberate ambiguity', exposing Israel's true position, protected by its US ally, inevitably put the Palestinian movement on a collision course with Israel and itself. Little was left to hide the incongruence of views and asymmetry in power, as the negotiations had run their course and Israel was not compelled to abide by any international legal norms. Fateh's strategic bet was also unfulfilled, as the former backers of international legitimacy norms refrained from holding Israel to account to comply with these norms when negotiations actually took place.

If the stance of Western peacemakers during the peace process and the Camp David negotiations was not enough of a disappointment to the Palestinian leadership let alone people, their position in the aftermath would be far worse.

Arafat's rejection of the US and Israeli offers at Camp David now cast him as 'not a partner for peace' to the US and Israel.[34] The off-budget financial dealings which facilitated his neopatrimonial rule, and which had been directly financed by Israeli transfers of monopoly rents into a Tel Aviv bank account, while Western donors looked the other way, would now become the subject of corruption charges by Western donors against the Palestinian leadership.[35] The World Bank and International Monetary Fund (IMF) would increasingly demand a wide series of 'good governance' reforms from the PA that sought to institutionally marginalise Arafat from his command over the apparatus that he had politically invested his charisma and legitimacy in. Donors demanded the creation of a prime ministerial position to hollow out the powers of the presidency; the exposure and consolidation of all PA investments; and the centralisation of all PA revenue streams into a single account overseen and audited by the IMF. Only then would legitimacy – and budgetary support to the PA – be reinstated.

These pressures would also simultaneously come at a time when Israel would launch its own military campaigns against the Palestinian intifada and the PA, destroying a great many of its buildings and reoccupying the 'A' Areas – the seat of PA power.

Between the two, the PA was being institutionally, financially and physically coerced to meet Western and Israeli demands that sought to eliminate Arafat from control over the PA, while Israel was equally content to use these measures to scupper the entire agenda of political negotiations with the Palestinians.

By the time Arafat mysteriously took ill and died in November 2004, most of the reforms to institutionally marginalise him had been adopted, legitimising the new structure and governance model the PA would embody in the post-Arafat era.

In retrospect, what the World Bank, the IMF and the Israeli army did to the PA between 2000 and 2004 constituted a hostile shakedown, instrumentalising international legitimacy and finance against a former ally – Arafat – who alone could have constructed the PA under the controversial political conditions of its birth. The result was to reconfigure this apparatus in a manner that could be controlled more directly, and which more efficiently fulfilled the tasks it was designed to fulfil, as determined by Western donors led by the US and Israel, not Israeli–Palestinian negotiations.

This instrumentalisation and leveraging of legitimacy to achieve certain institutional and political goals represented a significant historical moment in the Palestinian movement. It symbolised the moment when the PA – as the creation of a temporary tri-partite set of interests of Israel, Western donors and Fateh – was extracted from the grip of the persona that Palestinians had entrusted to steer the Palestinian course through the 'bet' on international legitimacy. But rather than deliver a return for the Palestinians, it birthed a set of institutions deemed vital to the survival of Israel as a 'Jewish democratic state', and which facilitated the heightened control and repression of Palestinians. Moreover, the persona entrusted by Palestinians to protect their lot throughout this bet/process, would die under curious circumstances.

Silent alarm bells began to sound within Palestinian circles as the asymmetrical power balance between the donors, Israel and the PA leadership was painfully obvious for Palestinians to see, and promised nothing new in a post-Arafat era.

Moreover, given that the institution of the PA had legitimacy production powers of its own, Western donors began to encourage the emergence of a new Palestinian leadership and governance arrangement, which could accept and internalise the new rules of the game. These actors had already succeeded to get Mahmoud Abbas to act as prime minister in the latter years of Arafat's rule, while former IMF resident director Salam Fayyad had also assumed the key role of Minister of Finance between 2002 and 2005. Both figures were considered closer to the Western donor agenda than Arafat, and were assumed to do well in a new round of national elections, seen as necessary to consolidate and legitimise the characters and orientation of the post-Arafat, post-Intifada era.

Western donor backing of national elections was also undertaken in a context where Israel's counterinsurgency moves had devastated popular mobilisation during the al Aqsa intifada, while 'democracy promotion' across the Middle East was still in vogue with the US administration at the time. Moreover, a network of Western-funded Palestinian NGOs was giving their funders assurances that Fateh remained the dominant political force in Palestinian politics, despite some strengthening of Hamas during the intifada. Little did these actors know that the opinion polls did not accurately reflect the true dynamics that Palestinian society had been undergoing since the failure of Camp David, the eruption of the Al Aqsa Intifada, and the death of Arafat.

Key to their blind spot was lack of appreciation for the multiple, hybrid layers of leveraged legitimacy the Palestinians experienced externally and internally, historically and throughout the peace process. Moreover, Palestinian society was undergoing a serious leadership vacuum in the wake of Arafat's passing, while the traumatic experiences produced across the OPT as a result of Israel's reoccupation of Area A, and repression of the intifada overall, left Palestinians feeling rudderless at a moment of critical challenges to their political and socio-economic existence. Fateh's larger failed bet on peace negotiations, together with Palestinian society's witnessing of the cynical legitimacy leverage game, made significant numbers of Palestinians feel like their cause was in danger of liquidation. Without effective power, resistance or counter-leveraging against this process, the Palestinian cause could be whittled away by Israel and Western donors through endless processes of coercive leveraging of one order or another.

Sensing its time to make moves in the political arena, Hamas would reverse its former opposition to participate in elections for PA bodies, asserting that the demands of a new era necessitated this. After Arafat's death, Hamas called for a joint national leadership to be established to make decisions until elections were held and openly began asserting that it intended to change the direction of Palestinian national politics. 'What was permitted to Yasser Arafat is forbidden to others and we must not let interested parties in the PA and PLO control the Palestinian destiny' noted a Hamas spokesman at the time.[36] 'Arafat derived his authority from being a symbol, but others don't have that privilege.'

What Hamas was really saying was that Palestinian tolerance for Fateh's historical bet, based on assurances anchored by the historical and political legitimacy of Arafat, and indirectly international legal norms, had ended with his passing. In his absence, no other Palestinian leader enjoyed similar stature, and it was now incumbent upon the movement to reassess its entire trajectory to take stock of what had happened as a consequence of this failed bet, and what needed to be done accordingly to re-establish the Palestinian project on a firmer political and strategic footing.

Hamas' 'Change and Reform' list in the 2006 PLC elections would subsequently promise wide-reaching internal and national reforms that fundamentally sought to realign the movement away from peace negotiations with Israel, and on a path to root out its internal corruption based on patronage-based networks, while claiming to reorient the movement around a 'resistance' agenda.[37]

Alternatively, Fateh was in organisational turmoil after Arafat's death, with competing former patronage strains vying for power and control at the expense of one another.

The subsequent splitting of Fateh votes in the PLC election would lead to a landslide victory for Hamas that overrepresented its true democratic power. Despite losing the popular election in real terms by a narrow three percentage points (Fateh's 41 per cent to Hamas' 44 per cent), Hamas took 59 per cent of all legislative council seats.[38]

The Hamas victory was a stunning blow to Western donors and the Fateh leadership, who never anticipated a loss to begin with, let alone one that was so large. It was almost as though both forces were blinded by such a possibility, having instrumentalised their monopolies over finance and legitimacy for so long.

Irrespective of the reasons behind this miscalculation and the poor performance of Fateh in the elections, the prospect of Hamas using its newfound control over the PA, armed with a democratic mandate, posed an immediate threat to the advances of the entire historical political process that had muscled the PLO to the negotiations table in the first place, and gotten it to accept UN resolution 242, the DOP, and the role of the PA on the ground as a civil administrator and Israeli security guarantor. Both Israel and Western donors would subsequently undertake immediate action to prevent such a possibility arising. The former would arrest dozens of Hamas PLC representatives, while the latter would cut financing to the PA, choosing to redirect all funds through a specially created mechanism that would go through the office of presidency controlled by Fateh, through Mahmoud Abbas. This move represented yet another overt contradiction to the credibility of Western donor efforts to ensure good governance, as only a few years earlier these forces had actually withheld financing from the PA, demanding the president not use personal accounts. Now donors were insisting on it yet again.

Concluding Thoughts

The hypocritical practices of the Western donor community towards the results of the 2006 PLC elections would subsequently confirm the opposition's earlier stance, that the 'political game' of the peace process, rooted in international legitimacy norms, was indeed a trap. Western donors could not tolerate either a genuine democratic Palestinian governance arrangement, nor were they keen to force Israel to abide by international law and human rights conventions. The instrumentalisation and leveraging of legitimacy by Western donors hence boomeranged, precisely at a moment when these powers believed they were victorious. Moreover, the entire ordeal would expose how international legitimacy functionally operated as a discursive and institutional technology that ultimately operated with colonial dimensions.

By the summer of 2007, a US-backed coup attempt directed at the Hamas government in Gaza, failed, forcing the particularly right-wing sections of Fateh who had backed it to flee to Ramallah under Israeli facilitation.[39] This led to the territorial political division between the Hamas-controlled Gaza strip and the Fateh-controlled West Bank, which persists to this day. The continued leveraging of international legitimacy against the Palestinian movement has functionally led to these policies now entrenching a divide and rule arrangement over Palestinian lives across the OPT with devastating consequences. The political, human and financial toll of these policies has functionally destroyed the institutional unity of the Palestinian movement – perhaps the most important accomplishment of the Palestinian movement in the post-1948 era. Now two sets of governing institutions, with two sets of legitimacy, preside over two non-sovereign territories, with two sets of tactics and strategies, and backed by two sets of financiers. Violence is routinely reproduced by this arrangement, with Palestinians its primary victims.

While the West Bank has undergone a concerted process of international statebuilding, Western donors continue to boycott the Hamas government in Gaza, while abstaining from acting to prevent Israel's devastating military and economic policies against the Strip. The launching of three unprecedented military assaults upon Gaza since 2008, destroying all of its productive capacities and killing more than 3,000 people, has nonetheless been ineffective in dislodging Hamas from power, or forcing the local community to turn against it. If anything, the movement's ability to withstand Israel's assaults has added to the movement's legitimacy, as it only justifies the movement's claim that the 'political game' always was a 'trap', and that the only way out is to attempt to construct an alternative model to that envisioned by Israel and international peacebuilders. At the very least, Hamas' power is seen as counterbalancing the former monopoly position of Fateh, thus providing Palestinians a 'fall-back' option. While Hamas' successful counter-leveraging of the former monopolisation of legitimacy by Fateh and Western donors modestly succeeded in erecting a new set of principles and institutions within the shell of the apparatus constructed by international statebuilders, the move would serve to hybridised Hamas' own legitimacy claims. Like Fateh before it, Hamas would use its democratic governance mandate, exercised exclusively within the Gaza Strip as the territory's now legitimate 'Palestinian Authority', to enforce a new local monopoly over governance, institutions and finance, while seeking to use this basis as the platform to advance its resistance agenda.

Thus, international peace and statebuilder attempts to instrumentalise legitimacy led to dual hybridised legitimacy claims and institutions while substantially complicating the challenges donors had initially hoped to resolve through their efforts.

Despite their position of commanding heights over a politically depen-dent and financially constrained people, penned in behind walls and checkpoints within a context of more than five decades of military occupa-tion, the capacity to control and leverage legitimacy as a critical frontier in the agenda of international peacebuilding and statebuilding practices remains unresolved. Domestic actors and movements will always be able to devise tactics and strategies to outflank the boundaries of international legitimacy leveraging if it is seen that this process is compromised by the politics of instrumentalisation. This is because the process of establishing boundaries to conform to instrumental needs necessarily comes in conflict with the perceived needs of the domestic constituency and right-bearers on whose behalf legitimacy is in principle, designed to serve. Once alien-ated, these actors can organise and challenge their marginalisation, expos-ing the efforts to instrumentalise legitimacy and counter-leverage them. The latter's ability to mobilise and organise is also primarily based on a set of collective moral and political convictions – and not only on power or finance – though these two can certainly be helpful. This means that their ability to appeal to grievance as a mobilisatory force is doubled in so far as they can appeal to the original sources of their grievance, together with the efforts to liquidate these.

In a context where the experience of the Oslo peace process demon-strated that refraining from resisting the Israeli occupation and accepting international legitimacy norms did not stop Zionist colonisation, which in turn threatens continued Palestinian presence on their land, there is every reason to believe that Palestinians will continue to seek ways to resist this fate. This will likely remain the case until the very moral con-cerns and political grievances of the Palestinians are addressed within a framework that embodies principles of legitimacy linked to fairness and inclusion, rather than just affiliation with power, coercion or financial co-optation.

Notes

1. The 2011 World Development report defines legitimacy as 'a broad-based belief that social, economic, or political arrangements and outcomes are proper and just' and 'international legitimacy' as relating to 'the discharge of values and responsibilities that international law view as the responsibility of states'. See World Bank, *World Development Report 2011: Conflict, Security and Development* (Washington, DC: World Bank, 2011), p. xvi, © World Bank, Available at <https://openknowledge.worldbank.org/handle/10986/4389>

2. Sayigh, Yezid, *Armed Struggle and the Search for State: The Palestinian National Movement 1949–1993*, (Oxford: Oxford University Press, 1997).

3. Cobban, Helena. *The Palestinian Liberation Organisation: People, Power, and Politics.* (Cambridge: Cambridge University Press, 1984), pp. 60–1.

4. See 'The Ten Point Program' Approved by the Palestine National Council at the 12th Session, 8th June 1974. Available at <http://www.ijs.org.au/The-Ten-Point-Program-/default.aspx>

5. Ibid. Article 8.

6. Gilbert Achcar, *Eastern Cauldron: Islam, Afghanistan, Palestine and Iraq in a Marxist Mirror*, (London: Pluto, 2004), pp. 129–53.

7. Yezid Sayigh, 'Struggle within, Struggle without: The Transformation of PLO Politics Since 1982', *International Affairs (Royal Institute of International Affairs 1944–)*, 1989, 65: 2, p. 248.

8. Achcar, *Eastern Cauldron: Islam, Afghanistan, Palestine and Iraq in a Marxist Mirror*, p. 135.

9. Hammond, J. 'The Myth of the UN Creation of Israel', *Foreign Policy Journal*, 26 October 2010, available at <http://www.foreignpolicyjournal.com/2010/10/26/the-myth-of-the-u-n-creation-of-israel/>; Pappé, Ilan, *The Ethnic Cleansing of Palestine*, (Oxford: Oneworld, 2006).

10. See UN Documents for Israel/Palestine, Security Council Report. Available at <http://www.securitycouncilreport.org/un-documents/israelpalestine/>

11. For an assessment of Israeli violations of international law, see <http://www.israellawresourcecenter.org/>

12. Faucon, Benoit, *West Bankers*, (London: Mashrek Editions Ltd., 2010), p. 90.

13. Said, E., 'The Morning After', *London Review of Books*, 21 October 1993, 15, pp. 20–1.

14. After the signing of the DOP, the incremental agreements reached between Israeli and Palestinian negotiators pertaining to the West Bank included the Gaza–Jericho Agreement (the Cairo Agreement) of 29 April 1994 or 4 May 1994, when including the Protocol on Economic Relations (Paris Economic Protocol); followed by the Early Empowerment Agreement of 29 August 1994; the Further Transfer Protocol (27 August 1995), the Israeli–Palestinian Interim Agreement (Oslo II, or Taba) of 24 September 1995; the Hebron Protocol of 7 January 1997; the Wye River Memorandum of 23 October 1998 to implement aspects of Oslo II; and the Sharm el-Sheikh Memorandum of 4 September 1999 to implement further aspects of Oslo II).

15. Achcar, *Eastern Cauldron: Islam, Afghanistan, Palestine and Iraq in a Marxist Mirror*, pp. 205–22.

16. Achcar, *Eastern Cauldron: Islam, Afghanistan, Palestine and Iraq in a Marxist Mirror*, p. 214.

17. Benvenisti, Meron, 'Border conflict', *Ha'aretz*, 16 December 1993.

18. Savir, Uri, *The Process: 1,100 days that Changed the Middle East*, (New York: Random House, 1998), p. 13.

19. See Annexes III and IV. The DOP can be read at <http://www.mfa.gov.il/mfa/ foreignpolicy/peace/guide/pages/declaration%20of%20principles.aspx>

20. Brynen, Rex J., *A Very Political Economy: Peacebuilding and Foreign Aid in the West Bank and Gaza* (Washington, DC: United States Institute of Peace, 2000).

21. Ghanem, A, 'Founding Elections in a Transitional Period: The first Palestinian General Elections', *Middle East Journal*, 1996, 50: 4, p. 515.

22. Jarbawi, Ali, *Al-Intikhabat wa-Nidham al-Hukum al-Falistini (The Elections and the Palestinian Regime)*, (Jerusalem: Palestinian Academy for International Affairs, 1994); Hamid, Alsosee Raed Abdul, *Legal Aspects of Palestinian Elections*, (Jerusalem: Israeli–Palestinian Center for Research and Information, 1995).

23. Jarbawi, *Al-Intikhabat wa-Nidham al-Hukum al-Falistini (The Elections and the Palestinian Regime)*, pp. 13–16.

24. Ghanem, 'Founding Elections in a Transitional Period: The first Palestinian General Elections', p. 525.

25. Based on a 3,200 person representative sample on Election Day across 148 voting centres describing. See Ghanem, 'Founding Elections in a Transitional Period: The first Palestinian General Elections'.

26. Roy, Sara M., *The Gaza Strip: The Political Economy of De-development*, (Washington, DC: Institute for Palestine Studies, 1995).

27. Usher, Graham, 'The Politics of Internal Security: The PA's New Intelligence Services', *Journal of Palestine Studies*, 1996, 25: 2, pp. 21–34.

28. CBS, 'Arafat's Billions', CBS News, *Sixty Minutes*, 9 November 2003, available at <https://www.cbsnews.com/news/arafats-billions/>

29. See Khan, M., 'Evaluating the Emerging Palestinian State: "Good Governance" versus "Transformation potential"', in Inge Amundsen, George Giacaman and Mushtaq Husain Khan (eds), State formation in Palestine: Viability and governance during a social transformation, (London: RoutledgeCurzon, 2004), pp. 13–63.

30. Zahhar, Mahmud, and Hussein Hijazi, 'Hamas: Waiting for Secular Nationalism to Self-Destruct. An Interview with Mahmud Zahhar', *Journal of Palestine Studies*, 1995, 24: 3, pp. 81–8.

31. Ibid. p. 88.

32. Ibid. p. 83.

33. See Malley, Robert, 'Fictions About the Failure at Camp David', *New York Times*, 8 July 2001; Malley, R. and H. Agha, 'Camp David: Tragedy of Errors', *New York Review of Books*, 9 August 2001; Reinhart, Tanya, *Israel/Palestine: How to End the 1948 War*. (New York: Seven Stories, 2002), pp. 21–60.

34. Honig-Parnass, Tikva and Toufic Haddad, *Between the Lines: Readings on Israel, the Palestinians and the US 'War On Terror'*, (Chicago and London: Haymarket, 2007), pp. 17–54.

35. Khan, 'Evaluating the Emerging Palestinian State: "Good Governance" versus "Transformation potential"', pp. 13 –63; Haddad, Toufic, *Palestine LTD.: Neoliberalism and Nationalism in the Occupied Territory*, (London and New York: I. B. Tauris, 2016), pp. 181–236.

36. Honig-Parnass and Haddad, *Between the Lines: Readings on Israel, the Palestinians and the US 'War On Terror'*, p. 264.

37. Hroub, Khaled, 'A "new Hamas" through its new documents'. *Journal of Palestine Studies*, 2006, 35: 4, pp. 6–27.

38. See National Democratic Institute, *Final Report on the Palestinian Legislative Council Elections*, January 25 (Washington, DC: NDI, 2006).

39. Rose, D., 'The Gaza Bombshell', *Vanity Fair*, April 2008.

FIVE

Peacebuilding as a Self-Legitimising System: The Case of Bosnia-Herzegovina

Stefanie Kappler

Introduction

The question of the legitimacy of peacebuilding is a fairly recent one given that the concept of 'peacebuilding' itself has long been assumed to be apolitical and technical in nature.[1] Richmond suggests that peace has been assumed to be extraordinarily legitimate by nature, arguing that 'almost inevitably thinking on peace has [. . .] followed the Platonic notion of an "ideal form," which is partly why the concept is so often imbued with such mystical legitimacy.'[2]

At the same time, the increasingly prominent acknowledgment in both policy circles and academia that peace is in fact 'political' has opened up the Pandora's box of legitimacy concerns around the mechanisms through which and ends to which peacebuilding is being conducted. The more critical literature on peace has therefore increasingly emphasised the power inherent in the policy projects that peacebuilding devises.[3] Academic debates have, at least to a small extent, started to reflect on the need of peacebuilding to be legitimate, not only from the perspective of the interveners and their host societies, but also the societies that 'receive' peacebuilding.[4] There have been debates around the tensions between local and international legitimacy.[5] There certainly also have been attempts to evaluate the success and thus, implicitly, the legitimacy of peacebuilding, for instance through its (in)ability to respond to the needs and interests of its recipients.[6] But even the more recent debates on 'hybrid legitimacy'[7] or everyday legitimacy[8] have tended to look at the manifestations of legitimacy as a relational phenomenon between local and international actors rather than the ways in which legitimacy discourses are constructed by the peacebuilding community itself and with reference to itself.

Given the self-referential nature of peace operations, the degree to which peacebuilding legitimacy has been tuned to the societies in which peace is being built has been rather limited in practice, as this chapter will argue. It will show with the example of the post-war peacebuilding process in Bosnia-Herzegovina (BiH) that instead, peacebuilding has been constructed by its architects as a self-perpetuating system within which legitimacy is assessed by the same networks that are at the very core of designing peacebuilding policies. The peacebuilding system can therefore be considered closed in itself and not open to external evaluation and challenge. As a result, its legitimacy is constructed through the feedback it produces for itself, which is bound to be positive and reproductive of its own discourses and practices. I argue in this chapter that this represents a mechanism through which the system can sustain itself in the long run, whilst avoiding fundamental critiques that might possibly result in the need to completely rethink the actors, tools and mechanisms through which peacebuilding operates.

Peacebuilding as a System of Self-Legitimation

Peacebuilding as a system of governance gained prominence in the 1990s, most notably with Boutros-Ghali's 'Agenda for Peace'.[9] If we reflect on the extent to which the system itself has changed ever since its confrontation with conflicts in BiH, Kosovo, Timor-Leste, Cambodia, Sri Lanka, Rwanda, and many others, it is interesting to note that the changes within the system – the actors that implement it, the organisations that fund it, the goals that are being developed – have remained rather minimal. This is not least due to what Lederach refers to as a 'cookie-cutter' approach, suggesting that 'our approaches have become too cookie-cutter-like, too reliant on what proper technique suggests as a frame of reference, and as a result our processes are too rigid and fragile'.[10] At this stage, one can ask why peacebuilding has developed such a rigid frame. Why has it not adapted and developed more against the background that it is being used and deployed all over the world?

I want to suggest in this chapter that this is largely due to what we can call an 'autopoietic logic' of peacebuilding. Luhmann has defined autopoiesis as a self-referential system that ultimately intends to reproduce itself.[11] In this, he relies to a certain extent on the work of the biologists Maturana and Varela who suggest that,

[a]n autopoietic machine is a machine organized (defined as a unity) as a network of processes of production (transformation and destruction) of components which: (i) through their interactions and transformations continuously regenerate and realise the network of processes (relations) that

produced them; and (ii) constitute it (the machine) as a concrete unity in space in which they (the components) exist by specifying the topological domain of its realisation as such a network.[12]

This, in turn, means that the social system in question, that is, the peacebuilding system, can be read as an 'ideal type', a closed social system,[13] and draws its references from within its own boundaries rather than from outside of those. It therefore derives both its logic and legitimacy from itself and therefore largely resists challenges from outside. At the same time, the closure of the system also means that it has retained a resilient spatial, temporal and sociological logic that has little need – or interest – to change over time or space. In that sense, the system's main ambition is to steer its knowledge creation and policy practice in a way that enables its stability and continuity, and the self-legitimising logic of the system fulfils exactly this purpose. As a result, feedback on the 'performance' of an autopoietic system is provided from the scripts and actors within its logic, that is, those who have a vested interest in the continuation of the system. Therefore, only agents who are in accordance with the underlying logic of the system are part of its design and feedback processes, so alternative notions and norms of peace tend to be dismissed through peacebuilding's structural setup.

In this context, Barker refers to self-legitimation as 'the cultivation of a distinguished identity'[14] as a potential goal in itself and 'a feature of all government'.[15] In that vein, we can read self-legitimation as a basic and necessary condition of governance, not only on the national, but also on the global level. If we then assume that peacebuilding is a form of governance, we have to acknowledge its ambition to legitimise its own goals, methods and actors. A lack of flexibility within peacebuilding thus does not come as a surprise, but is a logical outcome of this mechanism of legitimising itself by reference to its own goalposts. The focus on continuity rather than rupture, on stability rather than change,[16] the inclusion of a rather small pool of participants, the subcontracting of peace to non-governmental organisations,[17] as well as the use of strong conditionality in funding practices, are all indicative of this trend. Even when there has now been a stronger focus on practices of 'local ownership',[18] this has primarily served to further legitimise the peacebuilding system rather than opening doors for a rethinking of the system from a perspective of its host societies or even challenging the operational goals of the respective mission.[19]

Hence, given that the peacebuilding missions in BiH have been deployed for over twenty years meanwhile, it is a particularly useful example to gauge the extent to which change in the system has remained rather limited and how self-perpetuating dynamics dominate the design and evaluation of peacebuilding in the country and beyond.

The Peacebuilding Jigsaw in Bosnia-Herzegovina

The 'recent' war in BiH took place from 1992 and 1995 and has to be seen in the context of the breakup of the former Yugoslavia. The collapse of socialism, symbolised by the death of Josip Broz Tito in 1980, increasing degrees of privatisation and internal struggles to fill the power vacuum left behind by Tito all led to the destabilisation of the political, economic and social situation. Followed by the independence of Croatia and Slovenia, the situation of BiH, caught in the middle of these struggles, deteriorated and experienced some of the worst violence during this war. The capital city Sarajevo was under siege from 1992 until 1996 with a number of international attempts at mediation failing until the signing of the Dayton Peace Accords in 1995.

Whilst the war, at the point of writing, ended more than twenty years ago, the ensuing peacebuilding mission, which was one of the most comprehensive from its very beginning and is represented through a quagmire of organisations, still shows only little signs of becoming redundant. Powerful international actors including the European Union (EU), the Office of the High Representative (OHR), the Organisation for Security and Cooperation in Europe (OSCE), the North Atlantic Treaty Organisation (NATO) and a plethora of middle-sized NGOs continue to highlight the necessity of their ongoing presence in preventing the re-escalation of violence and keeping the country stable. In that sense, it can be argued that the legitimacy of the long-standing international engagement rests largely on the argument that there is a *need* for further engagement in the light of the potential *local* and *national* threats that the system in BiH might produce, with the OHR as the formerly most powerful external institution still present more than twenty years after the end of the war. If one takes a closer look at the types of 'problems' that international actors and donors strive to eliminate and tackle in their engagement in BiH, we can see that these range from security sector reform to education, from economic transformation to demining. And whilst these efforts cover such a vast range of policy and societal sectors, what is interesting is that the overall state structure remains largely untouched. In a way, the political system was created by the Dayton Peace Agreement, that is, a system that subdivides the country into two entities, the self-governing district Brčko and ten cantons, creates at times insurmountable obstacles to political change and can be said to engrain the structures of the war in the post-conflict environment. It also means that the constitution, part of the peace agreement, has empowered nationalists more than moderates and rewards ethnic identification. The famous 'Sejdić Finci' case, for instance, saw a Bosnian Roma and Jew sue the Bosnian state for discriminating against those who do not identify as Bosnian Serb, Bosnian Croat or Bosnian Muslim and denying them important political offices. Although Sejdić and Finci won the case in 2009 at the European Court of Human Rights and may represent a locally-grounded alternative vision of a post-war state structure, the latter remains largely unchanged and the majority of international organisations seem to accept the deadlock inherent in BiH's constitutional arrangements as well as the extent to which political elites keep benefiting from a system of division.[20]

In that vein, it is interesting to note that very often, when international organisations speak about Bosnian institutions or politics, they refer to them as 'complex' or 'very complicated'.[21] This implies an imagination of the international system, created by the Dayton Peace Agreement, subject to being derailed through the existence of *national* complexity, neglecting the fact that much of this complexity has been created by the intervention project itself. This is in line with Autesserre's observation that local mechanisms of conflict resolution have often been labelled as illegitimate, while liberal peacebuilding has much more often been labelled as a legitimate device through which change and social transformation can be catalysed.[22] Such a discourse defends international peacebuilding intervention as necessary and long-term, creating a self-sustaining field with very little variance over time. Anecdotally, this is visible through the make-up of the peacebuilding community that tends to mainly socialise with each other rather than more broadly with wider society. The OSCE office in Sarajevo, ironically, has for many years had an advertisement poster at its lifts by an international moving company – just one anecdote reflecting the fact that employees tend to be kept close to the headquarters rather than their host societies. The policy of job rotation, used at the majority of international organisations, is indicative of this problem. It means that international staff members are denied the opportunity to socialise and integrate within the respective host societies and instead ensures maximum loyalty to their organisation. This practice further ensures the continuity of the mechanics at play in the peacebuilding field as well as creating a system that is closed itself.

Against this background, the lack of flexibility and change of approach in international peacebuilding is perhaps little surprising. This became particularly obvious during the 2014 protests across the country that, in very vocal ways, suggested a need to combat corruption. The protests emerged from a medium-sized movement of factory-workers in the small town of Tuzla to a larger social movement against corruption, unemployment and more social justice.[23] Protesters formed 'plenums', smaller participatory bodies that dealt with issues of public interest and, amongst others, spoke out against corruption and ethno-nationalism in political arenas. Whilst these plenums started hosting debates that were very relevant for peacebuilding and the future development of BiH as a country, they were quickly brushed aside by the international community and dismissed as undemocratic, not sustainable and sometimes even violent. Whilst this is not to say that the plenums represented the population as a whole, it was still striking to see how little strategic attention this movement was given by the peacebuilders who have long claimed to strive to empower Bosnian society. I have argued elsewhere that the plenums were in fact quickly dismissed, both by Western European media as well as international diplomats in Bosnia, as being violent or lacking leadership.[24] It has to be said that, specifically within EU policy in BiH, there has ever since been a slightly higher degree of attention towards the material and economic aspects of peacebuilding, which were vocally highlighted by the plenums. At the same time, we have seen only little to no integration of the non-ethnic structures of the plenum into the peacebuilding process, thus allowing continuing manifestations of corruption and ethno-nationalism in the public sphere. Indeed, when now speaking to international organisation staff in BiH, the overall consensus is still to consider the ethnic division of the political system as an obstacle to the further development of peacebuilding rather than more strategic attention to this strong movement of the plenums (one among others) as evidence of the unifying forces across the country. The momentum that the abovementioned Sejdić–Finci case had brought into breaking up these ethnic categories only figures marginally in these debates.

Peacebuilding in BiH therefore remains in limbo between local and international, between unifying and segregating forces. It tends to take the divided, nationalistic forces as a given and feeds on those structures almost as the country was still in the midst of the war and its associated dividing lines.

This is the background against which this chapter asks how this system that rests on the perpetuation of the dividing structures of the war has ensured its survival for more than twenty years. Analysing where the system draws its legitimacy from, the chapter explores in more detail the mechanics of the peacebuilding system. It asks which actors, spaces, temporalities and logics are evoked to create legitimacy, how the peacebuilding field is structured and conditioned to ensure its continuous reproduction.

The Logics of Legitimacy

The actors that establish peacebuilding legitimacy

Although there is no clear career path to becoming a peacebuilding professional and actors involved in peacebuilding emerge from a number of
career trajectories, there is still a particular 'type' of staff who are found in
both headquarters and field offices that engage in peacebuilding. In this
context, Goetze has conducted a relevant study on the ways in which the
peacebuilding field generates power not only through the ways in which
it produces knowledge, but also in its mechanisms of expert production.[25]
Goetze shows how the world of peacebuilding has long tended to privilege
those already privileged, those with degrees from high-ranking universities,
thus precluding a rather large pool of the world population from participating in the design and implementation of peacebuilding.[26] Indeed, when
visiting international organisations in post-conflict contexts, and particularly BiH, it is rather striking how many staff members hold higher education qualifications from Western Europe, and mainly the UK. In addition,
one can notice a pattern in which responsibilities are usually such that
non-locals are given higher positions than their local counterparts, with
the latter often serving as assistants. As mentioned above, organisations
such as the EU or the OSCE, for instance, often hold policies that are based
on the principle of job rotation, a process throughout which an organisation can 'prevent' individuals from associating too closely with the local
context and being kept at maximum loyalty to the institution as they tend
to stay with the institution, but in different geographical contexts. The
wage gap between the 'locals' and the 'internationals', in turn, ensures that
international staff members stay loyal to the institution instead of looking for jobs elsewhere in the country in which they are deployed. Lemay-
Hébert et al. link this to the phenomenon of brain drain during the course
of which locals are 'co-opted' into the development system, made part of
it and thus unable or unwilling to return to the world outside it that has
worse working conditions and much lower salaries.[27] This can be considered a strategy through which the central peacebuilding actors are made
part of a system that leaves them almost unable to resist. The trainings
they go through – often at international elite universities – and the institutional constraints therefore deploy strong centripetal forces and only let
those participate who are in favour of the system and its policies to begin
with. Green, for instance, points to the particular training that peacebuilders should go through.[28] Not only does she point to the multicultural competences that are to be expected as core skills of peacebuilders, but also a

set of 'functional skills' and problem-solving oriented skills.[29] In a sense, she distils some key competencies that are basic necessities for successful peacebuilders and makes the case even for an 'army' of peacebuilders.[30] In-depth knowledge of local context and history is thus often considered a secondary skill that can be learnt on the job, although such skills can be crucially important if an organisation is to have a sustainable and meaningful presence in its host society.

As a result, it could be argued that participating actors will generally be trained in a way that will prevent them from putting the system into question as a whole and criticism will remain within the limits of the system. The selection of staff thus fulfils a self-legitimising promise and serves to hold the system together, even on the very large scale on which it operates. This is further reinforced by a trend to 'bunkerize' peacebuilding, that is, the tendency for those in positions of power in the field to stay in a contained or gated environment.[31] Such developments are not only true for environments with low security ratings for international actors, linked to a lifestyle of what Fisher calls 'defensive living'.[32] At least symbolically, it can also be observed in contexts such as post-war BiH where international actors are not forced to live in a compound for security reasons, but still tend to socialise in rather closed circles.

In analysing the ways in which actors design and legitimise peacebuilding policies in BiH more specifically, Kostić goes even further, suggesting that shadow peacebuilders engage in the establishment of narratives that, in turn, are the result of the strategic networks they are situated in.[33] Kostić's analysis of such networks in BiH suggests that these necessarily include a personal component in terms of who knows whom and who will be consulted within the network.[34] If we assume what I have argued above, namely that the bulk part of socialisation happens between actors who are part of the international community, then we also have to assume that their 'shadow network' is the strongest in terms of the narrative that perpetuates peacebuilding policy. As a result, the type of knowledge that is produced from these established connections is the knowledge that will keep reinforcing the necessity of further intervention – not least to ascertain international organisations' right to stay. Bliesemann de Guevara and Kostić situate this problem within a landscape of the neo-liberalisation of knowledge production, which in itself narrows the political space through which the knowledge of peacebuilding we hold can be challenged or even revised.[35] Again, this means that agency within the peacebuilding system faces strict limitations due to the setup of its internal processes.

The spaces of legitimation – where peacebuilding takes place

Peace seems to be confined to particular physical spaces in which it is expected to take place by the international peacebuilding community. Often, such spaces are formal and scripted and bear little surprise. A typical example in BiH is the famous bridge in Mostar which, after the World Bank's reconstruction efforts in 2004, tends to be presented as a major success in reconciling the divided city.[36] At the same time, there tends to be little emphasis on the fact that the bridge does not link the Bosniak with the Croat part of the city, but instead represents a connection within the Bosniak community. In fact, today Mostarians hardly cross the bridge and we can mainly observe tourists, tourist guides and the famous bridge divers on it, ready to jump into the water for a donation. In that sense, whilst the reconstruction of the bridge was important for the city in terms of its symbolic character and symbolises an important contribution by the World Bank, it has a limited social function in terms of reconciliation. This indeed seems to be true for many of the spaces that are deemed 'traditional' peace spaces: bridges, offices, dialogue fora, reconciliation centres and so on. They are usually closed, in a contained space with clear boundaries. This also means that particular forms of agency are promoted, facilitated and empowered in those spaces: agency that will, at the end of the day, only challenge the surface of peacebuilding, never its foundational assumptions and principles. They are spaces in which no unpredictable outcome can occur, where the actual setting and physical location set the parameters of interaction and frame what can and will be said. In BiH, this means a strong emphasis on urban, rather than rural, peacebuilding as well as projects within the Federation rather than Republika Srpska, the political environment of which is often deemed more prone to conflict than the one of the Federation.[37] It also means that spaces in which peace formation is happening beyond the public sphere of international peacebuilding are overlooked. As I have argued elsewhere,[38] the sphere of the arts that is often situated 'underground' in BiH has the potential to act as an alternative arena in which political legitimacy is created. The arts and culture have indeed a long history of acting a unifying factor in Bosnian society.[39] It is therefore somewhat surprising that there is a lack of engagement with this space as a potential reference to international peacebuilding. This is not least the case against the background that the sphere of the arts has tended to act as one that challenges and critiques international peacebuilding.[40] Using the arts as a sphere of engagement would thus, by its very nature, risk producing a de-legitimising discourse against international peace intervention. Its exclusion, instead, means that the overall peacebuilding discourse can remain stable and avoid facing challenges from the sphere of the arts. The statement that the arts cannot be used as a partner for peacebuilding as they are ethnically divided[41] can therefore also be read as a *justification* of why they are not included, rather than a statement of fact.

Peacebuilding legitimacy and timing – when peacebuilding takes place

There is also always a question of timing, that is, when peacebuilding takes place. This not least contributes to the ways in which it legitimates itself. It has indeed been suggested that peacebuilding is built on the assumption of linearity in terms of following a step-by-step logic, or what Paris refers to as the need to institutionalise before liberalising a post-conflict political environment.[42] 'Time' in the discipline of Political Science has indeed often been analysed in the light of sequencing and path dependencies.[43] This implies that 'peacebuilding' is necessarily a positive intervention and its success is mainly a matter of time. It is therefore no coincidence that the seminal study of Doyle and Sambanis codes peacebuilding intervention to assess the degree of success, but without allowing for a negative outcome of peacebuilding intervention in the coding method.[44]

In such linear imaginaries, peace is situated in the future, as an end goal, temporarily distant from war. This, in turn, also means that peacebuilding is assumed to be successful and thus legitimate as long as it moves along this assumed linear path of progress. As suggested above, this also means that peacebuilding sets its own benchmarks as moving away from whatever is the status quo. This is, for instance, obvious with the World Bank's statement on their engagement in BiH, in which they state that 'the transition process in BiH, and the Bank's efforts to support transition, had to confront the complex government structure and the unique characteristics of the SFRY system – social ownership and worker self-management'.[45] As a result, what the World Bank wants is to move away from the 'old' system (independent of its political and economic value) and legitimise its own policies through its ability to transform complexity into a straightforward, linear process. Legitimacy thus derives from linearity and consistency with its own approaches. The latter are devised independent of the context in which they are deployed and thus, again, evidence the closed nature of the peacebuilding system. This is not dissimilar from the European Commission's approach to peacebuilding in BiH, a mission that is focused on transforming BiH into a more EU-like country. In fact, the Commission Staff Working Paper Bosnia and Herzegovina/Stabilisation and Association Report 2004 over twenty pages mentions the word 'progress' forty-five times.[46] The benchmark of 'progress' again stems from the peacebuilding system itself and is immune to external challenge. The success and legitimacy of intervention therefore derives from the logic of the system itself and is translated into the host society, usually via project cycles. In this context, it is also interesting to note that the actors that are being made part of the peacebuilding system – being funded or empowered by it – are often those who have had no role in the past of the conflict. Hence, while the former war time leaders were made key actors in the peacemaking process and in the signing of the Dayton Peace Accords, the peacebuilding process is keen on empowering 'new' actors. The 'mushrooming' of NGOs, known from various other post-conflict zones,[47] is indicative of this trend to expect to paint a new peacebuilding image on a new blank canvas.[48] This is linked to the ambition to move to a better future detached from the past, but at the same time labels this past as a state in need of change. Again, there is no space for the past to challenge the vision of the future through the in-built assumption that the externally devised peacebuilding system will be better than what was there in the past. A deliberate ignorance of workers' or women's rights that Yugoslavia was proud of,[49] or the levels of equality that the country can today only dream of, thus becomes part and parcel of the peacebuilding project in its attempt to legitimise itself by delegitimising the past. The frame of reference in peacebuilding discourses is therefore rarely situated in the past of the former Yugoslavia. Instead, this era is often considered as 'backward' or torn by ancient hatreds – a representation that the famous book *Balkan Ghosts* by Robert Kaplan clearly illustrates, thus, perhaps inadvertently, setting the canvas on which peacebuilding paints its own assumptions of civilisation and progress.[50] Peacebuilding therefore assumes to take place *after* situations or even eras of 'uncivility', thus implying that its own policies can bring only improvement. This assumption inherently claims legitimacy as it foregrounds peacebuilding as a necessary intervention in order to rid a region, country or town from the troubles of its own past. This can be understood as symbolised by the ever-postponed proposal to close the OHR in BiH,[51] as the time is never quite considered ripe for the withdrawal of one of the most powerful international institutions in BiH. In that sense, the legitimacy of the continuing cycle of heavy-handed international peacebuilding rests on the assumption that, otherwise, BiH might just go to war again.[52]

The logics of the system – how the agent is supposed to act

The above-outlined factors facilitate a particular logic through which the peacebuilding system is expected to operate. This logic of operating concerns the 'who', 'where', 'when', and also the 'how'. Autesserre outlines in her recent book how the interaction of peacebuilders with 'the field' is shaped by practices, habits and narratives.[53] The everyday politics that result from this interplay of doing and telling things then feed into the very logics through which peacebuilding is being conducted. They identify roots and causes of violence, they organise and categorise them and they create 'order' in a complex situation – from the perspective of the peacebuilders. Such practices categorise and structure a 'field' of violence.[54] The structures that emerge from the practices, habits and narratives of the peacebuilders, in turn, are intended to provide fertile conditions on which peace can 'grow'. Put differently, it creates conditions under which peace *has* to grow.

In this context, it is meanwhile well known that peacebuilding has had a tendency to rely on 'log frames', that is, a highly-structured way of planning, designing, implementing and evaluating peacebuilding in projects rather than on a continuum, and presented in a matrix. This means that policies have to be packaged, given a time limit and be closed in themselves. This potentially risks the sustainability of the programme beyond its life cycle and has been critiqued as a Western way of going about peacebuilding.[55] Indeed, there has been rather limited variance over time in the ways in which peacebuilding is being packaged and organised, with the log frame being the sticky point that has often driven 'alternative' actors away from it. At the same time, the log frame format demands that every project's success can be evaluated after the usual three to four years of its lifecycle. Therefore, projects that do get funding and that do go ahead tend to have measures in place that will guarantee a controlled outcome. Their projects will be set according to what can be achieved – and that can, but does not have to be, in tune with the contextual givens in the context in which they operate. Hummelbrunner refers to this lack of flexibility and fixation of the project givens as 'lock-frame' to point to the closed nature of this approach.[56]

This is also why, in order to obtain funding, projects need to demonstrate chances of success before even having begun. This means that the probability of engaging with new, alternative and untested approaches is rather low as this might undermine their chances of measurable 'success'. As an indirect result, projects tend to obtain funding if they are in line with the dominant peacebuilding ideology and vision and, in order to obtain funding, the organisations proposing projects will likely be in line with peacebuilding's wider ambitions. Performance indicators will be developed accordingly and in line with this. Such practices rarely draw on input from the society in which they are deployed and contextualised. To quote but one example from BiH: Experienced in different types of civil society work in BiH, Šavija-Valha and Milanović-Blank produced a satirical piece in the format of an 'absolutely unnecessary guide to civil society building and project management for locals and internationals in BiH and beyond' in which, amongst others, they refer to the log frame as something a layman cannot understand.[57] The intended target group of such log frames are therefore actors who are able, willing and trained to comply with the basic tenets of the peacebuilding field.

In addition to the log frame as a format, peacebuilding projects, in order to obtain funding, also have to speak to particular key words, again set by the larger funding organisations. These key priorities will direct the way in which the overall peacebuilding landscape develops and will leave little flexibility in terms of adjusting the project to suddenly arising needs. Such dynamics that come with funding streams attached ensure the survival of the peacebuilding system and, at the same time, help defend and legitimise its ongoing presence in the respective host country. The logic of the system makes sure it reproduces itself through its self-appraisal. In that sense, the system is built to perpetuate itself and, by dictating the rules of the game, it sets its own conditions for evaluating its success and ensuring its continuing presence. In this context, Mac Ginty refers to the 'technocracy' of peacebuilding.[58] He suggests that the increasing technocratisation of funding and operating processes within the peacebuilding field risks minimising the agency of a variety of actors,[59] thus shaping what can and cannot be imagined, designed and implemented. In a country that is shaped by long-standing and often heavy-handed international intervention such as BiH, this tendency has wide-ranging repercussions for what type of change is possible. In fact, as described above, despite the creative potential in the sphere of the arts in the country, numerous officials working in international funding organisations have made it clear to me[60] that they cannot fund such projects given that the latter do not tend to comply with their own funding requirement and matrices.

This is not to say that there is no reflection in the peacebuilding world about such issues – indeed, there is an increasing acknowledgement of the need to develop participatory approaches or involve secondary audiences into the ways in which projects are assessed.[61] Mac Ginty also acknowledges the creativity of individuals and organisations involved in peacebuilding in coming up with innovative approaches to dealing with conflict.[62] At the same time, there are limited attempts to rethink the structure of the peacebuilding system *as a whole*, beyond a mere involvement of wider representative samples of actors and projects. Instead, there is mainly a tweaking of assumed errors that only goes so far as to prevent the system from collapsing whilst reaffirming the necessity to keep it in place. Again, the legitimacy of the system relies on the mechanics and benchmarks it keeps producing itself, in the success indicators inherent in log frames as well as the conditions on which funding hinges. Proposed innovation that cannot be measured in log frames (or at least in a modified version of a log frame) thus stands rather little success of obtaining funding or even policy contacts to the big international players.

Conclusion

These reflections on the ways in which the peacebuilding system in BiH legitimises itself mirror its self-referential nature. The system is so engrained that it offers little flexibility and is thus reliant on a constant reassertion of being necessary and beneficial. At this stage, we could even ask whether we can talk of agents in the peacebuilding system. Are they not mainly structurally conditioned by the field? First, if we assume this to be true, then these peacebuilding 'agents' have limited agency at best as their ability to transform or influence the system itself would be very marginal. Second, would that then mean that challenge, criticism and improvement of the field cannot come from inside but has to come from outside? In fact, many of the smaller moves within the system have had their origin outside its normal boundaries – from artists or the activists of the plenums in 2014, some of whom are still engaged in smaller protest actions. Locally-grounded authority indeed can be linked to systems of the past (for instance, in the form of 'Yugonostalgia'), challenge seemingly unchangeable national categories (as with the Sejdić-Finci case) or be derived from actors not prominently acknowledged in the peacebuilding system (such as artists). Yet as far as the peacebuilding system itself is concerned, there is a focus on the status quo and a fear of fundamental change. In BiH, this has led to what Bojičić-Dželilović calls an 'ethnic security paradox', that is, a situation in which ethnic identity and segregation becomes the given in the process of intervention and are even reinforced by the latter.[63] Peacebuilding policies have therefore largely been unable to prevent social cohesion from being based on ethno-national clientelistic networks.[64]

I would suggest that, at least partially, the lack of openness of the peacebuilding system is the result of an underlying global system of inequality, in terms of how chains of accountability are created, how the system is built to perpetuate itself and, to that end, which knowledge counts as valuable. Sassen argues that, although different types of actors work transnationally in the global economy, we still tend to assume a hierarchy between 'local < national < global'.[65] Such hierarchies are equally mirrored in the peacebuilding economy and policy and reflect the extent to which the assumed global structures of legitimation weigh heavier than the benchmarks of those at the receiving end of intervention.

It is only when the spaces, time frames and logics of peacebuilding are openly put up for a genuine political debate that the mechanisms of legitimation can be rethought and the system can better respond to the needs arising out from its host societies, rather than those political communities operating the system. In that sense, change in the sense of a move towards a higher degree of hybridity of legitimacy, requires a dialogue between the different stakeholders of the system and is dependent on the input from various sides. Thus, legitimacy is a relational concept that must not be viewed in isolation of neither actor that is part of its construction and reception. If international peacebuilding actors are to build legitimate forms of peace, they are necessarily dependent on local actors translating it into the context in which it is to be deployed. Against this background, it is central to understand transversal representations of and responses to peacebuilding legitimacy, deriving from a spatial and temporal reference frame outside the established field. This requires the integration of a diverse set of actors to transform processes of legitimisation rather than considering host societies as passive recipients of those. Creative and challenging initiatives are already happening, and it is time that international peacebuilders take more notice and are prepared to deviate from their own scripts.

Notes

1. Mac Ginty, 'Routine peace: technocracy and peacebuilding', pp. 287–308.
2. Richmond, 'Critical research agendas for peace: the missing link in the study of international relations', p. 264.
3. Chandler, 'The responsibility to protect? Imposing the 'Liberal Peace'', pp. 59–81; Kappler, Local Agency and Peacebuilding. EU and International Engagement in Bosnia-Herzegovina, Cyprus and South Africa; Mac Ginty, 'Indigenous Peace-Making Versus the Liberal Peace', pp. 139–63; Stokke and Uyangoda (eds), Liberal peace in question: politics of state and market reform in Sri Lanka.
4. Berdal, 'Chapter Two: Peacebuilding operations and the struggle for legitimacy', pp. 95–134.
5. Heathershaw, 'Peacebuilding as practice: discourses from post-conflict Tajikistan', pp. 219–36.
6. Talentino, 'Perceptions of peacebuilding: the dynamic of imposer and imposed upon', pp. 152–71.
7. Boege et al., 'On hybrid political orders and emerging states: state formation in the context of 'fragility'', p. 10.
8. Roberts, 'Post-conflict peacebuilding, liberal irrelevance and the locus of legitimacy', pp. 410–24.
9. Boutros Ghali, An Agenda for Peace: Preventive Diplomacy, Peacemaking and Peacekeeping.

10. Lederach, *The Moral Imagination: The Art and Soul of Building Peace*, p. 73.
11. Luhmann, 'The autopoiesis of social systems', pp. 172–92.
12. Maturana and Varela, *Autopoiesis and cognition: The realization of the living*, pp. 78–9.
13. Cf. Luhmann, 'The autopoiesis of social systems', pp. 172–92.
14. Barker, *Legitimating Identities: The Self-Presentations of Rulers and Subjects*, p. 4.
15. Ibid. p. 6.
16. Cf. Mac Ginty, 'Against Stabilization', *Stability: International Journal of Security and Development*, vol.1, no.1: pp.20–30.
17. Cf. Richmond and Carey (eds), *Subcontracting Peace: The Challenges of the NGO Peacebuilding*.
18. Cf. Lemay-Hébert and Kappler, 'What attachment to peace? Exploring the normative and material dimensions of local ownership in peacebuilding', pp. 895–914.
19. Von Billerbeck, 'Local ownership and UN peacebuilding: discourse versus operationalization', pp. 299–315.
20. Cf. Jenne, 'The Paradox of Ethnic Partition: Lessons from de facto Partition in Bosnia and Kosovo', *Regional and Federal Studies*, vol.19 (2): 273-89.
21. field observations, March 2017.
22. Autesserre, Severine (2009), 'Hobbes and the Congo: Frames, Local Violence, and International Intervention', *International Organization*, vol.63, pp.249-280.
23. Cf. Plenum gradjana i gradjanki Sarajeva (2014), 'Zahtjevi Plenuma gradjana i gradjanki Sarajeva prema Skupstini Kantona Sarajevo'. Available at http://plenumsa.org/zahtjevi-plenuma-gradana-i-gradanki-sarajeva-prema-skupstini-kantona-sarajevo/ (last accessed 08 August 2014).
24. Kappler, Stefanie (2017), 'The Securitization of International Peacebuilding', in *Securitization in Statebuilding and Intervention*, Bonacker, Thorsten, Distler, Werner & Ketzmerick, Maria (eds.), Baden-Baden: Nomos.
25. Goetze, Catherine (2017), *The Distinction of Peace. A Social Analysis of Peacebuilding*, Michigan: University of Michigan Press.
26. Ibid.
27. Lemay-Hébert et al., 'The internal brain drain: foreign aid, hiring practices, and international migration'.
28. Green, 'CONTACT: Training a new generation of peacebuilders', pp. 97–105.
29. Ibid. p. 100.
30. Ibid. p. 105.
31. Fisher, 'Reproducing remoteness? States, internationals and the co-constitution of aid 'bunkerization' in the East African periphery,' pp. 98–119; Smirl, *Spaces of Aid: How Cars, Compounds and Hotels Shape Humanitarianism*.
32. Fisher, 'Reproducing remoteness? States, internationals and the co-constitution of aid 'bunkerization' in the East African periphery,' p. 191.
33. Kostić, 'Shadow peacebuilders and diplomatic counterinsurgencies: informal networks, knowledge production and the art of policy-shaping', pp. 120–39.
34. Ibid.

35. Bliesemann de Guevara and Kostić, 'Knowledge production in/about conflict and intervention: finding "facts", telling "truth"', pp. 1–20.
36. Björkdahl and Kappler, *Peacebuilding and Spatial Transformation: Peace, Space and Place*, p. 26.
37. See, for instance, Chivvis, 'Back to the brink in Bosnia?', pp. 97–110.
38. Kappler, 'Everyday legitimacy in post-conflict spaces: the creation of social legitimacy in Bosnia-Herzegovina's cultural arenas', pp. 11–28.
39. Zelizer, 'The role of artistic processes in peacebuilding in Bosnia-Herzegovina', pp. 62–75.
40. Cf. Kappler, *Local Agency and Peacebuilding: EU and International Engagement in Bosnia-Herzegovina, Cyprus and South Africa*.
41. Confidential source, international community, Sarajevo, March 2017.
42. Paris, *At War's End: Building Peace After Civil Conflict*.
43. Pierson, *Politics in Time. History, Institutions, and Social Analysis*, p. 64.
44. Doyle and Sambanis, 'International peacebuilding: a theoretical and quantitative analysis', pp. 779–801.
45. World Bank, *Bosnia and Herzegovina: Post-Conflict Reconstruction and the Transition to a Market Economy. An OED Evaluation of World Bank Support*, p. 6.
46. European Commission, 'Commission staff working paper Bosnia and Herzegovina stabilisation and association report 2004'. Available at <http://ec.europa.eu/enlargement/pdf/bosnia_and_herzegovina/cr_bih_en.pdf> (last accessed 24 June 2016).
47. Cf. Jad, 'NGOs: between buzzwords and social movements', pp. 622–9.
48. Pugh, 'Transformation in the political economy of Bosnia since Dayton', p. 450.
49. Cf. Ramović, 'Maximum profit, minimal peace: insights into the peacebuilding potential of the workplace'.
50. Kaplan, *Balkan Ghosts: A Journey Through History*.
51. Cf. Tirak, 'The Bosnian Hiatus: A Story of Misinterpretations'.
52. Less, 'The next Balkan wars'; Lyon, 'Is war about to break out in the Balkans?'.
53. Autesserre, *Conflict Resolution and the Everyday Politics of International Intervention*.
54. Cf. Richmond et al., 'The "field" in the age of intervention: power, legitimacy, and authority versus the "local"', pp. 23–44.
55. Körppen, 'Re-politicising the strategies and methods of the liberal peacebuilding discourse', p. 34.
56. Hummelbrunner, 'Beyond logframe: critique, variations and alternatives', pp. 1–33.
57. Šavija-Valha and Milanović-Blank, 'Ubleha za idiote – apsolutno nepotrebni vodič kroz izgradnju civilnog društva i vođenje projekata za lokalce i internacionalce u BH i šire', pp. 46–73.
58. Mac Ginty, 'Routine peace: technocracy and peacebuilding', pp. 287–308.
59. Ibid. p. 292.
60. Interviews between 2008 and 2017.
61. Lemon and Pinet, 'Measuring unintended effects in peacebuilding: innovative approaches shaped by complex contexts', p. 14.

62. Mac Ginty, 'Routine peace: technocracy and peacebuilding', p. 301.
63. Bojičić-Dželilović, 'The politics, practice and paradox of "ethnic security" in Bosnia-Herzegovina', pp. 1–18.
64. Divjak and Pugh, 'The political economy of corruption in Bosnia and Herzegovina', pp. 373–86.
65. Sassen, 'Spatialities and temporalities of the global: elements of a theorization', p. 226.

Bibliography

Autesserre, Severine, 'Hobbes and the Congo: frames, local violence, and international intervention', *International Organization*, 2009, 63: pp. 249–80.

Autesserre, Severine, *Conflict Resolution and the Everyday Politics of International Intervention* (Cambridge: Cambridge University Press, 2014).

Barker, Rodney, *Legitimating Identities. The Self-Presentations of Rulers and Subjects*, (Cambridge: Cambridge University Press, 2001).

Berdal, Mats, 'Chapter Two: Peacebuilding operations and the struggle for legitimacy', *The Adelphi Papers*, 2009, 49: 407, pp. 95–134.

Björkdahl, Annika and Stefanie Kappler, *Peacebuilding and Spatial Transformation: Peace, Space and Place* (Abingdon, UK: Routledge, 2017).

Bliesemann de Guevara, Berit and Roland Kostić, 'Knowledge production in/about conflict and intervention: finding 'facts', telling 'truth'', *Journal of Intervention and Statebuilding*, 2017, 11: 1, pp. 1–20.

Boege, Volker, Anne Brown, Kevin Clements and Anna Nolan, 'On hybrid political orders and emerging states: state formation in the context of "fragility"', *Berghof Handbook Dialogue No. 8* (Berlin: Berghof Research Center for Constructive Conflict Management, 2008).

Boutros Ghali, Boutros, *An Agenda for Peace: Preventive Diplomacy, Peacemaking and Peacekeeping* (New York: United Nations, 1992).

Chandler, David, 'The responsibility to protect? Imposing the "Liberal Peace"', *International Peacekeeping*, 2004, 11: 1, pp. 59–81.

Chivvis, Christopher S., 'Back to the brink in Bosnia?', *Survival*, 2010, 52: 1, pp. 97–110.

Doyle, Michael W. and Nicholas Sambanis, 'International peacebuilding: a theoretical and quantitative analysis', *The American Political Science Review*, 2000, 94: 4, 779–801.

European Commission, 'Commission Staff Working Paper Bosnia and Herzegovina Stabilisation and Association Report 2004', 2004. Available at <http://ec.europa.eu/enlargement/pdf/bosnia_and_herzegovina/cr_bih_en.pdf> (last accessed 24 June 2016).

Fisher, Jonathan, 'Reproducing remoteness? States, internationals and the co-constitution of aid "bunkerization" in the East African periphery,' *Journal of Intervention and Statebuilding*, 2017, 11: 1, pp. 98–119.

Goetze, Catherine, *The Distinction of Peace. A Social Analysis of Peacebuilding* (Ann Arbor: University of Michigan Press, 2017).

Green, Paula, 'CONTACT: Training a new generation of peacebuilders', *Peace & Change*, 2002, 27: 1, pp. 97–105.

Heathershaw, John, 'Peacebuilding as practice: discourses from post-conflict Tajikistan', *International Peacekeeping*, 2007, 14: 2, pp. 219–36.

Hummelbrunner, Richard, 'Beyond logframe: critique, variations and alternatives', in Nobuko Fujita (ed.), *Beyond Logframe; Using Systems Concepts in Evaluation*, (Tokyo: Foundation for Advanced Studies on International Development, 2010), pp.1–33. Available at <http://www.perfeval.pol.ulaval.ca/sites/perfeval.pol.ulaval.ca/files/publication_129.pdf#page=8> (last accessed 18 May 2017).

Jad, Islah, 'NGOs: between buzzwords and social movements', *Development in Practice*, 2007, 17: 4–5, pp. 622–9.

Kaplan, Robert, *Balkan Ghosts: A Journey Through History* (New York: Picador, 2005).

Kappler, Stefanie, 'Everyday legitimacy in post-conflict spaces: the creation of social legitimacy in Bosnia-Herzegovina's cultural arenas', *Journal of Intervention and Statebuilding*, 2013, 7: 1, pp. 11–28.

Kappler, Stefanie, *Local Agency and Peacebuilding. EU and International Engagement in Bosnia-Herzegovina, Cyprus and South Africa* (Basingstoke: Palgrave Macmillan, 2014).

Kappler, Stefanie, 'The securitization of international peacebuilding,' in Thorsten Bonacker, Werner Distler & Maria Ketzmerick (eds), *Securitization in Statebuilding and Intervention*, (Baden-Baden: Nomos, 2017).

Körppen, Daniela, 'Re-politicising the strategies and methods of the liberal peacebuilding discourse', in Janel B. Galvanek, Hans J. Giessmann and Mir Mubashir (eds), *Norms and Premises of Peace Governance. Socio-Cultural s and Differences in Europe and India*, 2012, Berghof Occasional Paper No. 32: pp. 31–6.

Kostić, Roland, 'Shadow peacebuilders and diplomatic counterinsurgencies: informal networks, knowledge production and the art of policy-shaping', *Journal of Intervention and Statebuilding*, 2017, 11: 1, pp. 120–39.

Lederach, John Paul, *The Moral Imagination: The Art and Soul of Building Peace* (Oxford University Press, 2005).

Lemay-Hébert, Nicolas & Stefanie Kappler, 'What attachment to peace? Exploring the normative and material dimensions of local ownership in peacebuilding,' *Review of International Studies*, 2016, 42: 5, pp. 895–914.

Lemay-Hébert, Nicolas, Louis Herns Marcelin, Stéphane Pallage and Toni Cela, 'The internal brain drain: foreign aid, hiring practices, and international migration', *Disasters*, 2019. Available at <https://doi.org/10.1111/disa.12382> (last accessed 17 February 2020).

Lemon, Adrienne and Mélanie Pinet, 'Measuring unintended effects in peacebuilding: innovative approaches shaped by complex contexts', Special Working Paper Series on 'Unintended Effects of International Cooperation', presented at Ministry of Foreign Affairs of the Netherlands, 16–17 January 2017.

Less, Timothy, 'The next Balkan wars', *The New Statesman*, 6 June 2016. Available at <http://www.newstatesman.com/world/2016/06/next-balkan-wars> (last accessed 18 May 2017).

Luhmann, Niklas, 'The autopoiesis of social systems,' in F. Geyer & J. van der Zouwen (eds), *Sociocybernetic Paradoxes* (London: Sage, 1986), pp. 172–92.

Lyon, James, 'Is war about to break out in the Balkans?', *Foreign Policy*, 26 October 2015. Available at <http://foreignpolicy.com/2015/10/26/war-break-out-balkans-bosnia-republika-srpska-dayton/> (last accessed 18 May 2017).

Mac Ginty, Roger, 'Indigenous peace-making versus the liberal peace', *Cooperation and Conflict*, 2008, 43: 2, pp. 139–63.

Mac Ginty, Roger, 'Against stabilization,' *Stability: International Journal of Security and Development*, 2012a, 1: 1, pp. 20–30.

Mac Ginty, Roger, 'Routine peace: technocracy and peacebuilding', *Cooperation and Conflict*, 2012b, 47: 3, pp. 287–308.

Maturana, Humberto and Francisco Varela, *Autopoiesis and cognition: The realization of the living* (Boston: D. Reidel, 1980).

Paris, Roland, *At War's End: Building Peace After Civil Conflict* (Cambridge and New York: Cambridge University Press, 2004).

Pierson, Paul, *Politics in Time. History, Institutions, and Social Analysis* (Princeton and Oxford: Princeton University Press, 2004).

Plenum gradjana i gradjanki Sarajeva, 'Zahtjevi Plenuma gradjana i gradjanki Sarajeva prema Skupstini Kantona Sarajevo', 2014. Available at <http://plenumsa. org/zahtjevi-plenuma-gradana-i-gradanki-sarajeva-prema-skupstini-kantona-sarajevo/> (last accessed 8 August 2014).

Pugh, Michael, 'Transformation in the political economy of Bosnia since Dayton', *International Peacekeeping*, 2005, 12: 3, pp. 448–62.

Ramović, Jasmin, 'Maximum profit, minimal peace: insights into the peacebuilding potential of the workplace', unpublished PhD thesis, University of Manchester, 2017.

Richmond, Oliver, 'Critical research agendas for peace: the missing link in the study of international relations', *Alternatives*, 2007, 32: pp. 247–74.

Richmond, Oliver and Henry F. Carey (eds), *Subcontracting Peace: The Challenges of the NGO Peacebuilding*, (Aldershot: Ashgate, 2005).

Richmond, Oliver, Stefanie Kappler and Annika Björkdahl, 'The "field" in the age of intervention: power, legitimacy, and authority versus the "local"', *Millennium – Journal of International Studies*, 2015, 44: 1, pp. 23–44.

Roberts, David, 'Post-conflict peacebuilding, liberal irrelevance and the locus of legitimacy', *International Peacekeeping*, 2011, 18: 4, pp. 410–24.

Sassen, Saskia, 'Spatialities and temporalities of the global: elements of a theorization', *Public Culture*, 2000, 12: 1, pp. 215–32.

Šavija-Valha, Nebojsa and Ranko Milanović-Blank, 'Ubleha za idiote – apsolutno nepotrebni vodič kroz izgradnju civilnog društva i vođenje projekata za lokalce i internacionalce u BH i šire', *Casopis za knjizevnost I kulturu Album*, 2004, 20: pp. 46–73.

Smirl, Lisa, *Spaces of Aid: How Cars, Compounds and Hotels Shape Humanitarianism* (London: Zed Books, 2015).

Stokke, Kristian and Jayadeva Uyangoda (eds), *Liberal Peace in Question: Politics of State and market reform in Sri Lanka* (London and New York: Anthem Press, 2011).

Talentino, Andrea K., 'Perceptions of peacebuilding: the dynamic of imposer and imposed upon', *International Studies Perspectives*, 2007, 8: pp. 152–71.

Tirak, Goran, 'The Bosnian hiatus: a story of misinterpretations', *CEPS Policy Brief no. 219*, 2010. Available at <https://www.ceps.eu/system/files/book/2010/11/PB219%20Goran%20Tirak%20on%20Bosnian%20Hiatus%20e-version%20latest.pdf> (last accessed 18 May 2017).

Von Billerbeck, Sarah B. K., 'Local ownership and UN peacebuilding: discourse versus operationalization,' *Global Governance: A Review of Multilateralism and International Organizations*, 2015, 21: 2, pp. 299–315.

World Bank, *Bosnia and Herzegovina: Post-Conflict Reconstruction and the Transition to a Market Economy. An OED Evaluation of World Bank Support*, (Washington, DC: The World Bank, 2004).

Zelizer, Craig, 'The role of artistic processes in peacebuilding in Bosnia-Herzegovina.' *Peace and Conflict Studies*, 2003, 10: 2, pp. 62–75.

SIX

'We Are There at Their Invitation': Struggles for Legitimacy during the US Coalition Invasion–Occupation of Iraq

Florian Zollmann

Introduction

On 1 May 2003, then-US President George W. Bush announced the end of the 2003 Iraq War during a speech on the aircraft carrier USS Abraham Lincoln. In his address, Bush said that from now on 'our coalition is engaged in securing and reconstructing' Iraq.[1] During its 'transition from dictatorship to democracy', Bush further said, the US-led Coalition would 'stand with the new leaders of Iraq as they establish a government of, by and for the Iraqi people'.[2]

In the so-called mission accomplished address cited above, Bush justified the occupation of Iraq with implicit reference to one of the tenets of liberal peacebuilding, which tends to be implemented in the form of statebuilding and aims to build a democratic state around liberal institutions.[3] Scholars argue that the statebuilding process enacted by the US coalition shortly after Bush had delivered his speech was, in fact, conducted in accord with the liberal peacebuilding paradigm.[4] Furthermore, it is widely recognized that this process abysmally failed.[5] It is, however, less researched how the US coalition statebuilding project can be understood with respect to legitimacy concerns. In this particular context, it is noteworthy that Bush's statement cited above further highlighted Iraqi agency: according to Bush, the US coalition would support Iraqis as *they* attempted to build a state *for the Iraqi people*. Bush's statement can thus be regarded as an attempt to obtain legitimacy for the US coalition led statebuilding project. Bush emphasised Iraqi agency in order to legitimise foreign occupation vis-à-vis the Iraqi people as well as the wider international community.[6] It turned out, however, that Iraqi agency was undermined during the statebuilding process. Firstly, US coalition statebuilding was primarily designed to serve US-business rather than Iraqi interest.[7] Secondly, statebuilding lacked legitimacy and this can be regarded as a root cause for its failures. However, these connections have not yet been considered by scholarship. Consequently, this essay will further assess how issues of legitimacy related to military intervention and statebuilding in Iraq. More specifically, the essay addresses the following questions: did the US coalition exercise legitimate authority for the 2003 invasion-occupation of Iraq? How did legitimacy relate to international norms, local practices and local perceptions? What kinds of institutions were established during statebuilding in Iraq? And, finally, to what extend were these institutions legitimate?[8] The essay attempts to answer these questions through the lens of a revised version of Max Weber's framework for legitimate authority.

The essay entails five sections: section one extends and refines Weber's categories of legitimate authority in the light of selected academic literature on legitimacy. The following sections are based on case studies applying Weber's framework in the context of the Iraq invasion–occupation, focusing on the years 2003 and 2004 when the US coalition administration set the course for its statebuilding project. More specifically, section two assesses the 2003 invasion of Iraq, conducted by US coalition forces on 20 March and formally ending with Bush's address on 1 May 2003, in the context of Weber's category of the rationality of the law as well as political and moral grounds for legitimacy. Section three scrutinises how during the early post-invasion phase, the US coalition attempted to legitimise the radical transformation of the Iraqi economy on legal grounds. Section four assesses legitimacy from a local perspective. Focusing on the occupation of the Sunni stronghold Fallujah, where Iraqi resistance against US coalition statebuilding efforts firstly materialised, this section will investigate how US coalition forces attempted to govern Iraqi municipalities that relied on local, traditional structures of legitimacy. Section five concludes the chapter by pointing out how statebuilding efforts could have won higher degrees of legitimacy and thus been proven to be more successful. The case studies utilise a range of primary sources from legal documents, governmental bodies and NGOs, as well as secondary sources from academic literature and human rights organisations.

Section 1: Grounds for Legitimacy

Legitimacy in the context of governance in society is concerned with questions about who rules, exercises power and has the authority to do so. Craig Matheson argues that because power tends to be monopolised by 'power-holders' vis-à-vis 'power-subjects' legitimacy relates to issues of command and obedience.[9] Of course, as Matheson writes, power-holders can rely on coercive or rewards-based systems of authority that do not make claims to legitimacy.[10] In such cases, compliance may be enforced via the 'prospect of punishment' or the 'offer of rewards'.[11] Because such systems of authority are very costly, power-holders aim to obtain obedience 'motivated by a belief in legitimacy'.[12] Thus, as Matheson further points out, grounds for legitimation can be classified 'according to the particular explanation or reason why command and obedience are said to be legitimate'.[13]

An early classification system for legitimacy was postulated by Max Weber who provided a three-tiered legitimacy framework, each category suggesting different reasons for legitimate authority.[14] Weber's framework is somewhat rigid and has, since its formulation, been elaborated and updated by a range of scholars. In the following section, I will blend Weber's categories of legitimate authority with Matheson's refinement of the underlying grounds for legitimacy. Such an updated framework better allows for an assessment of forms of authority and the claims to legitimacy they make.

Weber coined three pure types of legitimate authority – (1) legal, (2) traditional and (3) charismatic – suggesting that these categories acquired legitimacy on different grounds.

1. Weber argued that legal authority derives legitimacy from rational grounds that rest 'on a belief in the "legality" of patterns of normative rules and the right of those elevated to authority under such rules to issue commands'.[15] Legal authority obtains legitimacy on the basis of binding and institutionalised regulations and procedures that define how laws may be created, enacted or changed. Legal authority, as part of governance, may further entail procedures such as elections, rotations, parliaments, cabinet governments and other governing rules and structures as specified in legislation.[16] According to Matheson, under legal authority, command–obedience relationships are regulated by legal norms. Furthermore, legal authority can be distinguished into two analytical categories that form its basis of legitimation: (i) convention and (ii) the rationality of law.[17] Legal authority also operates, at least technically, in the context of international relations where national as well as international state- and non-state actors aim to present their activities as legitimate within the framework of international society and its shifting norms, which are ultimately governed by the United Nations.[18]

2. According to Weber, traditional authority derives legitimacy from grounds that are based 'on an established belief in the sanctity of immemorial traditions and the legitimacy of the status of those exercising authority under them'.[19] Traditional authority thus claims legitimacy on the basis of 'personal loyalty' derived from customary obligations.[20] In the context of governance, authority is upheld by a ruler whose ability to exercise power is two-fold: on the one hand, a ruler is constrained by the inviolability of tradition as the basis of their legitimate authority. On the other hand, a ruler's power encompasses a sphere of despotism governed by nepotism and patronage.[21] Matheson argues that under traditional authority, command–obedience relationships are regulated according to customary norms. Furthermore, traditional authority can be separated into three categories that spell out its bases for legitimacy: (i) the sanctity of tradition, (ii) convention, as well as (iii) personal relationships.[22]

3. Weber wrote that charismatic authority derives legitimacy from charismatic grounds that relate to 'devotion to the specific and exceptional sanctity, heroism or exemplary character of an individual person, and of the normative patterns or order revealed or ordained by him'.[23] Charismatic authority rests on people's beliefs in the qualities of a leader.[24] In the area of governance, a ruler and their administrative staff are selected on the basis of peoples' faith in their virtues.[25] Charismatic governance may also comprise a 'wise man' responsible for legal issues, including conflict resolution, by virtue of his 'charismatic validity'.[26] As Matheson writes, under charismatic authority, command–obedience relationships emerge during times of crisis when stable structures collapse and people look for a 'leader'. Moreover, this category entails two analytical bases for legitimacy that can be separated for inquiry: (i) the sanctity of 'persons, groups, or norms' as well as (ii) 'the extraordinary quality of an individual *person* [original emphasis]'.[27]

Based on Weber's framework for legitimate authority, this section has mapped out seven categories that specify grounds for why authority may be legitimately exercised: legal convention, the rationality of law, the sanctity of tradition, traditional convention, personal relationships, the sanctity of persons, groups or norms, and the quality of a person.

The following case studies will analyse the US coalition invasion of and statebuilding project in Iraq in the light of its legal components, and in line with Weber's framework, with reference to political and moral grounds for legitimacy.

Section 2: The 'Rationality of Law' During the 2003 Invasion of Iraq

This section looks at the short-term *invasion* phase starting with the US coalition military intervention on 20 March 2003. This is important because under consideration of the rationality of the law the legitimacy of the invasion is crucially linked to the legitimacy of the occupation.

Advocates of the 2003 invasion of Iraq attempted to legitimise military intervention on several grounds. For instance, the main official justification for the 2003 Iraq War provided by the Bush and then-British Prime Minister Tony Blair administrations constituted the threat of Iraq's alleged possession of weapons of mass destruction (WMD).[28] Others argued that intervention might have been justified on grounds of moral or political necessity.[29] This perspective regarded intervention as legitimate if it *de facto* accrued from humanitarian imperatives or demonstrably led to favourable outcomes.[30] In their justification for military intervention in Iraq, proponents of this approach pointed to then-Iraqi President Saddam Hussein's dictatorial regime and its human rights record as a sufficient condition for intervention.[31]

Whatever one thinks about the validity of the justifications outlined above, they are not able to claim legitimacy on legal grounds because they have no basis in international law as codified in the United Nations Charter (UN Charter). Thus, even if Iraq had possessed WMDs or engaged in human rights breaches, the US coalition was *de jure* not entitled to intervene. As the late legal scholar Michael Mandel wrote, the Iraq intervention fell short 'of any justification in self-defence or authorisation by the Security Council of the United Nations, the only two accepted legal grounds for war in international law'.[32] This matter of fact was substantiated as the number of legal experts who saw the Iraq invasion as a violation of international law far exceeded the few who depicted it as legal.[33]

If we accept this as valid legal opinion, then the US coalition invasion of Iraq can hardly be framed in benign terms that imply legitimacy. In fact, legal reasoning adopted by the UN General Assembly Resolution 3314 in 1974 would suggest that the Iraq invasion should have been classified as a *prima facie* case of aggression because it constituted a military attack against a sovereign state.[34] According to General Assembly Resolution 3314, which aimed to 'contribute to the strengthening of international peace and security', aggression entails 'the most serious and dangerous form of the illegal use of force'.[35] The major precedent of a case of aggression constitutes the illegal wars of Nazi Germany. The judges of the Nuremberg Tribunal, at which the German Nazis were convicted, explained the graveness with the fact that aggression 'contains within itself the accumulated evil of the whole'.[36] The Nuremberg verdict holds initiators of unlawful wars accountable for all of the outcomes of their wars. The judges established this legal principle arguing that the major crimes committed by Nazi Germany had actually accrued from its initial military interventions.[37] Consequently, war as a means of policy was outlawed after World War II. Today, the UN Charter, which spells out binding law for its signature states including the US and the UK, regards military intervention as a last resort only to be applied in exceptional cases and with a high burden of proof – subject to UN Security Council authorisation. This binding statute of the UN Charter was reaffirmed at the 2005 World Summit, stating that 'the relevant provisions of the Charter are sufficient to address the full range of threats to international peace and security' further stressing 'the importance of acting in accordance with the purposes and principles of the Charter'.[38]

The legal framework outlined above is important in the context of Iraq. Well in line with the reasoning established at Nuremberg, the 2003 invasion facilitated a devastating chain of events: mass civilian deaths, the breakup of society, and ethnic conflict creating a breeding ground for terrorist entities such as ISIS. One estimate suggests that the invasion and subsequent occupation 'triggered an episode more deadly than the Rwandan genocide'.[39]

The legal principles and facts outlined above hence demonstrate that if authority for intervention derives its justification from the rationality of law, as conceptualised by Weber, then the 2003 US coalition invasion of Iraq was not only illegal but also illegitimate.[40] Yet, scholars and the media rarely question the legitimacy of the Iraq invasion on legal grounds. In fact, the dominant discourse on Iraq circulates around the validity of a range of secondary grounds that have been used to legitimise intervention. It is thus worth considering further whether political or moral grounds could have made valid claims to legitimise intervention. As discussed above, some actors had argued that the 2003 Iraq invasion was legitimate on political (the WMD issue) or moral (human rights issues in Iraq) grounds. In the following, I will look at both sets of arguments.

The WMD issue has served as a powerful political discourse to legitimise intervention in Iraq outside of the legal limits set by the UN Charter. Yet, the WMD threat was not only exaggerated but also based on the deceptive use of intelligence.[41] Moreover, well before the actual invasion phase, evidence by the United Nations Special Commission (UNSCOM), headed by Scott Ritter, suggested that Iraq had already been disarmed by 1998.[42] Additionally, no

WMD stockpiles were found.[43] Hence, the argument that the Iraq invasion obtained legitimacy on the grounds of political necessity (i.e. security) was weak and could never be substantiated. The Iraq War was in fact not about security. Well before the invasion phase, analysts and intelligence agencies suggested that an intervention would actually increase the support for political Islam thus risking blowback from 'retail' terrorists.[44]

Similarly, several caveats spoke against intervention on moral grounds. Firstly, the major crimes conducted by Saddam Hussein's regime took place during the 1980s when Iraq was still an ally of the US and the UK. At the time, Iraqi massacres of the Kurds did not elicit indignation or calls for intervention in US and UK government circles. In fact, the then-US President Ronald Reagan administration blocked congressional initiatives to condemn the Iraqi regime and continued to supply it with weapons.[45] Secondly, Iraqi society had been in relatively good shape, particularly in the late 1980s. Despite Saddam Hussein's repressive dictatorship, Iraq comprised an advanced welfare state and was among the countries with the highest living standards in the Arab world.[46]

While the Iraqi state had disintegrated during the 1990s, international agencies and scholars are broadly in agreement that this was the result of a UN-sanctions regime imposed on Iraq under the auspices of the US and upheld by three consecutive US administrations.[47] According to Gordon, most of the studies undertaken by researchers found that 'at least 500,000 children under age five who died during the sanctions period would not have died under the Iraqi regime prior to sanctions'.[48] Three senior UN career officials, Dennis Halliday (who described the sanctions as 'genocidal'), Hans von Sponeck and Jutta Burghardt, resigned their UN posts in Iraq in protest against the sanctions.[49] In 2000, the UN Sub-Commission on the Promotion and Protection of Human Rights appealed to the International Community demanding a lifting of the embargo, which it considered 'to be a flagrant violation of the economic, social and cultural rights and the right to life of the people concerned and of international law'.[50] However, as Gordon documented, the US administrations and Congress did not factor the human damage of the sanctions in their actions and 'the leadership, of both parties, had little tolerance for any advocacy regarding the humanitarian issues in Iraq'.[51] This episode further illustrates why Western proponents for intervention in Iraq could hardly claim legitimacy on moral grounds since their own governments kept silent about and then were the main cause of a genocidal humanitarian crisis in Iraq.

This discussion of political and moral grounds for intervention reminds us as to why the rationality of law (i.e. the UN Charter with its emphasis on state sovereignty) provides an appropriate benchmark for assessing the legitimacy of military intervention. As Slaughter comments: '[. . .] the most important lesson of the invasion of Iraq is that the safeguards built into the requirement of the *multilateral* authorisation of the use of force by UN members are both justified and necessary [original emphasis].'[52] This, even more so as in the contemporary unipolar world an approach to intervention based on elastic grounds, is problematic because it allows powerful states to intervene as they please and no matter the consequences.[53]

Having discussed the legal, political and moral dimensions of legitimacy with respect to the short-term *invasion* of Iraq, I now turn to the claims for legitimacy in regard to the *occupation* and associated statebuilding project.

Section 3: The Occupation of Iraq: Claiming Legitimacy on Legal Grounds

After the official ending of the invasion of Iraq on 1 May 2003, the US coalition set the course for a military occupation that would formally end with the withdrawal of US troops in 2011. This section investigates the early phase of the occupation in the year 2003 during which the US coalition cemented the design for its statebuilding project.

If we go back to the rationality of the law as a ground for legitimacy, then the US coalition occupation of Iraq was illegitimate in the same fashion as the invasion was. Again, this is plain fact from UN General Assembly Resolution 3314, which states that 'The invasion or attack by the armed forces of a State against the territory of another State, *or any military occupation, however temporary, resulting from such invasion or attack* [. . .] qualify as an act of aggression [emphasis added]'.[54] This reasoning suggests that legitimate governing authority cannot be obtained by an occupying power if the initial invasion that preceded the occupation was conducted in violation of the law.

Yet, the US coalition used the law to *ex post facto* legitimise the occupation of Iraq through the ratification of various UN Resolutions. Most notably, UN Resolution 1483, adopted by the Security Council shortly after the end of the invasion phase on 22 May 2003, recognized the US and the UK as occupying powers subject to the 'specific authorities, responsibilities, and obligations under applicable international law'.[55] The ratification of Resolution 1483 highlighted how the US coalition could use its power in the UN Security Council to legitimise an occupation that followed an illegal invasion. This was possible because the rationality of international law has largely been excluded from policy debates about the US and the UK's use of force abroad.[56] Additionally, binding international norms of non-intervention, as specified in the UN Charter or UN Resolution 3314, are rarely enforced by the Security Council, which is dominated by the US and its NATO allies. Thus, the text of UN Resolution 3314 was not evoked or otherwise turned into practice in consideration of the US coalition occupation of Iraq. This was further encouraged by the agenda of international law enforcement bodies such as the International Criminal Court (ICC) as well as human rights organisations such as Amnesty International and Human Rights Watch, which have not factored the crime of aggression in their jurisdiction.[57] As a consequence, powerful states are able to act in defiance of and remain exempt from the law.

This enabled the US coalition to impose its preferred statebuilding design on Iraq. In the wake of Resolution 1483, the Coalition Provisional Authority (CPA), led by then-US civilian administrator L. Paul Bremer III, was established. The creation of the CPA was a crucial move by the US coalition: because UN Resolution 1483 formally introduced the US and the UK as occupying powers, the CPA concurrently obtained legal authority as the agency designated to oversee the political process.[58] As Ali A. Allawi highlights, the formation of the CPA had two further implications: firstly, the US could mitigate criticism of and lawsuits against its policies with reference to the CPA and its status under international law. At the same time, the US maintained direct control over the political developments in Iraq as it levered the CPA's executive structures.[59] In practice, the CPA was part of US federal government while Bremer reported to the US Department of Defence.[60] Secondly, the establishment of the CPA effectively prevented the building of a provisional Iraqi government as demanded by Iraqi civil society.[61] Thus, the CPA took away Iraqi agency and allowed the US coalition to set the course for the statebuilding process in accord with its members' interests.

Although the CPA hardly represented the Iraqi people, it would enact and implement legal decisions locking Iraqi society in a devastating trajectory. Most significantly, Bremer's *Order Number 39*, from September 2003, determined to replace 'all existing foreign investment law' to privatise Iraq's largely state-owned economy.[62] The US provided BearingPoint, Inc., a Virginia-based corporation, with a $250 million contract to facilitate the transition. The contract demanded to 'establish the basic legal framework for a functioning market economy' and envisioned the restructuring 'in the areas of fiscal reform, financial sector reform, trade, legal and regulatory and privatisation.'[63]

On paper, the statebuilding initiated by the CPA was reminiscent of liberal-democratic 'market reforms' that are regarded as benevolent tenets of liberal peacebuilding.[64] In effect, the policies constituted a neo-colonial state intervention geared towards securing lucrative investor rights and market access for transnational corporations. Accordingly, at a congressional hearing, on 4 November 2003, M. Peter McPherson, economic advisor of the CPA, described the outcome of the legislation as follows: 'A new law allows for foreign investment up to 100 per cent of foreign ownership, full repatriation of investment and profits, national treatment and no screening committee.'[65] It is well documented by Naomi Klein and Jonathan Steele how this legislation configured the Iraqi economy as a corporate haven: corporate tax was reduced from 45 per cent to 15 per cent. Foreign businesses were allowed to own 100 per cent of any Iraqi firm. Investors received grants to export all profits without reinvestment or taxation requirements. One order lifted all import tariffs, thus undoing potential economic advantages of local Iraqi over foreign producers. Contracts could be codified with duration of forty years so that future governments had to accept the conditions established by the CPA. Only the oil sector was not supposed to be immediately privatised because the US coalition expected strong resistance to such a policy.[66]

Iraq's state economy was consequently opened up for foreign investment. During this course, major parts of Iraq's economy collapsed, forcing the country into a downturn spiral of unemployment and economic depression leading to the decline of the small-business sector (local enterprises and farms). At the same time, Bremer's so-called de-Ba'athification programme, which heralded the dismantlement of the Iraqi state apparatus and the dissolution of the Iraqi armed forces, decreased the purchase power of a large segment of the population.[67] Additionally, the US-instituted reconstruction programmes, which received a $73 billion stimulus, were not able to provide appropriate levels of restoration. The fund was used by the US and subsidised foreign companies such as Halliburton and Bechtel to 'invest' in the new Iraqi economy while Iraqi companies did not receive any pay-outs.[68] The radical shift to private enterprise also inhibited the reconstruction and maintenance of the already weakened public institutions like electrical, hospital, water and sewage facilities.[69] Allawi described the economic developments as follows:

> The CPA rushed into passing a mass of worthy investor-friendly laws, but none had the desired effect of stimulating investment or encouraging the inflow of foreign capital. Foreign investors were hesitant about visiting the country, let alone investing in it. [. . .] Iraq became a magnet for foreign charlatans and adventurers who came into the country on the back of the CPA, and were given unrestricted access to Iraqi ministries and institutions. Some surfaced as instigators and beneficiaries of major scams financed by the uncontrolled flood of cash that moved around the economy in the early days of occupation.[70]

In terms of the rationality of the law, Bremer's *Order Number 39* justified the transformation of the Iraqi economy and state with reference to the 'laws and usages of war' as well as 'relevant UN Security Council Resolutions including Resolution 1483 (2003)'.[71] It could thus be argued that the policies outlined above had obtained legitimacy on legal grounds. There are two reasons why such an argument does not hold ground: firstly, Resolution 1483 emphasised Iraqi ownership of the reconstruction process stressing 'the right of the Iraqi people freely to determine their own political future and control their own natural resources'.[72] Furthermore, UN member states were merely encouraged to 'assist' the Iraqi people 'in their efforts to reform their institutions and rebuild their country'.[73] It is thus questionable as to whether the CPA was mandated to engage in the comprehensive remodelling of the Iraqi economy without democratic oversight. Secondly, Resolution 1483 as well as *Order Number 39* clearly recognized the US coalition and CPA's obligations under international law as well as the laws of war. Under such legislation, Iraq's economic reconfiguration was disputable. Accordingly, Article 43 of the fourth section of the Hague Convention concerning the Laws and Customs of War on Land demands that if 'the authority of the legitimate power having in fact passed into the hands of the occupant, the latter shall' respect 'unless absolutely prevented, the laws in force in the country'.[74] Dave Whyte further comments on the CPA's statebuilding and the legal implications:

> A key effect of neo-liberal hegemony building is the subjugation of the norms of international law to the norms and values of the 'free' market. The economic transformation of Iraq was made possible only because the Anglo–American occupation was prepared to ignore international law (specifically the *jus cogens* sovereign right of a people to determine their own social, economic and cultural future) in the rush to establish a WTO-compatible economy. The neo-liberal regime imposed upon the Iraqi people by the CPA facilitated the transferral of Iraqi oil revenue into the hands of Western corporations with no mandate from the Iraqi people. The economic occupation is therefore clearly definable as a war crime under the terms of The Hague and Geneva treaties [emphasis in the original].[75]

As outlined in this section, the leaders of the US coalition did not adhere to major tenets of international law. The US coalition occupation and statebuilding project did thus not obtain legitimacy on grounds embedded in the rationality of law.

Having discussed the legal dimensions of legitimacy with regard to the long-term *occupation* and associated statebuilding project, I will now address how the US coalition governed local municipalities in Iraq. This will shed further light on how the occupation related to local Iraqi structures of legitimate governances that interacted with the wider statebuilding project.

Section 4: Local Resistance in Fallujah: Undermining Structures of 'Traditional Authority'

This section further interrogates the legitimacy of US coalition actions in Iraq focusing on the Sunni stronghold in Fallujah. The following case study demonstrates how the US coalition undermined legitimate authority based on traditional grounds.[76]

The US coalition envisioned Iraqi acceptance of the newly engineered society and state. When such approval did not materialise, the occupation regime resorted to force. This would start a cycle of violence in the Sunni dominated al-Anbar governorate which largely harboured the state facilities and government employees most heavily affected by the economic downturn instigated during the statebuilding process. It was also in these cities where the earliest demonstrations against the US coalition occupation recognisably took place.[77]

On 23 April 2003, two weeks after the regime of then-President Saddam Hussein had been toppled, US coalition forces established a basis in Fallujah. A battalion of the US Army's 82nd Airborne Division established a command post at Fallujah's Ba'ath party headquarters and about 150 soldiers occupied the al-Qa'id primary school nearby.[78] The soldiers were tasked to provide security for the city. Yet, the people of Fallujah had already established independent structures of local governance. An investigation by Human Rights Watch found that,

> by the time US forces arrived, tribal and religious leaders in al-Falluja had already selected a Civil Management Council, including a city manager and mayor. The quickly-formed local government was having success in minimising the looting and other crimes rampant in other parts of Iraq. Different tribes took responsibility for the city's assets, such as banks and government offices. In one noted case, the tribe responsible for al-Falluja's hospital quickly organized a gang of armed men to protect the grounds from an imminent attack. Local imams urged the public to respect law and order. The strategy worked, in part due to cohesive family ties among the population. Al-Falluja showed no signs of the looting and destruction visible, for example, in Baghdad.[79]

In the context of Weber's framework, local governing authority in Fallujah derived its legitimacy on traditional grounds rooted in long-lasting conventions and personal relationships. Located in the Sunni dominated al-Anbar governorate, Fallujah was considered to be a strong base of former Iraqi president Saddam Hussein and his Ba'athist party. Many residents from Fallujah had worked for the former Iraqi government's military and security services.[80] But the situation was more complex. The main beneficiaries of Saddam Hussein's regime were the residents of his hometown, Tikrit – particularly his ancestral village, Al Awja.[81] The 350,000 people of Fallujah were, on the other hand, embedded in tribal, religious and political clan structures that primarily cemented their traditional allegiance to the al-Dulaim tribe that dominated the region.[82] Hence, the investigation by Human Rights Watch found that Fallujah used to be a strong and supportive base for the Sunni Ba'athist party and former Iraqi president Saddam Hussein. At the same time, Human Rights Watch did not identify overwhelming support for Hussein. Many residents 'told Human Rights Watch that they considered themselves victims and opponents of his repressive rule'.[83] In fact, it is even assumed that some of the attempted coups against Hussein emanated from the city.[84] The people of Fallujah had also resisted against British occupation during the 1920s and World War II.[85] According to some commentators, Fallujah had a conservative nationalist outlook and 'a reputation as an independent city'.[86]

But independence was not accepted by the US coalition, which quickly claimed governing authority. Reflecting on the developments, investigative journalist Jonathan Steele cited a policeman in Fallujah:

> Fallujans don't like the Americans coming into the market area. They don't like the checkpoints they put up everywhere. The Americans said they would only stay for two or three days, but every day the number of soldiers is increasing. We can control Fallujah without the Americans. I want them to leave now.[87]

Thus, when US coalition forces remained in Fallujah, tensions rose between the soldiers and Fallujah's people. Residents took offense in what they regarded as aggressive street patrols and cultural insensitivities. Others objected to the occupation of the school, which should have reopened for classes on 29 April. The people also felt intimidated by the soldiers' use of binoculars and night-vision equipment. Some rumours spread that the Americans were watching Iraqi women.[88] The investigation by Human Rights Watch summarised the situation as follows: 'US soldiers may have believed that they were simply engaging in standard security and patrolling practices, but some in the local community resented their presence and actions.'[89]

As a consequence, a series of demonstrations where held against the occupation of the town.[90] On 28 April, a demonstration developed into a major incident, when US forces killed seventeen people. According to

Human Rights Watch, US soldiers said they came under 'effective fire [. . .] from gunmen in the crowd and on the roofs'.[91] The soldiers said they had only responded. In contrast, Iraqi demonstrators and eye-witnesses interviewed by Human Rights Watch said that they 'had been attacked without provocation' and that all the demonstrators had been unarmed, although some shootings had occurred in nearby neighbourhoods and on the main street.[92] A ballistic investigations by Human Rights Watch concluded that 'the physical evidence at the school does not support claims of an effective attack on the building' sheltering the soldiers.[93] Thousands of demonstrators joined together on 29 and 30 April to denounce the shootings and to 'demand the immediate withdrawal of American forces'.[94] Yet, another demonstration claimed the lives of three Iraqis who were shot by US fire. Further rebellious incidents continued on a regular basis during May and June 2003. Iraqi militancy significantly escalated when killings, house arrests and the detention of people from Fallujah into Abu Ghraib prison increased.[95] According to the scholar Allawi, in late summer of 2003, 'the people of Fallujah were openly boasting that they were in outright rebellion against the occupation'.[96] In the following month, a consolidated resistance with strong ties to the population waged many attacks on US coalition troops.[97] Graham argued that US coalition policies had fuelled the resistance because,

> all the civilian deaths would have caused a population anywhere to react: on Bloody Sunday in 1972, for example, only thirteen Irish Catholics were killed by British troops, but the incident set off decades of fighting. In the Sunni Triangle, an honour-based tribal society where revenge killings are integral to the culture, the cycle, once started, was almost impossible to stop. And it was only when the occupation was presented as a binary choice – you are either with us or against us – that the Sunni circled the wagons.[98]

One of the main causes of the uprising in Fallujah was the US coalition's forceful negligence of local structures of traditional authority. Furthermore, cultural insensitivities and a quick resort to military force further encouraged Iraqi resistance. Thus, on 29 June 2003, Bremer explained to the BBC's Peter Sissons how the US coalition would handle the growing militancy of the Iraqis: '[. . .] we are going to fight them and impose our will on them and we will capture or, if necessary, kill them until we have imposed law and order on this country [. . .]'.[99]

These developments took place at about the same time when the CPA instigated the radical transformation of Iraqi society and thus further contributed to the crisis in Iraq. Moreover, Iraqis were well aware about the underlying goals of the US coalition statebuilding project. Already shortly after US troops had entered Baghdad in late March 2003, opinion polls indicated that nearly 50 per cent of Iraqis believed the US coalition interest in Iraq was 'to get oil'.[100] Consequently, the US coalition attempted to further legitimise the occupation through 'Iraqisation'. On 28 June 2004, the Iraqi Interim Government (IIG) and its head, Prime Minister Ayad Allawi, were instituted as an Iraqi transitional government. The IIG formally inherited the government powers from the CPA, and was tasked with the mandate to pave the way for nationwide elections scheduled for January 2005.[101] Iraq's new status was established by UN Resolution 1546, codified on 8 June 2004. The resolution recognised the sovereignty of Iraq. Furthermore, its annex included letters by Ayad Allawi and United States Secretary of State, Colin L. Powell. In the writing of the letters, Allawi requested and Powell approved the maintenance of Multi National Forces (MNF) in Iraq.[102]

The transfer of sovereignty was an attempt by the US coalition to legitimise occupation on the ground of Iraqi approval. This policy related to the issue of traditional authority in the sense that the US coalition attempted to formally account for Iraqi agency and self-determination. Thus, David Brooks highlighted in the *New York Times* that 'the US had to transfer sovereignty precisely so it could stay. This was the only way to get enough legitimacy to fight the insurgents'.[103]

Evidence suggests, however, that the IIG was not an independent entity. As scholar Allawi writes, Iraq remained *de facto* under foreign occupation because the most important administrative powers were not relegated to the IIG, but to the US Embassy headed by Ambassador John Negroponte.[104] Moreover, the IIG had no democratic mandate: its members were largely selected by US coalition authorities without consent from the Iraqi population or the United Nations.[105] Hence, Andrea Carcano further remarked how 'it is difficult to consider the Interim Government as sovereign, at least under traditional international law, because it is lacking both independence/internal legitimacy and effective control'.[106] This lack of legitimacy directly linked to Iraqi perceptions about the occupation project. In October 2003, a National Intelligence Estimate (NIE), an assessment of the various US intelligence agencies, concluded that Iraqi resistance 'was fueled [sic] by local conditions – not foreign terrorists – and drew strength from deep grievances, including the presence of US troops'.[107]

But the US coalition had addressed these local conditions only by means of establishing a façade.[108] Thus, shortly before US coalition forces launched a devastating attack against Fallujah that would claim thousands of Iraqi civilian lives, Bush said the US coalition would act on behalf of Iraq: 'It's their government; it's their country. We're there at their invitation.'[109]

Conclusion

This study has demonstrated that the US coalition invasion and subsequent occupation project in Iraq were illegitimate if we consider the rationality of the law as well as tradition as grounds for legitimacy. Furthermore, in accord with the refined framework for legitimate authority derived from Weber, it could be demonstrated that the reason why many Iraqis regarded the US coalition statebuilding project as such was that it served US coalition rather than Iraqi needs and interests. Richmond and Mac Ginty have highlighted this problem:

> Positive peace in an emancipatory form cannot be achieved without a recognition of, and support for, subjects' rights, representation and material situation. The exclusion of the local scale means the liberal peace is an unequal peace benefiting the West/North, being little more than pacification in other contexts. Prejudging the norms, laws, institutions and architecture of peace, as well as the nature of the state and its position in global markets indicates that the theory and policy of peacebuilding is driven by realist and strategic rationalities.[110]

As demonstrated in this chapter, the main policy drift has led the US coalition on a path that undermined its legitimacy. Additionally, there have been limited ambitions to restore legitimacy retrospectively. This is obvious up to this date where possible policy options such as reparations or other forms of compensation for Iraq are rarely being discussed.[111] So far, there have been few substantive initiatives about opening up criminal proceedings let alone establishing an international criminal tribunal for Iraq or a referral to the ICC to prosecute any persons responsible for grave violations of the law in the context of Iraq post 2003.[112]

Finally, as this chapter suggests, United Nations led statebuilding efforts could have obtained higher degrees of legitimacy vis-à-vis the Iraqi population and international community, if Western actors had implemented policies in accord with the rationality of the law. In turn, this would have allowed for Iraqi agency because legal clauses enabling Iraqi ownership of and democratic participation during the statebuilding are clearly inscribed in the relevant UN Resolutions as well as Geneva and Hague Conventions. In conclusion, the best outcome for the Iraqi people would have been if the US coalition had adhered to international law and not executed the invasion–occupation in the first place.

Notes

1. CNN.com, 'Bush makes historic speech aboard warship', 2 May 2003. Available at <http://edition.cnn.com/2003/US/05/01/bush.transcript/> (last accessed 24 March 2017).
2. Ibid.
3. See Barnett, Michael, 'Building a republican peace: stabilizing states after war', *International Security*, 2006, 30: 4, p. 88.
4. See Richmond, Oliver P. *The Transformation of Peace* (Basingstoke: Palgrave Macmillan, 2005).
5. See Dodge, Toby, 'Intervention and dreams of exogenous statebuilding: the application of liberal peacebuilding in Afghanistan and Iraq', *Review of International Studies*, 2013, 39: 5, pp. 1189–1212.
6. For agency see Kappler, Stefanie, *Local Agency and Peacebuilding: EU and International Engagement in Bosnia-Herzegovina, Cyprus and South Africa* (Basingstoke: Palgrave Macmillan, 2014).
7. See Schwartz, Michael, *War Without End: the Iraq War in Context* (Chicago: Haymarket Books, 2008).
8. These questions were derived from Richmond, Oliver P. and Roger Mac Ginty, 'Introduction: legitimacy and peace in the age of intervention', in Oliver P. Richmond and Roger MacGinty (eds), *Local Legitimacy and International Peace Intervention* (Edinburgh: Edinburgh University Press, 2020), pp. 1–18.
9. See Matheson, Craig, 'Weber and the classification of forms of legitimacy', *The British Journal of Sociology*, 1987, 38: 2, p. 200.
10. Ibid.
11. Ibid.
12. Ibid.
13. Ibid. This is not to say that that coercive and rewards based claims to authority are irrelevant today.
14. See Weber, Max, *The Theory of Social and Economic Organization* (Glencoe, IL: The Free Press, [1947] 2012), p. 328. See also Whimster, Sam (ed.), *The Essential Weber: A Reader* (London: Routledge, 2004), p. 133.
15. Weber, *The Theory of Social and Economic Organization*, p. 328.
16. This section draws from Whimster, *The Essential Weber: A Reader*, pp. 133–5.
17. Matheson, 'Weber and the classification of forms of legitimacy', pp. 211, 213.
18. See Clark, Ian, *Legitimacy in International Society* (Oxford: Oxford University Press, 2005), p. 30.
19. Weber, *The Theory of Social and Economic Organization*, p. 328.
20. Ibid.
21. Whimster, *The Essential Weber: A Reader*, p. 135.
22. Matheson, 'Weber and the classification of frms of legitimacy', pp. 207, 213.
23. Weber, *The Theory of Social and Economic Organization*, p. 328.
24. Ibid.
25. Whimster, *The Essential Weber: A Reader*, pp. 138–9.
26. Ibid. p. 139.

27. Matheson, 'Weber and the classification of forms of legitimacy', p. 209, 213.

28. See Zollmann, Florian, 'Iraq and Dahr Jamail: war reporting from a peace perspective', in Richard Lance Keeble, John Tulloch and Florian Zollmann (eds), *Peace Journalism, War and Conflict Resolution* (New York: Peter Lang, 2010), pp. 139–56. Also Herring, Eric and Piers Robinson, 'Report X marks the spot: the British government's deceptive dossier on Iraq and WMD', *Political Science Quarterly*, 2014–2015, 129: 4, pp. 551–83.

29. For a critical discussion of this argument and its proponents in relation to Kosovo in 1999, see Falk, Richard, 'Legality and legitimacy: the quest for principled flexibility and restraint', in David Armstrong, Theo Farrell and Bice Maiguashca (eds), *Force and Legitimacy in World Politics* (Cambridge: Cambridge University Press, 2005), p. 37.

30. See Ibid. pp. 37–9, 41–2.

31. For some of these arguments that emphasised liberation of the Iraqi people, democracy promotion and similar ideological discourses see Chomsky, Noam, *Failed States: The Abuse of Power and the Assault on Democracy* (New York: Metropolitan Books, 2007), pp. 28, 130–2.

32. Cited in Zollmann, 'Iraq and Dahr Jamail: war reporting from a peace perspective', p. 141.

33. See Mandel, Michael, *Pax Pentagon: Wie die USA der Welt den Krieg als Frieden Verkauft* (Frankfurt am Main: Zweitausendeins, 2005), p.33 and the extensive references to legal opinions on Iraq in footnote 31. Also, Norton-Taylor, Richard, 'Law Unto Themselves', *The Guardian*, 14 March 2003. Available at <https://www.theguardian.com/world/2003/mar/14/iraq.richardnortontaylor> (last accessed on 22 May 2017).

34. See United Nations General Assembly, *A/RES/3314 (XXIX). Definition of Aggression, 1974*, p. 143. Available at <https://documents-dds-ny.un.org/doc/RESOLUTION/GEN/NR0/739/16/IMG/NR073916.pdf?OpenElement> (last accessed 4 June 2017).

35. Ibid. pp. 142–3.

36. Judgment, Trial of the Major War Criminals Before the International Military Tribunal, Nurnberg [sic], Germany, 1947 (Official Text), cited in Eugene C. Gerhart, *World Reference Guide to More than 5,500 Memorable Quotations from Law and Literature* (New York: William S. Hein and Co., 1998), p. 1109.

37. See Mandel, *Pax Pentagon: Wie die USA der Welt den Krieg als Frieden Verkauft*.

38. United Nations General Assembly, *A/RES/60/1. 2005 World Summit Outcome*, 2005, p. 22. Available at <http://www.un.org/womenwatch/ods/A-RES-60-1-E.pdf> (last accessed 24 May 2017).

39. Roberts, Les, 'Iraq's Death Toll Is Far Worse than Our Leaders Admit', *The Independent*, 14 February 2007, p. 32.

40. See also Slaughter, Anne-Marie, 'The use of force in Iraq: illegal and illegitimate', in Richard Falk, Irene Gendzier and Robert Jay Lifton (eds), *Crimes of War Iraq* (New York: Nation Books, 2006), pp. 111–2.

41. See Zollmann, 'Iraq and Dahr Jamail: war reporting from a peace perspective'. Also Herring and Robinson, 'Report X marks the spot: the British government's deceptive dossier on Iraq and WMD'.

42. For a discussion of the evidence provided by the UN weapons inspectors from UNSCOM, see Edwards, David and David Cromwell, *Guardians of Power: The Myth of the Liberal Media* (London: Pluto Press, 2006), pp.33–7.

43. See Herring and Robinson, *'Report X marks the spot: the British government's deceptive dossier on Iraq and WMD'*, p. 551.

44. See examples provided by Chomsky, *Failed States: The Abuse of Power and the Assault on Democracy*, p. 18.

45. See Chomsky, Noam and Gilbert Achcar, *Perilous Power: The Middle East and US Foreign Policy* (Boulder, CO: Paradigm Publishers, 2007), pp. 120–3.

46. According to the Center for Economic and Social Rights: 'Over 90% of the population had access to primary health care, including laboratory diagnosis and immunizations for childhood diseases such as polio and diphtheria. During the 1970s and 80s, British and Japanese companies built scores of large, modern hospitals throughout Iraq, with advanced technologies for diagnosis, operations and treatment. Secondary and tertiary services, including surgical care and laboratory investigative support, were available to most of the Iraqi population at nominal charges. Iraqi medical and nursing schools emphasized education for women and attracted students from throughout the Middle East. A majority of Iraqi physicians were trained in Europe or the United States, and one-quarter were board-certified specialists'. See Center for Economic and Social Rights, *Unsanctioned Suffering: A Human Rights Assessment of United Nations Sanction on Iraq*, May 1996, p. 8, Available at <http://www.cesr.org/sites/default/files/ Unsanctioned%20Suffering%201996.pdf> (last accessed 24 May 2017). See also the studies cited in Edwards, David and David Cromwell, *Guardians of Power: The Myth of the Liberal Media*, p. 21. For further evidence, see Normand, Roger, 'Sanctions against Iraq: new weapons of mass destruction', *CovertAction Quarterly*, Spring 1998, 64: pp. 4–10.

47. See Gordon, Joy, *Invisible War: The United States and the Iraq Sanctions* (Cambridge, MA: Harvard University Press, 2010), p. 3. For further evidence on the well-documented record of the sanctions and their effects see also Alnasrawi, Abbas, 'Iraq: economic sanctions and consequences, 1990–2000', *Third World Quarterly*, 2001, 22: 2, pp. 205–18; Anthony Arnove (ed.), *Iraq Under Siege: The Deadly Impact of Sanctions and War* (London: Pluto Press, 2000); Center for Economic and Social Rights, *Unsanctioned Suffering: A Human Rights Assessment of United Nations Sanction on Iraq*; Edwards and Cromwell, *Guardians of Power: The Myth of the Liberal Media*, and Normand, 'Sanctions against Iraq: new weapons of mass destruction'.

48. Gordon, *Invisible War: The United States and the Iraq Sanctions*, p. 87.

49. Ibid. p. 3. Halliday's statement was cited in Cromwell, David, 'Letter – BBC's Bias in Favour of War', *The Independent*, 11 January 2004, p. 26. Estimates of the amount of people who died as a result of the sanctions range up to 1.5

million, see Alnasrawi, 'Iraq: economic sanctions and consequences, 1990–2000', p. 214.

50. SUBCOM, *Humanitarian Situation of the Iraqi Population*, 18 August 2000. Available at <http://ap.ohchr.org/documents/alldocs.aspx?doc_id=7861> (last accessed 24 May 2017). In fact, several reports have emphasised that the sanctions violated basic tenets of human rights and international law. See studies in Gordon, *Invisible War: The United States and the Iraq Sanctions*, p. 2; also Center for Economic and Social Rights, *Unsanctioned Suffering: A Human Rights Assessment of United Nations Sanction on Iraq*, and Normand, 'Sanctions against Iraq: new weapons of mass destruction'.

51. Gordon, *Invisible War: The United States and the Iraq Sanctions*, p. 4.

52. Slaughter, 'The use of force in Iraq: illegal and illegitimate', p. 112.

53. See Falk, 'Legality and legitimacy: the quest for principled flexibility and restraint', p. 47. It should be further noted that recent so-called 'humanitarian interventions' were either conducted in violation of the UN Charter as in Kosovo (1999) or went beyond their legal mandate as in Libya (2011). Moreover, both interventions turned out to be far more deadly than the violence that had preceded them and which had initially served as a justification for intervention. See Zollmann, Florian, *Media, Propaganda and the Politics of Intervention* (New York: Peter Lang, 2017). For Kosovo, see Chomsky, Noam, *A New Generation Draws the Line: Humanitarian Intervention and the 'Responsibility to Protect' Today* (Boulder, CO: Paradigm Publishers, 2012) and Mandel, *Pax Pentagon: Wie die USA der Welt den Krieg als Frieden Verkauft*. For Libya, see Kuperman, Alan J., 'A Model Humanitarian Intervention? Reassessing NATO's Libya Campaign', *International Security*, 2013, 38: 1, pp. 105–36.

54. United Nations General Assembly, *A/RES/3314 (XXIX). Definition of Aggression, 1974*, p. 143.

55. See United Nations Security Council, *S/RES/1483*, 2003, p. 2. Available at <https://documents-dds-ny.un.org/doc/UNDOC/GEN/N03/368/53/PDF/N0336853.pdf?OpenElement> (last accessed 31 May 2017).

56. See Friel, Howard and Richard Falk, *The Record of the Paper: How the New York Times Misreports US Foreign Policy* (London: Verso, 2007), pp. 6–7.

57. See Herman, Edward S. and David Peterson, *The Politics of Genocide* (New York: Monthly Review Press, 2010), pp. 17–27.

58. See Allawi, Ali A., *The Occupation of Iraq: Winning the War, Losing the Peace* (New Haven and London: Yale University Press, 2007), pp. 105–7.

59. See Ibid. pp. 105–6.

60. Ibid, p. 106.

61. See Ibid. p. 105.

62. Coalition Provisional Authority, *Order Number 39*, 19 September 2003, p. 2. Available at <http://govinfo.library.unt.edu/cpa-iraq/regulations/20031220_CPAORD_39_Foreign_Investment_.pdf> (last accessed 31 May 2017)

63. Juhasz, Antonia, 'The economic colonization of iraq: illegal and immoral', *International Forum on Globalization*, New York, 8 May 2004. Available at <http://

www.ifg.org/analysis/globalization/IraqTestimony.html> (last accessed 1 May 2011).

64. See Barnett, 'Building a republican peace: stabilizing states after war', p. 88.

65. US Senate Committee on Banking, Housing, and Urban Affairs, 'Testimony of Mr. M. Peter McPherson', 2003. Available at <http://banking.senate.gov/ public/index.cfm?FuseAction=Hearings.Testimony&Hearing_ID=aef48487-6338-4352-9624-c1b1403bc2ed&Witness_ID=6b20012d-392e-413a-808e-e9c2ff1c05cd> (last accessed 10 June 2011). For a shortened version of this quote, see also Zollmann, Florian, 'Managing the elite consensus: a critical analysis of press discourses over warfare in Iraq', *Global Media and Communication*, 2011, 7: 3, pp. 265–6.

66. Klein, Naomi, *Die Schock Strategie: der Aufstieg des Katastrophen-Kapitalismus* (Frankfurt am Main: S. Fischer Verlag, 2007), pp. 480–1. See also Steele, Jonathan, *Defeat: Why They Lost Iraq* (London: I. B. Taurus, 2008), p. 236.

67. See Allawi, *The Occupation of Iraq: Winning the War, Losing the Peace*, p. 177 and Chapter 6. See also Schwartz, *War Without End: the Iraq War in Context*, pp. 42–9.

68. See Klein, *Die Schock Strategie: der Aufstieg des Katastrophen-Kapitalismus*, pp. 482–6.

69. See Allawi, *The Occupation of Iraq: Winning the War, Losing the Peace*, pp. 125; Klein, *Die Schock Strategie: der Aufstieg des Katastrophen-Kapitalismus*, Chapter 17, and Schwartz, *War Without End: the Iraq War in Context*, pp. 44, 71. See also Chatterjee, Pratap, *Iraq, Inc.: A Profitable Occupation* (New York: Seven Stories Press, 2004).

70. Allawi, *The Occupation of Iraq: Winning the War, Losing the Peace*, pp. 125–6. Generally, the monetary policies applied in Iraq ran counter the Marshall Plan instituted after World War II. The latter was based on strengthening the German and Japanese economies and had not allowed for foreign investment in these countries. See Klein, *Die Schock Strategie: der Aufstieg des Katastrophen-Kapitalismus*, pp. 482–6.

71. Coalition Provisional Authority, *Order Number 39*, p. 1.

72. United Nations Security Council, *S/RES/1483*, p. 1.

73. Ibid. p. 2.

74. International Conferences, *Hague Convention (IV) Respecting the Laws and Customs of War on Land and Its Annex: Regulations Concerning the Laws and Customs of War on Land*, 18 October 1907. Available at <http://www.refworld.org/ docid/4374cae64.html> (last accessed 6 June 2017).

75. Whyte, Dave, 'The crimes of neo-liberal rule in occupied Iraq', *British Journal of Criminology*, 2006, 47: 2, p. 191.

76. Some of the material used in this section draws from Zollmann, Florian, 'Warfare as remedy: how the independent framed the first US assault on Fallujah', *Occasional Working Paper Series*, 2008, 1: 1. Available at <http://eprints.lincoln.ac.uk/16189/> (last accessed 4 June 2017).

77. See Schwartz, *War Without End: the Iraq War in Context*, pp. 45–6.

78. For this context, see Human Rights Watch, *Violent Response: The US Army in al-Falluja*, 16 June 2003. Available at <https://www.hrw.org/report/2003/06/16/violent-response/us-army-al-falluja> (accessed 23 March 2017).

79. Ibid.

80. See Ibid.

81. See Graham, Patrick, 'Beyond Fallujah: a year with the Iraqi resistance', *Harper's Magazine*, June 2004. Available at <http://www.harpers.org/archive/2004/06/0080071> (last accessed 8 October 2007).

82. These issues are discussed in Steele, *Defeat: Why They Lost Iraq*, p. 56. See also Allawi, *The Occupation of Iraq: Winning the War, Losing the Peace*, pp. 169–78 and Schwartz, *War Without End: the Iraq War in Context*, pp. 88–91.

83. Human Rights Watch, *Violent Response: The US Army in al-Falluja*.

84. See Graham, 'Beyond Fallujah: a year with the Iraqi resistance'.

85. Steele, *Defeat: Why They Lost Iraq*, p. 56.

86. Ibid.

87. Cited in Ibid, p. 55.

88. See Human Rights Watch, *Violent Response: The US Army in al-Falluja*.

89. Ibid.

90. See Allawi, *The Occupation of Iraq: Winning the War, Losing the Peace*, p. 169.

91. Human Rights Watch, *Violent Response: The US Army in al-Falluja*.

92. Ibid.

93. Ibid.

94. Holmes, Jonathan, *Fallujah: Eyewitness Testimony from Iraq's Besieged City* (London: Constable, 2007), p. 5.

95. See Holmes, *Fallujah: Eyewitness Testimony from Iraq's Besieged City*, pp. 6–7. See also Allawi *The Occupation of Iraq: Winning the War, Losing the Peace*, and Graham, 'Beyond Fallujah: a year with the Iraqi resistance'.

96. Allawi, *The Occupation of Iraq: Winning the War, Losing the Peace*, p. 169.

97. See Allawi, *The Occupation of Iraq: Winning the War, Losing the Peace*; Holmes, *Fallujah: Eyewitness Testimony from Iraq's Besieged City*.

98. Graham, 'Beyond Fallujah: a year with the Iraqi resistance'.

99. BBC News 'Breakfast with Frost', *BBC News*, 29 June 2003. Available at <http://news.bbc.co.uk/1/hi/programmes/breakfast_with_frost/3029904.stm> (last accessed 7 June 2017).

100. Cited in Schwartz, *War Without End: the Iraq War in Context*, p. 52.

101. See Filkins, Dexter, 'US Transfers Power to Iraq 2 Days Early', *New York Times*, 29 June 2004, p. 1.

102. United Nations Security Council (2004) *S/RES/1546. Resolution 1546*. Available at <https://documents-dds-ny.un.org/doc/UNDOC/GEN/N04/381/16/PDF/N0438116.pdf?OpenElement> (last accessed 4 June 2017).

103. Brooks, David, Bush's Winning Strategy, *The New York Times*, 3 July 2004, p. 15.

104. Allawi, *The Occupation of Iraq: Winning the War, Losing the Peace*, p. 287.

105. Carcano, Andrea, 'End of the occupation in 2004? The status of the multinational force in Iraq after the transfer of sovereignty to the interim Iraqi government', *Journal of Conflict & Security Law*, 2006, 11: 1, p. 5.
106. Ibid. p. 6.
107. Strobel, Warren P. and Jonathan S. Lanay, 'Intelligence agencies warned about growing local insurgency in late 2003', *Knight Ridder Newspapers*, 28 February 2006. Available at <http://www.mcclatchydc.com/news/special-reports/iraq-intelligence/article24463582.html> (last accessed 4 June 2017).
108. Cf. Berit Bliesemann de Guevara and Florian P. Kühn, *Illusion Statebuilding: Warum Sich der Westliche Staat So Schwer Exportieren Lässt*, Hamburg: Körber Stiftung, 2010.
109. The New York Times, '"I'm ready for the job", Bush says in news conference after election', *New York Times*, 5 November 2004, p. 20.
110. Richmond, Oliver P. and Roger Mac Ginty, 'Where now for the critique of the liberal peace?' *Cooperation and Conflict*, 2015, 50: 2, p. 178.
111. Grounds for reparations and compensation have been documented. See, for example, Whyte, 'The crimes of neo-liberal rule in occupied Iraq', p. 191. See particularly the 'Declaration of the jury of conscience at the world tribunal on Iraq', 27 June 2005, in Richard Falk, Irene Gendzier and Robert Jay Lifton (eds), *Crimes of War Iraq* (New York: Nation Books, 2006), pp. 168–79.
112. For such an example, see 'Declaration of the jury of conscience at the world tribunal on Iraq', in Falk et al. (eds).

SEVEN

Inclusion and Performance as Sources of Legitimacy – the UN Mediation on Syria

Sara Hellmüller

Introduction

In his press briefing following discussions on Syria in April 2018, the president of the United Nations (UN) Security Council said that 'only the UN has the legitimacy and credibility needed for a viable, enduring political solution'.[1] This statement indicates the importance attributed to legitimacy in UN mediation. As Arnault says, the legitimacy of a peace process is 'critical to public support, always threatened by the inevitable setbacks, delays and impasses that are common in any civil war settlement'.[2]

The judicial legitimacy of the UN to mediate is enshrined in its Charter.[3] Articles 2 (§3) and 33 urge member states to settle disputes by peaceful means and article 99 confers to the UN Secretary-General good offices responsibilities. The Secretary-General usually appoints mediators as his Special Representatives or Special Envoys and drafts their terms of references. The UN Security Council further specifies their political mandate in resolutions related to the conflict they mediate.[4] Whereas the attention of international actors has for a long time almost exclusively remained on this judicial legitimacy focusing on the legal-rational dimensions of the term (see introduction to this book), since the so-called 'local turn' in peacebuilding,[5] inquiries into local legitimacy have increased.

One of the most prominently mentioned sources of such local legitimacy of peace processes is the participation of civil society. Pouligny defines civil society as 'the arena of voluntary – uncoerced – collective action around shared interests, purposes and values'.[6] This broad definition can include a wide range of actors collectively engaging around shared values, such as women's group, business actors, elders, local leaders and youth.[7] Participation of these actors is considered to increase the legitimacy of a peace process provided that they can relevantly influence it.[8] This is based on the argument that for a peace agreement to be sustainable, not only the actors who are able to stop the fighting should be included, but also those needed to build peace in the long term.[9]

While civil society participation has become considered as an important source of local legitimacy, it is only one part of the story. This is because whether the broader population in a given context considers a peace process as legitimate does not only depend on whether civil society actors participate or people feel represented through them, but also what results it produces. This type of legitimacy, defined as the performance of a peace process to produce tangible results for the population, has been neglected in the scholarly literature.[10] Drawing on the literature on statehood, 'performance legitimacy' refers to a state achieving its legitimacy through 'institutionalised procedures to produce benevolent results through its performance'.[11] In that sense, inasmuch as the state pursues and achieves goals that coincide with those of the broader society, its rule can be justified.[12] Applied to mediation, the UN's legitimacy is thus contingent on producing outcomes that are expected by the broader population. This does not only relate to the post-agreement phase, but also to the mediation process. As Arnault says, performance as source of legitimacy is indicated in the 'need for a protracted peace negotiation to perform in the public eye without waiting for the conclusion of the peace talks'.[13] When violence is still ongoing, the expectation is for the peace process to help reduce and eventually stop the fighting as this directly connects to the everyday lives of people living in the conflict context (see the conclusion of this book). Thus, even though a sustainable agreement goes beyond the mere ending of violence, the performance of an ongoing mediation process is often assessed in terms of its efficiency in reducing violence on the ground.

Thus, both inclusion and performance are sources of local legitimacy. Yet, authors often pit them against each other. They assert that civil society inclusion can reduce the efficiency of a mediation process because an increase in the number of actors in the process may delay the finding of an agreement.[14] Therefore, scholars point to a dilemma between ensuring the legitimacy of a process through civil society inclusion and its efficiency.[15] Consequently, they often interpret mediators' choices for an exclusive process as grounded in a concern for efficiency and a neglect of local legitimacy.

Based on the case study of the UN mediation in Syria from 2012 to 2018,[16] this chapter provides a different account of the interplay between inclusion, performance and legitimacy. It shows that pitting inclusion and

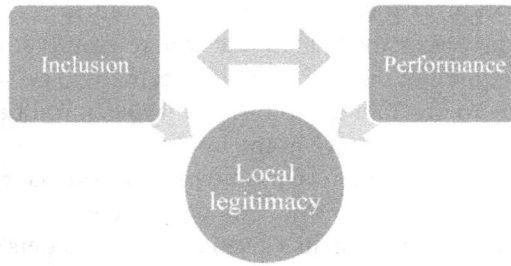

Figure 7.1 Illustration of relation between inclusion, performance and local legitimacy.

performance against each other overlooks two important points, illustrated in Figure 7.1. First, that both inclusion and performance are sources of local legitimacy and, second, that these two factors are not necessarily at odds with each other. Thereby, the chapter makes an important contribution to scholarly debates on mediation by untangling the complex relation between inclusion, performance and legitimacy.

In what follows, the chapter starts by assessing the approaches to local legitimacy of the first two UN mediators on Syria, Kofi Annan and Lakhdar Brahimi. Analysing their strategies shows that when mediators opt for exclusive processes, they do not necessarily decide *against* legitimacy. Rather, as this chapter demonstrates, depending on the context, mediators may prioritise performance over inclusion as source of legitimacy, therefore focusing on efficiency rather than inclusion. In its second part, the chapter analyses the strategy of the third UN mediator on Syria, Staffan de Mistura. It assesses his approach to pursue legitimacy through both inclusion and performance and thereby shows that inclusion does not automatically hamper performance, but can also potentially increase it. Inclusion and performance are thus not mutually exclusive, but a mediator's choice for inclusion may be taken based on an attempt to increase the performance of a process and thereby also its legitimacy. Lastly, the chapter examines the relation between inclusion, performance and legitimacy from the perspective of Syrian civil society. It demonstrates that although inclusion and performance are important sources of legitimacy, the link is not automatic but depends on how inclusion is managed.

Besides scholarly literature, the chapter is based on an analysis of mediators' briefings to the UN Security Council, transcripts of mediators' press conferences, policy papers and reports published by civil society organisations. It is also inspired by insights gained in the author's role as co-manager of a project implemented with the UN Office of the Special Envoy for

Syria (OSE) to facilitate civil society participation in the Intra-Syrian Talks during Staffan de Mistura's term.

From Kofi Annan to Lakhdar Brahimi: Performance as source of legitimacy

The Syrian armed conflict started with peaceful demonstrations for democratic reforms in the context of the Arab Spring in 2011. Upon violent suppression by government forces, the political opposition increasingly militarised and violence escalated into a full-blown civil war. Kofi Annan was the first mediator appointed as Joint Special Envoy for Syria by the League of Arab States (LAS) and the UN in February 2012. At the time, the international community was fundamentally divided over Syria. The LAS had adopted a Plan of Action that was openly in favour of government change and was calling for an end to violence, the release of detainees, and the start of a national dialogue.[17,18] Moreover, many Western countries and observers had indicated that they considered the Syrian president Bashar al-Assad as illegitimate, being convinced that his departure was imminent.[19] Russia, in contrast, was fundamentally opposed to any action that could lead to regime change as the Western-led intervention in Libya was still fresh on their memory.

To counter this polarised environment, Annan rejected the second action plan that the LAS proposed[20] and instead submitted a Six-Point Plan to the UN Security Council in March 2012. The plan called on the Syrian authorities to commit to work with the Special Envoy, cease fighting and provide urgent humanitarian assistance to the population.[21] Upon Assad's acceptance of the document,[22] a ceasefire was established and the UN deployed a Supervision Mission to Syria (UNSMIS).[23] Yet, the parties did not respect the ceasefire and Annan subsequently convened the Action Group for Syria consisting of external actors with stakes in the Syrian conflict[24] to discuss possible solutions to it. In a meeting later termed Geneva I, the Action Group developed the Geneva Communiqué on 30 June 2012. It stated that a 'new constitutional order' shall be set up through a 'transitional governing body' with 'full executive powers'.[25] However, Russia and China vetoed the first attempt to adopt the Geneva Communiqué in a UN Security Council chapter VII resolution.[26] At the same time, violence increased further and UNSMIS was withdrawn.[27] Given these gloomy perspectives, Annan resigned on 2 August 2012.

In terms of local legitimacy, Annan led a highly exclusive process prioritising performance over inclusion. The Geneva I meeting had no involvement of Syrian actors at all. This was despite the fact that Annan underlined the importance of civil society participation. Annan said, for instance, that 'the international community is determined to work with the Syrian people to support this process'.[28] He also indicated that he considered inclusion to be a key factor in any peace process, saying, 'I'm definitely opposed to mediation that brings the elite together, where you rearrange the chairs for the political elite and then you say you've solved it [. . .], never dealing with the problems of the people'.[29]

The reason why he did not include civil society is linked to his reading of the political situation. As documented by Hill, Annan saw the opposition movements as encompassing civil society.[30] His long-term strategy was to weaken the government through external pressure and to give the peaceful opposition time to organise to form a strong and unarmed counterweight to the government. In other words, as Hinnebusch and Zartman called it, 'inclusivity was part of his strategy of mobilising civil society to shift the power balance in favour of change'.[31] This was also visible in the Geneva Communiqué, which stated that 'all groups and segments of society in Syria must be enabled to participate in a National Dialogue process'.[32]

Therefore, Annan's choice to start with an exclusive process does not necessarily indicate indifference about local legitimacy. Rather, he wanted the process to perform as soon as possible in terms of stopping the violence, precisely because he wanted to allow for a legitimate process. Indeed, in all his official statements, he referred to the urgent need to stop the bloodshed. As he mentioned, for instance: 'I think the biggest priority, as I said, first of all we need to stop the killing. We need to stop the killing and we are pushing very hard for that, not only with the government and the parties on the other side, but also talking to governments with influence to support us in this process'.[33] He also specifically pointed out that his central concern had always been 'the welfare of the Syrian people'[34] and that the first thing to do was 'to do everything we can to stop the violence and the killing'.[35] He thus prioritised performance as the source of legitimacy over inclusion.

Lakhdar Brahimi succeeded Annan. The LAS and the UN appointed him as joint Special Representative in August 2012. He found a deeply entrenched conflict situation with a UN Security Council still deadlocked due to the division amongst its five permanent members (P5). During his time in office, the situation became increasingly grim on the ground. Even though a four-day ceasefire was negotiated on 24 October 2012 backed by a UN Security Council statement,[36] it soon collapsed.[37] Almost a year passed until the situation unblocked after the use of sarin gas in the Damascus suburb of Ghouta on 21 August 2013, which was an alarming illustration of how violent the conflict had become.[38] The UN Security Council passed

Resolution 2118 on 27 September 2013, in which it eventually endorsed the Geneva Communiqué and called for talks to discuss how to implement it. Brahimi invited the conflict parties to the Geneva II conference from 22 to 31 January and 10 to 15 February 2014. Yet, the talks collapsed. The parties were deeply mistrustful of each other as well as of the process. After the breakdown of the talks and acknowledging the impasse of the situation, Brahimi resigned on 13 May 2014.

Concerning local legitimacy, Brahimi – like Annan – led an exclusive process. He did not invite civil society actors to the Geneva II talks.[39] Yet, he underlined the importance of inclusive processes and indicated his opposition to elite-driven negotiations for instance when he mentioned that 'the future of Syria will be built by its people and none other'.[40] He also consulted civil society on the sidelines of the negotiations. Brahimi attended, for instance, a gathering of Syrian women convened by UN Women before the talks.[41] He mentioned that 'this meeting conveys to both parties that will sit together at the negotiating table the importance of listening to the voices of Syrian women and incorporating women as a key player in the efforts leading to a peaceful resolution of the Syrian crisis'.[42]

The reason behind this strategy was that he focused on getting the conflict parties to the table. He did not want to jeopardise this priority considering that the government and the opposition, as well as their external backers, were opposed to civil society participation in the Geneva II talks. As was stated, 'the regime did not want civil society to be there, the opposition did not want civil society to be there, and Americans and Russians did not want civil society to be there'.[43] Moreover, the fact that the conflict had started as a popular uprising made many observers define civil society as represented by an increasingly organised opposition, the Syrian National Council (SNC). As reported in Al-Monitor during the talks, 'Western powers are encouraging the SNC to reach out to Syrian civil-society groups'.[44] They hence saw the SNC as in charge of ensuring civil society participation and did not feel the need to invite additional civil society actors to the Geneva II negotiations.

The above shows that Brahimi's choice for an exclusive process does not indicate a neglect of legitimacy. Rather, he wanted to achieve local legitimacy through a performant process that stopped the violence as fast as possible. He made this clear in statements, for instance when he said that 'we all stressed the need for a speedy end to the bloodshed, to the destruction and all forms of violence in Syria'.[45] Moreover, when he ended the Geneva II conference, he apologised to the Syrian people for a lack of performance. He said, 'I am very, very sorry, and I apologise to the Syrian people [. . .], I apologise to them that on these two rounds we haven't helped them very much'.[46]

In conclusion, both Annan and Brahimi prioritised performance, rather than inclusion, as a source of local legitimacy. Staffan de Mistura, the third mediator, had a different approach.

Staffan de Mistura: Inclusion and performance as sources of legitimacy

The UN appointed Staffan de Mistura as Special Envoy for Syria in July 2014. In contrast to his predecessors, he only had a UN mandate and did therefore not inherit the legacy of the LAS stance on the conflict. De Mistura started his term with a decentralised approach attempting to achieve a ceasefire from the bottom up, beginning in Aleppo and then extending it to other areas.[47] This so-called 'freeze initiative' was met with high hopes for the situation to improve, especially because it could be linked to initiatives by local actors to negotiate ceasefires that often had only limited success.[48] The 'freeze initiative' could have supported these processes. However, the initiative was also criticised as playing into the government's hands and its 'effort to reclaim territory and rehabilitate its international standing'.[49] In the end, the initiative failed as no lasting ceasefire could be established in Aleppo.

In the meantime, the international stance on Syria shifted because two developments made it increasingly clear that government change was not likely to happen before political negotiations. First, the rise of ISIS and its terrorist attacks on European territory made Western states reassess the urgency of government change because they came to consider Assad the 'lesser of two evils'.[50] Second, Russia militarily intervened in support of the Syrian government in September 2015, decisively strengthening its military power, which further indicated that Assad would not be easily defeated. This made the interests of the P5 converge around a limited set of issues and enabled renewed diplomatic efforts to find a political solution to the Syrian conflict. In November 2015, foreign ministers of seventeen countries, the UN, the European Union and the LAS convened in Vienna. The meeting laid the foundation for the so-called International Syria Support Group (ISSG), co-chaired by Russia and the US, which devised a peace plan calling for renewed talks in Geneva. The UN Security Council endorsed the plan in its Resolution 2254 adopted on 18 December 2015. The so-called Intra-Syrian Talks formally started on 29 January 2016 in Geneva and proceeded in several rounds.

In terms of local legitimacy, and in contrast to his predecessors, de Mistura had a conscious strategy to include civil society in the Intra-Syrian Talks.[51] As he mentioned shortly before the talks started, 'the invitations will clearly want to be also addressed to women and civil society'.[52] For this purpose, he created the so-called Civil Society Support Room (CSSR) and the Women's Advisory Board (WAB). The CSSR has the objective to bring civil society to Geneva during rounds of talks. It provides them with a space to meet, discuss, prepare position papers and interact with the Office of the Special Envoy, member states delegations, different UN agencies, and potentially also the conflict parties' delegations.[53] The WAB consists of twelve Syrian women who directly advise the mediator.[54]

De Mistura's strategy to include civil society in the Intra-Syrian Talks indicates that inclusion and performance are not mutually exclusive. He said, for instance, that civil society actors 'make a remarkable contribution to our work' and that they 'will help me to do my job'.[55] More specifically, de Mistura mentioned three main motivations for including civil society that illustrate how inclusion can be used as a strategy to increase the performance of a mediation process.

De Mistura's first stated motivation was representation in that civil society actors could bring the voice of the broader Syrian population to the peace process. He said that 'both women and civil society organisations can provide [. . .] insight to the talks, by presenting the views and recommendations of important segments of Syrian society'.[56] Moreover, after the second round of Intra-Syrian Talks, de Mistura mentioned that civil society actors gave them 'the voice of the Syrian people'.[57] The mechanism he chose to ensure broad representation was that to each round of talks, he invited both civil society actors who had attended previous rounds as well as civil society actors who had never attended. This allowed the inclusion of as many different voices as possible while still maintaining some continuity of the discussions. Thereby, de Mistura and his team were informed about a broader spectrum of views and ideas that were, in their collectiveness, more representative than just listening to the conflict parties. At the same time, he was also aware that representation was never perfect, for instance, when saying, 'I can tell you that the groups we are talking to represent a lot of people, never perfect, never perfect, but let's start talking with them'.[58] De Mistura thus saw representation as helping the peace process to perform better in the sense that it took into account a broader variety of perspectives.

De Mistura's second declared motivation was that civil society could bring specific knowledge and expertise to the table. As stated by Alzoubi, civil society had become a major service-provider in many areas inside Syria.[59] As a result, they were often very close to the people and highly knowledgeable about the needs on the ground. Indeed, de Mistura underlined, for instance, that 'Syrian civil society provided the Special Envoy with information on the concrete daily challenges facing the Syrian people'.[60] Moreover, he consulted them on important issues and documents, for instance, on twelve principles that he had identified as consensus points between the conflict parties.[61] He mentioned that 'these are the principles that we have been working on and preparing for over a year and discussing with everyone, including civil society.'[62] Moreover, he also said that he used 'civil society's expertise on the four baskets[63] to unlock progress in the talks and move to concrete discussions towards transition'.[64] In that sense, he framed the knowledge civil society bought as improving the substance, and thereby the performance, of the peace process.

The third motivation de Mistura mentioned was that civil society actors could indirectly pressure the conflict parties since their participation showed support for a political solution to the conflict rather than for a military victory of one side or the other.[65] For instance, he cited a civil society actor he had met by underlining that *hudna, hudna, hudna* (truce, truce, truce) was their main priority and that there could be no military solution to the conflict.[66] Thus, civil society presence conferred upon him a stronger credibility when underlying the urgency of finding a solution to the conflict to the parties. Indeed, frustrated by the lack of progress after the eighth round of talks, he used civil society as a way to contrast the stalling by the parties with the willingness of civil society to move the process forward. More specifically, he said that 'two weeks have not been wasted' only because he 'had the opportunity of hearing many Syrian voices, the civil society, the Syrian Women's Advisory Board, and even [. . .] refugees'.[67] He thereby used civil society participation to pressure the parties to seriously engage in the peace process.[68] This shows that he saw the presence of civil society actors indicating their support to a political solution as crucial for the performance of the process.

Staffan de Mistura used civil society inclusion as both a direct source of legitimacy as well as an indirect one. By increasing representation, knowledge and expertise and putting indirect pressure on the parties, he used inclusion to make the process perform better and thereby become more legitimate. Civil society inclusion and performance are thus not mutually exclusive.

Civil society actors' perspectives: the link between inclusion, performance and legitimacy

While the above shows that civil society inclusion is an important source of legitimacy, it is not automatic. Rather, the specific way in which civil society participation is organised and how the process performs is crucial in terms of local perceptions of legitimacy. Analysing Staffan de Mistura's three motivations outlined above from the perspective of civil society actors helps to illustrate this point.

With regard to representation, the extent to which civil society actors felt representative of the broader population varied substantively. Some invited civil society groups established mechanisms to select representatives to attend the Intra-Syrian Talks and consulted widely before attending a round of talks in Geneva to make sure to convey points from a broad range of actors.[69] Others underlined that they only represented their own views and not those of others. At the same time, not all civil society actors wanted or were able to participate in the Intra-Syrian Talks. Some declined invitations based on political or personal considerations, others were prevented due to logistical or security reasons.[70] Thus, representation in the sense of including the view of a broad – and balanced – variety of actors is sometimes at odds with civil society interests and possibilities. If representation of specific societal groups is claimed, but the latter do not feel included, it can harm rather than help local legitimacy. Moreover, it can reinforce conflict cleavages in case civil society actors are put into strict political, religious or ethnic categories. This shows that representation and the corresponding selection procedure need to be handled delicately if they are to increase legitimacy.[71]

Second, in terms of the knowledge and expertise that civil society actors were supposed to bring, they sometimes remained frustrated with the limited influence they could exert on the political process. In an online statement, civil society actors underlined that 'from the onset of the Geneva talks we have pressed for an active role in shaping the process given our links to the ground'.[72] However, they raised concerns that they could not engage substantively due to the short time of the meetings and because the mediation team did not take up their knowledge and expertise in the way they expected. For example, some organisations declined the invitation to a CSSR meeting in December 2017 based on a concern that the discussions were not thorough enough to allow for substantive engagement.[73] There was also criticism about the fact that the UN did not share the outcomes of the discussions in a systematic matter. Based on consultations with more than 250 Syrian organisations, the Syrian Civil Platform recommended that 'the content and process of discussions [be shared] periodically and transparently with [an] even wider list of organisations' and that the UN had 'to publish periodic reports about outcomes during and after every meeting' of the CSSR.[74] This shows that in order for the process to be more legitimate, civil society actors need to see that their discussions advance from one meeting to another and be assured that their knowledge is having an impact on the peace process.

Concerning the indirect pressure on the conflict parties, civil society actors themselves referred to their important role in underlining the necessity of finding a political solution. As mentioned in a statement signed by 169 Syrian civil society organisations, the UN OSE should 'draw from the legitimacy and unique contribution of Syrian civil society to ensure a sustainable political agreement for Syria'.[75] As confirmed by one civil society actor, 'we should be able to apply pressure on the negotiating sides'.[76] Yet, this role does not come without challenges for civil society actors as it can create friction between them and the conflict parties. Civil society actors report to have been pressured by the official delegations not to attend the Intra-Syrian Talks. Thus, those who are – at least symbolically – aligned with one of the negotiating parties are cautious about how the mediator uses their presence with the conflict parties as it can inadvertently make their participation even more difficult.

More generally, it is difficult for civil society actors to justify their participation in a peace process when there are no tangible results, in other words, when it does not perform in terms of violence reduction. This was illustrated in a letter sent by civil society organisations to then-Secretary-General Ban Ki-moon stating, 'while we were asked to talk peace in Geneva, the civilians we represent were bombed in Syria'.[77] They threatened to end their participation in the Geneva process 'unless the international community takes major steps to protect civilians and enforce a cessation of hostilities in the country'.[78] This constitutes a dilemma: if civil society actors stop attending because the process does not deliver, the process further loses legitimacy. If they continue to attend without the process producing tangible outcomes, their participation loses legitimacy and their constituencies will increasingly feel alienated, so the process will equally lose legitimacy.[79] This is a further illustration of how performance and inclusion go hand in hand to produce legitimacy.

Conclusion

This chapter disentangled the relation between inclusion, performance and legitimacy. A comparison of the three subsequent UN mediators, Kofi Annan, Lakhdar Brahimi and Staffan de Mistura showed that both inclusion and performance are sources of legitimacy and that they are not necessarily at odds with each other.

First, the chapter demonstrated that if mediators decide for exclusive processes it does not imply that they ignore legitimacy. Kofi Annan and Lakhdar Brahimi both decided not to include civil society because they prioritised the performance of the peace process. Their statements indicate that they were aware of the important role of civil society, but they focused on getting the buy-in from the main conflict parties and their external backers, so that violence could be stopped as fast as possible. Thus, their decisions were not taken against, but in favour of legitimacy.

Second, the chapter showed that civil society participation does not necessarily lead to a less efficient mediation process, as often stated in the literature, but it can also be used as a strategy to increase its performance. Indeed, Staffan de Mistura pursued legitimacy through both inclusion and performance and his decision to include civil society was also based on his concerns for the peace process to perform.

Third, the chapter demonstrated that participation does not automatically lead to legitimacy. Indeed, civil society participation can hamper the legitimacy of a peace process if representation is not handled delicately, civil society actors do not feel that their knowledge is taken seriously, or if the mediator creates more friction between them and the conflict parties. More generally, if the political process shows no tangible progress in terms of violence reduction, meaning if it does not perform, it is difficult for civil society actors to sustain their presence.

Therefore, arguing in favour or against civil society inclusion does not necessarily indicate a choice for or against legitimacy. Rather, it is a judgment call by mediators about the most appropriate source of legitimacy to focus on. This choice is influenced by the context they act in, an aspect that the literature has insufficiently considered so far.[80] Comparative research on how the conflict setting influences sources of local legitimacy of a peace process is thus required to further nuance the debate.

Notes

1. Press elements by the President of the Security Council following discussions on Syria at the retreat at Backåkra, Sweden, on 22 April 2018, available at <https://www.government.se/statements/2018/04/press-elements-by-the-president-of-the-security-council-following-discussions-on-syria-at-the-retreat-at-backakra-sweden-on-22-april-2018/> (last accessed 14 October 2019).
2. Arnault, 'Legitimacy and peace processes: international norms and local realities', p. 23.
3. Nathan calls this judicial foundation the constitutional mandate, see Nathan, 'Marching orders: exploring the mediation mandate', pp. 158–9.
4. Ibid.
5. Mac Ginty and Richmond, 'The local turn in peace building: a critical agenda for peace', pp. 763–83.
6. Pouligny, 'Civil society and post-conflict peacebuilding: ambiguities of international programmes aimed at building 'new' societies', p. 497.

7. The term civil society remains contested. See Hellmüller, 'The changing role of civil society actors in peacemaking and peacebuilding', pp. 407–19, for an elaborate reflection on the concept of 'civil society' and its theoretical and practical implications.
8. Wanis-St. John and Kew, 'Civil society and peace negotiations: confronting exclusion', pp. 11–36; Nilsson, 'Anchoring the peace: civil society actors in peace accords and durable peace', pp. 243–66; Paffenholz, 'Civil society and peace negotiations: beyond the inclusion–exclusion dichotomy', pp. 69–91.
9. Hellmüller, 'The ambiguities of local ownership: evidence from the Democratic Republic of Congo', pp. 236–54; von Burg, 'On inclusivity: the role of norms in mediation'.
10. Zanker, 'The legitimisation of peace negotiations: a role for civil society?'
11. Zhu, '"Performance Legitimacy" and China's Political Adaptation Strategy', pp. 123–40.
12. Beetham, *The Legitimation of Power*.
13. Arnault, 'Legitimacy and peace processes: international norms and local realities', p. 23.
14. Raiffa, *Negotiation Analysis*; Cunningham, 'Responding to multi party civil wars: designing peace processes that make peace more likely'; Wanis-St. John and Kew, 'Civil society and peace negotiations: confronting exclusion'; Nilsson, 'Anchoring the peace: civil society actors in peace accords and durable peace'.
15. Belloni, 'Civil society in war-to-democracy transitions', pp. 182–210; Nilsson, 'Anchoring the peace: civil society actors in peace accords and durable peace'; Zanker, 'The legitimisation of peace negotiations: a role for civil society?'
16. This period covers the mediation by Kofi Annan, Lakhdar Brahimi and Staffan de Mistura. It does not cover the more recent mediation by Geir Pedersen.
17. Arab League, 'Council Resolution 7438 [Plan of Action]'.
18. The LAS had suspended Syrian membership, approved sanctions and sent an observer mission to Syria in November 2011. See Crocker et al., 'Why is mediation so hard? the case of Syria', p. 143.
19. Gowan, 'Kofi Annan, Syria and the uses of uncertainty in mediation', pp. 1–6.
20. Lundgren, 'Mediation in Syria: initiatives, strategies and obstacles, 2011–2016', pp. 273–88.
21. Six-Point Proposal of the Joint Special Envoy of the United Nations and the League of Arab States Security Council as annexed to Security Council Resolution 2042 (2012) of 14 April, available at <https://www.un.org/en/peacekeeping/documents/six_point_proposal.pdf> (last accessed 14 October 2019).
22. See UN News report, available at <https://news.un.org/en/story/2012/03/407392-syrian-government-accepts-un-arab-league-envoys-six-point-plan-end-crisis> (last accessed 14 October 2019).
Gowan sees two reasons for this. One was the pressure from Russia, which Annan had managed to convince. The second was that the threat of a military intervention similar to Libya still loomed on the horizon, instilling fear in the

government and inducing it to cooperate (see Gowan, 'Kofi Annan, Syria and the uses of uncertainty in mediation', p. 3).

23. UN Security Council Resolution 2043, available at <https://undocs.org/S/RES/2043(2012)> (last accessed 14 October 2019).

24. The following actors were present: Foreign Ministers of China, France, Russia, United Kingdom, United States and Turkey; the UN, LAS and the European Union; as well as Iraq, as Chair of the Summit of the League of Arab States; Kuwait, as Chair of the Council of Foreign Ministers of the League of Arab States and Qatar, as Chair of the Follow-up Committee on Syria of the League of Arab States.

25. Action Group for Syria, 'Final Communiqué'.

26. France, the US and the UK insisted on having it as part of a chapter VII resolution including the option of non-military sanctions on the government in case the peace plan was not implemented. For Russia and China, this was reminiscent of what happened in Libya, where they felt that France and the UK had used a chapter VII resolution stressing the protection of civilians as a basis for a Western-led military intervention aimed at regime change. They thus vetoed this first attempt to adopt the Geneva Communiqué by the UN Security Council.

27. Hill, 'Kofi Annan's multilateral strategy of mediation and the Syrian crisis: the future of peacemaking in a multipolar world?', pp. 444–78.

28. Statement by the Joint UN/LAS Special Envoy for Syria, Kofi Annan – Geneva, 12 April 2012, available at <http://www.un.org/apps/news/infocus/Syria/press.asp?NewsID=1208&sID=41> (last accessed 14 October 2019).

29. Cited in Hill, 'Kofi Annan's multilateral strategy of mediation and the Syrian crisis: the future of peacemaking in a multipolar world?', p. 457.

30. Ibid.

31. Hinnebusch and Zartman, 'UN mediation in the Syrian crisis: from Kofi Annan to Lakhdar Brahimi', p. 19.

32. Action Group for Syria, 'Final Communiqué'.

33. Transcript of the press encounter by the Joint Special Envoy on the Syrian crisis – Geneva, 8 May 2012, available at <http://www.un.org/apps/news/infocus/Syria/press.asp?NewsID=1211&sID=41> (last accessed 14 October 2019).

34. Kofi Annan, Press Conference (in Geneva), 2 August 2012, available at <http://webtv.un.org/news-features/news-story/watch/kofi-annan-joint-special-envoy-for-syria-press-conference-in-geneva/1768228719001> (last accessed 14 October 2019).

35. Secretary-General's joint press encounter with UN-Arab League Joint Special Envoy for Syria, Mr. Kofi Annan, New York, 29 February 2012, available at <http://www.un.org/sg/offthecuff/?nid=2253> (last accessed 14 October 2019).

36. Security Council Press Statement on Ceasefire in Syria, 24 October 2012, available at <https://www.un.org/press/en/2012/sc10800.doc.htm> (last accessed 14 October 2019).

37. Hinnebusch and Zartman, 'UN mediation in the Syrian crisis: from Kofi Annan to Lakhdar Brahimi'.

38. Crocker et al., 'Why is mediation so hard? The case of Syria'.

39. Hilal, 'The United Nations and a peace process strategy for Syria'; Krause and Enloe, 'A wealth of expertise and lived experience', pp. 328–38.

40. Remarks to the General Assembly on the Situation in Syria, 4 September 2012, available at <http://www.un.org/apps/news/infocus/Syria/press.asp?NewsID=1247&sID=45> (last accessed 14 October 2019).

41. Moreover, more than fifty Syrian women established the Syrian Women's Initiative for Peace and Democracy (SWIPD) with the objective to influence the talks. Alzoubi, 'Syrian civil society during the peace talks in Geneva: role and challenges', p. 1.

42. See 'Conference of Syrian women, convened by UN Women and the Netherlands, ends with strong recommendations for upcoming peace talks', Press Release, UN WOMEN, 13 January 2014, available at <http://www.unwomen.org/en/news/stories/2014/1/press-release-on-syrian-women-meeting> (last accessed 14 October 2019).

43. Brandenburg, 'Syria's civil society: Wael Sawah on the push for influence'.

44. Issa, 'Syrian civil society pushes for role at Geneva II'; see also Lowrie, 'Geneva II: Syrian civil society & women's groups'.

45. Transcript of press conference by Joint Special Representative for Syria, Lakhdar Brahimi – Geneva, 11 January 2013, available at <http://www.un.org/apps/news/infocus/Syria/press.asp?NewsID=1258&sID=45> (last accessed 14 October 2019).

46. Transcript of press conference by Joint Special Representative for Syria (JSRS) Lakhdar Brahimi, Geneva, 15 February 2014, available at <http://www.un.org/apps/news/infocus/Syria/press.asp?NewsID=1285&sID=45> (last accessed 14 October 2019).

47. Transcript of a press encounter by Staffan de Mistura, the UN Special Envoy for Syria, Damascus, Syria, 11 November 2014, available at <http://www.un.org/sg/offthecuff/index.asp?nid=3718> (last accessed 14 October 2019).

48. swisspeace et al., 'Inside Syria: What Local Actors Are Doing for Peace'.

49. Hilal, 'The United Nations and a peace process strategy for Syria'; see also Hallaj, 'Syria: an eye on peace: assessing options and entry points for peacebuilding and national dialogue(s)', pp. 115–220.

50. See for instance 'Western powers accept Assad as the lesser of two evils', *Middle East Monitor*, 11 February 2015, available at <https://www.middleeastmonitor.com/20150211-western-powers-accept-assad-as-the-lesser-of-two-evils/> (last accessed 14 October 2019).

51. In his approach, he refers to UN Security Council Resolution 2254, which states that 'the only sustainable solution to the current crisis in Syria is through an inclusive and Syrian-led political process that meets the legitimate aspirations of the Syrian people', Resolution 2254, adopted by the Security Council at its 7,588th meeting, on 18 December 2015, available at <http://www.securitycoun-

cilreport.org/atf/cf/%7B65BFCF9B-6D27-4E9C-8CD3-CF6E4FF96FF9%7D/s_
res_2254.pdf> (last accessed 14 October 2019).

52. Transcript of the press conference given in Geneva by the United Nations Special Envoy for Syria, Staffan de Mistura, on the Intra-Syrian Talks, 25 January
2016, available at <http://www.unog.ch/unog/website/news_media.nsf/ %28http
NewsByYear_en%29/AE403703D8CB5F53C1257F45006D48C7?OpenDocum
ent> (last accessed 14 October 2019).

53. Hellmüller and Zahar, 'Against the odds: civil society in the Intra-Syrian
Talks'; 'UN-led mediation in Syria and civil society: inclusion in a multi-
layered conflict'.

54. Alzoubi, 'Syrian civil society during the peace talks in Geneva: role and challenges'.

55. Staffan De Mistura, Special Envoy for Syria – Briefing to the Security Council pursuant
to Resolution 2254(2015), 27 February 2016, available at <http://www.unog.ch/
unog/website/news_media.nsf/(httpPages)/DE41A46692A9D300C1257F66000
3F8AD?OpenDocument> (last accessed 14 October 2019).

56. Office of the Special Envoy for Syria Press Statement, 2 February 2016, available
at <http://www.unog.ch/unog/website/news_media.nsf/%28httpNewsByYear_
en%29/7699AC3D3F5AB5C3C1257F4D0058C528?OpenDocument> (last
accessed 14 October 2019).

57. Transcript of press encounter by UN Special Envoy for Syria, Staffan de Mistura,
21 March 2016, available at <http://www.unog.ch/unog/website/news_media.
nsf/%28httpNewsByYear_en%29/7667D40E7768A946C1257F7D006D0B0E?
OpenDocument> (last accessed 14 October 2019).

58. Transcript of Press Conference by UN Special Envoy, Staffan de Mistura – Geneva,
14 December 2017, available at <https://www.unog.ch/80256EDD006B9C2E/
(httpNewsByYear_fr)/CB030AA3D9D07157C12581F7002F92A3?OpenDocu
ment> (last accessed 14 October 2019).

59. Alzoubi, 'Syrian civil society during the peace talks in Geneva: role and
challenges'.

60. Mediator's Summary of the 13–27 April Round of UN Facilitated Intra-Syrian
Talks, 28 April 2016, available at <http://www.unog.ch/unog/website/news_
media.nsf/(httpPages)/F37F7E194B2AF1B7C1257FA30027E636?OpenDocum
ent> (last accessed 14 October 2019).

61. Note to Correspondents: Statement on behalf of the UN Special Envoy for Syria,
Staffan de Mistura, available at <https://www.un.org/sg/en/content/sg/note-
correspondents/2017-12-01/note-correspondents-statement-behalf-un-special-
envoy> (last accessed 14 October 2019).

62. Briefing to the Security Council by UN Special Envoy for Syria, Staffan de Mistura,
19 December 2017, available at <https://www.unog.ch/80256EDD006B9C2E/
(httpNewsByYear_en)/14E1941EA7273E41C12581FB0067F0B4?OpenDocum
ent> (last accessed 14 October 2019).

63. The four baskets were thematic clusters to structure the talks. They were 1) a
credible non-sectarian transitional government, 2) a future constitution, 3)

early and free parliamentary elections within 18 months and 4) a united war against terrorism within Syria.

64. See 'Syrian civil society call for credible Syrian-led political process for Syria', Save Our Syria, 2 August 2017, available at <http://www.saveoursyria.org/letter-to-un-special-envoy-from-civil-society.html> (last accessed 14 October 2019).

65. See also Orjuela, 'Building peace in Sri Lanka: a role for civil society?', pp. 195–212; Wanis-St. John and Kew, 'Civil society and peace negotiations: confronting exclusion'.

66. Transcript of press remarks by Staffan de Mistura, UN Special Envoy for Syria Geneva, 27 April 2016, available at <http://www.unog.ch/unog/website/news_media.nsf/(httpPages)/000D36A774282696C1257FA3002BA4E4?OpenDocument> (last accessed 14 October 2019).

67. Transcript of Press Conference by UN Special Envoy for Syria, Staffan de Mistura, 14 December 2017, available at <https://www.unog.ch/80256EDD006B9C2E/(httpNewsByYear_fr)/CB030AA3D9D07157C12581F7002F92A3?OpenDocument> (last accessed 14 October 2019).

68. At the same time, de Mistura showed his awareness of the fragility of their support when shortly before interrupting the talks between two rounds, he said, 'the Syrian people [. . .] expect me and they expect all of us to produce something while we are talking. Since I am not seeing that, I have to be honest and say with myself, it is time now to have a pause'. (Note to Correspondents: Transcript of Press Stakeout of the Special Envoy for Syria, Staffan de Mistura, New York, 3 February 2016, available at <http://www.un.org/sg/offthecuff/index.asp?nid=4356> (last accessed 14 October 2019).

69. Hellmüller and Zahar, 'Against the odds: civil society in the Intra-Syrian Talks'.

70. Ibid.

71. A more adequate objective than representation may be diversity, in the sense that mediators strive for the highest possible variety of views without expecting those attending to represent a broader actor's category.

72. See 'Syrian civil society call for credible Syrian-led political process for Syria', Save Our Syria, 2 August 2017, available at <http://www.saveoursyria.org/letter-to-un-special-envoy-from-civil-society.html> (last accessed 14 October 2019).

73. See 'Statement by Syrian human rights organisations on the invitation to the Civil Society Support Room in Geneva', Syrians for Truth & Justice, 28 November 2017, available at <https://www.stj-sy.com/en/view/337> (last accessed 14 October 2019).

74. See 'Civil society participation in the political process', Syrian Civil Platform, 15 August 2016, available at <http://www.scplatform.net/en/wp-content/uploads/2016/08/Civil-society-participation-in-the-political-process-1.pdf> (last accessed 14 October 2019).

75. See 'Syrian civil society call for credible Syrian-led political process for Syria', Save Our Syria, 2 August 2017, available at <http://www.saveoursyria.org/

letter-to-un-special-envoy-from-civil-society.html> (last accessed 14 October 2019).
76. See 'The voices missing from Syria's peace talks', available at <https://www.aljazeera.com/indepth/features/2017/03/syria-war-missing-voices-syria-peace-talks-170322073131728.html> (last accessed 14 October 2019).
77. Lederer, 'Syrian civilian groups threaten to pull out of peace talks'.
78. Ibid.
79. See also Hellmüller and Zahar, 'Against the odds: civil society in the Intra-Syrian Talks'.
80. Hellmüller and Zahar, 'Context matters: theorising the relation between the context of armed conflicts and the inclusion of civil society in peace processes'.

References

Action Group for Syria, 'Final Communiqué' (Geneva: United Nations, 2012).
Alzoubi, Zedoun, 'Syrian civil society during the peace talks in Geneva: role and challenges', *New England Journal of Public Policy*, 2017, 29: 1, pp. 1–4.
Arab League, 'Council Resolution 7438 [Plan of Action]', 2011.
Arnault, Jean, 'Legitimacy and Peace Processes: International Norms and Local Realities', in Achim Wennmann and Alexander Ramsbotham (eds), *Legitimacy and Peace Processes: From Coercion to Consent* (London: Conciliation Resources, 2014), pp. 21–5.
Beetham, David, *The Legitimation of Power* (Houndsmills: Macmillan, 1991).
Belloni, Roberto, 'Civil society in war-to-democracy transitions', in Anna K. Jarstad and Timothy D. Sisk (eds), *From War to Democracy: Dilemmas of Peacebuilding* (Cambridge: Cambridge University Press, 2008), pp. 182–210.
Brandenburg, Rachel, 'Syria's Civil Society: Wael Sawah on the Push for Influence' (Washington, DC: United States Institute of Peace, 2014).
Crocker, Chester A., Fen Osler Hampson, Pamela Aall, and Simon Palamar, 'Why is mediation so hard? The case of Syria', in *Handbook of International Negotiation: Interpersonal, Intercultural, and Diplomatic Perspectives*, Mauro Galluccio (ed.) (Cham: Springer, 2015), pp. 139–56.
Cunningham, David E., 'Responding to multi party civil wars: designing peace processes that make peace more likely', Paper presented at the American Political Science Association's Annual Meeting, Chicago, IL, 2007.
Gowan, Richard, 'Kofi Annan, Syria and the uses of uncertainty in mediation', *Stability: International Journal of Security and Development*, 2013, 2: 1, pp. 1–6.
Hallaj, Omar Abdulaziz, 'Syria: an eye on peace: assessing options and entry points for peacebuilding and national dialogue(s)', in Charlotta Collén and Elisa Tarkiainen (ed.), *National Dialogues and Internal Mediation Processes: Perspectives on Theory and Practice* (Helsinki: Ministry of Foreign Affairs of Finland, 2014), pp. 115–220.
Hellmüller, Sara, 'The ambiguities of local ownership: evidence from the Democratic Republic of Congo', *African Security* 2012, 5: 3–4, pp. 236–54.

Hellmüller, Sara, 'The changing role of civil society actors in peacemaking and peacebuilding', in Fen Osler Hampson, Alpaslan Özerdem and Jonathan Kent (eds), *Routledge Handbook of Peace, Security and Development* (Abingdon: Routledge, 2020, pp. 407–19).

Hellmüller, Sara, and Marie-Joëlle Zahar, 'Against the odds: civil society in the Intra-Syrian Talks', in *Issue Briefs* (New York: International Peace Institute, 2018).

Hellmüller, Sara, and Marie-Joëlle Zahar, 'Context matters: theorizing the relation between the context of armed conflicts and the inclusion of civil society in peace processes', Paper presented at the *Annual Conference of the International Studies Association*, San Francisco, 2018.

Hellmüller, Sara, and Marie-Joëlle Zahar, 'UN-led mediation in Syria and civil society: inclusion in a multi-layered conflict', *Accord*, 2019, 28: pp. 84–7.

Hilal, Leila, 'The United Nations and a peace process strategy for Syria' (Oslo: NOREF, 2014).

Hill, Tom, 'Kofi Annan's multilateral strategy of mediation and the Syrian crisis: the future of peacemaking in a multipolar world?' *International Negotiation* 2015, 20: 3, pp. 444–78.

Hinnebusch, Raymond, and I. William Zartman, 'UN mediation in the Syrian crisis: from Kofi Annan to Lakhdar Brahimi' (New York: International Peace Institute, 2016).

Issa, Antoun, 'Syrian civil society pushes for role at Geneva II', (Beirut: Al-Monitor, 2013).

Krause, Jana and Cynthia Enloe. 'A wealth of expertise and lived experience', *International Feminist Journal of Politics*, 2015, 17: 2, pp. 328–38.

Lederer, Edith M., 'Syrian civilian groups threaten to pull out of peace talks', (New York: Associated Press, 2016).

Lowrie, Will, 'Geneva II: Syrian civil society & women's groups', (Gaziantep: Integrity Research, 2014).

Lundgren, Magnus, 'Mediation in Syria: initiatives, strategies, and obstacles, 2011–2016', *Contemporary Security Policy*, 2016, 37: 2, pp. 273–88.

Mac Ginty, Roger and Oliver Richmond, 'The local turn in peace building: a critical agenda for peace', *Third World Quarterly*, 2013, 34: 5, pp. 763–83.

Nathan, Laurie, 'Marching orders: exploring the mediation mandate', *African Security*, 2017, 10: 3, pp. 155–75.

Nilsson, Desirée, 'Anchoring the peace: civil society actors in peace accords and durable peace', *International Interactions*, 2012, 38: 2, pp. 243–66.

Orjuela, Camilla, 'Building peace in Sri Lanka: a role for civil society?' *Journal of Peace Research* 2003, 40: 2, pp. 195–212.

Paffenholz, Thania, 'Civil society and peace negotiations: beyond the inclusion-exclusion dichotomy', *Negotiation Journal*, 2014, 30: 1, pp. 69–91.

Pouligny, Béatrice, 'Civil society and post-conflict peacebuilding: ambiguities of international programmes aimed at building 'new' societies', *Security Dialogue*, 2005, 36: 4, pp. 495–510.

Raiffa, Howard, *Negotiation Analysis* (Cambridge: Belknap, 2004).

swisspeace, Conflict Dynamics International, and FarikBeirut.net, 'Inside Syria: what local actors are doing for peace' (Bern: swisspeace, 2016).

von Burg, Corinne, 'On inclusivity: the role of norms in mediation' (Bern: swisspeace, 2015).

Wanis-St. John, Anthony and Darren Kew, 'Civil society and peace negotiations: confronting exclusion', *International Negotiation* 2008, 13: 1, pp. 11–36.

Zanker, Franzisca, 'The legitimisation of peace negotiations: a role for civil society?' Eberhard Karls Universität Tübingen, Germany, 2015.

Zhu, Yuchao, '"Performance legitimacy" and China's political adaptation strategy', *Journal of Chinese Political Science* 2011, 16: 2, pp. 123–40.

EIGHT

Agonisation to Re-Legitimise the Postcolonial, Post-Conflict Somaliland

Yoshi Nakagawa

Introduction

This chapter highlights deliberation as a socio-political means of re-legitimatising the postcolonial, post-conflict polity in a contractarian tra-dition, and explores an empirical inquiry into the case of Somaliland, the breakaway state of northern Somalia, in the short to medium term. While political philosophers have often viewed legitimacy as the entitlement of rulers to rule without coercive means, a classical school of contractarians hypothesised social contract as the source of political legitimacy.[1] Hobbes[2] conceptualised the social contract as emanating from individuals surren-dering their rights to the mighty state for the sake of their liberties, while Locke[3] considered it to lie between individuals and the constitutional government that saves the former's liberties from the Leviathan state. Rousseau,[4] in turn, upheld democracy as a systemic cause for legitimation given that the elected government treats its citizens free from inequal-ity and oppression. Extending this, Kant[5] rationalised the monadic and dyadic cause for peace under liberal democracies. The Kantian rationale for perpetual peace has underpinned the charters of the League of Nations and the United Nations, and more recently the discourse of liberal peace.[6] On the other hand, Weber[7] underlined empirical reasoning for political legitimacy. His contention for legitimacy of the state which delivers public services and secures the rule of law in whatever form of regime has been pivotal in the discourse of statebuilding.[8] The warfare which has prevailed since the end of the Cold War has conflated the discourses of liberal peace and statebuilding as the policy foundation of external intervention for peacebuilding.[9]

The global consensus on liberal statebuilding has, however, overlooked the implications of (post)colonial historicity and culture for the legitimation problem with vertical and horizontal inequalities/differences in the non-Western context. Colonisation, in an attempt to build modern statehood in the traditional stateless societies, has effected socio-political ramifications although it is geopolitically, historically and culturally contingent. The colonisers' introduction of indirect rule to employ the traditional leaders (e.g. kings, chiefs, elders) for the effective control of indigenous subjects formed the vertical inequality/difference between the colonial state and the colonised society at the polity level.[10] Their measures, including Western/modern education and employment, to civilise their subjects and economise the running of the colonial state, also stratified the modern elite and the traditional non-elite within the subjects, leading to horizontal inequality/difference between the modern and the traditional segments at the agency level.[11] The colonisation project thus experienced a legitimation problem with the vertical (state–society) and horizontal (modernity–tradition) inequalities/differences. The postcolonial state undermined this, reproducing, deforming and radicalising the inherited inequalities/differences. As the crisis escalated, the postcolonial state securitised the polity yet radicalised the inequalities/differences.[12]

Postcolonial, post-conflict Somaliland has similarly faced the legitimation problem. Since pre-colonial times, the Northern Somali have structured everyday life based on kinship, and explored societal deliberation to mediate inter/intra-clan tensions at the elder council (*guurti*).[13] Lewis[14] has styled societal deliberation as the foundation of 'pastoral democracy' vis-à-vis Western liberal democracy. Yet, (post)colonisation has formed, deformed and radicalised the vertical and horizontal inequalities/differences. It was in the late nineteenth century that Britain's indirect rule divided the pre-colonial society, with the vertical inequality/difference between the colonial state and the colonised society and with the horizontal inequality/difference between the modernised urban few and the traditional rural majority[15]. The postcolonial regime, in Scientific Socialism, exacerbated these divisions, promoting the modern, educated technocrats yet marginalising the societal majority who had respected traditional norms and values.[16] The regime's strategy of *divide and rule* radicalised this legitimation problem, pushing the Northern Somali to armed resistance under the Somali National Movement (SNM) alongside other movements across Somalia. Peacebuilding in Somaliland thus required deliberating on the legitimation problem as the historical and cultural cause of conflict.

This chapter reviews how the socio-political agencies based on different sources of legitimacy in Somaliland have deliberated on the legitimation problem in view of changing power relations between the state and society over a decade after the end of the Somali civil war in 1991. In doing so, the first section briefly reviews the existing arguments on deliberation, legitimacy and peacebuilding. It indicates that approaches to deliberation are reflexive to multiple dimensions of power, generating implications for political legitimation and peacebuilding. The second section explores the evidence of deliberation on the legitimation problem in Somaliland between the end of the Somali civil war in 1991 and the first cycle of local and national elections in 2005. Deliberating on the legitimation problem in Somaliland required the societal agencies to exercise the emancipatory dimension of power, establish and deepen argumentation, and address the radicalised socio-political inequalities/differences. Yet, it also indicates that the advent of the electoral regime has formed a new form of inequality. While the electoral regime forms winners and losers in electoral politics, home-grown democratisation attracts external intervention, which has exacerbated the societal divisions and increased the risk of delegitimising the postcolonial, post-conflict polity.

Multiple approaches of deliberation to legitimation and peacebuilding

What approaches effectively address the legitimation problem in the post-colonial, post-conflict polity? Discussions among contemporary contractarians can serve as a good starting point. They have contended for deliberation as a socio-political means of reaching consensus in the politics of difference in view of the legitimation crisis in pluralising Western societies.[17] They have often underlined approaches to deliberation, among others: 1) a rational approach, 2) an agonistic approach, 3) a hybrid approach, and 4) an approach to engaging disagreement in reflexion to changing state–society relations. While the first three assume that deliberation is a means of reaching a certain form of consensus over difference, the last highlights deliberation to transform difference into disagreement given the protracted and irreducible nature of difference.

Above all, linking the legitimation crisis in Western democracies to an exclusive, winner-take-all form of politics, deliberation scholars, such as Rawls[18] and Habermas[19], have underlined rationalising socio-political argumentation, making a rational consensus in the politics of difference. Their essentialist contentions for rationality over irrationality, regardless of the Rawlsian overlapping/ethical or the Habermasian communicative methods of reasoning, however, risk the irrational other being excluded from deliberation and leading them to antagonistic dissensus against rationality.

With this concern, Mouffe[20] has problematised the coercive dimension of power (*power-over*) of rationality over irrationality, and advocated empowering the irrational yet agonal other for self-determination in a bottom-up, Foucaudian sense. Given that inter-subjective asymmetry enables agonal agencies to construct an ever-renegotiable, conflictive consensus over a non-negotiable, rational consensus, she argues that the agonistic approach to deliberation transforms the antagonistic dissensus into an agonistic consent.[21] Yet, such a linear view of an antagonism–agonism nexus based on the emancipatory yet resistive dimension of power (*power-against*) also risks the uneasy inter-agential/discursive clash (re-)antagonising agonism when their differences are protracted and irreducible. In this sense, negating binary divisions between rationality and irrationality, between power-over and -against, and between antagonism and agonism, and so on, Benhabib[22] underlines the cooperative or cooped dimension of power (*power-to/with*) which enables the deliberating agencies not to either rationalise or agonise over the difference, but to explore their 'betweenness', reaching a third, hybrid consensus that displaces either a rational or a conflictive consensus in the hybrid approach. In turn, Ranciere[23] has problematised the consensus system that pushes the deliberating agencies to reach any form of consensus. Instead, he promotes radical disagreement over consensus, reframing deliberation to seek the mutually agreed disagreement over the difference. The constructivist view of difference underlines inter-subjective recognition and equality between the deliberating agencies as the key conditions to reach radical disagreement.

A critical strand of peacebuilding has interplayed with these contentions of multiple approaches to deliberation in view of the different dimensions of power (*power-over, power-against, power-to/with*). With a view that peacebuilding is consensus-building between the warring parties, Barnett[24] is one of the few scholars to have highlighted a nexus between deliberation and peacebuilding. For him, a republican ethos for publicity urges the warring parties to rationalise the conflict of interest, transcend it and thus render the war-torn state legitimate.[25] Yet, questions remain. Among others, if a republican ethos is the precondition for deliberation, how can the warring parties acquire it? Otherwise, are those who lack it unable to deliberate? Although Shinko[26] argues that deliberation itself nurtures a certain ethos (e.g. agonistic respect and critical responsiveness in her contention), critical scholars have turned to the agonistic approach to peacebuilding. Ramsbotham,[27] for instance, adopts the Mouffean view of the antagonism–agonism nexus, highlighting agonistic dialogue between agonal agencies to transform inter-agential enmity into adversary. In taking this line, he delineates the ideal procedure for agonistic dialogue as follows: 'acknowledging radical disagreement; clearing up the immediate misunderstanding; aligning the arguments to promote engagement; uncovering the moments of radical disagreeing; and exploring radical disagreement'.[28] Yet, such a methodological focus on how to proceed with agonistic dialogue risks the dialogue falling to become a mere managerial tool of seeking radical disagreement, masking the intractability of antagonism and the commutability between antagonism and agonism given the asymmetrical power between the agonal agencies. In this sense, Aggestam et al.[29] are more critical of the Mouffean view, underlining institutional measures for agonisation, not only setting up the socio-political agora for agonistic dialogue, but also keeping the agonal agencies engaging in agonisation and preventing them from antagonising their inequalities/differences.[30]

Empirical inquiry into establishing and deepening agonisation in Somaliland

These contentions for multiple approaches to deliberation and their nexus with legitimation and peacebuilding seem largely normative in the Western context, obscuring the reality of deliberation and postcolonial implications in the non-Western context. What approaches of deliberation are processed given the changing dimensions of power in the postcolonial, post-conflict polity? How do the diverse socio-political agencies address (or fail to address) the legitimation problem with the vertical and horizontal inequalities/differences, and re-legitimise (or delegitimise) the postcolonial, post-conflict polity? This section reviews the emancipatory process in which agonisation emerged and consolidated in upscaling societal argumentation to the state realm in two stages: establishing and deepening it, in the relative absence of external intervention in the postcolonial, post-conflict Somaliland.

Establishing agonisation in the hybrid polity

The state collapse of Somalia in 1991 enabled a clique of the SNM elite to effect a political project to build modern statehood in Somaliland. The overall absence of external intervention in Somaliland, due to the overwhelming attention of the UN and Western donors to political and humanitarian crises in Mogadishu, allowed the SNM to fill the political vacuum in Somaliland, declare independence from Somalia, establish the breakaway state and elevate its chairman to the Presidency and its central committee to comprising the National Assembly.[31] The rational approach to state-led deliberation, however, exacerbated the inherited legitimation problem. As the Barre regime, the common enemy in Mogadishu, disappeared, political tension soon emerged between the modern-educated civilian faction led by President 'Tuur' and the army-oriented military conservatives, which had been largely masked during the Somali civil war. As matters became exacerbated, the desperate President did not engage with the latter, but dismissed them from the cabinet. The civilian-led deliberation in the state, however, aggrieved, expelled the other and their clan constituency and cemented their resistance. As a small arms and war culture prevailed, the power struggle within a clique of the SNM was soon radicalised in 1992. The outbreak of political violence can be thus interpreted as a by-product of political delegitimation in connection with the malaise of modernity and the dissensus of tradition in elite-led, state-oriented rationalisation in the postcolonial, post-conflict polity.

The failure of rationalisation, however, paved the way for societal forces built upon cultural and relational legitimacy to take the lead in agonising antagonism in a bottom-up approach. Local elders, whom the Barre regime had undermined for years, rapidly restored authority in societal deliberation. They led the councils of elders (*guurtis*) in more than twenty inter-clan meetings held nationwide from 1991 to 1993,[32] deliberating on grassroots disputes and exploring inter-clan mediation and reconciliation. Religious leaders, who had been running schools, clinics and mosques, also witnessed elder-led deliberation and made it legitimate in the view of the societal majority.[33] Women's dual kinships between natal and affinal clans also facilitated inter-clan dialogues despite male dominance in deliberation.[34] Poets even acted as agents of social media in the Somali oratory culture, reciting poetry to set the agenda and summarise collective decisions made in the inter-clan meetings.[35] The resurgence of societal deliberation built upon cultural tradition and relationality empowered the societal forces to meet, mediate and intervene in the embattling political elite over difference. Societal argumentation in a series of socio-political encounters throughout 1992 culminated in the 'Conference of Elders of the Communities of Somaliland' in Boroma in 1993, where more than 2,000 participants from across society, including elders, religious leaders, women and the diaspora, deliberated on a broad range of issues with the embattling political elite over five months, largely through self-help effort. Their eventual agreements on the National and Peace Charters as the provisional constitution and the setting up of the *Guurti* (the Council of Elders) as the highest authority for political deliberation into the state realm replaced the SNM-origin President and the National Assembly with the non-SNM President and the national *Guurti*.[36]

Postmodern scholars linked this institutional invention of hybrid polity and the political stability thereafter as the cause of a 'hybrid political order'.[37]

Creating the national agora in the hybrid polity, however, failed to perpetuate an agonistic peace, reflecting changing dynamics in international–state–society relations. In the meantime, the *Guurti* had eroded political relevance and legitimacy. Given the *Shahad* ('begging to those whom you know', a derogative term) culture, President Egal, a veteran politician and former Prime Minister of Somalia, with whom the elders had opted to replace President 'Tuur' in the Boroma Conference, had explored measures to buy peace, paying monthly salaries to the *Guurti* members and employing bribery to patronise his allies yet disempower his foes in high politics. The monetisation of politics boosted rents in eldership and proliferated the offices of elders, yet undermined the integrity of the *Guurti* in the eyes of the societal majority.[38] Meanwhile, ousted President 'Tuur' and his clan constituency had been aggrieved by their political demotion and increased their involvement in high politics in Southern Somalia, where the UN had promoted liberal statebuilding to re-centralise Somalia. A growing tension between the UNOSOM in Mogadishu and the Egal administration in Hargeisa urged the former to invite 'Tuur' and his allies to represent Somaliland in Mogadishu. The discursive and material manoeuvre from Mogadishu, however, exacerbated antagonism in Hargeisa between the government and the opposition and between the nationalists and the federalists, and intertwined them,[39] leading to the breakout of political violence in 1994. Despite the escalation of violent conflict, the tamed and cajoled *Guurti* had been largely on the side of the government, being dysfunctional in mediating the radicalised difference in the divided society.

As conflict reached a stalemate, another round of home-grown initiatives had arisen. Among others, a volunteer group of diaspora set up the 'Peace Committee for Somaliland'[40] in 1995 to bridge the government and the opposition and deliberate on the radicalised differences.[41] Although its actual impact has been contentious,[42] the Committee assembled the antagonising agencies and explored discursive ambiguity between them in a series of societal meetings, and echoed the local elders who had also led inter-clan meetings elsewhere.[43] Meanwhile, President Egal had carefully monitored the resurgence of agonistic dialogue with his fresh memory of the fact that societal argumentation in the Boroma process ended up ousting his predecessor. While he had waited for his moment to push back the society-led initiatives, this came when the withdrawal of UN peacekeepers from Somalia in 1995 disgraced the federalist claim of 'Tuur' and his allies and the diminished material support from Mogadishu and elsewhere led the opposition to be technically defeated in the warfare in Somaliland.[44] Capturing the momentum, President

Egal demanded that the Peace Committee dissolve itself and the societal agencies discontinue societal deliberation, and rejected a societal call for another 'clan conference'.[45] Instead, he was determined to organise a government-led conference for his political survival. The government set the agenda and participants for the 'National' Conference in Hargeisa in 1996. This indicates the changing power relations between the *Guurti* and the government in political deliberation after the 'Clan' Conference in Boroma. The proposal of the President for extensive power-sharing with the opposition in the government and the *Guurti* ameliorated the radicalised difference among the political elite to some extent, although it did not address the emerging asymmetry between the state and society, largely excluding the societal majority from political deliberation in the Conference and beyond.

In the meantime, the *Guurti* had faced continuous criticism from the society. Its failure to agonise on political antagonism raised a societal question about the legitimacy of the *Guurti* as the national 'guardian'. Its rubber-stamping attitude to the government caused the political opposition and societal majority discontent at the lack of 'rule of the game' to unseat the executive and the legislature in the state. As the *Guurti* continued to erode its relevance, it was the home-grown democratisation that reactivated and deepened socio-political agonisation. Societal argumentation emerged following the costly deal on extensive power-sharing and public employment in the government. As the absorption of clan militias made the national security forces double or triple what was actually required, the enlarged ministerial positions increased the civil service.[46] Budget constraints pushed the government to seek taxation on the societal forces, including the wealthy capitalists and local entities that had run business and public functions locally, operating small enterprises, trading goods, collecting private tax, financing clan militias and maintaining the rule of law. As the government established local administration and appointed governors and mayors to approach these societal forces, the increased intervention from Hargeisa made state-society, central-local relations increasingly frictional and conflictive, given the lack of a legal framework authorising the government to intervene in the local economy and governance. In socio-political contestation, the local entities pushed back against the government, contesting 'no taxation without representation' and demanding political liberation and democratisation.[47]

Deepening agonisation in home-grown democratisation

The sudden advent of the electoral regime after the public referendum on the Constitution in 2001, however, led to renewed political tension in high politics, among others, between the modernists who were largely in the

executive, attempting to capitalise on the elections to consolidate their legitimacy, and the traditionalists who were largely in the *Guurti*, fearing to lose
their vested interests in the hybrid polity. Their struggle over power continued until the latter accepted the electoral contest as an effective means
to unseat the interim president after the sudden death of President Egal in
2002.[48] The proposed electoral system was the proportional party-list system in multi-member local constituencies to limit the number of political
parties to three, given the socio-political dominance of the three clan families in Somaliland (the Haber Jalo, the Haber Awal and the Haber Yunis in
the Isaaq clan).[49] It relaxes obstacles to the creation of political organisations to contest the local elections, yet qualifies only three of them to turn
into political parties to contest the national elections, depending on the
results of the local elections. The condition for a political organisation to
upgrade to political party is to acquire more than 20 per cent of the votes
cast in all regions, or otherwise the highest number of the votes cast in the
local elections.[50] In order to prevent political fragmentation into clan-based
politics, those which fail to meet this must be dissolved and merged into
the qualified ones.[51] Although such a measure for forced dissolution and
merger could undermine ideological cohesion within the political parties
and limit the voters' political choice in a single electoral cycle,[52] this would
be offset by some merits. First, limiting the number could facilitate the three
parties to enhance inter-party interaction for political deliberation. Second,
it could also encourage the party members to increase intra-party interaction and cooperation. According to the contact hypothesis,[53] a growing
inter-/intra-party contact between elites from different societal backgrounds
would alleviate the inter-clan antagonism and regional polarisation which
repeatedly caused political violence in the past. Third, electing local representatives at the national elections could force the political parties to be
accountable to their local constituents, restoring the eroded link between
the state and society.

The first electoral cycle from 2002 to 2005 was effective in forming and
transforming the political parties and the *Guurti* into the new agora for
socio-political interaction and deliberation. In the local elections in 2002,
six political organisations contested, blending modernity in party politics
and tradition in electoral operations. As 70% of the voters were allegedly
clan constituents, most of the political organisations were formed on a clan
basis.[54] The clan origin of party leaders was determinant in recruiting and
selecting the party candidate since the clans were pivotal to mobilising their
affiliates for electoral campaign. Given this, the populous clans opted to
diversify their resources across the political organisations/parties to minimise
the risk of electoral defeat. As a result, most organisations/parties contained

some factions from the major clans and formed inter-clan coalitions.[55] This inter-clan, intra-party power-sharing deal urged the clan factions to deepen agonistic respect in deliberating on party agenda and electoral activities, even if it remained at the elite level, making the political organisation/party not mono-ethnic, but multi-ethnic.[56] This facilitated the inter-party transfer of politicians from the disqualified organisations to the qualified parties to agonise the political difference in the multi-ethnic parties.

Agonistic respect emerging in and across the political parties benefitted the resolution of a close race in the presidential elections in 2003. The opposition seriously challenged the miniscule margin of eighty votes between the incumbent and the opposition candidates. In response, the clan leaders urged the opposition not to provoke the dispute and accept the defeat in the end. Although the opposition's self-restraint was the key to not having radicalised the dispute, the clan leaders had averted the risk of electoral defeat, diversifying their clan affiliates across the political parties. As a result, despite the concern about one party rule after the elections, the inter-clan, intra-party coalition in the ruling party urged the state to allocate its power and resources to the major clans, and thus share common ground with the opposition to some extent.[57] Indeed, despite the growing inter-party competition in relation to the upcoming parliamentary elections, the three parties had been relatively cooperative in political deliberation on the key issues, including the demarcation of regional constituencies for the next elections and the handling of political conflict with Puntland that led to the first armed confrontation between Somaliland and Puntland in 2004.[58]

Subsequently, the parliamentary elections for the Lower House took place in 2005. The result reflected the merit of the inter-clan, intra-party coalition in the multi-ethnic parties. Despite a visible correlation between the party leaders and their clan constituencies, all parties gained at least two seats from all regions and one representative from more than seven sub-clans.[59] This result indicates that all parties acquired inter-clan support nationwide to some extent. Also, the defeat of the ruling party in the elections urged the minority government to deepen cooperation with the opposition for political deliberation. Above all, the new Lower House became largely modernised, including more MPs who were professionals, women and youths.[60] While about one third of the MPs were from the professional diaspora, their average age was lower than ever.[61] As a result, the new legislative structure was transformed into the new national agora, juxtaposing the *Guurti* (the Upper House) to promote societal tradition in the consensual politics with the Lower House to represent political modernity in majority rule. The home-grown, bottom-up democratisation in the transition from the hybrid polity to the multi-party system reformed the national deliberative space, which enabled the traditional/societal and the modern/political to re-engage in, and re-agonise on, the socio-political differences.

The Somali-own electoral regime has, however, also engendered a new form of inequality between the 'winners' and 'losers', undermining deliberative quality. In the modern segment, the wealthy capitalists have increased their stake in high politics. While the average cost of an electoral campaign reached US$70,000 per candidate,[62] the monetisation of elections elevated the cost of entry to high politics and caused adverse side-effects. First, it allowed the capitalists to patronise the political parties,[63] exacerbating *Shahad* culture and preserving political corruption. Although the code of conduct on the elections was signed by all parties, it was not legally binding but a mere 'gentlemen's agreement', and the lack of a legal framework, institutional weakness in the judiciary, and socio-political culture impelled the capitalists, party candidates and elected politicians to employ bribery and vote-buying.[64] Second, the financial burden constrained the resource-poor actors, notably women and youths, from running for election. While electoral campaigns require the female and young candidates to travel widely to reach out to women/youth voters nationwide, they often failed to afford these expenses.[65] Third, besides the political parties, the material power of the capitalists has prevailed in the civil society. As with political parties, local NGOs and media were often funded by the capitalists in their setting up and running. Their dependency on the capitalists, however, led the civil society to be self-restrictive or even co-opted by the state on the capitalist side, rather than being agonal to the state.[66] Otherwise, they increased dependency on foreign aid for liberal statebuilding.[67]

The emergence of modernity in the state has, however, not retreated from tradition, but revived and reinforced it. As the most viable way for the electoral candidates to secure the popular vote is to mobilise the affiliated clan constituencies, the clan leaders have increased their stakes in not only nominating clan candidates, but also re-indoctrinating women and youths on clannism.[68] Also, proportional representation assisted major (sub-)clans in maximising benefit from the elections. The results of the parliamentary elections in 2005 showed that the Isaaq clan, including the three major sub-clans, increased their presence in the Lower House.[69] Isaaq domination in high politics made the intra-Isaaq dynamics more significant than ever. The electoral politics, however, increase the risk of breaking the intra-Isaaq balance. The electoral defeat may aggrieve the 'loser', radicalise their claim and put political legitimacy in jeopardy. In turn, the marginalised other, for instance, the Darood clan in the eastern regions, were aggrieved, associating with the neighbouring Puntland state and causing security concerns.[70] Also, the continued male dominance in political deliberation has disempowered women and youths. Women's candidacy was often unsupported by the clan elders who viewed it as challenging tradition and splitting clan constituency between natal and marital clans.[71] The age limit (over 35) for candidacy for MP also prevented youths under 30, who reportedly amount to 70% of the entire population, from running for election.[72] As a result, while only two women were elected in the local (out of 332) and national (out of eighty-two) elections, the age of the youngest MPs remained in the late 30s. The civic plea for electoral quotas for women has, however, repeatedly been rejected as unconstitutional by the male-dominated *Guurti*.[73]

In the meantime, democratisation has attracted donor attention. Although the figure is unknown, foreign aid to Somaliland is estimated to be more than double the national budget.[74] Accordingly, the government published the first national development plan in 1997, urging donors to align their activities with the government's priorities,[75] yet donors have been largely unresponsive, not only bypassing the unrecognised state, but also aiding the modern segment while undercutting the traditional segment, and thus exacerbating the segmental division across the polity.[76] Also, their remote operations from Nairobi have increased indirect costs (e.g. staff salaries, travel costs, and so on), and caused a contention that only 20 per cent of the total aid reached local populations.[77] The rapid inflow of aid for the elections has caused tension between donors and locals. Claiming 'a vote for peace',[78] donors have financed key electoral expenses, covering 68 per cent and 77 per cent of the administrative costs in the 2002 and 2005 elections, respectively.[79] Yet, this aid dependency has undermined the local ownership of democratisation as donors have pressed the government to adopt a rigid template on the electoral schedule and benchmarks. As a result, one of the electoral commissioners lamented, 'from the President to the Minister of the Interior, all beg donors for money, relying and reflecting on their agendas and priorities on the electoral operations. Is this still a bottom-up approach to democratisation?'[80] The increasing external interventions have deformed the Somali way of emancipatory democratisation.

Conclusion

The empirical inquiry in Somaliland indicates the multiple sources of legitimacy in the non-Western society, including culture, tradition, relationality, positionality and material power, and the effectiveness of these societal holders of legitimacy to exercise the emancipatory dimension of power, and establish and deepen agonistic argumentation for political legitimation.

Yet, their relationships are dynamic, complex, transformative, conflictive and even contradictory. Indeed, after the failed attempt of the state elite to rationalise the polity after the Somali civil war, traditional leaders with cultural and relational sources of legitimacy effectively agonized with the embattling political elite, which led to the incorporation of the *Guurti* into modern statehood to share the power and resources of the state with the political elite. This consociational measure to establish the national agora in the hybrid polity was instrumental in transforming socio-political antagonism into agonism, yet failed to perpetuate an agonistic peace. The dark side of the societal sources of legitimacy, including the cultural (e.g. *Shahad* culture and kin-based patronage) and structural (e.g. rents in eldership) causes, eroded the authority of the *Guurti* in the eyes of the societal majority. Rather, it was the wealthy capitalists and local entities with material power who led to re-agonising political deliberation on taxation and restructuring the hybrid polity in home-grown democratisation. The centripetal measure for the electoral system promoted inter-clan, intra-party coalitions in the political organisations/parties as the emerging agora for state–society interaction, and transformed the *Guurti* into the two-house council to juxtapose the modern/political and the traditional/societal and make them interact to re-address the legitimation problem. Yet, the electoral regime has formed a new form of inequality/difference across the polity. In between, the external interveners with discursive and material power from Mogadishu, Nairobi and elsewhere manoeuvred and exacerbated the endogenous inequalities/differences. In this sense, the two-staged institutional measures for 'inclusion before moderation' in Somaliland – a consociational measure to establish socio-political interaction before a centripetal measure to moderate agonal clashes – were reflexive to changing relations of power in the postcolonial, post-conflict polity between the societal holders of legitimacy at the horizontal level, between the political and societal agencies in the state at the vertical level, and between the Somalilander and external interveners at the international level. Societal legitimacy is thus effective, but not a panacea, for the nexus between agonisation and political legitimation given its subjection to the entangled international–state–society relations and its implications for whether the societal agencies succeed or fail in their attempt to agonise with the state and international agencies in the era of liberal statebuilding.

Acknowledgement

This research has been partly funded by the University of Manchester.

Notes

1. See Richmond and Mac Ginty in the Introduction, pp. 2, 8.
2. Hobbes, *Leviathan*.
3. Locke, *The Second Treatise of Government and A Letter Concerning Toleration*.
4. Rousseau, *The Social Contract and Discourses*.
5. Kant, *Kant's Political Writings*.
6. For example, Doyle, 'Kant, Liberal Legacies, and Foreign Affairs', pp. 205–35; Russett, *Grasping the democratic peace*.
7. Weber, *From Max Weber: Essays in Sociology*.
8. For example, Huntington, *Political Order in Changing Societies*; Tilly, 'Reflections on the History of European State-Making', pp. 3–83.
9. For example, UN, *An agenda for peace*; OECD, *Principles for Good International Engagement in Fragile States & Situations*; World Bank, *World Development Report 2011*.
10. For example, Bayart, *The State in Africa: The Politics of the Belly*; Mamdani, *Citizen and Subject: Contemporary Africa and the Legacy of Late Colonialism*.
11. Bayart, *The State in Africa: The Politics of the Belly*.
12. Ninsin, 'Three levels of state reordering: the structural aspects', pp. 265–81.
13. Farah & Lewis, *Somalia: The Roots of Reconciliation*.
14. Lewis, *A Pastoral Democracy*.
15. Geshekter, 'Anti-colonialism and class formation: the Eastern Horn of Africa before 1950', pp. 1–32.
16. Samatar, *Socialist Somalia*.
17. Held, *Models of Democracy*, pp. 191–6.
18. Rawls, *A Theory of Justice*.
19. Habermas, *The Theory of Communicative Action*.
20. Mouffe, 'Deliberative democracy or agonistic pluralism?', pp. 745–58.
21. Ibid. p. 755.
22. Benhabib, 'Feminist Theory and Hannah Arendt's Concept of Public Space', pp. 97–114.
23. Ranciere, *Disagreement*.
24. Barnett, 'Building a republican peace: stabilizing states after war', pp. 87–112.
25. Ibid. pp. 97–9.
26. Shinko, 'Agonistic peace: a postmodern reading', pp. 473–91.
27. Ramsbotham, *Transforming Violence Conflict*.
28. Ibid. pp. 105–6, 109.
29. Aggestam et al., 'Towards agonistic peacebuilding? Exploring the antagonism-agonism nexus in the Middle East Peace process', pp. 1736–53.
30. Ibid. p. 1749.
31. Interpeace, *Peace in Somaliland*.
32. Farah & Lewis, *Somalia: The Roots of Reconciliation*.
33. Ibid.
34. Jama, 'Somali women and peacebuilding', pp. 62–5.

35. Ducaale, 'The Role of the Media in Political Reconstruction', pp. 123–88.
36. Interpeace, *Peace in Somaliland*.
37. Boege et al., *On Hybrid Political Orders and Emerging States: State Formation in the Context of 'Fragility'*.
38. Jimcaale, 'Consolidation and decentralization of government institutions', pp. 76–7.
39. Bryden & Farah, *The Peace Committee for Somaliland*.
40. Abdi, 'Report on peace-making initiative in Somaliland: April 1995–January 1997', available at <http://www.c-r.org/sites/default/files/ReportonPeacemakingSomaliland_199609_ENG.pdf> (last accessed 19 May 2015).
41. Bryden & Farah, *The Peace Committee for Somaliland*.
42. Walls, PhD thesis: *State Formation in Somaliland: Bringing Deliberation to Institutionalism*, p. 144.
43. Abdi, 'Report on peace-making initiative in Somaliland: April 1995–January 1997', available at <http://www.c-r.org/sites/default/files/ReportonPeacemaking-Somaliland_199609_ENG.pdf> (last accessed 19 May 2015).
44. Balthasar, 'Somaliland's best kept secret: shrewd politics and war projects as means of state-making', pp. 218–38.
45. Abdi, 'Report on peace-making initiative in Somaliland: April 1995January 1997', available at <http://www.c-r.org/sites/default/files/ReportonPeacemaking-Somaliland_199609_ENG.pdf> (last accessed 19 May 2015).
46. Forberg & Terlinden, *Small Arms in Somaliland*, pp. 29, 32, 44; Jimcaale, 'Consolidation and cecentralization of government institutions', p. 72.
47. Eubank, 'Taxation, political accountability and foreign aid: lessons from Somaliland', pp. 465–80.
48. Bradbury et al., 'Somaliland: choosing politics over violence', pp. 455–78.
49. Jama, *Somaliland Electoral Laws*.
50. Jama, *Somaliland Electoral Laws*, pp. 94–6.
51. Ibid. p. 56.
52. Yusuf, 'The Saga of the Pursuit of Women's Quota in Somaliland', pp. 94–104.
53. Allport, *The Nature of Prejudice*.
54. Yusuf, 'Somaliland's political culture: challenges to democracy', p. 18.
55. Lindeman and Hansen, 'Somaliland: presidential election 2003'.
56. Ibid.
57. Bradbury et al., 'Somaliland: Choosing Politics over Violence', pp. 455–78.
58. APD, *A Vote for Peace*, p. 22.
59. Ibid. pp. 41–2.
60. Progressio, *Further Steps to Democracy*, p. 23; Personal interview, The Lower House, Hargeisa, 20 October 2015.
61. Ibid. p. 10.
62. Ibid. p. 10.
63. Ibid. p. 10.
64. Verjee et al., *The Economics of Elections in Somaliland: The Financing of Political Parties and Candidates*, pp. 39–40.
65. Warsame, 'Swimming against the current: a women's experience in running for the first Somaliland parliament elections in 2005', p. 49.

66. Ibrahim, *Somaliland's Investment in Peace: Analysing the Diaspora's Economic Engagement in Peace Building*, p. 51.
67. Moe, *Somaliland Report*.
68. APD, *A Vote for Peace*, p. 37.
69. Ibid. p. 44.
70. Hoehne, *Between Somaliland and Puntland: Marginalization, Militarization and Conflicting Political Visions*. More recently, the Khatumo State has challenged Somalilandor Puntland due to the power vacuum.
71. Warsame, 'Swimming against the current: a women's experience in running for the first Somaliland parliament elections in 2005', p. 49.
72. Ahmed, 'The salient role of youth in Somaliland development', p. 100.
73. Yusuf, 'The Saga of the Pursuit of Women's Quota in Somaliland', pp. 94–104.
74. Bradbury, *Becoming Somaliland*, p. 157.
75. Renders, *Consider Somaliland: State-Building with Traditional Leaders and Institutions*, p. 168.
76. Hammond et al., *Cash and Compassion: The Role of the Somalil Diaspora in Relief, Development and Peace-Building*, 67; Moe, *Somaliland Report*, pp. 39–40.
77. Moe, *Somaliland Report*, pp. 51–2.
78. APD, *A Vote for Peace*.
79. Verjee et al., *The Economics of Elections in Somaliland: The financing of political parties and candidates*, p. 14.
80. Personal interview, The University of Hargeisa, 26 September 2015.

References

Abdi, S. D., 'Report on peace-making initiative in Somaliland: April 1995–January 1997', 1996, available at <http://www.c-r.org/sites/default/files/ReportonPeace-makingSomaliland_199609_ENG.pdf> (last accessed 19 May 2015).
Aggestam, K., Cristiano, F. & Strombom, L., 'Towards agonistic peacebuilding? Exploring the antagonism-agonism nexus in the Middle East Peace process', *Third World Quarterly* 2015, 36: 9, 1736–53.
Allport, G. W., *The Nature of Prejudice*, London: Addison-Wesley, 1954.
APD, *A Vote for Peace* (Hargeisa: APD, 2006).
Balthasar, D., 'Somaliland's best kept secret: shrewd politics and war projects as means of state-making', *Journal of Eastern African Studies* 2013, 7: 2, 218–38.
Barnett, M., 'Building a republican peace: stabilizing states after war', *International Security*, 2006, 30: 4, 87–112.
Bayart, J.-F., *The State in Africa: The Politics of the Belly* (London: Longman, 1993).
Benhabib, S., 'Feminist theory and Hannah Arendt's concept of public space', *History of the Human Sciences*, 1993, 6: 2, 97–114.
Birnir, J. K., *Ethnicity and Electoral Politics* (Cambridge: Cambridge University Press, 2007).
Boege, V., Brown, A., Clements, K. P. & Nolan, A., *On Hybrid Political Orders and Emerging States: State Formation in the Context of 'Fragility'*, Berlin: Berghof Research Centre, 2008.

Bradbury, M., *Becoming Somaliland* (Oxford: James Currey, 2008).

Bradbury, M., Abokor, A. Y. & Yusuf, H. A., 'Somaliland: choosing politics over violence', *Review of African Political Economy*, 2003, 30: 97, 455–78.

Brock, K., McGee, R. & Gaventa, J., *Unpacking policy: knowledge, actors, and spaces in poverty reduction in Uganda and Nigeria* (Brighton: Fountain Publishers, 2004).

Bryden, M. & Farah, A. Y., *The Peace Committee for Somaliland* (Addis Ababa: UNDP Emergencies Unit for Ethiopia, 2000).

Chandra, K. *Why Ethnic Parties Succeed* (Cambridge: Cambridge University Press, 2004).

DFID, *Building Peaceful States and Societies: A DFID Practice Paper* (London: DFID, 2010).

Doyle, M. W. 'Kant, liberal legacies, and foreign affairs', *Philosophy & Public Affairs* 1983, 12: 3, 205–35.

Drake, A. & McCulloch, A., 'Deliberative consociationalism in deeply divided societies', *Comparative Political Theory*, 2011, 10: 3, 277–94.

Dryzek, J., 'Deliberative democracy in divided societies: alternatives to agonism and analgesia', *Political Theory* 2005, 33: 2, 218–42.

Ducaale, B. Y., 'The role of the media in political reconstruction', in WSP International (ed.), *Rebuilding Somaliland: Issues and Possibilities* (Lawrenceville, NJ: The Red Sea Press, 2005), pp. 123–88.

Eubank, N., 'Taxation, political accountability and foreign aid: lessons from Somaliland', *Journal of Development Studies* 2012, 48: 4, 465–80.

Farah, A. Y. & Lewis, I. M., *Somalia: The Roots of Reconciliation* (London: Action Aid, 1993).

Ferme, M., 'Staging Politisi: The Dialogics of Publicity and Secrecy in Sierra Leone', in J. L. Comaroff & J. Comaroff (eds), *Civil Society and the political imagination in Africa* (Chicago: University of Chicago Press, (1999), pp. 161–91.

Forberg, E. & Terlinden, U., *Small Arms in Somaliland* (Berlin: Berlin Information Center for Transatlantic Security, 1999).

Geshekter, C. L., 'Anti-colonialism and class formation: the Eastern Horn of Africa before 1950', *The International Journal of African Historical Studies* 1985, 18: 1, 1–32.

Habermas, J., *The Theory of Communicative Action* (Cambridge: Polity Press, 1984).

Habermas, J., *Between Facts and Norms: Contributions to a Discourse Theory of Law and Democracy* (Oxford: Polity Press, 1996).

Hammond, L., Awad, M., Dagane, A. I., Hansen, P., Horst, C., Menkhaus, K. & Obare, L., *Cash and Compassion: The Role of the Somali Diaspora in Relief, Development and Peace-Building* (New York: UNDP, 2011).

Hashim, Y. & Walker, J.-A., 'Constructing spaces for poverty reduction: politics, religion and poverty reduction policies in Jigawa state', in K. Brock, R. McGee & J. Gaventa (eds), *Unpacking Policy* (Brighton: Fountain Publishers, 2004), pp. 238–54.

Held, D., *Models of Democracy*, 3rd edn (Oxford: Polity, 2006).

Hobbes, T., *Leviathan* (Harmondsworth: Penguin, 1968).

Hoehne, M. V., *Between Somaliland and Puntland: Marginalization, Militarization and Conflicting Political Visions* (Nairobi: The Rift Valley Institute, 2015).

Huntington, S. P., *Political Order in Changing Societies* (New Haven: Yale University Press, 1968).

Ibrahim, M. H., *Somaliland's Investment in Peace: Analysing the Diaspora's Economic Engagement in Peace Building* (Brussels: DIASPEACE, 2010).

Interpeace, *Peace in Somaliland* (Hargeisa: APD, 2008).

Interpeace, *Background Paper: Voices of Civil Society Organization (CSOS) on Peace-building and Statebuilding* (Geneva: Interpeace, 2010).

Jama, F., 'Somali women and peacebuilding', in M. Bradbury & S. Healy (eds), *Whose Peace Is It Anyway?* (London: Conciliation Resources, 2010), pp. 62–5.

Jama, I. H., *Somaliland Electoral Laws*, 2005, available at <www.somalilandlaw.com/Somaliland_Electoral_Laws_Handbook_2008PP.pdf> (last accessed 27 May 2015).

Jimcaale, C., 'Consolidation and decentralization of government institutions', in WSP International (ed.), *Rebuilding Somaliland* (Lawrenceville: The Red Sea Press, 2005), pp. 49–121.

Kant, I., *Kant's Political Writings*, 2nd edn (Cambridge: Cambridge University Press, 1991).

Lemarchand, R., 'The state, the parallel economy, and the changing structure of patronage systems' in D. Rothchild & N. Chazan (eds), *The Precarious Balance: State and Society in Africa.* (Colorado: Worldview, 1988), pp. 149–70.

Lewis, I. M., *A Pastoral Democracy* (London: Oxford University Press, 1961).

Lindeman, B. N. & Hansen, S. J., 'Somaliland: Presidential Election 2003', available at <http://www.somalilandlaw.com/NORDEM_Report_on_the_2003Pres_Elections.pdf> (last accessed 28 May 2015).

Locke, J., *The Second Treatise of Government and a Letter Concerning Toleration* (Oxford: Blackwell, 1948).

Mamdani, M., *Citizen and subject: contemporary Africa and the legacy of late colonialism*, (London: James Currey, 1996).

Marx, K., *Karl Marx and F. Engles. Selected Works Vol. 1* (Moscow: Foreign Language Publishing House, 1962).

Migdal, J. S., 'The state in society: an approach to struggles for domination', in J. S. Migdal, Joel, A. Kohli and V. Shue (eds), *State Power and Social Forces: Domination and Transformation in the Third World* (Cambridge: Cambridge University Press, 1994), pp. 7–34.

Moe, L. W., *Somaliland Report* (Brisbane: The University of Queensland, 2013).

Mouffe, C., 'Deliberative democracy or agonistic pluralism?' *Social Research* 1999, 66: 3, 745–58.

Nagle, J., 'From the politics of antagonistic recognition to agonistic peace building: an exploration of symbols and rituals in divided societies', *Peace & Change* 2014, 39: 4, pp. 468–94.

Ninsin, K. A., 'Three levels of state reordering: the structural aspects', in D. Rothchild & N. Chazan (eds), *The Precarious Balance: State and Society in Africa* (Boulder: Westview, 1988), pp. 265–81.

OECD, *Principles for Good International Engagement in Fragile States & Situations* (Paris: OECD, 2005).

O'Flynn, I., 'Divided societies and deliberative democracy', *British Journal of Political Science*, 2007, 37: 4, pp. 731–51.

Progressio, *Further Steps to Democracy* (London: Progressio, 2006).

Ramsbotham, O., *Transforming Violence Conflict* (Abingdon: Routledge, 2010).

Ranciere, J., *Disagreement* (Minneapolis: The University of Minnesota Press, 1999).

Rawls, J., *A Theory of Justice* (Cambridge: Belknap Press, 1971).

Renders, M., *Consider Somaliland: State-Building with Traditional Leaders and Institutions* (Leiden: Brill, 2012).

Renders, M. & Terilinden, U., 'Negotiating statehood in a hybrid political order: the case of Somaliland', *Development and Change*, 2010, 41: 4, pp. 723–46.

Rousseau, J.-J., *The Social Contract and Discourses*, new edn (London: Dent, 1973).

Russett, B. M., *Grasping the Democratic Peace* (Princeton: Princeton University Press, 1993).

Samatar, A. I., *Socialist Somalia* (London: Zed Books, 1988).

Schaap, A., 'Agonism in divided societies', *Philosophy & Social Criticism* 2006, 32: 2, pp. 255–77.

Shinko, R., 'Agonistic peace: a postmodern reading', *Millennium* 2008, 36: 3, pp. 473–91.

Tilly, C., 'Reflections on the history of European state-making', in C. Tilly, ed., *The formation of National States in Western Europe* (Princeton: Princeton University Press, 1975), pp. 3–83.

UN, *An Agenda For Peace* (New York: UN, 1992).

Verjee, A., Abokor, A. Y., Yusuf, H. A., Warsame, A. M., Farah, M. A. & Hersi, M. F., *The Economics of Elections in Somaliland: The financing of political parties and candidates*. (Nairobi: The Rift Valley Institute, 2015).

Walls, M., PhD thesis: *State Formation in Somaliland: Bringing Deliberation to Institutionalism* (London: University College London, 2011).

Warsame, A. M., 'Swimming against the current: a women's experience in running for the first Somaliland parliament elections in 2005', in Social Research and Development Institute (SORADI) (ed.), *Somaliland: Facing the Challenges of Free and Fair Elections* (Hargeisa: SORADI, 2010), pp. 46–52.

Weber, M., *From Max Weber: Essays in Sociology* (London: Routledge, 1975).

World Bank, *World Development Report 2011* (New York: Oxford University Press, 2011).

Young, I. M., *Inclusion and Democracy* (Oxford: Oxford University Press, 2000).

Yusuf, H. A., 'Somaliland's political culture: challenges to democracy', in Social Research and Development Institute (SORADI) (ed.), *Somaliland: Facing the Challenges of Free and Fair Elections* (Hargeisa: SORADI, 2010), pp. 16–21.

Yusuf, H. A., 'The saga of the pursuit of women's quota in Somaliland', in Social Research and Development Institute (SORADI) (ed.), *Reflections and Lessons of Somaliland's Two Decades of Sustained Peace, Statebuilding and Democratization* (Hargeisa: SORADI, 2012), pp. 94–104.

NINE

Third Party Legitimacy and International Mediation: Peacemaking through Pan-Africanism in Sudan

Allard Duursma

Introduction

A dominant view within the field of international mediation is that the most effective type of third party to resolve civil wars is a high-leverage, manipulative power broker that can provide sticks and carrots in order to persuade the conflict parties to make peace.[1] This dominant view, which is based on a materialist logic, overlooks the role of ideational factors. In this chapter, I argue against the dominant materialist view of mediation success by illustrating that ideational factors matter in peace processes. More specifically, I show how a preference among the Government of Sudan (GoS) and the Sudan People's Liberation Movement (SPLM/A) for 'African solutions to African conflicts' provided the Intergovernmental Authority on Development (IGAD) with a high degree of legitimacy. This high degree of legitimacy allowed the IGAD mediation team to remain involved in mediation from 1994 onwards, eventually pulling the conflict parties towards peace in 2005.

Like other chapters in this volume, this chapter thus contributes to the literature on legitimacy and peace processes. Yet, rather than considering how legitimacy is the product of perceptions of local-level actors as several other chapters in this volume, this chapter is concerned with how the legitimacy of an international third party was the product of the perceptions of national-level elites. This approach also entails a departure from the Weberian understanding of legitimacy as a justification for rule,[2] but on an international level rather than a local level. Since mediation efforts in civil wars are based on the consent of the conflict parties, the legitimacy of third parties mediating civil wars does not rest on international law or the capacity of the third party to deliver its objectives. Instead, third parties with legitimacy in these contexts can have social influence because the change in behaviour they ask of the conflict parties is congruent with the value system of both the influencing third party and the conflict parties being influenced. In civil wars in Africa, the African solutions to African conflict is a major part of this collective value system.

This chapter proceeds as follows. The next section provides a brief overview of the materialist-dominated literature on international mediation, after which I put forward a legitimacy-based perspective on mediation success. Next, I assess the merit of this legitimacy-based perspective of mediation success on the basis of the IGAD-led peace process to end the north–south Sudan civil war. I show how the normative structure of the society of African states provided African third parties with a high degree of legitimacy during their mediation efforts between the Government of Sudan and rebels in southern Sudan. The final section concludes.

Towards a Legitimacy-Based understanding of Mediation Success

Scholars studying third party peacemaking have traditionally focused on the incentives that can be provided to move conflict parties towards a negotiated settlement.[3] In one of the first comparative case studies on international mediation, Zartman argues that leverage, based on economic and military capabilities, is the ticket to mediation success.[4] I refer to this way of understanding mediation success as a capacity-based perspective, because of the importance attached to the tangible resources of third parties. At the core of the capacity-based perspective of mediation is thus a realist conception of power, in which power is understood as 'the ability of states to use material resources to get others to do what they otherwise would not'.[5]

The far majority of subsequent studies on mediation have followed the capacity-based perspective of mediation success in which the material resources of a third party are understood as determining the prospects of mediation success. For instance, Rothchild argues how providing material incentives to conflict parties can move them towards compromise. This leads Rothchild to conclude that 'in highly intense conflicts, many of which have spread across international borders, strong external mediators with enormous resources at their disposal become an essential part of the conflict management process. Only these external actors have the capacity to wield the necessary pressures and incentives to encourage local rivals to reconsider their alternatives and then to enforce the peace during the post-negotiation phase'.[6] Similarly, in one of the first quantitative studies on international mediation, Bercovitch argued and found that the 'possession of resources and an active strategy provide the basis for successful media-tion'.[7] This finding is supported by later statistical studies.[8] Based on the current quantitative mediation literature, Greig and Diehl assert in their literature review that mediation by a weak mediator is not effective as it is 'limited in the resources that can be brought to bear in the talks as a means of pushing the parties to make concessions and leverage an agree-ment between the two sides'.[9]

In spite of capacity-based explanations of mediation success domi-nating the literature, several authors have noted that the success of third parties is also based on ideational sources of social control. In his book published in 1967, Young described both tangible and intangible charac-teristics of a third party that he deemed necessary for effective intervention in international crises.[10] Rubin has noted that 'almost any third party, in almost any setting, is likely to rely on some measure of legitimate power in excising influence', but he also added that some mediators are more likely to rely on legitimacy than others.[11] Princen's work on mediation by the Vatican in the Beagle Channel Dispute between Argentina and Chile suggests that the legitimacy of the pope contributed to the resolution of this conflict.[12]

However, few scholars have tried to explain what third party legitimacy exactly entails and how it operates in mediation processes. A common element in most studies on international legitimacy is that it is discussed in relation to other forms of social control.[13] For instance, in his seminal piece on legitimacy in international politics, Hurd considers three possible ideal-types of social control.[14] The first two of these ideal-types are in line with the capacity-based perspective of mediation and address the ability of a superior actor to get a subordinate actor to obey because of fear of punishment or because of providing benefits. By contrast, the third type of social control identified by Hurd relates to how an actor complies with another actor because they feel that what this actor wants is legitimate and therefore ought to be obeyed.[15] Based on this last type of influence, Hurd defines legitimacy simply as the 'normative belief by an actor that a rule or institution ought to be obeyed'.[16] From this perspective, legitimacy is thus necessarily a subjective quality.

Beetham also asserts that legitimacy is socially constructed on the basis of certain beliefs, but he identifies two additional elements: the power rela-tion needs to conform to established rules and there should be evidence of consent by the subordinate to the particular power relation.[17] These two additional elements of legitimacy are fundamental characteristics of *every* international mediation effort. First, international mediation is per defini-tion based on consent. Without consent, third party involvement should

rather be classified as coercive intervention. Second, international mediation always conforms to established rules, since from an international law
perspective, any state or international organisation – regardless of geographical location – has, in principle, the right to mediate armed conflicts.[18]
Hence, two of Beetham's criteria of legitimacy – the procurement of consent
and the invocation of international law – apply to all mediation efforts.
Consequently, when assessing the degree of legitimacy of a third party in
any mediation effort, one has to assess to what extent compliance with the
third party can be justified on the basis of beliefs by the conflict parties that
complying with the mediator is the right thing to do.[19]

Applying this theoretical argument to the resolution of civil wars in
Africa, I argue that African third parties are effective in resolving civil wars
in Africa because of the norm of African solutions to African challenges.
From Africa's early post-colonial period onwards, the norm of African solutions to African conflicts has consistently been recognised as a strong international norm in the African state system.[20] These African solutions norm
results in a normative pull towards compliance with African third parties.
Several scholars on Africa's international politics have reflected on this normative pull. For instance, Červenka has noted that the search for compromises is 'regarded as a moral obligation on the conflicting parties to settle
their dispute in the interests of African unity'.[21]

Connecting this reflection to the broader literature on norms and the
impact of legitimacy reveals how African third parties have a comparative
advantage when involved in mediation in civil wars in Africa. Franck points
out that an actor or rule that is perceived as legitimate 'exerts a pull toward
compliance on those addressed normatively because those addressed believe
that the rule or institution has come into being and operates in accordance
with generally accepted principles of right process'.[22] The social processes
that underlie this normative pull have been well documented within the
field of social psychology. For example, Kelman shows how social influence
is accepted because the change in behaviour is congruent with the value
system of both the influencing agent and the ones being influenced.[23] Similarly, Tyler concludes that 'people internalise group values. They take on
the values of the group as their own values. This leads them to voluntarily
follow the decisions of group authorities. Breaking rules and disobeying
decisions made by authorities has greater negative implications for the self,
whereas rule following has greater positive implications'.[24]

The next section shows how the legitimacy of IGAD – which is a result of
the African solutions norm – allowed the IGAD mediation team to remain
involved in mediation from 1994 onwards, eventually pulling the conflict
parties towards peace in 2005.

Peacemaking through Pan-Africanism in Sudan

In early 1994, IGAD became involved in mediation in the conflict between the GoS and the SPLM/A, which had been ongoing since 1983. IGAD stepping into the fray was preceded by the adoption of the Organisation of African Unity (OAU) Mechanism for Conflict Prevention, Management and Resolution in Cairo in June 1993. This landmark in the development of a more robust peace and security architecture in Africa reaffirmed the legitimacy of African third parties. Indeed, Cohen explains that a significant effect of these mechanisms was 'the collective pressure brought to bear on individual governments to accept OAU interference'.[25] While this statement by Cohen is meant as a general observation, he adds that the IGAD mediation in Sudan during the mid-1990s is a telling example of the normative pressure put on conflict parties to accept mediation: 'Although both the Sudanese government and the southern insurgents of the Sudan people's Liberation Army have good tactical reasons not to negotiate, they have faithfully turned up at IGAD negotiating sessions because of this OAU peer pressure'.[26] Indeed, the GoS remained superior on the battlefield in the early 1990s, but it also wished to show commitment to the resolution of the conflict. Chief government negotiator Mohamed el-Amin Khalifa states that 'Al-Bashir did not refuse mediation by IGAD because an African third party that genuinely wanted to help to make peace in Sudan just had to be welcomed'.[27] In addition, the IGAD mediation was seen by the GoS as shielding the peace process from strong external pressures from non-African actors. Commenting on the peacemaking effort of IGAD, President Omar al-Bashir suggested that 'Africans have become mature enough to resolve their own problems and are no longer in need of a foreign guardian' and further stated that the IGAD mediation efforts would be 'without loopholes through which colonialism can penetrate on the pretext of humanitarianism'.[28] Former Presidential adviser Ghazi Salah al-Din al-Atabani confirms that this was not mere rhetoric: 'President al-Bashir believed that African mediation would protect us vis-à-vis western powers'.[29] Al-Bashir's statement shows how the GoS justified the involvement of IGAD using normative arguments related to IGAD's legitimacy.

The SPLM/A was initially hesitant to accept mediation by IGAD. Since IGAD is an interstate organisation, the southerners perceived the organisation as likely to favour the government side in the conflict.[30] Yet, declining mediation by IGAD would risk alienating the entire region. Senior SPLM/A member Bona Malwal notes how because of 'the regional commitment to peace, to be seen to resist peace was extremely difficult, if not impossible, for the SPLM/A'.[31] Similarly, senior SPLM/A member Lual Deng acknowledges that part of the reason the SPLM/A accepted mediation by IGAD was that they did not want to be seen as warmongers by African leaders.[32]

In addition, a strong commitment to peaceful conflict resolution mitigated some of the concerns among the SPLM/A leadership that the mediation effort would favour the GoS. Indeed, Cirino Hiteng Ofuho, a senior SPLMA negotiator, reflected that a major reason for accepting IGAD mediation was that 'it had a clear incentive to see a peaceful solution in Sudan'.[33] Similarly, prior to the negotiations mediated by IGAD, John Garang stated that 'I expect a lot from these states because they are our neighbours and the sense they are affected by our problem whether through the exodus of refugees or instability on the borders'.[34]

Based on this idea of legitimate involvement, the IGAD mediation team started proximate consultations with the conflict parties in January 1994 in order to determine the issues that would be put on the agenda for the formal talks. Yet, after four rounds of negotiations throughout the first half of 1994, the conflict parties had still not agreed on an agenda. The major stumbling block was the refusal by the GoS mediation team to put the issue of self-determination on the agenda, arguing that the issues of self-determination and religion and state are not within the mandate of the IGAD mediation team.[35] During the fourth round of negotiations in September 1994, the new head of the negotiation team, Ghazi Salah al-Din al-Atabani, argued that 'self-determination-alias-separation of southern Sudan is bound to elicit a chain-reaction afflicting the rest of Africa. This is an eventuality that the founding fathers of the OAU consciously tried to avoid'.[36]

The refusal by the GoS to discuss self-determination led to a significant deterioration in relations between Khartoum and the IGAD member countries, but the leaders of the mediating IGAD member states decided that they would remain involved in mediation.[37] This continued involvement proved fruitful, as Kenyan President Moi succeeded in convincing President al-Bashir to finally accept the Declaration of Principles (DoP) at an IGAD summit in Nairobi in July 1997.[38] Although the DoP does not qualify as a peace agreement, the signing of it was a significant step in the mediation process. It reflected the growing consensus among the major conflict parties what the underlying issues of the conflict were that needed to be tackled. The signing of the DoP also confirmed the legitimate involvement of IGAD. Indeed, Mutrif Siddiq highlights that 'the acceptance of the DoP reflected that IGAD was perceived as a viable and legitimate forum to resolve the conflict. We fully supported the IGAD initiative'.[39]

After the conflict parties had agreed on the DoP, negotiations took place at some point every year between 1997 and 2000, but little progress was made. While it was clear what the conflict issues were, the positions of adversaries seemed truly incompatible. The support provided to the SPLM/A by the third parties involved in mediation could not change this fundamental obstacle to peace. Nevertheless, while the signing of the DoP initially might have been considered a purely rhetorical commitment by the conflict parties, it created a normative benchmark which greatly contributed to formulating a mutual acceptable solution to the war in the early 2000s.

Indeed, when Kenyan General Lazaro Sumbeiywo was mandated by IGAD in January 2002 as the new chief mediator, he intended to address each issue in the DoP through negotiations until all issues were addressed. Sumbeiywo later reflected that when he became the chief mediator he believed that the 1997 concluded 'DoP was a complete diagnosis but some-body had to do the prescription for every problem'.[40] After almost a month of negotiations, on 17 July 2002, Sumbeiywo instructed GoS negotiator Sayed el-Tayeb and SPLM/A negotiator Deng Alor to engage in discussions on the two sides' red lines, without any other representatives of the con-flict parties or the mediators present. It became apparent from the discus-sion between el-Tayeb and Alor that the SPLM/A leadership would never compromise on the option of secession in a referendum, whereas the GoS would never sign an agreement that would turn Sudan into a secular state.[41] Consequently, on 20 July 2002, the conflict parties signed the Machakos Protocol, in which the conflict parties agreed on the principles of self-deter-mination for the South, Sharia law for the North, and the common goal of building a united Sudan. The conclusion of the Machakos Protocol high-lighted that the conflict parties wanted to settle the conflict, as well as that a mutual satisfactory solution to the conflict could be found as long as a legitimate third party provided the environment in which the parties could look for solutions.

Expectations were briefly tempered when the SPLM/A attacked Torit in September 2002.[42] Yet, this attack only temporally stalled the peace process. President Moi consulted with Garang, obtaining a promise of the SPLM/A leader that he would not conduct attacks like these in the future. Sumbeiywo talked to President al-Bashir and managed to regain the commitment of the GoS to the peace process.[43] According to Sumbeiywo, it was already clear by then that the conflict parties had confidence in the peace process: 'Neither delegation was really keen to run away'.[44] After the SPLM/A attack on Torit, both sides realised the negative impact fighting could have on the peace process.[45] This led to the signing of the Memorandum of Understanding on Cessation of Hostilities on 15 October 2002.[46]

A major turning point in the peace process occurred at an IGAD summit in Nairobi on 2 April 2003 when President Omar al-Bashir and SPLM/A leader John Garang met and shook hands, both expressing their confidence in the IGAD-led mediation process and stressing the need to maintain momentum towards the conclusion of a final settlement.[47] To move the process forward, Sumbeiywo tried to get Vice-President Ali Osman Taha and John Garang engaged in direct talks, which took place for the first time on 4 September 2003. From this first meeting between Taha and Garang onwards, the mediation process gained momentum.[48] After almost a month of talks between Taha and Garang, on 25 September 2003, the conflict parties concluded the Agreement on Security Arrangements during the Interim Period, which stipulated that an internationally monitored ceasefire would take effect once a final agreement was signed. Taha and Garang reached an agreement on how to distribute the oil wealth of southern Sudan on 7 December 2003.

After the Framework on Wealth Sharing had been concluded in January 2004, negotiations started to focus again on the three areas. To move the parties towards compromise on this issue, US representatives intervened in these negotiations, proposing that Southern Kordofan and the Blue Nile States would remain two federal states of Sudan; but that Abyei would be granted an interim self-administering status, while organising a referendum on whether to join the North or the South.[49] The conflict parties agreed to this proposal and subsequently signed two separate agreements on 26 May 2004.[50]

On 26 May 2004, the same day as when the two agreements on the three areas were concluded, the adversaries also concluded a protocol on power-sharing. This agreement established a Government of Southern Sudan (GoSS) for the interim period.[51]

The Comprehensive Peace Agreement (CPA) was signed in Naivasha on 9 January 2005.[52] In essence, the CPA put together the six partial agreements that had been signed on the basis of the Machakos Protocol.[53] The CPA stipulated that the South was to be given an autonomous status for six years and a referendum to be held in 2011 regarding possible secession from Sudan, the North and South were to maintain separate armed forces, the positions in the central government were to be split equally between the North and the South, and Sharia Law would only be applicable in the North.[54]

The final phase of the Naivasha process suggests that the legitimacy of a third party and the capacity of another third party can supplement each other. As a result of a coordinated mixed mediation effort led by an African third party, the conflict parties finally terminated the conflict in 2005. IGAD provided the peace process with an air of legitimacy. This, in turn, allowed the IGAD mediation team to provide a problem-solving forum to resolve the underlying conflict issues. In addition, from early 2001 onwards, western diplomats started playing an active role in the peace negotiations, when the cooperation between the US, the UK and Norway – which came to be known as the Troika – was formalised at a meeting in London on 24 October 2001. The Troika representatives supported the IGAD initiative by occasionally putting pressure on the conflict parties, upon request by Sumbeiywo, in order to break deadlocks.[55]

Several mediators closely involved in the process agree that while the Troika provided crucial pressure, it was the sustained effort of IGAD that lies at the heart of the successful mediation effort. For instance, Susan Page, a US advisor within the IGAD secretariat for peace in Sudan, notes that the while the donors are claiming credit, it was the presidents of the region who succeeded in resolving the conflict.[56] Similarly, Luca Zampetti, an Italian observer to the Naivasha process, argues that 'it was the IGAD mediation team led by Sumbeiywo that made the CPA happen. While the work of IGAD enjoyed a sound supporting structure provided by international parties, I believe there is no doubt that only an African institution could have pulled this off. Naivasha was an African success. Full stop'.[57] In short, pressure and inducements by the Troika helped to move the conflict parties towards compliance, but this capacity-based mediation strategy would not have been sufficient by itself. Pressure and inducement cannot adequately explain the conclusion of the CPA. It was the high degree of legitimacy of IGAD that allowed the IGAD mediation team to maintain the commitment of the conflict parties towards finding a mutually acceptable agreement that could end the war.

In spite of a conflict over the contested Abyei area, the conflict parties remained committed to the referendum stipulated in the CPA. Against a background of a promise by the conflict parties that they would accept any outcome and strong diplomatic involvement both from the African Union (AU) and the US, the referendum on self-determination for Southern Sudan took place between 9 and 15 January 2011. A couple of days prior to the start of this referendum, President al-Bashir gave a speech in Juba on 4 January 2011, in which he emphasised how his commitment to pan-Africanism made him highly committed to abide by the referendum results: 'Whatever be the choice of the Southerners, we will accept it and say welcome . . . But let us provide a good example for brothers in Africa, even if we separate and we will do it peacefully, we will cooperate and provide them with the example of how the United States of Africa could be'.[58] Indeed, the referendum was held peacefully and it was officially announced on 7 February 2011 that 98.83 per cent of the Southerners that had voted chose an independent South Sudan. Moreover, the voter turnout was close to 100 per cent in most locations. The referendum held in early 2011 led to secession of South Sudan on 9 July

2011. This ended almost six decades of conflict, which had taken the lives of around 2 million people.[59]

Conclusion

In conclusion, considering that mediation is a voluntary process, it is striking that third party legitimacy has received almost no scholarly attention. Conflict parties need to give their consent to both the involvement of the mediator and the final outcome of the mediation process, yet mediation in civil wars has predominantly been studied from a materialist perspective that prescribes that conflict parties need to be coerced or induced. A government concedes part of its sovereignty when it accepts international mediation, yet few studies have addressed what factors contribute to legitimate third party involvement and how this level of legitimacy affects the subsequent mediation process.

More generally, as noted in the introduction to this volume, legitimacy is still often equated with a justification for rule. This chapter has gone beyond this Weberian understanding of legitimacy. This chapter has also gone beyond the dominant understanding of international legitimacy as resting on the common maintenance of the state-system, international law and norms of human rights. Instead, taking a sociological perspective, this chapter takes belief systems, norms, and identity as the starting point for the international legitimacy of third parties involved in civil wars in Africa.

The norm of African solutions to African conflicts – which itself is based on various other norms, including the norms of anti-colonialism, non-alignment, and African unity – puts moral pressure on conflict parties in civil wars in Africa to make peace in the interest of Africa. Indeed, the commitment of the IGAD to the African solutions norm provided the IGAD mediation team with a high degree of legitimacy, which allowed the IGAD mediation team to maintain the commitment of the conflict parties to the mediation process and pull the conflict parties towards making peace. The diplomatic involvement of IGAD in the conflict between the GoS and the SPLM/A thus demonstrates how third party legitimacy contributes to mediation success. As such, this chapter shows – similar to scholarly work that shows that legitimacy matters on the local level – that legitimacy can pull elites embroiled in national-level civil wars towards peace.

In conclusion, I have argued that third party legitimacy – which in the case of African third parties flows from their commitment to the African solutions norm – makes third party involvement more acceptable. This legitimacy-based perspective on the understanding of mediation success is quite different from that consistently pursued in the contemporary literature, opening up a new research agenda.

Notes

1. See: Touval, 'The Superpowers as Mediators'; Zartman, *Ripe for Resolution: Conflict and Intervention in Africa*; Rothchild, *Managing Ethnic Conflict in Africa: Pressures and Incentives for Cooperation*; Sisk, *International Mediation in Civil Wars: Bargaining with Bullets*; Smith and Stam, 'Mediation and peacekeeping in a random walk model of civil and interstate war'; Favretto, 'Should peacemakers take sides? Major power mediation, coercion, and bias'.
2. Weber, *Gesammelte Politische Schriften*.
3. Duursma, 'A current literature review of international mediation', pp. 81–98; Duursma 'When to get out of the trench: using smart pressure to resolve civil wars', pp. 43–61.
4. Zartman, *Ripe for Resolution: Conflict and Intervention in Africa*.
5. Barnett and Duvall, 'Power in international politics', p. 40.
6. Rothchild, *Managing Ethnic Conflict in Africa: Pressures and Incentives for Cooperation*, p. 109.
7. Bercovitch, 'International mediation and dispute settlement: evaluating the conditions for successful mediation', p. 28.
8. See Beardsley et al., 'Mediation style and crisis outcomes'; Svensson, 'Mediation with muscles or minds? Exploring power mediators and pure mediators in civil wars'.
9. Greig and Diehl, *International Mediation*, War and Conflict in the Modern World, p. 71.
10. Young, *The Intermediaries: Third Parties in International Crises*, pp. 80–91.
11. Rubin, 'Conclusion: international mediation in context', p. 255.
12. Princen, *Intermediaries in International Conflict*; 'Mediation by a transnational organization: the case of the Vatican'.
13. Wendt distinguishes between coercion, calculation and belief. Wendt, *Social Theory of International Politics*, pp. 247–50. Kratochwil identifies institutional sanctions, rule-utilitarianism and emotional attachment as distinct types of social control. Kratochwil, *Rules, Norms and Decisions: On the Conditions of Practical and Legal Reasoning in International Relations and Domestic Affairs*, p. 97. March and Olson talk about a logic of expected consequences and a logic appropriateness. March and Olsen, 'The institutional dynamics of international political orders', p. 54.
14. Hurd, 'Legitimacy and authority in international politics', p. 381.
15. Ibid. p. 379.
16. Ibid. Other scholars also emphasise the normative dimension of legitimacy. Franck, *The Power of Legitimacy among Nations*, p. 235; Beetham, *The Legitimation of Power*, Issues in Political Theory, p. 5; Clark, *Legitimacy in International Society*, p. 2.
17. Beetham, *The Legitimation of Power*, p. 6.
18. See Convention (I) For the Pacific Settlement of International Disputes (The Hague I), (29 July 1899); Charter of the United Nations, (26 June 1945), Article 33.
19. Duursma, 'Partnering to make peace: the effectiveness of joint African and non-African mediation effort', pp. 590–615.

20. See Zartman, 'Africa as a subordinate state system in international relations'; 'The OAU in the African state system: interaction and evaluation', p. 29; Foltz, 'The organization of African unity and the resolution of Africa's conflicts'; Williams, 'From non-intervention to non-indifference: the origins and development of the African Union's security culture', p. 261; Dersso, 'The quest for pax Africana: the case of the African Union's peace and security regime'.

21. Červenka, *The unfinished quest for unity: Africa and the organisation of African unity*, p. 65.

22. Franck, *The Power of Legitimacy among Nations*, p. 24.

23. Kelman, 'Compliance, identification and internalization: three processes of attitude change'.

24. Tyler, 'The psychology of legitimacy: a relational perspective on voluntary deference to authorities', p. 336.

25. Cohen, 'African capabilities for managing conflict: the role of the United States', p. 78–9.

26. Ibid. endnote 4.

27. Interview with Mohamed el-Amin Khalifa in Khartoum, 18 December 2014.

28. Khadiagala, *Meddlers or Mediators? African Interveners in Civil Conflicts in Eastern Africa*, p. 194.

29. Interview with Ghazi Salah al-Din al-Atabani in Khartoum, 7 December 2014.

30. Iyob and Khadiagala, *Sudan: The Elusive Quest for Peace*, p. 104.

31. Interview with Bona Malwal in Oxford, 11 November 2014.

32. Interview with Lual Deng in Addis Ababa, 3 February 2015.

33. Ofuho, 'Negotiating peace: restarting a moribund process', p. 20.

34. Khadiagala, *Meddlers or Mediators? African Interveners in Civil Conflicts in Eastern Africa*, p. 195.

35. Interview with Mohamed el-Amin Khalifa in Khartoum, 18 December 2014; Interview with Mutrif Siddiq in Khartoum, 13 January 2015. See also Iyob and Khadiagala, *Sudan: The Elusive Quest for Peace*, p. 106; Khadiagala, *Meddlers or Mediators? African Interveners in Civil Conflicts in Eastern Africa*, pp. 199–200; El-Affendi, 'The impasse in the IGAD peace process for Sudan: the limits of regional peacemaking?', p. 586.

36. Khadiagala, *Meddlers or Mediators? African Interveners in Civil Conflicts in Eastern Africa*, pp. 200–1.

37. Wöndu and Lesch, *Battle for Peace in Sudan: An Analysis of the Abuja Conferences, 1992–1993*, p. 162.

38. Ibid. pp. 166–7; Khadiagala, *Meddlers or Mediators? African Interveners in Civil Conflicts in Eastern Africa*, p. 206; Barltrop, *Darfur and the International Community: The Challenges of Conflict Resolution in Sudan*, pp. 46–7; El-Affendi, 'The impasse in the IGAD peace process for Sudan: the limits of regional peacemaking?', p. 588.

39. Interview with Mutrif Siddiq in Khartoum, 13 January 2015.

40. Simmons and Dixon, 'The mediator's perspective: an interview with General Lazaro Sumbeiywo', p. 23.

41. Interview with Sayed el-Tayeb in Khartoum, 8 January 2015; Johnson, *Waging Peace in Sudan: The Inside Story of the Negotiations That Ended Africa's Longest Civil War*, p. 49; Stiansen, 'How important is religion? The case of the Sudan peace negotiations'; Rolandsen, 'A quick fix? A retrospective analysis of the Sudan comprehensive peace agreement'.

42. Young, *The Fate of Sudan: The Origins and Consequences of a Flawed Peace Process*, p. 101.

43. Waihenya, *The Mediator*, pp. 96–8; Rolandsen, 'Sudan: the role of foreign involvement in the shaping and implementation of the Sudan comprehensive peace agreement', p. 80.

44. Simmons and Dixon, 'The mediator's perspective: an interview with General Lazaro Sumbeiywo', p. 24.

45. Ibid.; Waihenya, *The Mediator*, p. 99.

46. Johnson, *Waging Peace in Sudan: The inside Story of the Negotiations That Ended Africa's Longest Civil War*, p. 63.

47. Iyob and Khadiagala, *Sudan: The Elusive Quest for Peace*, pp. 122–3; Johnson, *Waging Peace in Sudan: The inside Story of the Negotiations That Ended Africa's Longest Civil War*, p. 70.

48. Khadiagala, *Meddlers or Mediators? African Interveners in Civil Conflicts in Eastern Africa*, p. 243.

49. Interview with Douglas Johnson in Oxford, 27 February 2015. Douglas Johnson acted as a resource person to the mediation team in the Comprehensive Peace Agreement negotiations over the Three Areas. See also Rothchild, 'Conditions for mediation success: evaluating us initiatives in Sudan and Liberia', p. 101; Rolandsen, 'Sudan: The role of foreign involvement in the shaping and implementation of the Sudan comprehensive peace agreement', p. 82.

50. Telephone interview with Jason Matus, 26 January 2015. See also Johnson, 'Why Abyei matters: the breaking point of Sudan's comprehensive peace agreement?'

51. Rolandsen, 'Sudan: The role of foreign involvement in the shaping and implementation of the Sudan comprehensive peace agreement', p. 82.

52. The text of the CPA is available at <http://www.ucdp.uu.se/gpdatabase/peace/Sud%2020050109.pdf>

53. Brosché, *Sharing Power – Enabling Peace? Evaluating Sudan's Comprehensive Peace Agreement*, p. 17.

54. Ibid. pp. 20–3.

55. Johnson, *Waging Peace in Sudan: The inside Story of the Negotiations That Ended Africa's Longest Civil War*, p. 42.

56. Martin, *Kings of Peace Pawns of War: The Untold Story of Peacemaking*, p. 151.

57. Interview with Luca Zampetti in Addis Ababa, 4 February 2015.

58. Young, *The Fate of Sudan: The Origins and Consequences of a Flawed Peace Process*, p. 211.

59. Copnall, *A Poisonous Thorn in Our Hearts: Sudan and South Sudan's Bitter and Incomplete Divorce*, p. 265; LeRiche and Arnold, *South Sudan: From Revolution to Independence*, p. 1.

References

Barltrop, R., *Darfur and the International Community: The Challenges of Conflict Resolution in Sudan* (London: I. B. Tauris, 2011).

Barnett, M. and R. Duvall, 'Power in international politics', *International Organization* 2005, 59: 1, pp. 39–75.

Beardsley, K., D. M. Quinn, B. Biswas and J. Wilkenfeld, 'Mediation style and crisis outcomes', *The Journal of Conflict Resolution* 2006, 50: 1, pp. 58–86.

Beetham, D., *The Legitimation of Power: Issues in Political Theory* (Basingstoke: Macmillan, 1991).

Bercovitch, J., 'International mediation and dispute settlement: evaluating the conditions for successful mediation', *Negotiation Journal* 1991, 7: 1, pp. 17–30.

Brosché, J., *Sharing Power – Enabling Peace? Evaluating Sudan's Comprehensive Peace Agreement* (Uppsala: United Nations Mediation Support Unit and Department of Peace and Conflict Research, 2009).

Červenka, Z., *The unfinished quest for unity: Africa and the Organisation of African Unity* (London: J. Friedman, 1977).

Charter of the United Nations, 26 June 1945.

Clark, I., *Legitimacy in International Society*, (Oxford: Oxford University Press, 2005).

Cohen, H. J., 'African capabilities for managing conflict: the role of the United States', in D. R. Smock and C. A. Crocker (eds), *African Conflict Resolution: The US Role in Peacemaking* (Washington, DC: United States Institute of Peace Press, 1995).

Convention (I) for the Pacific Settlement of International Disputes (The Hague I), 29 July 1899.

Copnall, J., *A Poisonous Thorn in Our Hearts: Sudan and South Sudan's Bitter and Incomplete Divorce* (Oxford: Oxford University Press, 2014).

Dersso, S. A., 'The quest for pax Africana: the case of the African Union's peace and security regime', *African Journal on Conflict Resolution* 2012, 12: p. 2.

Duursma A., 'A current literature review of international mediation', *International Journal of Conflict Management* 2014, 25: pp. 81–98.

Duursma, A., 'Partnering to make peace: the effectiveness of joint African and non-African mediation efforts', *International Peacekeeping* 2017a, 24: 4, pp. 590–615.

Duursma A., 'When to get out of the trench: using smart pressure to resolve civil wars', *Civil Wars* 2017b, 17: pp. 43–61.

El-Affendi, A., 'The impasse in the IGAD peace process for Sudan: the limits of regional peacemaking?' *African Affairs* Oct 2001, 100: 401, pp. 581–99.

Favretto, K., 'Should peacemakers take sides? Major power mediation, coercion, and bias', *The American Political Science Review* 2009, 103: 2, pp. 248–63.

Foltz, W. J. 'The organization of African unity and the resolution of Africa's conflicts', in F. M. Deng and I. W. Zartman (eds), *Conflict Resolution in Africa* (Washington, DC: Brookings Institution, 1991).

Franck, T. M., *The Power of Legitimacy among Nations* (Oxford: Oxford University Press, 1990).

Greig, J. M. and P. F. Diehl, *International Mediation*, War and Conflict in the Modern World (Cambridge: Polity, 2012).

Hurd, I., 'Legitimacy and authority in international politics', *International Organization* 1999, 53: 2, pp. 379–408.

Iyob, R. and G. M. Khadiagala, *Sudan: The Elusive Quest for Peace* (Boulder: Lynne Rienner Publishers, 2006).

Johnson, D. H., 'Why Abyei matters: the breaking point of Sudan's comprehensive peace agreement?' *African Affairs* Jan 2008, 107: 426, pp. 1–19.

Johnson, H. F., *Waging Peace in Sudan: The Inside Story of the Negotiations That Ended Africa's Longest Civil War* (Eastbourne: Sussex Academic Press, 2011).

Kelman, H. C., 'Compliance, identification and internalization: three processes of attitude change', *Journal of Conflict Resolution* 1958, 2: 1, pp. 51–60.

Khadiagala, G. M., *Meddlers or Mediators? African Interveners in Civil Conflicts in Eastern Africa* (Leiden: Martinus Nijhoff, 2007).

Kratochwil, F. V., *Rules, Norms and Decisions: On the Conditions of Practical and Legal Reasoning in International Relations and Domestic Affairs*, Cambridge Studies in International Relations (Cambridge: Cambridge University Press, 1989).

LeRiche, M., and M. Arnold, *South Sudan: From Revolution to Independence* (Oxford: Oxford University Press, 2013).

March, J. G. and J. P. Olsen, 'The institutional dynamics of international political orders', *International Organization* 1998, 52: 4, pp. 943–69.

Martin, H., *Kings of Peace Pawns of War: The Untold Story of Peacemaking* (London: Bloomsbury Academic, 2006).

Ofuho, C. H., 'Negotiating peace: restarting a moribund process', in M. Simmons and P. Dixon (eds), *Peace by Piece: Addressing Sudan's Conflicts* (London: Conciliation Resources, 2006), pp. 18–19.

Princen, T., *Intermediaries in International Conflict* (Princeton: Princeton University Press, 1992).

Princen, T., 'Mediation by a transnational organization: the case of the Vatican', in J. Bercovitch and J. Z. Rubin (eds), *Mediation in International Relations: Multiple Approaches to Conflict Management* (Basingstoke: Macmillan, 1992), p. 283.

Reus-Smit, C., 'International crises of legitimacy', *International Politics* 2007, 44: 2–3, pp. 157–74.

Rolandsen, O. H., 'A quick fix? A retrospective analysis of the Sudan comprehensive peace agreement', *Review of African Political Economy* 2011, 38: 130, pp. 551–64.

Rolandsen, O. H., 'Sudan: the role of foreign involvement in the shaping and implementation of the Sudan comprehensive peace agreement', in M. Eriksson (ed.), *Mediation and Liberal Peacebuilding: Peace from the Ashes of War?* (London: Routledge, 2013), pp. 76–91.

Rothchild, D., 'Conditions for mediation success: evaluating US initiatives in Sudan and Liberia', in T. Lyons and G. M. Khadiagala (eds), *Conflict Management and African Politics: Ripeness, Bargaining, and Mediation*, xii (London: Routledge, 2008), p. 154.

Rothchild, D. S., *Managing Ethnic Conflict in Africa: Pressures and Incentives for Cooperation* (Washington, DC: Brookings Institution Press, 1997).

Rubin, J. Z., 'Conclusion: international mediation in context', in J. Bercovitch and J. Z. Rubin (eds), *Mediation in International Relations: Multiple Approaches to Conflict Management* (Basingstoke: Macmillan, 1992), p. 283.

Simmons, M. and P. Dixon, 'The mediator's perspective: an interview with General Lazaro Sumbeiywo', in M. Simmons and P. Dixon (eds), *Peace by Piece: Addressing Sudan's Conflicts* (London: Conciliation Resources, 2006), pp. 18–19.

Sisk, T. D., *International Mediation in Civil Wars: Bargaining with Bullets* (London: Routledge, 2009).

Smith, A. and A. Stam, 'Mediation and peacekeeping in a random walk model of civil and interstate war', *International Studies Review* 2003, 5: 4, pp. 115–35.

Stiansen, E., 'How important is religion? The case of the Sudan peace negotiations', International Peace Research Institute Oslo (PRIO), Oslo Forum 2006.

Svensson, I., 'Mediation with muscles or minds? Exploring power mediators and pure mediators in civil wars', *International Negotiation* 2007, 12: 2, pp. 229–48.

Touval, S., 'The superpowers as mediators', in J. Bercovitch and J. Z. Rubin (eds), *Mediation in International Relations: Multiple Approaches to Conflict Management* (Basingstoke: Macmillan, 1992) p. 283.

Tyler, T. R., 'The psychology of legitimacy: a relational perspective on voluntary deference to authorities', *Personality and Social Psychology Review* 1997, 1: 4, pp. 323–45.

Waihenya, W., *The Mediator* (Nairobi: Kenway Publications, 2006).

Weber, M., *Gesammelte Politische Schriften*, Johannes Winckelmann (ed.), Vol. 2 (Tobingen: Mohr Paul Siebeck, 1958).

Wendt, A., *Social Theory of International Politics*, Cambridge Studies in International Relations (Cambridge: Cambridge University Press, 1999).

Williams, P. D., 'From non-intervention to non-indifference: the origins and development of the African Union's security culture', *African Affairs* 2007, 106: 423, pp. 253–79.

Wöndu, S. and A. M. Lesch, *Battle for Peace in Sudan: An Analysis of the Abuja Conferences, 1992–1993* (Lanham: University Press of America, 2000).

Young, J., *The Fate of Sudan: The Origins and Consequences of a Flawed Peace Process* (London: Zed Books, 2012).

Young, O. R., *The Intermediaries: Third Parties in International Crises* (Princeton, NJ: Princeton University Press, 1967).

Zartman, I. W., 'Africa as a subordinate state system in international relations', *International Organization* 1967, 21: 3, pp. 545–64.

Zartman, I. W., 'The OAU in the African state system: interaction and evaluation', in Y. El-Ayouty and I. W. Zartman (eds), *The OAU After Twenty Years* (New York: Praeger, 1984).

Zartman, I. W., *Ripe for Resolution: Conflict and Intervention in Africa* (Oxford: Oxford University Press, 1985).

TEN

Post-War Legitimacy: A Framework on Relational Agency in Peacebuilding

Florian Krampe and Lisa Ekman

Introduction

There is increasing interest in the role of legitimacy as an indicator of social and political stability in post-war societies. In this chapter we provide an analytical framework to examine peacebuilding interventions from a legitimacy perspective. The relationship between the state and society is conceived as crucial to international peacebuilding interventions seeking to assist conflict-torn countries toward a self-sustaining peace – or a situation where external support is unnecessary.[1] The literature on peacebuilding primarily has discussed the importance of legitimacy *of* peacebuilding interventions. However, we argue that contemporary peacebuilding interventions and the scholarly assessments of them have largely overlooked the relationship between the domestic actors involved in, and affected by, the conflict.

Instead of focusing on the principal purpose of peacebuilding processes, which is to build sustainable peace within a country, peacebuilding interventions deal with legitimacy as a tool to justify the peacebuilding agenda and approaches of international actors. The international quest for legitimacy has paradoxically redirected attention away from addressing the important challenge facing domestic peacebuilding processes, namely the peaceful relationship between the domestic state and society. We conceive of peacebuilding as founded in the relational agency between politics and society, i.e. between state and non-state actors (both military and civilian). We define peacebuilding as the *process* where in a post-war situation the structural-normative setup of the state in relation to society becomes renegotiated through the *interactions* of domestic state and non-state actors with, or without, the involvement of international or other external actors. We maintain that perceived legitimacy of the relationship between the domestic state and society constitutes the foundation of the social and political post-war order.

In this chapter we begin by discussing the existing peacebuilding literature and practices, before articulating our framework on legitimacy, actors and relational agency in peacebuilding. Thereafter, we present an extended application of the framework on two recent peacebuilding processes. The chapter concludes by stressing the necessity to refocus peacebuilding interventions to the relational dynamics and legitimacy of domestic state and non-state actors.

From liberal peacebuilding to broader peacebuilding

In the early post-Cold War period, the UN Security Council, with newfound confidence, authorised an unparalleled number of multilateral military operations broadly referred to as peace operations to intervene in internal armed conflicts.[2] Concurrently, the UN's 'Agenda for Peace' introduced the concept of peacebuilding, which had salient impact on the discourse and practices of international intervention.[3] The notion of peacebuilding was rooted in liberal ideals of fostering democratic peace by supporting post-war states to establish strong democratic institutions and macroeconomic growth based on a capitalist market economy.[4] The liberal agenda was envisioned as the key instrument of the international community to bring about lasting peace. In the process of liberal peacebuilding, the host state's sovereignty would often be suspended and an international trustee – typically in form of a UN mission – would shoulder all state institutions and functions until the host state was fit to resume its sovereign responsibilities.[5]

However, with the repeated failures of international peacebuilding interventions in the late 1990s, the literature grew increasingly critical, highlighting especially three main areas. The first relates to the normative agenda of peacebuilding interventions, its content and meaning; the second to the practice and implementation of peacebuilding; and the third to the complex and multidimensional relationships of different actors in the context of peacebuilding interventions.[6]

The explicit and underlying normative content of liberal peacebuilding has sparked a lively debate among scholars. Pugh argues that international peacebuilding interventions are simply a tool to safeguard Western capitalism because they are 'not simply about promoting good governance and reducing chaos (...), but also to sustain hegemonic power over the global economic future'.[7] Similarly, Noam Chomsky argues that peacebuilding interventions of the 1990s were, in fact, a form of neo-imperialism, as they sought to shape the new liberal post-war order by transferring assumed international norms and values onto local recipients.[8] Scholars frequently describe this relationship as external imposition because local actors are treated as 'objects to be transformed'.[9] Whereas this critique may appear as a rebuttal of liberalism as such, David Chandler, one of the foremost critics of liberal peacebuilding, has argued that the norms guiding today's liberal peacebuilding interventions are, in fact, anything but liberal.[10] Critics of the liberal peace agenda continued to work within the normative frame-work they critiqued, as 'there is no realistic alternative to some form of liberal peacebuilding strategy'.[11] In this vein of thought, James D. Fearon and David Laitin argued that international assistance was necessary and justified in weak and post-war states because even though locally built peace would be the most 'natural' pathway to rebuilding states after war, 'the local and international costs and risks of such "natural" processes of state formation can be very high'.[12]

Multiple studies have illustrated how the explicit and underlying norma-tive content of liberal peacebuilding has inevitably shaped the practices of different actors in the context of peacebuilding interventions. Roland Paris argued that peacebuilding interventions focused too strongly on implement-ing a quick post-war transition toward democratic rule, thereby effectively inflicting renewed conflict by introducing a competitive political system in already weak states.[13] In addition, the predominance of the liberal agenda has been argued to cause an over-reliance on international ownership and top-down character of peacebuilding practices. Even though well-intended,[14] the strong normative and practical (or social-material) influence actively suppresses the agency of local actors, and thereby produces a set of new problems.[15] While successful at pacifying active fighting in many cases, peace-building interventions have nevertheless contributed to 'un-ending' or 'freez-ing' conflicts, leaving post-war societies in a 'no-war, no-peace' situation.[16]

The increased complexity of contemporary post-war contexts has raised the issue of alternative approaches to peacebuilding. Especially the work by Roger Mac Ginty demonstrates that liberal peacebuilding interventions have met local resistance. This resistance is argued to generate a hybrid peace that is neither the liberal peace that external actors intended, nor the peace envisioned by local actors.[17] Subsequently, studies increasingly focus on the agency of local actors in peace processes, which has been shown to exist and persevere during peace processes.[18] This strand of research advo-cates for a 'multidimensional' framework of peacebuilding that works from different understandings of peace as an alternative to the prevalent liberal peacebuilding agenda.[19]

Analytical Framework

Legitimacy has been a central concept in the understanding of politics, the state and societies for centuries.[20] Drawing on existing scholarship, this chapter puts forth an analytical framework to study peacebuilding interventions through an actor-oriented approach. The framework rests on three basic assumptions about post-war peacebuilding: i) peacebuilding is an actor-driven, relational process to establish a legitimate form of governance; ii) the matter of legitimacy is largely rooted in the matter of perceived ownership in the peacebuilding process, namely who has the authority to design and implement peacebuilding practices and whom are perceived to be the main beneficiary of its reforms; iii) domestic and international actors both have agency to influence the principal relationship in post-war peacebuilding, namely that between the domestic state and its population.

Relational Agency in Post-war Peacebuilding

Peacebuilding is rooted in the relationship between politics, namely the state in particular, and the wider society.[21] We define peacebuilding as the process wherein the structural-normative setup of the post-war state vis-à-vis society is renegotiated through various interactions between domestic state and non-state actors with, or without, the involvement of international or other external actors. The stability of this new social and political order is dependent upon its legitimacy among the people it governs.

In the context of international peacebuilding interventions, the domestic relationship between the state and society is shaped by the relational dynamics between different domestic and international actors. Ideally, local citizens perceive the involvement of foreign peacebuilders as not only necessary, but legitimate.[22] However, the issue of legitimacy is closely linked to that of ownership, and what actors are viewed to exert influence on the conditions and implementation of the national peacebuilding process. Existing literature generally approaches ownership as either 'local' (or domestic) that emphasises a 'bottom-up approach' and communitarian decision-making or 'international', whereby external actors exert significant influence on the peacebuilding process in accordance with the liberal peace agenda. In terms of the latter, international actors commonly still referred to it as 'local ownership' based on the prevalent assumption of local compliance to international, universal norms. As such, ownership in terms of local agency and control is the envisioned outcome of peacebuilding, not necessarily the principal focus during the peacebuilding process.[23]

This has sparked debate between the proponents of domestic owner-ship[24] and those in favour of international ownership.[25] David Chandler argues that any international involvement constitutes an external imposi-tion that obstructs domestic agency.[26] Anna Jarstad and Louise Olsson argue that domestic ownership appears impossible as long as the peacebuilding intervention is characterized by a tangible power asymmetry between inter-national and domestic actors, which creates 'a partly symbiotic and partly destructive relationship'.[27] Similarly, others add nuance to the perceived dichotomy of domestic and international ownership by arguing that the dynamics between international and domestic agency, ultimately, generate a form of hybrid peace.[28]

We argue that the current focus on ownership limits the analytical reach to study agency in a descriptive manner, rather than a normative, prescrip-tive standpoint. The reason for this is that it does not help us identify whom the citizens and society in the post-war country identify as the legitimate owners of peace. Instead, applying an actor-oriented approach enables a more nuanced understanding of the peacebuilding process. The common vertical distinction of actors between local and global is misleading, as it conflates different actors groups with important distinguishing features; in particular, it treats state and society as one and the same social system. Thereby it negates the existence of multiple identities in favour of 'a singular set of social values and norms'.[29]

We therefore suggest following Holsti's definition of high-level of legiti-macy, as contingent on both vertical legitimacy (between the state and society) and horizontal legitimacy (among different communities within the state).[30] Thereby, we disaggregate actors along additional dimensions and sharpening the study of peacebuilding 'beyond the broad categories of conflict between the local and the global'.[31] This actor-oriented approach demonstrates that legitimate authority may establish in alternative spaces, generating different, 'multi-dimensional' understandings of what consti-tutes a legitimate post-war peace.[32] As such, it recognises the limits of tradi-tional understandings of social contracts as confined to a single authority, while exploring the alternative of multiple and, perhaps conflicting, author-ities as important to conceptions of post-war legitimacy.

For the purpose of this framework, we disaggregate actors along two axes: vertical and horizontal, as well as domestic and international, creating four different categories of actor groups of particular interest to post-war peace-building (see Figure 10.1). The division of actors into these four categories has a number of advantages: i) it provides a more nuanced disaggregation of both the international and domestic actors involved in the peacebuild-ing process; ii) it enables a shift in focus to the principal relationship in the

	State actor	*Non-state actor*
International	State actors and intergovernmental organizations (civilian and military) that act across national platforms at the international level of peace-building operations	Non-governmental organizations or groups (civilian and military) that work across national platforms at the international level of peacebuilding operations
Domestic	Local actors (civilian and military) that are affiliated with or representing the government in the post-conflict country	Non-governmental organizations or groups (civilian and military) living in the post-conflict country

Figure 10.1 Matrix of actor groups in post-war peacebuilding.

peacebuilding process, namely that between the state and society; iii) it provides more accurate grounds for illustrating dynamics of agency in post-war peacebuilding. Nevertheless, merging vastly different types of actors within the same category holds some important limitations. Although conceived as ideal types, in reality, the distinction between different actor groups is usually elusive. Yet, we argue that the diversity contained *within* each category is best addressed in the scope of individual research endeavours that can discuss at greater length the distinguishing features of the specific actors and relationships of interest.

Post-War Legitimacy

The role of legitimacy in post-war peacebuilding has gained increased attention in the literature, both at the domestic and international levels.[33] Legitimacy offers a 'midterm definition of peace' that is broader than the more frequently used concept of peace as 'the absence of armed conflict', but more substantive than the open-ended notion of 'positive peace'.[34] Moreover, legitimacy is less normatively biased and allows for a broader array of political systems to be recognised as locally acceptable structures of peace.[35] As such, we recognise the existence of multiple understandings of legitimacy in different societies and contexts. To that end, legitimacy constitutes an emancipatory concept that stresses the importance of local societies in determining the legitimacy of post-war political systems.[36] This relational understanding of legitimacy neither excludes nor challenges the role of the state, as done by some other post-Westphalian perspectives. Nor does it understate the agency of society in shaping the post-war order.

In existing scholarship, legitimacy is either defined by a set of normative criteria, such as a legal framework, or empirical criteria, such as actors' perceptions, belief systems, attitudes and behaviour. These understandings are widely believed to interact in mutually influential ways. For instance, Kalevi Holsti understands legitimacy as defined by the linkages between the physical, attitudinal and institutional components of a state.[37] Moreover, legitimacy is a relational concept closely linked to the notion of authority, as it gives authorities the perceived right 'to act', 'to exist', or to 'perform an activity in a certain way'.[38] Belief in the legitimacy of the state constitutes the core of well-functioning state–society relations with peaceful and voluntary transitions of power, as '[i]t is an acceptance, even approbation, of the state's rules of the game, its social control, as true and right . . . It indicates people's approval of the state's desired social order through their acceptance of the state's myth'.[39] Weber famously wrote, 'the basis of every system of authority, and correspondingly of every kind of willingness to obey, is a belief, a belief by virtue of which persons exercising authority are lent prestige'.[40] Thus, the importance of a belief in legitimacy is not to be understated. Resultantly, existing scholarship has recognised the role of perceptions in shaping peacebuilding dynamics in post-war countries.

Challenges to Post-War Legitimacy

In countries affected by internal armed conflict, the social contract between local citizens and state authorities is corrupted, compromised or more often completely eroded. Peacebuilding activities are intended to influence, shape and support the process of rebuilding the broken social contract, which is why the legitimacy of the state–society relationship, namely the consensual and peaceful conferral of political authority, is of the utmost importance.

There are a number of ways in which actors involved in peacebuilding affect the perceived legitimacy of state–society relations. In this section we briefly outline the actor groups between which relational dynamics influence, and possibly challenge, the legitimacy of domestic state–society relations (see Figure 10.2). By sketching out these different sets of relations, we suggest that 'post-war' contexts are likely to experience multiple and fluctuating understandings of what constitutes a legitimate authority depending on the changing dynamics of the conflict at hand. Unlike traditional liberal notions of legitimate authority based on international law and norms, this suggests that peacebuilders – both domestic and international – need

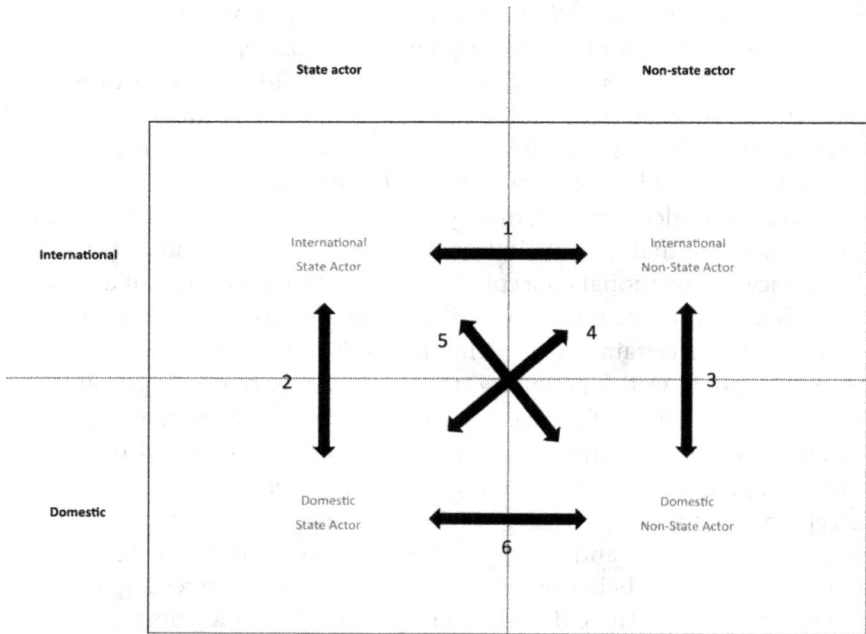

Figure 10.2 Relational dynamics and challenges to legitimacy.

to find ways to work more productively with the expected plurality and hybridity of locally-perceived legitimate authorities, as well as more critically address their own roles in shaping these, possibly conflict-reinforcing, relationships.

(1) International state and international non-state actors. In the mid-1990s, a set of 'new' external state actors – regional organisations and coalitions of the willing – entered the realm of peacebuilding alongside the UN. The literature on inter-organisational collaboration expanded to address the relationship between intervening state and non-state actors in the context of post-war multidimensional peacebuilding interventions. Intervening actors with different institutional objectives, structures and cultures were expected to coordinate their activities, which added further complexity of the peacebuilding setting.[41] The principal divide concerned the relationship between civilian and military actors,[42] principally deployed armed forces and non-governmental humanitarian organisations.[43] Increasingly close interaction and collaboration between military actors and humanitarian agencies is identified to challenge the legitimacy of traditionally 'neutral' actors.[44] More recently, the literature has also recognised the relational dynamics

between militaries of different national contingents and mission structures, or between private contractors and state militaries.[45] Moreover, it reveals how, instead of focusing on the critical endogenous challenges of post-war countries and the domestic relationship, international actors debate among themselves legitimacy concerns tied to the implementation of the peace-building intervention rather than the conflict at hand.[46]

(2) International state actors and domestic state actors. Existing literature on peacebuilding interventions centres on the relationship between external state actors and host–state authorities. This focus has generated an understanding of post-war legitimacy as a largely top-down, state-centric and legalistic phenomenon, measureable with indicators such as host–state consent, UN Security Council authorisation, and a broad representation among troop-contributing countries. The widespread appeal of this approach is understandable, as it resonates with the liberal peace agenda that external actors have the power to intervene in post-war countries and thereby change local perceptions of state legitimacy and effectiveness,[47] echoing the Western understanding of armed forces as suitable actors to implement 'policy by other means'. Although existing scholarship presents convincing empirical evidence to support the claim that international peacekeepers are relatively effective in shortening the duration of armed conflict, curbing its lethality and prolonging (negative) peace after war,[48] there is also a growing critique of both intended and unintended influence of international intervention on domestic state actors, typically labelled as dynamics of a hybrid peace.[49] While again occupied with the manufactured challenge for legitimacy deriving from the intervention, this line of inquiry has highlighted what Oliver Richmond calls the 'infrapolitics of peacebuild-ing', namely the existence of 'significant agency at the local level'.[50]

(3) International non-state actors and domestic non-state actors. There is now a strong emphasis in the peacebuilding literature on the inclusiveness of non-state actors, stressing the benefits of domestic and international non-state actors.[51] However, several scholars contend that this has not translated into actual inclusion of those actors in peacebuilding practice.[52] Research on international negotiations suggests that non-state actors are a positive complement to state actors, but their inclusion and exclusion in negotiated processes is highly dependent on the host government's motivation and interest.[53] Moreover, as previously argued, international non-state actors and state actors have been found to compete for influence in post-war countries, resulting in tensions that further aggravate the exclusion of domestic actors and challenge the perception of international non-state actors' legitimacy.[54] International and domestic non-state actors may cater to international state actors by a) using them as a source of income,[55] or b) by serving

as legitimating agents by producing specific knowledge of interest to international state actors. For example, an analysis of the International Crisis Group (ICG), an international non-state actor, shows how ICG reports on peacebuilding in Bosnia and Herzegovina (BiH) served as an instrument for 'US diplomats to shape the course of intervention in BiH'.[56]

(4) International non-state actors and domestic state actors. Particularly in the transitional justice debate surrounding today's peacebuilding interventions, there is strong emphasis on the role that international non-state actors play in influencing domestic state actors. In Afghanistan, the transitional justice community has objected to and criticised attempts by the Afghan government to develop autonomous policies to deal with transitional justice issues. This is mostly because internationals are convinced that their policy solutions hold the answers to the problems faced by the Afghan people but lack political space for implementation. Hence, they criticise international state actors for having a narrow approach to security and peacebuilding. Yet, in essence, while advocating themselves as the legitimate advocate of the Afghan people, the transitional justice community exerts strong influence on the Afghan government under the umbrella of good governance, peacebuilding and dealing with the past. As such, international non-state actors exert influence on perceptions of the legitimacy of domestic state actors in post-war countries.[57]

(5) International state actors and domestic non-state actors. For a long time, research, policy, and practice on peacebuilding intervention neglected the relationship between international state actors and non-state actors in the host-nation, including the relationship with the local civilian population. With the changing dynamics of international interventions since the 1990s, local citizens are now widely recognised as principal actors to post-war peacebuilding. Therefore, international support of the development of legitimate state–society relations has developed into a moral and political obligation of international actors, as well as a key premise for mission effectiveness. Resultantly, a growing number of UN Security Council Resolutions call for increased measures of civilian protection and local capacity building as part of international peacebuilding interventions.[58] At the same time, there is growing critique of international state actors' influence on local non-state actors. Although the performance of international state actors, principally in terms of establishing security, has been important to improve local perceptions of the intervention, it does not necessarily improve local perceptions of domestic state authorities. For instance, intervening military forces may run the risk of being perceived as an illegitimate intrusion if locally perceived to support host–state reforms and authorities that, in fact, are deemed threatening to local norms, values and ways of life.[59]

(6) Domestic state and domestic non-state actors. A persistent gap in the critique of the liberal peace debate is the absence of possible alternatives to the ideals of a liberal peace after armed conflict.[60] Peacebuilding, as a concept, was developed to focus international and domestic efforts toward solving the root causes of conflict. The principal relationship in peace-building is that between the domestic state and society, namely first and foremost those involved in, and affected by, the armed conflict. Yet, recent scholarly contributions have effectively exposed widespread and systemic neglect of non-state and 'local' dimensions of conflict.[61] Considering that boundaries between state and non-state actors, as well as civilian and mili-tary actors, are oftentimes blurred in civil wars, this principal relationship cuts across all segments of the population in the affected nation, as well as possible regional and international dimensions. We argue, and previous empirical studies suggest, that legitimate domestic actors are not necessar-ily absent because the internationally initiated post-war political order is locally rejected.[62] For instance, in Bosnia, Somalia and Nepal, local gover-nance structures have emerged to fill the legitimacy gap in the absence of a functioning state.[63] Similarly, a similar decentralised process of conflict resolution exists in Kenya, wherein the legitimacy of local actors is arguably more important than that of the state.[64]

The above examples of the various relational dynamics in contempo-rary peacebuilding settings provide a brief illustration of the applicability of the framework. In the following section, we extend the application of the framework to examine peacebuilding efforts in Afghanistan and Nepal.

External Challenges to Local Legitimacy in Afghanistan: A Failed Host-citizen Contract

Afghanistan arguably constitutes the most protracted, invasive and complex case of international intervention of this generation. The international and US-led military components of the intervention were proclaimed as means to support the development of a viable peace and legitimate Afghan state authorities. This ambitious objective constituted a key component of the 'host–citizen contract',[65] namely the perceived social contract governing the relationship between external military forces and Afghan citizens. By exam-ining this relationship more closely, we illustrate how different relational dynamics in peacebuilding interact and exert salient, and possibly negative, influence on the legitimacy of domestic state–society relations.[66]

At the outset of international intervention, Afghan citizens appeared cautiously optimistic to the presence of international and US military forces. Despite Afghanistan's troubled past with foreign militaries, the dire security situation in the country at the time led some Afghans to view international forces as liberators.[67] During the first few years of international intervention, external military forces were perceived to fulfil local expectations of improving physical security and deterring the Taliban from political leadership. As a result, public support of the international intervention was reinforced along with increasingly positive perceptions of Afghan state authorities.[68]

However, beginning around the time of the first Afghan elections in 2004, local perceptions of international and US military forces grew increasingly complex. The newly elected national government, supported by the international intervention, was perceived as both reluctant and incapable of meeting the expectations and needs of Afghan citizens. As a result, Afghans grew critical of the influence of international intervention on domestic state–society relations. For instance, many Afghans seemed to blame the pervasive state of national political and economic corruption on the intervention.[69]

Over time and based on local experiences of the ongoing armed conflict, Afghans came to re-evaluate the relationship with external military forces. The rapidly deteriorating security situation in the country led to the expansion of international and US-led military operations. Throughout Afghanistan, combat operations intensified and contributed to a surge in both foreign and Afghan civilian and military casualties. What is more, the provision of basic security and livelihood services, which constituted objectives of the international intervention, was widely perceived as neither particularly effective nor sustainable.[70] Following this negative development in the overall dynamics of the armed conflict, Afghans perceived that external military forces had not only changed the ways in which they conducted military operations, but also how they interacted with Afghan people.

Afghan citizens reported that relational dynamics became increasingly characterized by distrust, aggression and culturally derogatory behaviour. International and US military forces were perceived to increasingly infringe on Afghan people and communities without due care to local preferences and needs. The combination of a perceived limited responsiveness to local needs and a tendency to act overtly aggressive and disrespectful toward Afghans, seemingly without repercussions, constituted a principal source of resentment toward international and US military forces. Combined with the perceived poor performance of the intervention in terms of meeting local expectations of social, political and economic progress in the country, Afghans began doubting the true intentions of external military forces. The sense of disillusionment was not limited to the military intervention, but also shaped local perceptions of the relationship with national authorities and reforms.[71] For example, some Afghans believed that international and US military forces had purposely brought insecurities and conflict to local communities to justify their continued control over Afghan authorities. What is more, Afghans reported being sceptical of the partnership between international and US military forces and Afghan security and defence forces, which they believed intentionally sought to weaken Afghan authorities to ensure a continued Afghan dependency on external armed forces.[72] Consequently, some Afghans reported placing their trust instead in interpersonal relationships, including family networks, community ties or local strongmen rather than relying on Afghan state officials and institutions supported by the international intervention.

However, when faced with the reality of imminent international and US troop withdrawal, local perceptions of international intervention grew more ambivalent. At this critical juncture, some Afghans felt that troop withdrawal could possibly help to encourage local conflict resolution between the Afghan state and non-state armed groups, and that it was time to give Afghan authorities the opportunity to shoulder the responsibility of principal guardian of the Afghan people.[73] However, others felt that Afghan authorities were not yet ready to manage the persistently dire state of national insecurities, in particular the threat of a 'resumption of full-scale civil war, the return of Taliban rule, or foreign occupations by either Pakistan or Iran'.[74] Therefore, even though external military forces were widely perceived as unable to establish a viable and legitimate peace, some Afghan citizens still considered a continued international military presence as the lesser of two evils. Similarly, some members of US military forces shared the understanding of military withdrawal as premature and, thus, not an accurate reflection of a self-sustaining social contract in Afghanistan, namely sufficient ability and willingness of Afghan state authorities to uphold their sovereign responsibilities toward the Afghan people.[75]

The case of Afghanistan elucidates the perception-based, dynamic and relational qualities of post-war legitimacy, and highlights that relational dynamics between external military forces and local citizens exert salient influence on local perceptions of the legitimacy of host state–society relations. In so doing, it raises the question of whether international military intervention is necessarily conducive to the development of viable and locally legitimate state–society relations, especially if external military forces are not themselves perceived as accountable to the local population.[76]

Endogenous Challenges to Local Legitimacy in Nepal: The State–Society Gap

This section illustrates the importance of the relationship between domestic state actors and domestic non-state actors in peacebuilding interventions by applying the framework to the example of service provision in Nepal, which was facilitated by the Nepali government, e.g. through the development of micro-hydropower stations in remote areas, in an attempt to address local grievances following the 1996–2006 civil war and support the peace process.[77]

In Nepal, the provision of ecologically sensitive services to communities by the state yielded tremendously positive socio-economic effects for rural communities. However, despite the positive performance by state actors, there has not been an equivalent positive political effect, especially with regard to the legitimacy of the Nepali state. This raises the question of whether state-led service provision, here in form of micro-hydropower development, is always conducive to the broader peacebuilding efforts. Applying the framework, the case of Nepal helps to identify critical domestic challenges to the peacebuilding process, which are often overlooked or become subordinate in discussions on global–local tensions. In Nepal, the example of micro-hydropower development unravelled the grave divide between state and society – fundamentally challenging the basis of a legitimate Nepali social contract.

The provision of energy in Nepal remains a pivotal challenge. In 2010, almost a quarter of the country did not have access to electricity, and even those households that were connected did not receive continuous power. The capital, Kathmandu, experiences scheduled power cuts up to fourteen hours a day during the drier winter season, when hydropower ebbs, and two to three hours a day in the water-rich monsoon months.

As a landlocked country in the Himalayas without fossil fuels, hydropower has been the key focus for increasing energy production. Small hydro projects, called micro-hydropower, are often the only way of providing remote communities with electricity. Funding of these projects is administered through the Nepali state. The projects are implemented through the Alternative Energy Promotion Centre of the Ministry of Environment, Science and Technology, with the United Nations Development Program and World Bank as principal donors.

The findings show that micro-hydropower development has had many positive effects for rural communities, especially in regard to socio-economic development. Along with micro-hydropower development come other public and private services, like cable internet and television. The improved socio-economic status of households in two communities reflects a clear reduction in vulnerability to poverty and even food security as the improved canals diverting water to the micro-hydropower station have improved irrigation of nearby fields. This indicates a strong performance of the implementing agencies, i.e. the Nepali government.[78]

Yet, when considering the political consequences of micro-hydropower development, assessed through household interviews in two communities in rural Nepal,[79] it becomes evident that it has facilitated local interactions that have resulted in more local autonomy rather than facilitating state building and consolidating the relationship between the Nepali government and its people. From a community-centred, human security perspective, such autonomy is without a doubt a positive development. However, when considering the broader post-war context and the all-important relationship between the state and its people, which we are suggesting is fundamental for peacebuilding, it is more problematic.

People's outlook regarding the Nepali state is an important measure of stability. Economic and social grievances were key aspects to the civil war.[80] Eventually the Maoists toppled the monarchy and gained power in the aftermath of the war. Yet, while local socio-economic gains have been visible from the electrification through the micro-hydropower projects and they are funded in part by the new government, these results have produced little change in people's outlook on the state.

Theoretically, the opposite is expected. The provision of services through state actors, in this case electricity, is anticipated to strengthen the stability and legitimacy of the relationship between the state and society. As Holsti argues, the economic effects of resource extraction are critical: 'If the state extracts to the point where livelihood is no longer possible, migration, resistance, rebellion, and secession attempts become alternatives to payment. In societies characterised by extensive poverty, virtually any government extraction imposes a severe threat'.[81] Yet, the case of Nepal indicates that the link between service provision in the form of electricity to local communities and the matter of state legitimacy is more complex.

The main reason for weak state legitimacy is the high degree of local autonomy, which stands in opposition to a reciprocal relationship between local and state actors. While this is a legacy of Nepali politics and a failure to hold community level elections in the last decade, the experiences around the micro-hydropower project have amplified the divide between rural and central actors by strengthening the cohesion of autonomous local networks. For example, in Rishmi, the success of local cooperation has reaffirmed the local community's ability to take charge of their own interests and confirmed that they can successfully do so. Yet, this has contributed to local perceptions of a widened gap between state actors and the community, while also contributing to the community's mistrust of state actors. Particularly, the successful implementation of the project by local citizens' own labour and financial contributions has been an important factor that strengthened the sense of self-reliance and being able to provide for themselves: 'The people from the village brought this. We all contribute money in this. We all brought it together. We all worked for it'.[82] Similar expressions of local solidarity and cohesion were echoed in Kharbang: 'In my experience, we can do it'.[83]

Ultimately, the successful implementation of the micro-hydropower projects created and consolidated new informal governance structures. These forms of self-governance were perceived locally as legitimate structures that replaced the role of formal state actors with local informal actors. The new governance structures gained a high degree of local support and legitimacy because they are perceived as having been the actual provider of socio-economic development. Of course, a strong local community is a positive development; it empowers actors and increases resilience to cope with disturbances to the community, contributes to socio-economic development, and reduces vulnerabilities. A recent strand in the peacebuilding literature looks favourably at such alternative traditional developments in the context of peace processes.[84] For instance, some might argue that such local developments are indicative of an alternative post-liberal peace, especially since local citizens tend to try to influence and transform external support according to their own necessities.[85]

However, taking the larger state–society relationship into account, a widened distance between state actors and the local community is likely to have negative implications for the peace process because it calls into question the legitimacy of the post-war state. The Nepali state exists despite its weak government actors and it also exists in the heads of villagers. Thus, the observed 'governance without government'[86] inadvertently complicates the consolidation of the post-war state building process.

In sum, in the case of service provision in Nepal, the framework allows us to identify that the legitimacy of informal self-governance structures and local order may constitute an important endogenous challenge to the Nepali peace process if the key objective of peacebuilding is to restore the legitimacy of the state–society relationship.[87]

Conclusion

In this chapter we have introduced a framework to better address the challenges of building self-sustaining peace in post-war societies. The framework advances a relational understanding of peacebuilding as rooted in the relationship between those principally involved in and affected by the conflict, namely the domestic state and society. Concurrently, it situates this principal relationship in the broader context of peacebuilding processes, which is recognised as influenced by a number of different actors and relational dynamics. Thus, the framework opens up to further study of each of the different, yet interlinked, relational dynamics identified in previous research to, in different ways, affect the legitimacy of the post-war order.

By recognising the importance of different sets of relational dynamics, the framework helps to illustrate potential areas of conflicting dynamics within peacebuilding processes, whether linked to domestic state–society relations, or introduced – intentionally or not – by the presence of international actors. Although more work is needed to address the different relational dynamics in post-war peacebuilding, increasing awareness of the broader picture is intended to encourage scholars, policymakers and practitioners to acknowledge the limitations of studying any relationship in isolation, as they all interact and together shape the conditions for peacebuilding.

Refocusing scholarly attention to the importance of domestic state–society relations is not intended to romanticise the role of the 'local', but rather to stimulate a curiosity to explore what constitutes or breaks legitimate state–society relations in the context of the specific post-war peacebuilding setting. This does not make peacebuilding any less difficult, but it may lead to the development of more realistic and sustainable foundations for peace that are urgently needed.

Notes

1. Stedman et al. (eds), *Ending Civil Wars – the Implementation of Peace Agreements*; and Toft, *Securing the Peace*.
2. Fukuyama, *The End of History and the Last Man*; Fortna & Howard, 'Pitfalls and prospects in the peacekeeping literature', pp. 283–301; and Zaum (ed.), *Legitimating International Organizations*.
3. Boutros-Ghali, 'An agenda for peace'.
4. Paris, *At War's End: Building Peace After Civil Conflict*; Jarstad & Sisk, *From War to Democracy: Dilemmas of Peacebuilding*; Newman et al. (eds), *New Perspectives on Liberal Peacebuilding*; and Pugh et al. *Whose Peace? Critical Perspectives on the Political Economy of Peacebuilding*.
5. Krasner, 'Sharing sovereignty: new institutions for collapsed and failing states', pp. 85–120; and Chesterman, *You, the People: the United Nations, Transitional Administration and State-Building*.
6. These areas of critique are not mutually exclusive.

7. Pugh, 'Post-war economies and the New York dissensus', p. 271; see also Tadjbakhsh, *Rethinking the Liberal Peace*.

8. Chandler, *International Statebuilding: The Rise of Post-Liberal Governance*; and Kostić, 'Education through regulation?', pp. 105–130.

9. Donais, 'Empowerment or imposition? Dilemmas of local ownership in post conflict peacebuilding processes', p. 19; see also Chandler, 'International statebuilding: the rise of post-liberal governance', p. 40.

10. Chandler, *International Statebuilding: The Rise of Post-Liberal Governance*.

11. Paris, 'Saving liberal peacebuilding', p. 340.

12. Fearon & Laitin, 'Neotrusteeship and the problem of weak states', p. 43; see also Krasner, 'Sharing sovereignty: new institutions for collapsed and failing states', pp. 85–120.

13. Paris, 'Peacebuilding and the limits of liberal internationalism', pp. 54–89; and Paris, 'At war's end: building peace after civil conflict'.

14. Fearon, Laitin, 'Neotrusteeship and the problem of weak states', pp. 5–43; Krasner, 'Sharing sovereignty: new institutions for collapsed and failing states', pp. 85–120; and Paris, 'Saving liberal peacebuilding', p. 337.

15. Mac Ginty, *No War, No Peace: the Rejuvenation of Stalled Peace Processes and Peace Accords*; Chesterman, 'Ownership in theory and in practice: transfer of authority in UN statebuilding operations', pp. 3–26; and Donais, 'Empowerment or imposition? Dilemmas of local ownership in post-conflict peacebuilding processes', pp. 3–26.

16. Duffield, *Development, Security and Unending War*; and Mac Ginty, 'No war, no peace: why so many peace processes fail to deliver peace', pp. 145–62.

17. Mac Ginty, 'Hybrid peace: the interaction between top-down and bottom-up peace', pp. 391–412.

18. Menkhaus, 'Governance without government in somalia spoilers, state building, and the politics of coping', pp. 74–106; Richmond, *A Post-Liberal Peace*; Krampe, 'Empowering peace: service provision and state legitimacy in Nepal's peace-building process', pp. 53–73; and Richmond, *Peace Formation and Political Order in Conflict Affected Societies*.

19. Kappler, *Local Agency and Peacebuilding*.

20. Weber, *Grundriss Der Sozialökonomik. III. Abteilung. Wirtschaft Und Gesellschaft*; Lipset, 'Some social requisites of democracy: economic development and political legitimacy', pp. 69–105; and Migdal, *Strong Societies and Weak States: State–society Relations and State Capabilities in the Third World*.

21. Migdal, *State in Society*.

22. Karlborg, 'The ambiguous host–citizen contract: an evolving notion of duty in the US military quest for local legitimacy', pp. 864–84.

23. Chesterman, 'Ownership in theory and in practice: transfer of authority in UN statebuilding operations', pp. 3–26; and Donais, 'Empowerment or imposition? Dilemmas of local ownership in post-conflict peacebuilding processes', pp. 3–26.

24. Lederach, *Building Peace – Sustainable Reconciliation in Divided Societies*.

25. Fearon, Laitin, 'Neotrusteeship and the problem of weak states', pp. 5–43; and Krasner, 'Sharing sovereignty: new institutions for collapsed and failing states', pp. 85–120.
26. Chandler, *International Statebuilding: The Rise of Post-Liberal Governance*.
27. Jarstad, Olsson, 'Hybrid peace ownership in Afghanistan: international perspectives of who owns what and when', p. 105.
28. Boege et al., 'Hybrid political orders, not fragile states', pp. 13–21; Hughes et al., 'The struggle versus the song – the local turn in peacebuilding: an introduction', pp. 817–24; and Krampe, Swain, 'Human development and minority empowerment'.
29. Migdal, *State in Society*, p. 5.
30. Holsti, *The State, War, and the State of War*.
31. Höglund, Orjuela, 'Friction and the pursuit of justice in post-war Sri Lanka', p. 300.
32. Kappler, *Local Agency and Peacebuilding*.
33. Lemay-Hébert, 'Statebuilding without nation-building? Legitimacy, state failure and the limits of the institutionalist approach', pp. 21–45; Lake, 'Building legitimate states after civil wars', pp. 29–51; Kappler, '*Everyday legitimacy in post-conflict spaces: the creation of social legitimacy in Bosnia-Herzegovina's cultural arenas*', pp. 1–18; Karlborg, 'Enforced hospitality: local perceptions of the legitimacy of international forces in Afghanistan', pp. 435–48; Ramsbotham, Wennmann, 'Legitimacy and peace processes'; and Krampe, 'Empowering peace: service provision and state legitimacy in Nepal's peace-building process', pp. 53–73.
34. Themnér & Ohlson, 'Legitimate peace in post-civil war states: towards attaining the unattainable', pp. 61–87.
35. Lipset, 'Some social requisites of democracy: economic development and political legitimacy', pp. 69–105.
36. Themnér, Ohlson, 'Legitimate peace in post-civil war states: towards attaining the unattainable', pp. 61–87; and Krampe, 'Empowering peace: service provision and state legitimacy in Nepal's peace-building process', pp. 53–73.
37. Holsti, *The State, War, and the State of War*. Underlying this is the conceptualisation of the state by Buzan that perceives states based on the idea of the state, the institutions of the state, and the physical base of the state (see Buzan, Barry *People, States, and Fear*).
38. Suchman, 'Managing legitimacy: strategic and institutional approaches', pp. 574 f; and Ahlstrom, Bruton, 'Learning From Successful Local Private Firms in China: Establishing Legitimacy', p. 73.
39. Migdal, *Strong Societies and Weak States: State–society Relations and State Capabilities in the Third World*, p. 33.
40. Weber, *The Theory of Social and Economic Organisation*, p. 382.
41. Moskos, et al., *The Postmodern Military: Armed Forces After the Cold War*.
42. Miller, 'From adversaries to allies: relief workers' attitudes toward the US military', pp. 181–97; and Franke, *The Peacebuilding Dilemma: Civil–Military Cooperation in Stability Operations*.

43. Aall, 'Nongovernmental organizations and peacemaking', pp. 433–44; and Byman, 'Uncertain partners: NGOs and the military', pp. 97–114.
44. Duffield, *Global Governance and the New Wars: the Merging of Development and Security.*
45. Rubenstein, *Peacekeeping Under Fire: Culture and Intervention.*
46. Krampe, 'The liberal trap – peacemaking and peacebuilding in Afghanistan after 9/11', pp. 57–75.
47. Wiharta, 'The legitimacy of peace operations', pp. 95–116.
48. Fortna, 'Does peacekeeping keep peace? International intervention and the duration of peace after civil war', pp. 269–92; Gilligan, Sergenti, 'Do UN Interventions Cause Peace? Using Matching to Improve Causal Inference', pp. 89–122; and Hegre et al., 'Peacekeeping works'.
49. Mac Ginty, 'Hybrid peace: the interaction between top-down and bottom-up peace', pp. 391–412.
50. Richmond, *A Post-Liberal Peace*, p. 14.
51. Paffenholz, *Civil Society, Peacebuilding: a Critical Assessment*; Richmond, *A Post-Liberal Peace*; and Hughes et al., 'The struggle versus the song – the local turn in peacebuilding: an introduction', pp. 817–24.
52. Chandler, *International Statebuilding: the Rise of Post-Liberal Governance*; Donais, *Peacebuilding and Local Ownership*; and Eriksson, Kostić, *Mediation and Liberal Peacebuilding*.
53. Albin, *Can NGOs Enhance the Effectiveness of International Negotiation?* pp. 371–87.
54. Krampe, 'The liberal trap – peacemaking and peacebuilding in Afghanistan after 9/11', pp. 57–75.
55. Polman, *The Crisis Caravan.*
56. Kostić, 'Transnational think-tanks: foot soldiers in the battlefield of ideas? Examining the role of the ICG in Bosnia and Herzegovina, 2000–01', p. 647.
57. Krampe, 'The liberal trap – peacemaking and peacebuilding in Afghanistan after 9/11', pp. 57–75.
58. United Nations, *Peacekeeping Operations: Principles and Guidelines*; and Hultman, 'UN peace operations and protection of civilians cheap talk or norm implementation?', pp. 59–73.
59. Karlborg, 'Enforced hospitality: local perceptions of the legitimacy of international forces in Afghanistan', pp. 435–48.
60. Paris, 'Saving Liberal Peacebuilding', pp. 337.
61. Autesserre, *The Trouble with the Congo: Local Violence and the Failure of International Peacebuilding.*
62. Kappler, 'Everyday legitimacy in post-conflict spaces: the creation of social legitimacy in Bosnia-Herzegovina's cultural arenas', pp. 15.
63. Menkhaus, 'Governance without government in Somalia: Spoilers, State Building, and the Politics of Coping', pp. 74–106; Kappler, 'Everyday legitimacy in post-conflict spaces: the creation of social legitimacy in Bosnia-Herzegovina's cultural arenas', pp. 1–18; and Krampe, 'Empowering peace: service provision and state legitimacy in Nepal's peace-building process', pp. 53–73.

64. Elfversson, 'Peace from below: governance and peacebuilding in Kerio Valley, Kenya', pp. 469–93.

65. Karlborg, *Enforcing Legitimacy: Perspectives on the Relationship Between Intervening Armed Forces and the Local Population in Afghanistan.*

66. This section condenses more extensive studies by one of the authors to exemplify the usefulness of the framework (Karlborg 2014).

67. Karlborg, 'Enforced hospitality: local perceptions of the legitimacy of international forces in Afghanistan', pp. 435–48.

68. Ibid.

69. Ibid.

70. Ibid.

71. Ibid.; Karlborg, *Enforcing Legitimacy: Perspectives on the Relationship Between Intervening Armed Forces and the Local Population in Afghanistan*; and Karlborg, 'Exploring noncombat contact and the sense of soldierly duty in Afghanistan', pp. 107–50.

72. Speaking to this dynamic, some US military members reported that when interaction with Afghan security and defence forces was characterised by positive interdependence and reciprocity rather than asymmetry and power imbalance, it seemed to foster loyalty and mutual trust, which had proved instrumental to achieving viable results on the ground (Karlborg 2015c).

73. Karlborg, 'Enforced hospitality: local perceptions of the legitimacy of international forces in Afghanistan', pp. 435–48.

74. Ibid. p. 439.

75. Karlborg, 'Exploring noncombat contact and the sense of soldierly duty in Afghanistan', pp. 107–50.

76. Karlborg, *Enforcing Legitimacy: Perspectives on the Relationship Between Intervening Armed Forces and the Local Population in Afghanistan*; and Karlborg, 'Exploring Noncombat Contact and the Sense of Soldierly Duty in Afghanistan', pp. 107–50.

77. This section condenses the more extensive study (Krampe 2016) to exemplify the usefulness of the framework.

78. Krampe, 'Empowering peace: service provision and state legitimacy in Nepal's peace-building process', pp. 53–73.

79. See Ibid.

80. Whelpton, *A History of Nepal.*

81. Holsti, *The State, War, and the State of War*, p. 109.

82. Author interview Rishmi, HH3 & HH4, 156

83. Author interview Kharbang03_Mitra

84. Clements et al., 'State building reconsidered: the role of hybridity in the formation of political order', pp. 45–56.

85. Richmond, *A Post-Liberal Peace.*

86. Menkhaus, 'Governance without government in Somalia: spoilers, state building, and the politics of coping', pp. 74–106.

87. Krampe, 'Empowering peace: service provision and state legitimacy in Nepal's peace-building process', pp. 53–73.

References

Aall, Pamela, 'Nongovernmental organizations and peacemaking', in Chester A. Crocker et al. (eds), *Managing Global Chaos: Sources of the Responses to International Conflict* (Washington, DC: United States Institute of Peace Press, 1996), pp. 433–44.

Ahlstrom, David & Garry D. Bruton, 'Learning from successful local private firms in China: establishing legitimacy', *Academy of Management Executive* 2001, 15: 4, pp. 72–83.

Albin, Cecilia, 'Can NGOs enhance the effectiveness of international negotiation?' *International Negotiation* 1999, 4: 3, pp. 371–87.

Autesserre, Séverine, *The Trouble with the Congo: Local Violence and the Failure of International Peacebuilding* (Cambridge: Cambridge University Press, 2010).

Boege, Volker, M. A. Brown & Kevin P. Clements, 'Hybrid political orders, not fragile states', *Peace Review* 2009, 21: 1, pp. 13–21.

Boutros-Ghali, Boutros, 'An agenda for peace', *International Relations* 1992, 11: 3, pp. 201–18.

Buzan, Barry, *People, States, and Fear* (Brighton: Wheatsheaf Books, 1983).

Byman, D., 'Uncertain partners: NGOs and the military', *Survival* 2010, 43: 2, pp. 97–114.

Chandler, David, *International Statebuilding: the Rise of Post-Liberal Governance. Critical Issues in Global Politics* (London and New York: Taylor & Francis, 2010).

Chesterman, S., *You, the People: the United Nations, Transitional Administration and State-Building.* (New York: Oxford University Press, 2005).

Chesterman, S., 'Ownership in theory and in practice: transfer of authority in UN statebuilding operations', *Journal of Intervention and Statebuilding* 2007, 1: 1, pp. 3–26.

Clements, Kevin P., Volker Boege, Anne Brown, Wendy Foley & Anna Nolan, 'State building reconsidered: the role of hybridity in the formation of political order', *Political Science'*, 59: 1, pp. 45–56.

Donais, Timothy, *Peacebuilding and Local Ownership* (London: Routledge, 2012).

Duffield, Mark, *Global Governance and the New Wars: the Merging of Development and Security* (London and New York: Zed Books, 2001).

Duffield, Mark, *Development, Security and Unending War* (Cambridge: Polity Press, 2007).

Elfversson, Emma, 'Peace from below: governance and peacebuilding in Kerio Valley, Kenya', *The Journal of Modern African Studies* 2016, 54: 3, pp. 469–93.

Eriksson, Mikael & Roland Kostić, *Mediation and Liberal Peacebuilding*, Mikael Eriksson & Roland Kostić (eds) (London: Routledge, 2013).

Fearon, James D. & David D. Laitin, 'Neotrusteeship and the problem of weak states', *International Security* 2004, 28: 4, pp. 5–43.

Fortna, Virginia P. 'Does peacekeeping keep peace? International intervention and the duration of peace after civil war', *International Studies Quarterly* 2004, 48: 2, pp. 269–92.

Fortna, Virginia P. & Lise M. Howard, 'Pitfalls and prospects in the peacekeeping literature', *Annual Review of Political Science* 11: 1, pp. 283–301.

Franke, V. 'The Peacebuilding Dilemma: Civil–Military Cooperation in Stability Operations', *International Journal of Peace Studies*, 2006, 11: 2.

Fukuyama, Francis, *The End of History and the Last Man* (New York: Simon and Schuster, 2006).

Gilligan, M. J. & E. J. Sergenti, 'Do UN interventions cause peace? Using matching to improve causal inference', *Quarterly Journal of Political Science* 2008, 3: pp. 89–122.

Hegre, Håvard, Lisa Hultman & Håvard M. Nygård, 'Peacekeeping Works', *Conflict Trends* 2015, 01.

Holsti, Kalevi J. *The State, War, and the State of War* (Cambridge: Cambridge University Press, 1996).

Höglund, Kristine & Camilla Orjuela, *Friction and the Pursuit of Justice in Post-War Sri Lanka. Peacebuilding* 2013, 1: 3, pp. 300–16.

Hughes, Caroline, Joakim Öjendal & Isabell Schierenbeck, *The Struggle Versus the Song – the Local Turn in Peacebuilding: an Introduction. Third World Quarterly* 2015, 36: 5, pp. 817–24.

Hultman, Lisa, 'UN peace operations and protection of civilians: cheap talk or norm implementation?' *Journal of Peace Research* 2013, 50: 1, pp. 59–73.

Jarstad, Anna K. & Louise Olsson, 'Hybrid peace ownership in Afghanistan: international perspectives of who owns what and when', *Global Governance* 2012, 18: 1, pp. 105–19.

Jarstad, Anna K. & T. Sisk, *From War to Democracy: Dilemmas of Peacebuilding* (Cambridge: Cambridge University Press, 2008).

Kappler, Stefanie, 'Everyday legitimacy in post-conflict spaces: the creation of social legitimacy in Bosnia-Herzegovina's cultural arenas', *Journal of Intervention and Statebuilding* 2012, 7: 1, pp. 1–18.

Kappler, Stefanie, *Local Agency and Peacebuilding* (Basingstoke: Palgrave Macmillan, 2014).

Karlborg, Lisa, 'Enforced hospitality: local perceptions of the legitimacy of international forces in Afghanistan', *Civil Wars* 2014, 16: 4, pp. 1–24.

Karlborg, Lisa, 'The ambiguous host–citizen contract: an evolving notion of duty in the US military quest for local legitimacy', *Studies in Conflict & Terrorism* 2015a, 38: 10, pp. 864–84.

Karlborg, Lisa, *Enforcing Legitimacy: Perspectives on the Relationship Between Intervening Armed Forces and the Local Population in Afghanistan* (Uppsala: Uppsala University, 2015b).

Karlborg, Lisa, 'Exploring noncombat contact and the sense of soldierly duty in Afghanistan', in *Enforcing Legitimacy: Perspectives on the Relationship between Intervening Armed Forces and the Local Population in Afghanistan* (Uppsala: Uppsala University, Department of Peace and Conflict Research, 2015c), 106: p. 55.

Kostić, Roland, 'Education through regulation?' in Hanne Fjelde & Kristine Höglund (eds), *Building Peace, Creating Conflict – Conflictual Dimensions of Local and International Peace-Building* (Lund: Nordic Academic Press, 2011), pp. 105–130.

Kostić, Roland, 'Transnational think-tanks: foot soldiers in the battlefield of ideas? Examining the role of the ICG in Bosnia and Herzegovina, 2000–01', *Third World Quarterly* 2014, 35: 4, pp. 634–51.

Krampe, Florian, 'The liberal trap – peacemaking and peacebuilding in Afghanistan after 9/11', in Mikael Eriksson & Roland Kostić (eds), *Mediation and Liberal Peacebuilding* (London: Routledge, 2013), pp. 57–75.

Krampe, Florian, 'Empowering peace: service provision and state legitimacy in Nepal's peace-building process', *Conflict, Security & Development* 2016, 16: 1, pp. 53–73.

Krampe, Florian & Ashok Swain, 'Human development and minority empowerment', in: Oliver P. Richmond, Sandra Pogodda & Jasmin Ramovic (eds), *The Palgrave Handbook of Disciplinary and Regional Approaches to Peace* (London: Palgrave Macmillan UK, 2016).

Krasner, Stephen D., 'Sharing sovereignty: new institutions for collapsed and failing states', *International Security* 2004, 29: 2, pp. 85–120.

Lake, D. A., 'Building legitimate states after civil wars', in Matthew Hoddie & Caroline Hartzell (eds) *Strengthening Peace in Post-Civil War States* (Chicago: The University of Chicago Press, 2010), pp. 29–51.

Lederach, John P., *Building Peace – Sustainable Reconciliation in Divided Societies* (Washington DC: United States Institute of Peace Press, 1997).

Lemay-Hébert, Nicolas, 'Statebuilding without Nation-Building? Legitimacy, State Failure and the Limits of the Institutionalist Approach', *Journal of Intervention and Statebuilding* 2009, 3: 1, pp. 21–45.

Lipset, Seymour M. 'Some social requisites of democracy: economic development and political legitimacy', *American Political Science Review* 1959, 53: 1, pp. 69–105.

Mac Ginty, Roger, *No War, No Peace: the Rejuvenation of Stalled Peace Processes and Peace Accords* (Basingstoke: Palgrave Macmillan, 2006).

Mac Ginty, Roger, 'No war, no peace: why so many peace processes fail to deliver peace', *International Politics* 2010a, 47: 2, pp. 145–62.

Mac Ginty, Roger, 'Hybrid peace: the interaction between top-down and bottom-up peace', *Security Dialogue* 2010b, 41: 4, pp. 391–412.

Menkhaus, Ken, 'Governance without Government in Somalia Spoilers, State Building and the Politics of Coping', *International Security* 2006, 31: 3, pp. 74–106.

Migdal, Joel S., *Strong Societies and Weak States: State–society Relations and State Capabilities in the Third World* (Princeton: Princeton University Press, 1988).

Migdal, Joel S. *State in Society* (Cambridge: Cambridge University Press, 2001).

Miller, Laura L. 'From adversaries to allies: relief workers' attitudes toward the US military', *Qualitative Sociology* 1999, 22: 3, pp. 181–97.

Moskos, Charles C., John A. Williams & David R. Segal, *The Postmodern Military: Armed Forces After the Cold War* (New York: Oxford University Press, 2000).

Newman, Edward, Roland Paris & Oliver P Richmond (eds), *New Perspectives on Liberal Peacebuilding* (Tokyo, New York, Paris: United Nations University Press, 2009).

Paffenholz, Thania, *Civil Society & Peacebuilding: a Critical Assessment* (Boulder: Lynne Rienner Publishers, 2010).

Paris, Roland, 'Peacebuilding and the limits of liberal internationalism', *International Security* 1997, 22: 2, pp. 54–89.

Paris, Roland, *At War's End: Building Peace After Civil Conflict* (New York: Cambridge University Press, 2004).

Paris, Roland, 'Saving Liberal Peacebuilding', *Review of International Studies* 2010, 36: 02, p. 337.

Polman, Linda, *The Crisis Caravan* (London: Picador, 2011).

Pugh, Michael, 'Post-war economies and the New York dissensus', *International Peacekeeping* 2006, 6: 3, pp. 269–89.

Pugh, Michael, N. Cooper & M. Turner, *Whose Peace? Critical Perspectives on the Political Economy of Peacebuilding* (Basingstoke: Palgrave Macmillan, 2010).

Ramsbotham, Alexander & Achim Wennmann, 'Legitimacy and peace processes', *Accord* 2014, 25: pp. 6–11.

Richmond, Oliver P. *A Post-Liberal Peace* (Abingdon and New York: Routledge, 2012).

Richmond, Oliver P. *Peace Formation and Political Order in Conflict Affected Societies* (Oxford: Oxford University Press, 2016).

Rubenstein, Robert A., *Peacekeeping Under Fire: Culture and Intervention* (Abingdon: Routledge, 2015).

Stedman, Stephen, Donald Rothchild & Elizabeth M. Cousens (eds), *Ending Civil Wars – the Implementation of Peace Agreements* (Boulder and London: Lynne Rienner Publishers, 2002).

Suchman, Mark C. Managing 'Legitimacy: strategic and institutional approaches', *Academy of Management Review* 1995, 20: 3, pp. 571–610.

Tadjbakhsh, Shahrbanou, *Rethinking the Liberal Peace* (London and New York: Taylor & Francis, 2011).

Themnér, Anders & Thomas Ohlson, 'Legitimate peace in post-civil war states: towards attaining the unattainable', *Conflict, Security & Development* 2014, 14: 1, pp. 61–87.

Donais, Timothy, 'Empowerment or imposition? Dilemmas of local ownership in post-conflict peacebuilding processes', *Peace & Change* 2009, 34: 1, pp. 3–26.

Toft, Monica D., *Securing the Peace* (Princeton: Princeton University Press, 2009).

United Nations, *Peacekeeping Operations: Principles and Guidelines* (New York: United Nations Department of Peacekeeping Operations and Department of Field Support, 2008).

Weber, Max, *Grundriss Der Sozialökonomik. III. Abteilung. Wirtschaft Und Gesellschaft* (Heidelberg: J. C. B. Mohr (Paul Siebeck), (1922)).

Weber, Max, *The Theory of Social and Economic Organisation*, Talcott Parsons (ed.) (New York: Oxford University Press, 1947).

Whelpton, John, *A History of Nepal* (Cambridge: Cambridge University Press, 2005).

Wiharta, Sharon, 'The legitimacy of peace operations', in *SIPRI Yearbook Armaments, Disarmament and International Security* (Solna: Stockholm International Peace Research Institute, 2009), pp. 95–116.

Zaum, Dominik (ed.), *Legitimating International Organizations* (New York: Oxford University Press, 2013).

ELEVEN

Legitimacy in Lebanon

Kristina Tschunkert and Roger Mac Ginty

Introduction

Lebanon's fraught history invites us to question the sources, character and necessity of legitimacy. It encourages us to open up legitimacy to more sociological analyses that move us beyond the potentially narrow confines of Newtonian links between the citizen, government and service delivery. While these transactional aspects of legitimacy are important, other issues such as heritage, identity and blunt power (sometimes force) play a significant role. This chapter seeks to unravel the complex 'swirl' that constitutes political legitimacy in Lebanon. It sees legitimacy as a hybrid construction that derives from a complex mix of identity and transactional politics. The chapter is influenced by Alex De Waal's concept of the political marketplace and uses a modified version of this to help explain the dynamism and trade-offs involved in constructing, maintaining, using and undermining legitimacy.[1]

The chapter proceeds by first unpacking legitimacy as a concept and then introducing the concept of the political marketplace. It then applies the political marketplace concept to Lebanon. It identifies five aspects of de Waal's political marketplace that are relevant for an analysis of legitimate political authority in Lebanon: monetised transactional politics; highly personalised politics; the international and transnational integration of the political marketplace; the structured and regulated nature of the marketplace; and the masculine nature of politics. In its final substantive section, the chapter examines the legitimacy of international and transnational actors in Lebanon. Given that Lebanon is hugely penetrated by international organisations and international non-governmental organisations, it seems appropriate to examine their sources of legitimacy. The chapter draws on a number of interviews undertaken by the authors jointly and separately in 2013 and 2017. The 2013 interviews were with a cross section of the population. While there is no claim that these are scientifically representative of the Lebanese population (a difficult claim to verify given that the last census was in 1932),[2] the authors are satisfied that opinions from the main identity groups were captured. The 2017 interviews were more targeted at opinion-formers and personnel from civil society and international organisations.

Legitimacy as a concept

Legitimacy is a fundamental aspect of state–citizen relationships and essentially all power relations. It thus lies at the core of the statebuilding agenda. Lebanon, it is argued in this chapter, is the site of unfinished and highly problematic statebuilding. There is broad consensus that legitimacy is a desirable quality for political entities.[3] Politicians and authorities invariably try to legitimise their decisions and actions,[4] as without legitimacy, power is exerted merely through coercion, a form of governance that is thought to result in instability precisely because of the lack of legitimacy.[5] Thus, legitimacy can be understood as acceptance of authority based mainly on compliance and consent. It consists of a two-way relationship and it is something that must be achieved through justifiable procedures rather than received, as it deals with the regulation of relationships between entities that exercise power and those over whom this power is exercised.[2] Thus it seems prudent to adopt a relational approach to legitimacy.

While there is broad agreement on the value of legitimacy, its sources and ways to assess it remain contested. Legitimacy can be assessed by taking a normative or an empirical approach. A normative approach is concerned with a set of standards with which an actor or an institution must comply in order to be recognised as legitimate. An actor or institution is considered legitimate if the right to rule is socially institutionalised[3] and if its exercise of power conforms to certain normative standards[2] which thus means that legitimacy is assessed on the basis of moral justifiability. One such normative standard is the ideal of democracy. According to this logic, legitimacy is given a functionalist definition which is assessed in terms of, for instance, provision of goods and services (such as security, healthcare, education and infrastructure). Fukuyama[6] claims that only a democratic state can be legitimate, which means that in this normative view, sources of legitimacy are put into hierarchies where the normative concept of democracy is given priority. Rotberg[7] seconds this view and states that 'it is according to their performances, according to the levels of their effective delivery of the most crucial political goods that strong states may be distinguished from weak ones'. This is sometimes characterised as 'neo-Weberian',[8] as this emphasis on the functionality of the state derives from a Weberian conceptualisation of the state. As we will see in relation to Lebanon, western notions of legitimacy do not always travel smoothly to other contexts.

Proponents of the empirical approaches to legitimacy, on the other hand, have criticised the normative approach for its view of legitimacy as a one-way relationship and its neglect of local knowledge and social dynamics. The empirical approach is based more on a Durkheimian conception of the state as 'the very organ of social thought'.[9] This approach is preoccupied with perceptions that people hold about an actor or institution, as well as the factors that incentivise people to consent to power and thus people's continuous assessment of whether actors and institutions function in an acceptable way.[10] Legitimacy is assessed inductively based on local processes and what people deem to be legitimate rather than deductively drawn from a normative regime.[11] Buzan,[12] for instance, emphasises the 'idea of the state', an implicit social contract and ideological consensus. He agrees that a state cannot exist without a physical base but neither can it function without a deeply rooted idea of the state among the citizens. 'Belief' plays a crucial role in this according to Weber. Lipset[13] agrees that legitimacy is the capacity 'to engender and maintain belief that the existing political institutions are the most appropriate ones for the society'. Hence, legitimacy needs to be assessed considering historical and social contexts rather than focusing on universal ideal relations. This point is worth bearing in mind in relation to the later material on Lebanon.

Thinking on legitimacy has been heavily influenced by Weber. He explored political legitimacy addressing the interrelation between objective and subjective meanings by studying the institutionalised right to legitimacy and the subjective interpretations of actors as functions of political stability. Weber distinguished three types of legitimacy: traditional, charismatic and legal-rational. The notion of legal-rational legitimacy rests on an ideal-type bureaucracy and formal rules which are seen to be prerequisites for a strong state that has the capacity to ensure the security and wellbeing of its citizens. Traditional legitimacy is based on customs and beliefs that are deeply engrained in a society. Charismatic legitimacy is based on the belief of people in the extraordinary qualities of an individual that makes them a role-model or leader.[14] The notion of legal-rational legitimacy is particularly linked to Western interpretations of legitimacy based on liberal democratic values that understand the state in terms of institutions and service delivery, implying that a state's legitimacy can be built and strengthened by supporting the development of institutions and service delivery. It also assumes that the state is technocratically proficient in order to build and maintain institutions and to deliver services.

More recently, the assumptions underpinning Weber's conceptualisation of political legitimacy have been problematised, with more weight being put on the social and contextual factors that help constitute legitimate political authority. Beetham[15] points to the reductionist conclusions that can be drawn from Weber's definition of legitimacy. He argues that a power relationship is not legitimate because people believe in it but because it can be justified according to their beliefs, in the sense that legitimacy is assessed according to the conformity of a power relation to people's values and expectations. Beetham[14] thus objects to the Weberian notion that 'reporting' people's belief in legitimacy is what counts but rather 'assessing' the level of coherence between an entity of power and the beliefs, values and expectations according to which it can be justified. Furthermore, Weber's definition lacks two things: first, components of legitimacy that are not a matter of belief such as legality and, second, the idea of consent by citizens expressed through actions that indicate consent. Beetham[14] argues that Weber's 'types' of legitimacy are rather all forms of 'beliefs' and are thus just one component of legitimacy. He therefore suggests an alternative framework with three distinct levels: conformity to rules, justifiability of rules in terms of shared beliefs, and legitimation through expressed consent. Lamb[4] proposes a multidimensional framework that shows five features which can be used to assess legitimacy: predictable, justifiable, equitable, accessible and respectful. This reflects an understanding of legitimacy as a two-way relationship where legitimacy is not merely a reflection of belief but is reflected in the interplay of individual beliefs and system features and is indicated by evidence of consent.

These dominant and alternative views of legitimacy are, however, rather rigid and narrow, neglecting the fact that legitimacy is dynamic as norms and values change, and legitimacy is hence always in a process of transformation, construction and deconstruction.[16] Local power relationships are often not considered and the focus on Western-type strong states neglects the reality of diverse non-Western governance structures.[13] There is a danger that Weber's categories of legal-rational, traditional and charismatic forms of legitimacy fall into a binary cliché in which the legal-rational is aligned with the modern, progressive and good, and the traditional and the charismatic are seen as backward, regressive and bad. In reality, and as will be demonstrated with the case study of Lebanon, hybridised forms of legitimacy are more likely to exist whereby societies develop their own set of legitimacies that make up an ethos and politico-cultural logic. Ideal types and binaries have little role in these modernities whereby institutions, citizens and a host of other bodies operating at different levels of society invent and reinvent legitimacy.

The next section explains the concept of the political marketplace or the transactional sphere in which legitimate political authority is developed and maintained. It is the contention of this chapter that the political marketplace concept is a useful way of understanding legitimacy in contemporary Lebanon.

The political marketplace

The notion of the political marketplace arises from work by Alex de Waal on the politics of the Horn of Africa.[17] For him, the political marketplace is a site of monetised transactional politics whereby those in power resemble 'skilful political business managers' who weave a deft course in political life. They extract and distribute resources to stay in power, and must chart a path that simultaneously makes them a client (of those who fund them) and a patron (of a constituency of voters and/or supporters). According to de Waal:

> The political marketplace is a system of governance run on the basis of personal transactions in which political services and allegiances are exchanged for material reward in a competitive manner. A ruler bargains with members of the political elite over how much he needs to pay – in cash, or in access to other lucrative resources such as contracts – in return for their support. They exert pressure on him using their ability to mobilise votes, turn out crowds or inflict damaging violence.[18]

De Waal's notion of the political marketplace calls into question the seriousness and utility of many internationally-sponsored statebuilding exercises. In theory, statebuilding is about the construction of a functioning state, one that in the mind of the liberal internationalist will be an iteration of a Weberian democratic state with an open economy. Yet many polities that have experienced significant international statebuilding interventions can be characterised as being political marketplaces. A Weberian state has not been built. Instead, international actors (including international organisations, donor governments and INGOs) have backed elites to act as a proxy for a state. This is the situation in Afghanistan, Iraq, South Sudan and many other polities. Sometimes there is a veneer of democracy but often the main criteria have been: that the current incumbent is not the last incumbent; that they do not threaten the international order; and that they are reasonably biddable. Thus, rather than statebuilding, there is deal-making with elites who have captured the state, or those parts of the state that they find attractive. The deal-making involves political elites delivering goods and services to international actors. These might include the provision of the façade of a legitimate government, or the control of factions and others who might threaten national or regional security, and the opening of markets to international and transnational actors. The return side of the transaction might involve the transfer of material resources (either directly or circuitously to political elites), international legitimacy, humanitarian and development assistance, and forms of security and political tenure. This transactional politics and deal-making fits within the notion of the political marketplace.

It is the argument of this chapter that political legitimacy in Lebanon can be explained through the lens of a political marketplace. Before going any further, it is worth noting that the notion of the political marketplace only goes so far in relation to our account of Lebanon and legitimate political authority. The aspect of Lebanon's political culture that is not fully taken account of by the idea of the political marketplace is identity politics. Lebanon is patterned by entrenched sectarian affiliations that mean that most people would self-identify with religious-political labels. This means that the political marketplace, in the case of Lebanon, is not an untrammelled scene of capitalism whereby politics is dictated by the highest bidder. Instead, we see a hybrid polity (as all polities are) whereby identity politics and transactional politics co-constitute each other to produce a context in which politics is marketised and monetised but also shaped by identity-claims and grievances. Lebanon's political marketplace allows for some transactions to cross over the main societal fissures. Indeed, Lebanon is a power-sharing democracy (although many caveats should be attached to such a description). The strength of identity politics, however, means that there are limits to the transactional nature of politics.

Five aspects of De Waal's notion of the political marketplace provide an analytical framework for this chapter[19] and are applied to Lebanon in the next section:

1. That politics is dominated by monetised transactional politics. This is true of Lebanon although, as just mentioned, it is true only up to a point. Identity politics will trump transactional politics in many instances.
2. The political marketplace relies on highly personalised forms of politics – with elite figureheads and families playing a prominent role.
3. The political marketplace is internationally and transnationally integrated.

4. The political marketplace is structured and regulated.
5. The political marketplace is characterised by hegemonic masculinity.

Taken together, these five points provide a way of understanding political legitimacy in contemporary Lebanon. Importantly, they help give an idea of the complexity and fluidity of transactional politics. The political marketplace is made and remade on a constant basis. It involves much insecurity and precariousness on the part of political elites, as well as their international sponsors.

Lebanon

This section takes each of the five points above and discusses them in turn in relation to Lebanon. As a collective, the five points build a picture of a Lebanon in which legitimate political authority is male, in the hands of a small clique and is, to some extent, for sale.

Dominance of transactional politics

This point can be modified from de Waal's emphasis on monetised transactional politics to take account of the identity politics that prevails in Lebanon, and the fact that many of the transactions that lubricate politics rely on goods in kind as well as money. Lebanon's politics rely on a series of trade-offs. At the national level, the current constitutional 'order' emanating from the 1989 Ta'if Accord can be described as a nationally agreed and internationally sanctioned trade-off. Within this national-level trade-off there are a series of sub-national trade-offs that make Lebanese politics the site of considerable transactional activity. The most obvious series of transactions occur at the intra-group level whereby Shiite, Sunni, Christian Orthodox and Druze political actors[20] act as brokers to channel resources (jobs, 'public' goods, security, prestige) to their own community. In the legal-rationalist scenario, this would be the function of the state and so capture of the state would be the logical route through which political leaders could access the resources required to channel resources to their supporters (thereby gaining and maintaining legitimacy). In Lebanon, however, the capture of the state is not regarded by political elites as a failsafe way to access resources. Access to the state helps – but only up to a point. Instead, most political leaders rely on extra-state routes to access resources and thus to achieve legitimacy. The most significant of these routes involve identity politics, the use of political dynasties, and support from external backers.

Lebanon, odd as it may seem to those accustomed to a legal-rational mind-set, is a site in which political leaders do not particularly identify with the idea of Lebanon, or the Lebanese state. Instead, most political leaders preside over a landscape primarily populated by networks (of their own loyalists and members of the same politico-religious identity group). This is also how many people see, and embody, their political lives. In the 2013 interviews with citizens, it was remarkable how few of them talked about Lebanon as a country. There was very little sense of the existence of the nation-state as, in reality, there is no singular nation of Lebanon. Nor is there much of a state. The consociational system is based, to a certain degree, on process-based, democratic legitimacy; however, power-sharing based on sectarian identity undermines the development of national identity and state-based legitimacy. Notions of a common Lebanese nationalism are subordinated to factionalised politico-religious identity groups. The Lebanese state is minimal – a husk with limited relevance given its inability to provide services and the unwillingness of political leaders to make it the conduit for public goods. Instead, politics is seen primarily through the lens of identity groups and the relations of that group with other groups. The Ta'if Accord, although ushering an end to the civil war, institutionalised and codified politico-religious politics. As one interviewee noted, 'The Accord reinforced sectarianism, and above all moved it from the street to the political and administrative structure of the government and country in general'.[21]

Political leaders are able to exploit this institutionalised sectarianism and rely on members of the respective identity groups to be exclusively supportive of in-group political leaders. But this only goes so far. Political constituencies require mobilisation, space for their grievances and aspirations to be aired, evidence of competence from their leaders, and – especially in a fractured society – evidence that their situation is more advantageous than rival groups. All of this requires resources and it is here that Lebanon can be seen as a political marketplace. As will be discussed in more detail in a subsequent sub-section, most Lebanese political leaders have external sponsors who – it is not completely unfair to say – have bought Lebanese clients (although these clients are not without agency). These resources (both monetary and symbolic) are then filtered down into the groups, being top-sliced along the way. As one interviewee remarked of former Prime Minister Rafik Hariri, 'He knew how to return the favours'.[22] On another currently active politician he said, 'It's all about jobs', meaning the political leader was able to secure jobs for his constituency.

Distribution of resources, including the allocation of jobs among leaders' constituencies, is a matter that cannot be analysed without referring to *wasta*. Lebanon's consociational political system is thought to undermine most forms of state legitimacy and instead supports a patronage-based legitimacy.[23] Referred to as *blat* in Russian and *Vitamin-B* in German, *wasta* can be defined as 'a type of favouritism that grants one with advantages, not because of merit, but because of the tribe (or in the case of Lebanon, sect) they belong to. Wasta is personalistic and most often originates from family, tribal (sectarian) relationships, or close friendship'.[24] Often described in Western cultures in negative ways connected to corruption, it can also be likened to a form of professional networking that is crucial if one wants to survive in Lebanon's political marketplace. According to Cunningham and Sarayrah, 'understanding *wasta* is key to understanding decisions in the Middle East, for *wasta* pervades the culture of all Arab countries and is a force in every significant decision'.[25] Due to this importance, it should not just be dismissed as a form of corruption but rather acknowledged as an important part of social capital in the marketplace. It is celebrated as a source of pride and prestige.[26] Interviews with small businesses in Lebanon have shown this importance also within the international aid system. When asked about access to resources, the common answer, given with a smirk was 'it's all about who you know (which is also the literal translation of *wasta*), it's all about *wasta*'.[27] This shows not only the importance of *wasta* and its omnipresence in everyday life, but also how it permeates traditional political spheres in Lebanon as well as international aspects of the marketplace. *Wasta* 'acts as an invisible hand that facilitates individuals engaged in complex exchanges within a social network'[25]. Furthermore, it is then also deeply linked to power relations, as those that are not well connected naturally cannot benefit as much as those who have established connections with important families/clans.

It is argued here that government policies are merely support actors compared to the deeply institutionalised relationship infrastructures embedded in *wasta*.[28] There is a profound public lack of trust in government and so, to get things done, many people rely on family connections.[29] Thus, *wasta* is the prominent way through which resources and markets are accessed which shows the pragmatic legitimacy entailed in *wasta*. Finally, *wasta* has gained moral legitimacy over the course of history as it is not only perceived to be beneficial but also as 'the right thing to do',[30] a notion that prevails in Lebanon still today.

Interviews among opinion-formers attested to how the buying of favours is ingrained into how Lebanese society operates. As a Lebanese employee of an INGO commented, 'Bribery is not a scandal. People are used to it . . . It is the system'.[31] One civil society interviewee noted how jobs in the army and civil service were bought.[32] A number of interviewees commented on how elections saw the mobilisation of constituencies, sometimes with cash inducements but also with promises of resources to come. Often the money to fund electoral campaigns came from outside – 'the Gulf, Iran and Saudi Arabia'.[33]

There is some political cross-over in Lebanon in the sense of members of one religious group voting for someone outside of their group. For example, Walid Jumblatt, the Druze leader, has secured votes from some Christians and Sunnis. In part, this is due to geography (they reside in an area 'controlled' by him and his supporters) and in part this is because he is the conduit for resources.[34]

Highly personalised forms of politics

One of the remarkable aspects of Lebanese politics is the importance and persistence of political dynasties. Emblematic figures have been able to maintain prominent positions on the political stage for long periods of time. At the time of writing, Hassan Nasrallah has been Secretary General of Hezbollah since 1992. Nahib Berri has led the Amal Movement since 1980 and has been Speaker of the Parliament since 1992. Walid Jumblatt (son of Druze leader Kamal Jumblatt) has been seen as the leader of Lebanon's Druze population since at least the 1980s, although he is in the process of stepping aside from active politics – but making sure his son replaces him. Michel Aoun, a Christian Maronite, was a General in the Lebanese Army in the 1980s, then became Prime Minister and is currently President. Saad Hariri, the former Prime Minister, is the son of assassinated former Prime Minister Rafik Hariri. The list of political dynasties (all dominated by males) could go on.

The essential point is that the political system is highly personalised, with dynastic figureheads regarded as the legitimate representative of a single community. As one interviewee noted, '. . . if you offend Saad Hariri that means you are offending the Sunnis'.[35] Another interviewee said 'I even stopped dealing with the grocery shop in the neighbourhood. I can't stand it anymore – every time [I] enter his shop, he insists on insulting Saad Hariri'.[36] The totemic status of Hariri is replicated in other communities with other figureheads. In some cases, dynastic leaders have engaged in drastic alliance shifts. These can be best explained by the need to protect their own position and to secure access to resources.

While the two main sources of legitimate political authority for political leaders are their dynastic heritage as community leaders, and their ability to secure and distribute goods and services, there is a third – difficult to define – factor: cultural status and significance. Political leaders are aware of the need to be seen as figureheads for their communities and so they live up to this. Often they have a lifestyle and entourage that signals their importance. As one interviewee noted, 'The road that takes you to the house of politicians is paved'.[37]

The political marketplace is internationally and transnationally integrated

It is worth noting that Lebanon's political marketplace is integrated into a series of international and transnational political economies. The marketplace is well-known by external actors and indeed these actors not only help fuel the marketplace, but they have helped construct it, too. Lebanon is a highly penetrated context, with multiple external actors – international organisations, states and INGOs – maintaining clients in Lebanon. Lebanese political actors are aware of this marketplace and in many instances have actively sought patrons. A short chapter does not afford enough space to map the complex web of patrons and clients. Moreover, the web of relationships is more complicated than a simple case of Iran supporting Hezbollah and Saudi Arabia and the US supporting the Sunnis to counterpoise Iranian influence.

The key point is that the marketplace is an accepted part of 'doing business' in Lebanon. External actors realise that as this is a marketplace it involves competition and thus they have to incentivise potential Lebanese clients. This involves, in some cases, cash. In other cases, the currency might be prestige or offers of security. The widespread international and transnational acceptance of a market is worth bearing in mind in relation to questions of legitimacy as it undercuts the legitimacy of those who may seek to justify their actions on the grounds of principle. Most of the discussions between international and transnational actors, and Lebanese political actors, will occur behind closed doors. Indeed, perhaps the most remarkable aspect of a statement by US Vice President Joe Biden during the 2009 Lebanese election was that it was made publicly. According to Biden, 'I do not come here to back any particular party or any particular person. I come here to back certain principles . . . We will evaluate the shape of our assistance programs based on the composition of the new government and the policies it advocates'. His comments were translated by headline writers to 'If you vote for Hezbollah, we'll cut your aid'.[38] Just for good measure, a US naval fleet was stationed just off the Lebanese coast, and within sight of Beirut, for the duration of Biden's visit.

The political marketplace is structured and regulated

All markets, even the so-called 'free market', have rules and limits. They rely on a certain degree of predictability of reward and censure to make it rational for actors to become involved in them. In a context in which trust is in short supply, actors may rely on observed evidence of past exchanges to engage in the market, and a virtuous cycle of reciprocity may develop.[39] Markets of this sort are system stabilising but still dependent on contingency (that an action by actor A will be reciprocated by an action by actor B).[40] Importantly, the rules of the market are rarely written down, yet they are well known.

From the outside, it may seem that societies prone to civil war and experiencing threat-laden politics are without regulation and order. Despite upheaval, Lebanese politics and society is highly structured and regulated. A fundamental structure comes in the post-Ta'if Accord constitutional arrangement, a form of consociationalism that preserves a rough balance between Sunnis, Shia and Christians. A key plank of the constitutional structure is based on the fiction that Lebanon's population is comprised of one third Sunnis, one third Shia and one third Christian. What is more, most politicians accept this fiction. To do otherwise risks bringing down the entire arrangement and raising the possibility of civil war.

Aside from the constitution, many other structures and types of regulation take the form of embedded norms that are widely accepted but not written down. Chief here is the restraint shown by political leaders. Certainly there are mobilisations, unwise words, and gestures that risk upsetting the balance. Yet, in large part, these occur within limits. Since the civil war, Lebanon has come close to the edge of civil war with mobilisations and counter-mobilisations, most notably in the wake of the 2005 assassination of former Prime Minister Rafik Hariri. There has been sectarian violence and constitutional crises (such as the failure to appoint a President and the bizarre 2017 on/off resignation of Prime Minister Saad Hariri). Yet this turbulence has occurred within limits. It can be said that there is awareness among many political leaders that they can rock the boat (often to keep their own supporters mobilised) but not capsize it.

The political marketplace is characterised by hegemonic masculinity

As discussed in the section on the highly personalised forms of politics, it is noticeable that the main political leaders in Lebanon are, and have been, men. Lebanese politics is strikingly male. Following the 2009 parliamentary election, a mere 3.1 per cent of members of the Lebanese Parliament were female.[41] This was more or less at the bottom of the world index of female parliamentary representation. The women's affairs minister is a man.[42] There has been no shortage of analysis on the male domination of Lebanese politics.[43] Nor has there been a shortage of women's participation-type programmes and projects by international actors.[44] Despite all of this campaigning and advocacy, the May 2018 election resulted in a very modest uplift of female parliamentarians to 4.7 per cent – and a number of them were related to prominent male politicians.

One area in which a hyper-masculine political culture is evident is in the tenor of political debate. This has tempered somewhat in recent years, perhaps in a realisation (and echoing the above sub-section) that the system needs some regulation lest it implode. The following quotation from Walid Jumblatt, a veteran Druze leader and former warlord, gives an idea of the masculine ultimatum style politics based on threats of violence:

> If you think that we will stand idly by, you are imagining things. We might be forced to leave scorched earth. Our existence, our honour, our survival, and Lebanon are more important than anything else. You want anarchy? We welcome anarchy. You want war? We welcome war. We have no problem with weapons. We have no problem with weapons or missiles. We will take the missiles from you, ready to fire. We have no problem with martyrdom or suicide.[45]

The masculine political culture is underpinned by a masculinised societal culture. The non-elite interviews conducted as part of this research attest to the fact that many (not all) households are male dominated, with the male deciding where the family live, and how relations with out-group members are to be conducted.[46] As one male interviewee noted, 'A wife can't be independent from the husband . . . at the end she is under my umbrella and should always be'.[47]

Taken together, the various components of Lebanon's political marketplace suggest a polity in which legitimacy is transactional. As such, it requires those in the market to be keen observers of their context and to move deftly. It places an emphasis on the optics of legitimacy. Legitimate political authority is as much about being seen to have legitimacy, and being seen to have the right to legitimacy. Thus, the visual aspect of politics matters – whether through the size of street protests or the various billboards seen around Lebanon attesting to the munificent philanthropy of various leaders in the Gulf States who sponsor reconstruction and development. But alongside this visual aspect of legitimate political authority are unseen aspects that will happen behind closed doors or rely on tacit understandings that support or compliance on one issue will necessitate some form of return.

International and transnational actors

Thus far, the chapter has examined legitimate political authority among Lebanese political actors. But Lebanon is a highly penetrated society, with multiple international and transnational actors holding significant power. The power of political patrons, such as the US, Saudi Arabia and Iran, has already been alluded to. This section will look at the legitimacy of international peace-support, humanitarian and development actors. International organisations, bilateral donors and INGOs have responded to a series of crises in Lebanon: the enormous destruction caused by the 2006 Israeli-Hezbollah war, the movement of approximately one million Syrians into Lebanon as a result of the Syrian civil wars, and the perceived need for Lebanon – as a deeply divided society – to have governance and pro-peace support. Through interviews with NGO and INGO personnel, we have identified seven sources of legitimacy claimed by external actors for their presence and activities in Lebanon:

- International legal framework
- Delivery and technical skill
- In country orientation
- Track record
- Technocratic standards
- Peer legitimacy
- External legitimacy

It should be said that in many of the interviews with NGO and INGO personnel, we began by talking about the sources of legitimate political authority in Lebanon. Interviewees were usually able to talk in an animated fashion about legitimacy in Lebanon and often talked in an exasperated fashion about sectarianism and corruption. When we changed tack and asked about the legitimacy of their organisations and their legitimacy to operate in Lebanon, there was often a lengthy pause and a clunking of mental gears. Interviewees spoke openly and at length about the legitimacy of their own organisations, but it was clear that many of them had not really given the issue much consideration.

The first issue, an international legal framework – such as a body of international law and norms or an internationally-approved mandate – was mentioned surprisingly infrequently by interviewees. International mandates, and particularly UN mandates, are of course political devices and, as such, have the potential to be divisive. UN Security Council Resolution 1701 that was introduced in the wake of the 2006 Israeli-Hezbollah war, for example, is regarded negatively by many Shia as a vehicle to curb Hezbollah. Some Sunnis and Christians, on the other hand, would see the mandate as a good thing. One interviewee working for a European-based humanitarian/development organisation noted that INGOs often had to remind the Lebanese government of their obligations in relation to human rights or the rights of the child.[48]

A second source of legitimacy for international actors rested in their technical skills. As one INGO worker noted, 'We can get shit done, sometimes'.[49] As he went on to explain, 'It depends on the INGO and what they have to offer. MSF (Médecins Sans Frontières) has a lot as they often have something the government has not'. This is a crucial contextual point and explains much of the legitimacy of international actors. Given that the Lebanese government cannot, or is not inclined to, deliver public goods then other actors – political parties, bilateral donors, NGOs and INGOs – become the default providers of these goods. Significant legitimacy follows from this. There is no doubting the technical competence of many international organisations and INGOs. The UN and some INGOs can scale up very quickly.[50] The UN in particular is able to collect high quality data – something that is of great use to the government and others.[51] It is worth noting, and this is a point made by a number of interviewees, that many Lebanese do not distinguish between INGOs and international organisations. For many, they are 'those foreign people in cars who bring us stuff'.[52] As a result, it may be difficult for international and transnational actors to benefit from legitimacy from the public.

A third source of legitimacy comes from the in-country orientation of the INGO. In other words, does it comport itself in a way that gains trust and respect from national employees of the INGO, the government and the various constituencies that constitute the Lebanese public? An in-country orientation that might enhance legitimacy may include the hiring of national staff and their inclusion in programme and project design, the compliance of an organisation with national protocols, and an attempt to respond to the needs of all communities.

A fourth source of legitimacy that was highlighted in the interviews was the track record of the organisation in Lebanon. Lebanon's repeated crises have meant that INGOs, NGOs and others have come and gone. Some organisations, however, have built up a track record – and relationships – over a number of decades. The representative of one organisation that has been present in Lebanon for a long period noted that the organisation still had 'kudos' from its assistance following the 2006 Israeli-Hezbollah war.[53] The interviewee went on to note that 'people have long memories'. In a similar vein, another interviewee noted, 'If you mess up they will not forget. The smaller the community, the longer they will remember'.[54]

A fifth source of legitimacy arose from the technocratic standards that intervening organisations could meet, or their activities in innovating such standards. A number of interviewees noted that the Lebanese government was tightening restrictions on expatriate workers. As one Lebanese employee of an NGO noted, 'INGOs and NGOs have to work in a framework provided by the Lebanese Government . . . before an NGO could do anything. Now there are visas for ex-pats'.[55] INGOs now have to register with the Ministry of Finance. Although there are still many unregistered organisations in Lebanon,[56] the government is becoming stricter. In addition to the controls imposed from without, a number of interviewees noted that an increasing number of INGOs were imposing their own strictures and accountability checks. Thus, for example, INGOs conducted due diligence checks on themselves or contracted others to do this. Some also developed and instituted SMS accountability mechanisms whereby the recipients of assistance could give feedback. This innovation is important in that most accountability mechanisms tend to miss out the recipients.

A sixth source of legitimacy was peer legitimacy or the 'political economy' of observation and ranking among bilateral donors, INGOs and NGOs. Organisations noticed when another organisation was effective and well run, and also noted the reverse. Much of this depended, according to interviewees, on the calibre of the country director of an INGO and their quality could vary considerably.[57] Rumour and subjective judgement played a large role in this, but given that Lebanon is a small area and that many INGO staff have a long track record of working in the sector, their professional assessments of peers were worth taking seriously.[58]

The final source of legitimacy mentioned by interviewees was external legitimacy coming from the donors themselves. One interviewee noted that his organisation's main source of legitimacy came from Brussels, as the organisation was chiefly funded through the European Union.[59] This position was echoed, not without awareness and discomfort, by a number of interviewees. Such legitimacy could, potentially, be self-assumed. This is not to suggest that INGOs act irresponsibly or do not respond to actual need that has been assessed with care. It is, instead, to highlight how national and sub-national actors can be bypassed and how legitimacy for many international actors lies outwith Lebanon.

Concluding discussion

This chapter comes to three conclusions in relation to political legitimacy. While the conclusions primarily stem from the analysis of Lebanon, they have wider implications for how we consider legitimate political authority.

The first point to make is that there is a multiplicity of sources and types of legitimacy. As a result, it is difficult to conceive of legitimacy as a discrete political currency or phenomenon. Instead it is a complex set of relationships, transactions and perceptions. This diffuse nature of legitimacy is doubtless analytically unsatisfactory to those who value a neatness of concepts and categories. But the case of Lebanon shows that a quest for such neatness is likely to be frustrated. By drawing on De Waal's concept of the political marketplace, this chapter highlighted the transactional nature of legitimacy – how it can be attained and held through the provision of material and non-material resources. The networked nature of legitimate political authority also became clear, particularly in relation to how networks map onto identity affiliations. This is also likely to be true of multiple other contexts in which political support is not only contingent on the provision of public goods but is also linked to race, religion, caste or tribe.

A recognition of legitimacies (rather than a singular legitimacy) calls for research methods capable of escaping the orthodoxy of political science and its concentration on formal institutions. Networked and transactional legitimacy points to the necessity of deploying research methods that draw on sociology and anthropology in order to capture the complex and textured nature of legitimacy.

A second conclusion from the case of Lebanon is to point to the minor role of the state and its formal institutions. In many contexts, and certainly in much of the orthodox literature on legitimate political authority, the state plays a central role as a clearing house for claims on legitimacy or as the chief disburser of public goods (that may lead to legitimacy). In the case of Lebanon, political actors do not necessarily see the state as the primary vehicle through which to exercise power. Instead, clan-based political parties and movements are the chief means of accumulating support, disbursing patronage and being seen to achieve tactical and strategic goals. Hezbollah plays a part in the power-sharing government, yet has its own patronage network independent of the state. Other parties have, or have tried to, emulate this configuration. The deeply divided nature of Lebanon means that actors taking the reins of the state (even under a power-sharing arrangement) have to show responsibility for citizens outside of their core identity group. This is an unattractive prospect for many political actors in Lebanon as it brings few rewards. Moreover, the Lebanese state – under successive governments – has acquired only limited governance capabilities. Massive international 'good governance' assistance over many decades has strengthened government capabilities in some functional areas, but the results have been patchy. To put it bluntly, the state has limited competence and technical ability. Lebanon is a neo-liberal state that has not gone through a prior phase of social welfare followed by austerity. Its original, and lasting, stance has been one of a parsimonious public offering.

The paucity of the state as a formal political actor sets Lebanon apart from a number of states, especially those in the formal Weberian tradition. Yet there is a significant category of states in which the state has a weak claim to popular loyalty or affiliation. These hollow or virtual states are often host to identity groups that have a greater hold over people. Legitimacy still matters to people in such contexts but they do not see the state as being the primary legitimate political entity.

The final concluding point is to note that the legitimacy of domestic and international actors in Lebanon was framed in quite different ways. This reinforces our other conclusion on the plurality of types of legitimacy. While there are some overlaps on how the legitimacy of actors is assessed, the frames of legitimacy – that is the calculation on whether an actor is legitimate or not – were made in different ways. The area of overlap was on technical ability and provision of public goods. Claims to legitimacy for both international and domestic actors are enhanced if they are able to provide goods. Yet *wasta*, or the 'who you know' culture, opens avenues of networking and transactional politics that, in large part, do not apply to international actors. Similarly, the political economies of INGOs that involve pleasing donors, maintaining a strict audit trail, and having a web presence that speaks to audiences back home, have limited relevance to the legitimacy calculations made about actors internal to Lebanon.

Notes

1. De Waal, Alex, *The Real Politics of The Horn of Africa: Money, War, and The Business of Power* (Cambridge: Polity, 2015).
2. Maktabi, R., 'The Lebanese census of 1932 revisited: who are the Lebanese?' *British Journal of Middle East Studies*, 1999, 26: 2, pp. 219–41.
3. Erman, E., 'Global political legitimacy beyond justice and democracy?' *International Theory*, 2016, 8: 1, pp. 29–62.
4. Netelenbos, B., *Political Legitimacy beyond Weber: an Analytical Framework* (London: Palgrave Macmillan, 2016).
5. Lamb, R., *Rethinking Legitimacy and Illegitimacy, a New Approach to Assessing Support and Opposition across Disciplines*, Center for Strategic & International Studies (Plymouth: Rowan & Littlefield, 2014).

6. Fukuyama, F., *State-Building – Governance and World Order in the 21st Century* (New York: Profile Books, 2004).
7. Rotberg, R., *When States Fail: Causes and Consequences* (Princeton: Princeton University Press, 2004), p. 6.
8. Lemay-Hérbert, N., Rethinking Weberian Approaches to Statebuilding, in D. Chandler and T. D. Sisk (eds.), *Routledge Handbook of International Statebuilding* (Abingdon: Routledge, 2013), pp. 3–14.
9. Durkheim, E., *Professional Ethics and Civic Morals* (London: Routledge, 1957), pp. 79–80.
10. Roos, K. and Lidström, A., 'Local policies and local government legitimacy, the Swedish case', *Urban Research & Practice*, 2014, 7: 2, pp. 137–52.
11. Andersen, M. S., 'Legitimacy in state-building: a review of the IR literature', *International Political Sociology*, 2012, 6, 205–19.
12. Buzan, B., *People, States and Fear: An Agenda for International Security Studies in the Post-cold War Era* (New York: Harvester Wheatsheaf, 1991).
13. Lipset, S. M., *Political Man, the Social Basis of Politics* (New York: Doubleday, 1959), p. 86.
14. Weigand, F., *Investigating the Role of Legitimacy in the Political Order of Conflict-torn Spaces*, Working Paper SiT/WP/04/15 (London: LSE, 2015).
15. Beetham, D., *The Legitimation of Power* (Houndmills: Palgrave, 1991).
16. Algappa, M., 'The anatomy of legitimacy', in Alagappa, M. (ed.), *Political Legitimacy in Southeast Asia. The Quest for Moral Authority* (Stanford: Stanford University Press, 1995).
17. De Waal, *The Real Politics of The Horn of Africa: Money, War, and The Business of Power.*
18. De Waal, Alex, 'Introduction to the political marketplace for policymakers', The Justice and Security Research Programme, World Peace Foundation, Policy Brief 1, 2016, p. 1. Available at <http://www.lse.ac.uk/internationalDevelopment/research/JSRP/downloads/JSRP-Brief-1.pdf> (last accessed 15 March 2018).
19. Drawn primarily from De Waal, 'Introduction to the political marketplace for policymakers'.
20. It is acknowledged that in Lebanon there are eighteen recognised religious sects, among which the ones mentioned here are the most prominent and powerful.
21. Interview with male Shia, Beirut, 17 July 2013.
22. Interview with NGO employee, Beirut, 26 June 2017.
23. Mourad, L. and Piron, L. H., *Municipal Service Delivery, Stability, Social Cohesion and Legitimacy in Lebanon, an Analytical Literature Review*, Background Paper, Issam Fares Institute for Public Policies (Beirut: American University of Beirut, 2016).
24. Kropf, A. and Newbury-Smith, T. C., 'Wasta as a Form of Social Capital? An Institutional Perspective', in Ramady, M. A. (ed.), *The Political Economy of Wasta: Use and Abuse of Social Capital Networking* (Cham: Springer, 2016), pp. 3–22.
25. Cunningham, R. and Sarayrah, Y., *Wasta: The hidden force in Middle Eastern societies* (London: Praeger, 1993), p. 3.

26. Barnett, A., Yandle, B. and Naufal, G., Regulation, trust and cronyism in Middle Eastern societies: the simple economics of *wasta*', *The Journal of Socio-Economics*, 2013, 44: pp. 41–46 at p. 26.
27. Interview with male shop owner, Majdel Anjar, 6 March 2018.
28. Weir, D. T. H., 'Human Resource Development in the Middle East: A Fourth Paradigm', in M. Lee (ed.), *HRD in a Complex World* (London: Routledge, 2003), pp. 69–82.
29. Alreshoodu, S. A., 'Negative Institutional Influences in the Saudi Public Sector: *Wasta*, Public Service Motivation and Employee Outcomes' (Doctoral Dissertation), (Cardiff: Cardiff University, 2016).
30. Sidani, Y. and Thornberry, J., 'Nepotism in the Arab world: an institutional theory perspective', *Business Ethics Quarterly: the Journal of the Society for Business Ethics*, 2013, 23: 1, pp. 69–96.
31. Interview with INGO employee, 26 June 2017.
32. Interview with NGO employee, Beirut, 26 June 2017.
33. Interview with INGO employee, Beirut, 26 June 2017.
34. Interview with NGO employee, Beirut, 26 June 2017.
35. Interview, Male Sunni, Beirut, 21 June 2013.
36. Interview, Female, Beirut, 6 July 2013.
37. Interview with INGOa employee, 28 June 2017.
38. Daragahi, Borzou, 'Joe Biden, in Lebanon, hints that US might cut aid if Hezbollah win election', *Los Angeles Times*, 23 May 2009. Available at <http://articles.latimes.com/2009/may/23/world/fg-biden-lebanon23> (last accessed 19 April 2018).
39. Lister, Andrew, 'Markets, desert, and reciprocity', *Politics, Philosophy & Economics*, 2017, 16: 1, pp. 47–69.
40. Manatschal, Anita, 'Reciprocity as a trigger of social cooperation in contemporary immigration societies?', *Acta Sociologica*, 2015, 58: 3, pp. 233–48.
41. International Parliamentary Union, 'Women in national parliaments', available at <http://archive.ipu.org/wmn-e/classif.htm> (last accessed 16 March 2018).
42. Kanso, Heba, 'Losing opportunities: Lebanon campaigns for more women in parliament', Reuters, 7 February 2018. Available at <https://www.reuters.com/article/us-lebanon-women-politics/losing-opportunities-lebanon-campaigns-for-more-women-in-parliament-idUSKBN1FR1Z8> (last accessed 18 March 2018).
43. Khoury, Doreen, 'Women's political participation in Lebanon', *Heinrich Böll Stiftung*, 25 July 2013. Available at <https://www.boell.de/en/2013/07/25/womens-political-participation-lebanon> (last accessed 18 March 2018).
44. Delegation of the European Union to Lebanon, 'Gender equity and empowerment of women in Lebanon, EU-funded project celebrates achievements at closing event', European External Action Service Press Release, 3 March 2017. Available at <https://eeas.europa.eu/delegations/lebanon_tk/26698/%22Gender%20Equity%20and%20empowerment%20of%20Women%20in%20Lebanon%E2%80%9D%20EU-funded%20project%20

260 / Kristina Tschunkert and Roger Mac Ginty

celebrates%20achievements%20at%20closing%20event> (last accessed 18
March 2018); Kiwan, Dina, Farah, May, Annan, Rawan and Jaber, Heather,
*Women's participation and leadership in Lebanon, Jordan and Kurdistan Region
of Iraq: Moving from individual to collective change*, Oxfam Research Report,
(Oxford: Oxfam, April 2016).
45. Walid Jumblatt cited on MEMRI TV website, 10 February 2008. Available at
<https://www.memri.org/tv/lebanese-druze-leader-walid-jumblatt-exchanges-
curses-and-threats-lebanese-rivals/transcript> (last accessed 18 March 2018).
46. Interview with female Sunni, Soujoud, 2 June 2013.
47. Interview with male Sunni, Beirut, 27 June 2013.
48. Interview with INGOb employee Beirut, 28 June 2017.
49. Interview with INGO employee Beirut, 27 June 2017.
50. Interview with an employee of a UN agency, Beirut, 27 June 2017.
51. Ibid.
52. Interview with national staff employee of INGO, Beirut, 26 June 2017.
53. Interview with INGOb employee Beirut, 28 June 2017.
54. Interview with INGO employee Beirut, 27 June 2017.
55. Interview with national staff employee of INGO, Beirut, 26 June 2017.
56. Interview with INGO employee Beirut, 27 June 2017.
57. Interview with INGOb employee Beirut, 28 June 2017.
58. Interview with Lebanese employee of NGO, Beirut, 26 June 2017.
59. Interview with INGO employee, Beirut, 27 June 2017.

Peacebuilding and Legitimacy: Some Concluding Thoughts

Oliver P. Richmond and Roger Mac Ginty

The simple horizontal and vertical alignment of multiple legitimacies into common, central authorities as the basis for an evolved and ethical peace appears to be an oversimplification of a very complex process. Too much substance is lost in its simplification, as is well illustrated in Roger Mac Ginty and Kristina Tschunkert's chapter on Lebanon, which follows Boege's deployment of hybridity in understanding the realities of legitimate authority in modern conflict-affected societies. Visoka's chapter on Kosovo underlines the relationality of contemporary legitimate authority, something which peacebuilding has mostly missed, and all of the other chapters confirm variations of this theme. Much of this argumentation indicates that effective peacebuilding needs to understand the special complexities of relational political legitimacy across life-worlds and levels of analysis far better if it is to be more successful. A localised view of legitimacy creates a number of different and contradictory demands in the context of the nature of the state and its performance, as well as towards the international community. These point beyond the usual understandings of modern legitimacy emanating from civil society and within a liberal social contract, which may be weakly extended to international institutions and law, however, including the balancing of social justice and human rights with identity, long-standing institutions, patterns of authority and law.

It is clear that social legitimacy – perhaps linked to kinship, religion or identity – is not always aligned with the state or with international norms. Yet, international actors have intervened in the post-Cold War environment as if local and state forms of legitimacy authority should be aligned with international law and norms. Indeed, enormous efforts have been made by international actors in multiple contexts to try to train, mentor and encourage local forms of legitimacy to adapt to internationally-recognised forms. This institutional isomorphism seems to have failed to recognise that different types of legitimacy are at work in different domains and that all of them contribute to a complex assemblage of power, legitimacy, patronage and logics. The empirical evidence amassed so far shows that convergence is an unlikely goal, if not impossible, and that in fact the multiple forms of legitimacy at work in post-war contexts normally diverge. This implies that legitimacy is likely to rest on a divergence rather than convergence between custom, practice, national or international law, a very tricky proposition indeed for any rationality-based international order.

Furthermore, notions of legitimacy require an acceptance that mobility across networks and scales is inevitably connected with security, development and peace, and that the old notion of fixed citizenship blocks these new and emerging rights.[1] This right and practice of mobility is also connected to discussions about historical and distributive legitimacy: it represents a micro-structural response as a form of recompense for both. Its impact on legitimacy is little understood so far. While the mobility of people, material, capital and ideas is by no means new, there is a sense that its pace and scale has increased in recent decades – thus bringing the rigidity of traditional thinking about peace and security into sharp relief. Because peacebuilding takes place in widely divergent societies, and involves a transfer of ideas and resources between them, there are significant complementarities and tensions between three key areas of legitimacy: local level, state and international legitimacy.

Local level legitimacy is connected with the organisation of everyday life and the cultural, social, economic and political power structures that maintain its integrity. It spans custom, tradition and identity to civil society, the social contract, and positionality vis-à-vis the state and the international community. This local legitimacy is often enacted and embodied at the hyper-local and micro-levels of the home, the immediate vicinity of the home and the family. It is often imbricated with gender and cultural relations that are at odds with widely accepted norms in the global North – many of which are reflected in international law. State legitimacy is related to legal and constitutional frameworks, and the maintenance of social, identity, and political processes. In many cases it exists simply because of 'stateness' – or the simple existence of the state and the power and claims that come with that. In an ideal case, it connects to debates about trust and community, the social contract and representation or elections. However, in many cases, the state has little interest in aligning its material power with immaterial claims such as representation or participation. International legitimacy rests on the common maintenance of the states-system, international law and norms of human rights, to varied extents. State and international forms of legitimacy are subject to questions of representation, efficiency and effectiveness (sometimes referred to as 'performance legitimacy'). They are both contested through different forms of statehood (authoritarian, non-secular, capitalist, development and so on) and competing sources of international legitimacy (say from the perspectives of the BRICS or IBSA, the UN system, the IFIs and so on). Perhaps one of the most interesting aspects of state and international legitimacy is the extent to which it is often unquestioned by many who live under these umbrellas.

Civil societies also have mixed perspectives on legitimacy, some aspiring to a liberal social contract, others influenced by identity, religion or different forms of community organisation, or economic positionality in the global economy. In many cases, parts of civil society might be captured by the state (for example, Nigeria) or by international actors (for example, Haiti) and so the independence of civil society, and thus its views on legitimacy, can be questioned.

The connections between local, state and international legitimacy are often seen as formative of state–society relations and of international society, both of which are necessary for peacebuilding's legitimacy. Thus, peacebuilding and intervention more broadly defined, is subject to tensions between local, state and global norms, interests and power structures. If the state follows social practice and the international follows consensus amongst states, this would probably be the optimal liberal peace scenario. Yet, a convergence between these different sources of legitimacy seems difficult in a post-colonial era. This is especially the case given their different scales. Can a hyper-local legitimacy based on a traditional family in Tajikistan be reconciled with a legitimacy based on conformity to international human rights law? As much as anything else, these different legitimacies are based on different logics or modes of thinking.

To understand the different bases and processes of local forms of legitimacy from different locations around the world, in their local, state and transnational forms requires that further research on legitimacy and legitimate political authority and must include local voices from different global regions. This requires research that enables different positionalities as a methodological approach to understanding how legitimate political authority is seen in different ways in different regions and contexts of the world. For western social scientists, jurists, policymakers and peacebuilding practitioners, it might also require seeking to understand beliefs and practices that are antithetical to basic rights that have been long normalised in the global north. This may allow a better understanding of how different forms of legitimacy,

formal or informal, material and immaterial, are related, entangled and potentially being mediated by multilateral or donor institutions, IFIs, INGOs, the
military or peacekeepers and other interventionary actors. It may help understand local, state and international forms of legitimacy and relationships, as
well as disaggregate, rational-legal, norm, power, trust, and context-centred
forms of legitimacy and their historical layers. Ontological and epistemological methods and approaches might be compared. Likewise, it may provide
grounded empirical knowledge and theory to explain where the mediation
of different forms of legitimacy has failed, or is in danger of failing. In fact,
this points beyond negative and positive (narrow and broad) forms of instrumental legitimacy, towards more relational and hybrid forms. This points to
the issue of whether peace can be made in situations where local, state and
international forms of legitimacy diverge? If local legitimacy is so important,
we cannot afford to ignore issues with regional security, geopolitics, global
capital, or other forces that are beyond the capacity of local systems of governance. Can different forms of political authority become more complementary rather than homogenous or subsidiary as subaltern, hybrid, and mobile
forms of political agency emerge on a large scale? This is necessary for peace
to be achieved under post-colonial conditions of hybridity, and yet, it is also
much more difficult to imagine an agonistic peace with alterity which would
be emancipatory and empathetic, than a homogenous peace in which power
underpins harmony (as with the liberal peace). However elegant the latter
may have seemed to its supporters, however, it has failed because it did not
undo entrenched power structures and inequalities, but rather has maintained
them through power-sharing arrangements, and exacerbated this through its
adoption of neoliberal forms of peace.

Subsidiarity and Complementarity

The understanding and practical implementation of two peacebuilding
principles is at stake in the more practical dimensions of this debate: principles that are widely endorsed by the UN, EU and the AU. These are:

(1) The principle of subsidiarity that a conflict should be managed
at the smallest, lowest or least centralised authority capable of
addressing matters effectively. The promise of respect for local
agency and ownership inherent in this principle is, however, in
practice often absent.

(2) The principle of complementarity refers to the need to address
conflict through close interaction between different groupings
within society. This principle undergirds the development of

peace architectures or infrastructures across the world and within states. It suggests an understanding that, even where a conflict is addressed at the most relevant level, local conflicts do not exist in isolation, and have to be addressed through collaboration with other groups of authority and legitimacy (meaning from the international down to the local and vice versa).

Both of these principles also relate to important norms, including human rights and social legitimacy (which may sometimes be contradictory), and to efficiency: that is the ability of governance and law to provide support and protection for citizens in a way they experience as reasonable and fair. In practice, however, complementarity is mostly developed in a top-down manner, partially denying the twin essentials of local agency and owner-ship, networked social relationality and inter-group relations, in favour of state or universal frameworks. This rights-based approach has often post-poned engaging with or overlooked pressing local needs, identities and existing (often unwritten and informal) law and institutions (or perceives them as an obstacle to peace). Furthermore, because the state is often con-trolled by political elites with a lot to lose from liberal reform (and more from critical restructuring), and its capacity is weak, it is unlikely that it has the capacity or the will to resolve such issues. Elites tend to see society as a resource to be managed rather than a political body to be represented in conflict affected societies.

Furthermore, when internationals delegate power to local actors through the state or through frameworks such as complementarity or subsidiarity they may dilute their own capacity to induce reform or support civil society. Thus, merely appealing to local forms of legitimacy is not enough, and may be counter-productive. It may be that more direct engagement is needed according to the political authority and processes local legitimacy suggests. Reconciling international, elite and local understandings of legitimacy is a very complex task but necessary if political authority is to be created and maintained, especially in view of the fact that authority can only be main-tained with social consent. It requires an acceptance that quite different views of legitimacy need to be negotiated and accommodated.

Finally, conflicts cannot be understood only on the scale of the state and its localised networks. Regional and global causal factors are also essential to any local or state conflict. Thus, a post-conflict form of legitimate authority must necessarily be related to all three scales, and the only way this can be relational, networked, and agonistically mediated, and engaged across the different authorities in existence, would be through networks of difference. Thus, post-conflict legitimate authority emerges through complex networks of mediated difference, rather than by assimilation into a homogenous legal, technical or bureaucratic system. Technical, bureaucratic, epistemic, legal, institutional, economic, identity or power-based forms of legitimate authority cannot capture these requirements alone: a complex combination is the practical reality. This means seeing legitimacy in the plural – as legitimacies that might interact in complex ways, draw on multiple sources of power and express themselves in very different ways. They would inevitably connect peace with global justice if their tensions could be resolved.

Legitimacy and Peacebuilding in Practice

The theoretical positions from a state-centric, positivist, liberal, structuralist and cosmopolitan perspective indicate that legitimacy must be constructed at the state and/or international level, based upon common interests or a supposed moral community at each level. Just about every case study one cares to examine indicates that this has not happened, nor been attempted, and indeed that legitimacies have often been in tension with each other rather than mutually mediated and constituted. This suggests that there should be a global or, at least, state-level formula for a common legitimacy, which must be discovered, implemented and enforced by constitutional and international law. In the absence of a framework allowing for the mobility of citizens across systems and scales, international, regional, state, and local institutions, laws, norms and interests would ultimately be aligned into a common set of positions, which each framework would have to accept and incorporate in order to become legitimate. Homogenous state level systems enable immobile citizenship in which resources and knowledge are mobile but legitimate authority is built on the centralised service delivery required by immobile citizenship in a territorialised setting. This may inadvertently contradict the attempt to stop nationalism and degrades rights, upon which liberal citizenship rests.

Trusteeship forms of external governance would resolve this in that they enforce the continuity of the system, as with UN governance in Timor after independence in 1999, Bosnia and Kosovo, and much literature of the era declares that a single system of legitimacy captured within a state system or liberal nature is desirable if not practical.[2] Clearly, the assumption of territorial sovereignty and the related lack of mobility supports some problematic outcomes, especially with respect to autonomy and self-determination, which counterposes the legitimate authority of the state and the international community. Palestine is a key example in political terms. Emblematic of the rational-bureaucratic-legal dimensions of this was the 'Standards Before Status' framework for Kosovo.[3] Similarly, the role of the Office of the

High Representative (OHR) in Bosnia and Herzegovina (BiH) was to make sure that domestic institutions aligned themselves with liberal peacebuilding, assuming a fixed territory and citizenry.[4] In a different manner, the US administration in Iraq followed neoliberal statebuilding frameworks.[5] In South Sudan, the Democratic Republic of the Congo (DRC) and Libya, the international presence has been much more cautious about taking over governance, or disaggregated aspects of it, but has taken on significant responsibilities over time. However, in Afghanistan and Iraq, internationals and particularly the US focused on their own legitimate authority as a medium for reconstructing a viable state.[6] As a consequence of failure in both these cases, intervention in Syria and Libya has been implausible or limited even under the terms of Responsibility to Protect (R2P),[7] and there has been very little engagement in the post-revolutionary states across the region, to support human rights or civil society, often leaving inhabitants to fend for themselves.[8] What is noticeable is that the rhetoric of liberal internationalism, so vocal in the late 1990s and early 2000s, has given way to embarrassed silence.[9] Or, where international actors, like the UK or EU, do make pronouncements on the future of a conflict-affected area it is often in terms of the need for security and stabilisation rather than in terms of human rights and representative forms of government.

This confused interplay of the legitimacy of liberal internationalism, elite nationalism, and social groupings has not prevented conflict in any of these cases: from the perspective of attaining a positive and hybrid form of peace, these are more or less raggedly governed or ungoverned spaces now in legitimate and consensual terms, under the forcible control of deep state, militarist, or corrupt elite actors. Locally legitimate authority is connected with the state through notions of self-determination, but ideologically, and in terms of global trade and international law, the relationship is minimal – and indeed often conflicting. It is conceptually elegant but hardly representative of empirical fact, and therefore the governance it develops rests on coercion rather than consent.

Such dynamics have been evolving over the history of UN involvement in peace matters, connecting intervention, the liberal international community, capital, civil society and deeper questions about the nature and sources of legitimate authority. Normally, rights and civil society are the most marginalised in the ensuing political framework, after war, even despite the discursive support of internationals.

For example, legitimacy in Cyprus during the early part of the conflict (1960s) was seen through two conflicting versions of nationalism (Greek aspirations for Enosis, and Turkish aspirations for independence or at least partition) in the Cold War context.[10] There was also a nascent third type of nationalism associated with some Greek Cypriots who wanted Cyprus to be an independent country, which many Greek nationalists also supported as an interim measure. In the 1970s, international law became especially important for the Greek Cypriot position in that it supported self-determination of the majority and independence. Later, the EU became prominent for both, though nationalism remained at the local level.[11] For the Turkish Cypriots, international law was not as helpful after 1974 because of the ambiguity about Turkish military intervention on their behalf and whether or not the war was legal in terms of protecting the Turkish Cypriots, or could be regarded as an invasion. What was particularly powerful was the legitimacy of Turkish state involvement and identity at the level of the Turkish Cypriot community.[12] Since the decolonisation movement of the 1950s, these different forms of legitimacy have tended to clash, meaning that multiple authorities across the island and region professed control of land, population, norms, institutions and military resources in ways that made it extremely difficult for proximate co-existence to occur.[13] This is more or less the prevailing situation, with several legitimate authorities appealing to different and contradictory arguments and population bases. This has proven impossible to resolve, and raises the question of whether or not it is actually possible to do so: this would imply hybrid and agonistic forms of legitimacy, connecting often opposed political systems with peaceful rather than violent methods of exchange, interim external guarantees, major territorial and other concessions. At the very least a toleration of difference, past injustice, and continuing clashing claims would be required. Many of these requirements are antithetical to the positions of both sides, in which they have invested much.

The approach to legitimacy during earlier phases of the Cyprus dispute were fairly similar to the very state-centric, rigid (and gendered) bargaining approach according to military and sovereign power on display in the Israel–Egypt conflict, leading up to the Camp David Accords, which reaffirmed boundaries, sovereignty, and territoriality under the guarantee of the US as a major superpower. Under this logic, authority was constructed in such a way as to put the state before human security for some groups such as the Palestinians, but not for the main state majorities.[14] In this way, legitimate authority is seen in realist guise, as a pragmatic choice to secure the greatest number according to fixed territory and boundaries. This is the basis for authority upon which Weberian notions of narrow legitimacy rest. However, this system of power, authority and legitimacy has clearly failed at several stages in Cyprus: colonial; post-colonial self-determination; and during a peace process designed to maintain that system but engineer a complex solution to accommodate conflicting nationalism since 1964.

Similarly, in the Middle East, the two state approach since the Oslo Accords has not been able to take control of legitimate authorities in order to displace them and modify them in liberal guise.

The later phases of the Cyprus and the Middle East peace processes, after the Cold War ended, began to operate more flexibly, meaning that the possibility of a solution appeared to be moving closer in both. Territoriality, power and sovereignty began to change with the encroachment of the EU into the Eastern Mediterranean and the related role of the US in the Middle East, softening power and boundaries and introducing pluralist attitudes to difference and identity. In Cyprus, for the international community and domestic actors, the reimagined post-conflict state would have to understand how legitimate authority across ethnic groups could be conceived in a heavily territorialised and nationalist environment. Various federal, confederal, cantonal and power-sharing approaches were consequently devised in order to maintain territorial sovereignty, and share authority. So far, the EU framework of integrated states has come closest to a common local, state, and international form of legitimacy, aligned across these scales of analysis. A similar model was envisioned after the Oslo process for the Israel Palestine conflict: some shared sovereignty and trusteeship but, on paper, two separate states. Legitimacy and its relationship with authority was thus becoming increasingly complicated and scalar. To connect the state, international law and global trade, locally legitimate authorities would have to divest themselves of ethno-nationalism and related economic patronage structures, or religion, and traditional hierarchies of power in both communities, as well as the expansionist goals of both motherlands. All of this is unlikely because these are the foundations of sovereignty and claims to sovereignty that notions of peace are connected with.

The modern state is now increasingly ambiguous in relation to peace and yet, as Cyprus and Palestine illustrate, there is no replacement concept that might be applied, other than a watered down sovereignty under the conditions of regional and global governance. But this does not satisfy nor resolve local, conflicting claims, demands for identity-recognition, rights, autonomy, restitution or self-determination. On paper, territorial sovereignty satisfies parochial claims for legitimate authority but then sets in place a chain reaction of conflicts which undermines it, forcing a shift of level to regional and international forms of neo-trusteeship to overcome the contradictions of nationalism. Yet, these forms of trusteeship suffer from low levels of legitimacy on the ground, even if they have access to resources, leverage and expertise from liberal or neoliberal epistemological frameworks.

One might see similar dynamics in the Northern Ireland conflict, though the alignment of legitimacy across scales is more ambiguous than the 'European solution' to the Cyprus problem envisioned. As in Cyprus, post-colonial legitimacy was construed in very different ways by the two constituent communities, as a sectarian political framework, which was connected to territorial sovereignty and independence. This was in acute tension with the UK's position and interests, as were the Cypriot's ethnonationalist positions with the regional hegemon, Turkey (as well as with Greece). Britain's position was, by the late 1990s, that legitimacy was contained in an EU integrated liberal framework of politics, in which territorialism and autonomy were curtailed by UK and EU integration, boundaries were porous, but also balanced with the confessional politics of the two main communities on the island. Protestant-unionist understandings of legitimacy were related to UK nationalism and associated territorial sovereignty. Catholic-nationalist understandings connected to the struggle for independence from UK hegemony and to be united with the south. What unpicked this circle of centripetal and centrifugal forces, was the framework and material resources offered by the EU, powerful support from the US political establishment, and flexibility on formal sovereignty from the UK government and from the loyalist political community. In particular, the territorial nature of political arrangements was left ambiguous. Legitimacy and all of its different levels and dynamics was thus somehow reconciled into a common framework connecting Ireland with Northern Ireland and the UK, as well as the EU, even though authority remains strongly contested in some pockets, and the territorial settlement, as well as intergroup relations, also remains fragile.

This complex arrangement is full of contradictions when viewed through the sharp corners of the states-system and Weberian notion of sovereignty, but much more feasible when viewed through the prism of rights and equality for individuals. For example, Northern Ireland's inhabitants have the right to identify as Irish, British or both. Thus fudging the local organisation of power and authority allows the liberal peace framework to maintain state and international relations, and supply security and material benefits (to some degree) directly to the population, meaning that ambiguity is more in their interest than sharp nationalist claims. The United Kingdom's 2016 decision to leave the European Union (a departure that did not command support among either of Northern Ireland's communities) constitutes a withdrawal from the constructive ambiguity that underpinned the 1998 Good Friday Agreement.

Similarly, legitimacy in Timor was locally construed through a number of different sources which were only indirectly congruent with the sort of state international actors had in mind after their intervention in 1999 as being legitimate.[15] The UN's role was to establish a liberal state fully integrated into the global economy, with the help of the World Bank.[16] In fact, some elements of locally legitimate authority were completely opposed to the liberal peace, including aspects of self-determination, custom and religion, and the socialist ideology of key political forces and organisations. The two main political parties, the resistance and independence movements, the Catholic Church and the *lisan* all represent key sources of legitimacy, some overlapping and some in conflict.[17] Political parties were problematic to externals because of their ideological components, which also affected the independence movements' positions. The churches and *lisan* were problematic because they conflicted with underlying assumptions of rationality and secularism. Furthermore, these aspects of legitimacy were community-based and propagated hierarchical forms of authority not selected through overt democratic processes nor connected with the state, international law and global economy.[18] These conflicting sources of legitimacy point to decentralised, multiple and plural forms of political authority, which also relate to disaggregated power.[19] They are messy and dynamic, and particularly in relation to their immaterial aspects – such as spiritual belief – defy the neat categories that international actors may prefer.

Yet, as in many other cases of peacebuilding and statebuilding after the end of the Cold War, from Cambodia to Sierra Leone, Liberia, and Bosnia, power and authority tends to be concentrated amongst centralising elites, which draw on international and state level systems of legitimacy, relating to the capture of donor aid, foreign capital, close regional alliances, or the command of the armed forces or national institutions, reverting to political populism and nationalism rather than genuine social legitimacy when elections near. This phenomenon might be described as a form of oligarchic or authoritarian democracy in which the chances that the population will vote for their own rights, equality or peace dividends are minimised by nationalism, sectarianism, the manipulations of elites and global capitalism. For example in Colombia, the peace process between FARC and the government has not queried the legitimacy of the state, though it has contested the legitimacy of the neoliberal economic model in the face of the deprivation of the general population.[20] The extended talks in Havana focused upon resolving this tension without changing the economic model of the state and to the overall detriment of justice claims in some cases. It is easy to see why resolving these different understandings of legitimacy is so difficult: justice issues may well have prevented the FARC from signing an agreement on several levels, and the redistribution of capital is strongly resisted by the country's elites.[21] It is difficult to imagine how law and legitimacy can be built in the face of such a dichotomy, but with the peace agreement in 2016 it looked possible that very significant compromises had been made that leave some, though not all, of these issues outstanding.

These oppositional dynamics are also clearly on view in Afghanistan in the contest between religious and secular forms of authority, and the control of resources for patronage in an environment of acute violence and poverty.[22] The problems of conflicting scales and concepts of legitimacy were most acute where local forms of legitimacy connected to Islamic law, structures of patronage, warlordism, superpower politics and the subsequent state structures, and various social patterns of behaviour did not sit well with liberalism or regulated forms of capitalism. Measured against the enormous military, political and economic resources thrust into the political environment, one can begin to understand the power of these localised and historical forms of legitimacy, authority and power, but also how much tension they are in with liberal norms and values.

Just as national elites have often captured the state in post-conflict contexts, another form of capture may also be at work. Those elites may then be able to capture the attention and resources of international elites. Thus, the governments in Iraq and Afghanistan are propped up by international assistance. To a certain extent, regimes and militias in other states are supported by international elites who use their diplomatic capital to ensure security and stabilisation. The scale of the 'sunk costs' in Afghanistan, Iraq, Myanmar and many other places means that international actors are loathe to walk away from their 'investments'. This is a factor exploited by national elites. They gain legitimacy from the patronage extended to them by international actors. Yet the international actors are so dependent on the national elites remaining in situ that they are hampered in the extent to which they can encourage emancipatory reforms. This 'double capture' – of the state by national elites and of international elites by national elites – is the paradox at the heart of legitimacy contests in post-conflict societies. The legitimacy of international actors (certainly among their domestic audience) is dependent on having reliable partners in the post-conflict country. But this reliability comes at a price. The national elites often become indispensable allies who cannot be pressed too hard on issues of justice and the redistribution of rights, material goods and land.

As Visoka and others haves argued,[23] the case of Kosovo hosts different types of local legitimisation and delegitimisation practices, some connected to intervention, and others to ethnicity. Liberal peacebuilding, state formation and peace formation indicate different centrifugal and centripetal forces, focusing on rights, power and identity or emancipation in often contradictory ways. These forces are legitimised from different quarters and bases, including different local groupings, the state and the international, and cannot be brought into alignment without a complex mixture of power and legitimacy, which cannot be aligned simply. Multiple and incompatible epicentres of local and international legitimacy are also not necessarily closely aligned to power even if they hold legitimacy. Most importantly, and as has often been the case around the world, local customary forms of governance and dispute management, as well as local cultural practices associated with legitimate political authority have been mostly ignored by international intervening actors. Thus peacebuilding has depended upon an external framework for legitimate political authority derived from a liberal political and neoliberal economic exemplar emanating from key western states and economic institutions, propagated by donors and INGOs. This has led to various forms of local resistance and contestation, producing a negative hybrid peace because it has not been able to engage with the presence of multiple centres of international and local authority. The generation of multiple legitimacies is what has led to the Kosovan state, in fact. It can be said that local and social legitimacies, some impacted by international intervention and others largely unchanged by it, have melded with international pressures and dynamics to produce a complex assemblage of legitimacies. For many of the international elites, local and social legitimacies are regarded as somehow backward and anti-modern. There are attempts, often shallow, to mould local and social forms of legitimacy so that they can conform to 'acceptable' forms of legitimacy that can be classed as resilience, social cohesion or indigenous technical knowledge.

In many ways, the 'conflict' between Israel and the Palestinians constitutes a contradiction between the modern state and historical communities, and the different forms of legitimacy they are connected to: international and national law and the organisation of communities.[24] There is a 'traditional' struggle of an impoverished indigenous people for self-determination against a technologically well-equipped settler colonial regime, both holding conflicting claims over the territorial sovereignty that could be established under modern international law. The proposed and generally-accepted 'solution' is based on international law and UN resolutions, both of which are subject to further contradictions. The law of the state versus the laws of the establishing post-colonial state clash, with each other and with popular notions of sovereignty. Legitimacy and authority have been at least discursively aligned for two states: Israel and Palestine living side-by-side. For that reason, in the aftermath of the 1993 Oslo Peace Accords between the PLO and Israel, huge amounts of resources were poured into peacebuilding activities to support the building of infrastructure in the occupied Palestinian territory and the creation of the Palestinian Authority (PA). The goal was to limit and redirect customary authority and its self-determina-tion claims for a new state, to limit the power of the existing state of Israel, in order to come to a compromise arrangement over power, authority, land and borders, whilst maintaining high levels of legitimacy across both communities.[25] But it seems apparent that this can only be achieved if the imbalances of power are moderated by an outside actor, with a higher level of legitimate authority (or power).

The restructured PA interim administration was to be the foundation for a Palestinian state in the areas occupied after 1967, signalling a resolu-tion of the tensions between these multiple claims to legitimate authority. However, almost two decades after the five-year interim period has ended, the peace process is moribund, the PA is unable to govern or provide ser-vices and resources effectively and the Israeli state continues its strategy of settlement.[26] Each framework claims legitimate authority for its own con-stituency and arrangements of power. The fiction of a peace process still has traction for some international actors such as the US and EU. The legiti-mate authority of the Israeli state's strategy of settlement expansion and counterinsurgency arises from its own internal political processes, in turn supported by the US and – to a large degree – the EU. Its controversial posi-tions are widely supported in its own internal politics. The PA position is even more complex because of its internal polarisation between the Gaza Strip (under the control of Hamas) and the West Bank (under the control of Fateh). In general, the PA has struggled to offer the public goods a modern state normally needs to in order to maintain legitimacy, but has been able to compensate with alternative local and international sources relating to dynamics of self-determination, identity and justice.

Hybrid forms of legitimacy have emerged in the interplay of local and international peacebuilding in the South Pacific, connecting to post-colonial forms of peace and state formation.[27] International peacebuild-ing interventions in post-conflict Timor-Leste, Bougainville (Papua New Guinea), the Solomon Islands and others rapidly turned to the develop-ment of local sensitivity about alternative forms of political authority, out-side of the experience of the western, liberal state framework, which in turn began to produce what might be described as hybrid forms of peace.[28] They have been confronted with local realities which have forced them to modify Weberian and modernisation oriented understandings of the state, more characterised by relationality and the co-existence and entanglement of a variety of legitimate political authorities and competing understandings of legitimacy. This is a regional phenomenon, which can also be discerned across much of the world's political systems if one looks hard enough, where different forms of authority are entangled with the state as the prime force by virtue of its sovereignty, military and economic capacity and provision of services. But the state is not the sole authority, even if it struggles to maintain a monopoly, a fact which is very clear in places such as Timor-Leste or the Solomon Islands. In particular, non-state local customary actors and institutions offer alternative and widely accepted forms of legitimacy that predate the modern state by a large margin. Sometimes they offer more services than the state can and are better able to connect the cultural expectations of many inhabitants. The type of state that is being constructed via external intervention is focused on alien concepts of human rights, democracy, and monetised and formal marketization, with little capacity to provide public services or security in return (as a form of modern state social contract). In the course of peace and state formation legitimacy, governance, and the state has been hybridised often in agonistic and awkward ways, with new forms and understandings of legitimacy emerging.[29] These hybrid legitimacies are often ungainly and contradictory. They offer citizens in post-conflict contexts a difficult path to navigate in the search for security and material goods, and in terms of fulfilling immaterial ambitions such as identity claims and religious recognition. Where they have agency, national elites, as well as individuals and groups of individuals, will move between routes and types of legitimacy.

These hybrid legitimacies also encourage us to think of the temporalities of legitimacy and how legitimacies originally established in one time period adapt and are overlaid with other legitimacies. Some what might be called 'legacy legitimacies' might last for a long period and remain relatively unchallenged and unchanged. Other forms of legitimacy might be disruptive to established legitimacies. The result is a complex assemblage of legitimacies that form a jumbled sedimentation. This might be especially problematic for international actors and others who might feel that a 'new start' is possible. The difficult task for interveners is to find a balance between pre-existing and emergent legitimacies in contexts that are likely to be fluid and be prone to a mix of local, national, international and transnational dynamics.

The centralisation and aggregation of power in the ideal liberal, neo-liberal, or authoritarian-capitalist states prevalent today have difficulty reconciling such multiplicities of legitimate authority, whether charismatic, historical, cultural or religious, or even if aimed at the accretion of high levels of rights beyond the basic human rights framework. This means that modern legitimate authority has come to rest on the accumulation of territory and wealth through self-help within fixed geopolitical boundaries. Capital is often unregulated but people are bureaucratically and legally constrained. This is seen as a short cut to a stable political order, but it has actually blocked the search for ever more sophisticated forms of justice and thus the reconstitution of legitimate political authority for the modern era in conflict-affected societies. This tension has caused the breakdown of both liberal internationalism and neoliberalism, leaving the modern state remaining as the final arbiter of authority and legitimacy. In other words, conflict-affected societies are afflicted by nineteenth century solutions to fast moving conflicts. They are barely governed, except in a unilateral and inconsistent manner by international peacebuilding and development, but often controlled more firmly by predatory local political actors. Modern legitimate authority is constrained by its own internal nationalism and geo-political position.

History has come full circle in some senses: the state was once the source of emancipation through nationalism and imperialism but this process produced negative forms of peace based upon local and international exclusion; then through internationalism, regionalism and neoliberalism, reducing the state to a night-watchman under the conditions of global governance in the hope of producing more positive forms of peace, which ended up being constrained by Eurocentric biases. The fragmentation of the state's power through both constitutional checks and balances and the liberal peace architecture was an intentional response to the failure of balancing and the emergence of industrial arms races and war. The goal was to foreground the rights and claims of conflict-affected citizens, to produce hybrid and positive forms of peace.

Now once again, the state is the site of security and closure, whilst exploiting or accommodating capital and technology. Debates about legitimacy are being once again connected to nationalism rather than rights and critical forms of emancipation. This, as can be seen from the cases in this volume, has made it difficult to achieve multi-dimensional, multi-level, and hybrid forms of legitimacy, and practice has diverged from scientific findings about the conditions now necessary for peace. Either international norms are the source of legitimacy, buttressed by weak or strong interventionism, or the state remains its key site, but raises support through nationalism. Where neither international nor state capacity is strong enough, local forms of legitimate authority are more prominent but challenge the dominance of international human rights norms or elite power. Yet, the hoped for liberal alignment of international, state and society, has not emerged. Instead, as our cases show, these three aspects of legitimacy remain in tense relationships, producing agonistic and hybrid forms, which are often exploited by state level actors, or rejected or appropriated by international level actors. However, what is clear from the last three decades' worth of peacebuilding experience is that state and international legitimacy are inadequate when measured against the claims connected to hybrid and positive forms of peace and their implied relationality, mobility and networked nature. This in fact connects legitimacy not to efficacy of provision or sovereignty and power, but to broader forms of global justice.[30]

The resolution of the tensions between liberal, neoliberal and capital-ist-authoritarian states are essential for peace, and it is clear that successful legitimate authority throughout history, measured in terms of peacefulness, has been relational and networked rather than centrifugally centred on a single state, government or charismatic figure. A broader and more local-ised perspective is politically necessary. Quite simply, this points to the fact that the capitalist and liberal modes of state development in the modern era may not be closely compatible with positive and hybrid forms of peace, or the expansion of rights necessary because they still perpetuate modes of domination, whether through liberal ontologies or capitalist rationalities. However, it is also clear that the state and the international communities have been platforms for an elucidation of ever more expanded notions of rights in order to capture legitimacy, especially from the more aspira-tional perspective of global and civil society. The 'local-local', however, often tends to be rather more suspicious of both. Furthermore, the ideal of an advanced state is itself contested and nowhere fully stable or complete without these relational but agonistic ontologies that require rights, equal-ity and justice to be seen in a regional or global perspective. Yet, more critical positions suggest that such common and cosmopolitan agendas are unlikely, and that it is futile to try to align local, state, and domestic legitimacy and authority into a common system of law and institutions, especially because of the remaining historical and distributive forms of injustice in the international system.

Thus, the practice of intervention under the framework of complemen-tarity and subsidiarity indicates that policymakers reject both the redressal required for global justice, and the notion that the liberal state is only legitimate under particular circumstances. Local legitimacy is still seen as marginal, the state is the key site of legitimacy, and should be aligned with international norms, governed by global institutions. This is not a relational, networked and hybrid system, but a hub and spoke, top-down framework. This position indicates that alignment is actually counterpro-ductive, and that governance must be more communitarian at the local and state level, but also that at the international level legitimacy can only be maintained in the light of progress towards global justice. This seems to be a workable contradiction, whereby local legitimacy is subsumed into a broader liberal-governmental project. In a range of our contemporary cases, both of these models can be seen in motion and in tension with each other, as outlined above. In practice, peacebuilding and statebuilding have sought to make local systems of law and institutions align themselves with international systems in a common system of legitimacy. Yet practice would have been better off mediated by a range of normative, cultural, political and structural differences, if stability and justice were the aim of societies, states, and international actors and leadership. In other words, top-down forms of legitimacy, otherwise known as norm-cascades, generally have failed to receive popular support unless they are compromised by self-determination or other local constraints, such as identity hierarchies. This produces a paradox: multiple forms of legitimacy must be balanced for sustainable peace and yet, as the liberal peace project has shown in the last thirty years, peacebuilding has tended to emanate from civil society and international actors whose legitimacy at popular, state and international levels is minimal. Neo-trusteeship oriented models of legitimacy have arisen as a consequence, but this has made it even more unlikely that legitimacy across the scales or levels of analysis can be reconciled fully in the architecture of the state. Both top-down and bottom-up frameworks for legitimacy are unlikely to be relational or without power imbalances, undermining authority rather than coalescing around a new peace project inherent in the state.

* * *

To conclude, the connection of power, ethnography, authority and legitimacy with existing forms of conflict-affected state and international frameworks (in the context of geo-economics) clearly indicates the limits of systems of top-down and bottom-up forms of domination and self-interest. It points to the logic of the Kantian, Roussean or Lockean social contract where legitimate authority, international law and a modern state connect closely with localised social practices and conventions as the basis for legitimacy in conflict-affected environments in far more relational terms. The limits of the liberal and realist form of social contract are also on display in that it neither has a single authority nor the power to reform or change systems of politics and authority under the legacy of multiple power-relations that conflicts often carry. Nor does it often have the vision necessary for post-colonial developments in the more relational and hybrid terms peace now seems to require. Fundamentally, as repeated violent conflicts and uprisings show, the traditional social contract allied to an inflexible state model keeps breaking down.

The case studies in this volume indicate a far more complex array of legitimacies, which are difficult to harness into a united and universal system, run by the state or the international community. Broader, relational, multi-scalar and hybrid forms of legitimacy are both necessary but complex, and are always in motion, backwards and forwards. This means that peace's connection with legitimate authority is shifting away from the state as its sole nexus, or the international community as its trustee, but the ethnographic, local perspective on legitimacy also indicates that it can no longer be thought of solely according to power or legal-bureaucratic relationalities. Increasingly, it would seem, claims for new legitimate authority are being connected to social, distributive and global justice, but also with community perspectives. These claims are networked, mobile and technological, not 'parochial'. They forge modernities that are different from the 'approved' modernities of the bureaucratic-rational model. This is a 'new' tension that peace and IR scholars might engage with, although to do so it would be prudent to take on methods and insights from anthropology, sociology and gender studies. From these perspectives, the modern state and the international communities diverge towards matters of territory, boundaries, centralised authority or neo-colonial forms of normative and political oversight.

The point of legitimate political authority and its association with the modern liberal international and state is to capture it for long enough to establish the ground for the next development. This is the moment of interregnum we currently inhabit where the old notion of peace through the liberal state and the liberal international system, allied with neoliberal forms of globalisation and cosmopolitanism, has become moribund: but the new is yet to emerge in anything other than disjointed form. A return to political nativism in the US and the UK, and the EU's introspective dynamic, means that the usual self-appointed leaders of the international community seem too pre-occupied to articulate a new vision. In the interregnum we see Russian and Chinese foreign policy assertiveness, but this has little say on political legitimacy. Where alternative forms of legitimacy are eked out, this is often in marginal and 'hard to see' spaces, and does not – as yet – constitute a systemic alternative with a joined up ideological prospectus. Despite well-intentioned reform initiatives, there is a sense of drift and few genuine moves to address power imbalances.

Questions such as who has the moral right to govern in the modern world (and how to connect this right with actual capacity) are open once again. If not international actors, political elites or financial actors, then societal actors? Some argue that peace as governance may not be run by experts anymore, but more likely by algorithms under new technological conditions,[31] but there is little sign of this so far: power and order are still humanly contested everywhere. In cases of war endings, it might be that international actors need to govern through a liberal-local system of trusteeship to maintain both local and international forms of hybrid legitimacy in the short term, while being protected from geopolitical and geo-economic forces that feed off conflict rather than cooperation, at least briefly, as in Afghanistan, Iraq, Bosnia, Kosovo or Timor-Leste. In cases of low-level violence, or the implementation of peace agreements, or for development purposes, national elites may rule. In the medium term, however, it is clear that such legitimate authority cannot survive for long (as can be seen in Kosovo). Where even this is difficult, local people organise their own systems of government where they can, but under these conditions, as in Syria recently, power, legitimacy and authority are fragmented, meaning that the capacity to provide major public goods – including security – is minimal. The legitimacy of governance in either set of cases is clearly connected to its norms, identity, historical resonance and effectiveness, and it now reaches across international networks and scales.

Political legitimacy in conflict affected regions and related to contemporary matters of peace now emanates from multiple sources in hybrid form, broadening conceptions of justice-making for what Lake has called 'relational authority'. This indicates legitimate authority and hierarchy develop across a range of local to global scales based upon mutually agreed rights, duties and responsibilities.[32] It points to the existence of a wide range of emergent forms of the social contract in a global context, dependent upon context, society and power structures. These are being mediated to produce narrow and unstable or broader forms of peace. This collection of essays indicates that the latter are increasingly connected to conceptions global justice and thus imply a reinvented conception of legitimate political authority across different scales.

Notes

1. Richmond and Mac Ginty, 'Mobilities and peace', pp. 606–24.
2. For example, Doyle, Michael W., *Ways of War and Peace* (New York: W. W. Norton, 1997).
3. Ker-Lindsay and Economides, 'Standards before status before accession: Kosovo's EU perspective'.
4. Parish, 'Demise of the Dayton Protectorate', pp. 11–23.
5. Dodge, 'Iraq: The contradictions of exogenous state-building in historical perspective', pp. 187–200.
6. See my earlier book, Richmond, *Failed Statebuilding*.
7. Thakur, 'R2P after Libya and Syria: engaging emerging powers', pp. 61–76.

8. Alvarez-Ossorio, 'Syria's struggling civil society: the Syrian uprising', pp. 23–32; Geha, 'Understanding Libya's civil society', <http://www.mei.edu/content/map/understanding-libya-s-civil-society>

9. Mac Ginty, 'Post-legitimacy and post-legitimisation: A convergence of western and non-western intervention', pp. 251–5.

10. Anastasiou, *The Broken Olive Branch: Nationalism, Ethnic Conflict and the Quest for Peace in Cyprus: The Impasse of Ethnonationalism*; Hannay, *Cyprus: The Search for a Solution*; Dodd, *The History and Politics of the Cyprus Conflict*.

11. Ker-Lindsay, James, *EU Accession and UN Peacemaking in Cyprus*.

12. Dodd, *The Political, Social and Economic Development of Northern Cyprus*.

13. Richmond, 'Decolonisation and post-independence causes of conflict: the case of Cyprus'.

14. Princen, *Intermediaries in International Conflict*.

15. Wallis, 'A liberal-local hybrid peace project in action? The increasing engagement between the local and the liberal in Timor-Leste', pp. 735–61; Trindade, 'Reconciling conflicting paradigms: an East Timorese vision of the ideal state'.

16. UNDP, *Building Blocks for a Nation: The Common Country Assessment for East Timor*.

17. Nixon, 'The crisis of governance in new subsistence states.'

18. Pereira and Lete Koten, 'Dynamics of democracy at the "suku" level', pp. 222–35.

19. Volker et al., *On Hybrid Political Orders and Emerging States: What is Failing – States in the Global South or Research and Politics in the West?*, pp.15–35.

20. Aviles, 'Paramilitarism and Colombia's Low-Intensity Democracy', pp. 379–408.

21. Franz, 'The ends of peace', <https://www.jacobinmag.com/2016/09/colombia-farc-santos-uribe-paramilitaries-drugs>

22. Higashi, *Challenges of Constructing Legitimacy in Peacebuilding: Afghanistan, Iraq, Sierra Leone, and East Timor*.

23. Visoka and Bolton, 'The complex nature and implications of international engagement after Kosovo's independence'; see also Lemay-Hébert, 'Everyday legitimacy and international administration: global governance and local legitimacy in Kosovo', pp. 87–104.

24. Aide, 'Violence and statebuilding in a borders conflict context: a study of the Israeli–Palestinian conflict', pp. 261–77.

25. Turner, 'Completing the circle: peacebuilding as colonial practice in the occupied Palestinian Territory', pp. 492–507.

26. Bishara, *Palestine/Israel: peace or apartheid*, p. 133.

27. See for example, Clements et al., 'State building reconsidered: the role of hybridity in the formation of political order', pp. 45–56; Wallis et al., 'Political reconciliation in Timor-Leste, Solomon Islands and Bougainville: the dark side of hybridity', pp. 159–78.

28. Richmond, *A Post-Liberal Peace*.

29. Ibid.

30. Pogge, 'World Poverty and Human Rights', pp. 1–7.

31. Harari, *Homo Deus*, p. 307.

32. Lake, *Hierarchy in International Relations*, pp. 8, 10.

References

Aide, Esu, 'Violence and statebuilding in a borders conflict context: a study of the Israeli–Palestinian conflict', *Journal of Intervention and Statebuilding*, 2016, 10: 2, pp. 261–77.

Alvarez-Ossorio, Ignacio, 'Syria's struggling civil society: the Syrian uprising', *Middle East Quarterly*, Spring 2012, pp. 23–32.

Anastasiou, Harry, *The Broken Olive Branch: Nationalism, Ethnic Conflict and the Quest for Peace in Cyprus: The Impasse of Ethnonationalism* (Syracuse: Syracuse University Press, 2008).

Anderson, Mary B., Dayna Brown and Isabella Jean, *Time to Listen: Hearing People on the Receiving End of International Aid* (Cambridge, MA: CDA, 2012).

Applebaum, Arthur Isak, 'Legitimacy without the Duty to Obey', Philosophy & *Public Affairs*, 2010, 38: 3, pp. 215–39.

Avilés, William, 'Paramilitarism and Colombia's low-intensity democracy', *Journal of Latin American Studies*, 2006, 38: 2, pp. 379–408.

Beetham, David, *The Legitimation of Power* (Houndmills: Palgrave Macmillan, 1991).

Bellina, Séverine, Dominique Darbon, Stein Sundstøl Eriksen, Ole Jacob Sending, *The Legitimacy of the State in Fragile Situations. Report for the OECD DAC International Network on Conflict and Fragility* (Paris: OECD, 2009).

Bishara, Marwan, *Palestine/Israel: peace or apartheid* (London: Zed Books, 2003), p. 133.

Boege, Volker, M. Anne Brown, Kevin Clements and Anna Nolan, *On Hybrid Political Orders and Emerging States: State Formation in the Context of 'Fragility'* (Berlin: Berghof Research Centre for Constructive Conflict Management, 2008).

Boege, Volker, M. Anne Brown, Kevin Clements and Anna Nolan, *On Hybrid Political Orders and Emerging States: What is Failing – States in the Global South or Research and Politics in the West?* Berghof Handbook Dialogue Series, no. 8 (Berlin, Berghof Research Centre for Constructive Conflict Management, 2009), pp. 15–35.

Buchanan, Allen and Robert O. Keohane, 'The Legitimacy of Global Governance Institutions', *Ethics and International Affairs*, 2006, 20: 4, pp. 405–37.

Clements, Kevin, Volker Boege, Anne Brown, Wendy Foley, and Anna Nolan, 'State building reconsidered: the role of hybridity in the formation of political order', *Political Science*, 2007, 59: 1, pp. 45–56.

Cook, Deborah J. 'Legitimacy and Political Violence: A Habermasian Perspective', *Social Justice*, 2003, 30: 3, pp. 108–26.

Di Palma, Giuseppe, *The Modern State Subverted* (Colchester: ECPR, 2013).

Dodd, Clement, *The Political, Social and Economic Development of Northern Cyprus* (Tallahassee, FL: Eothen Press, 1993).

Dodd, Clement, *The History and Politics of the Cyprus Conflict* (London: Palgrave Macmillan, 2010).

Dodge, Toby, 'Iraq: The contradictions of exogenous state-building in historical perspective', *Third World Quarterly*, 2006, 27: 1, pp. 187–200.

Englebert, Pierre, *State Legitimacy and Development in Africa* (Boulder: Lynne Rienner, 2000).

Finnemore, Martha and Kathryn Sikkink, 'International norm dynamics and political change', *International Organization* 1998, 52: Autumn, pp. 887–917.

Franz, Tobias, 'The ends of peace', *Jacobin,* 26 September 2016, <https://www.jacobinmag.com/2016/09/colombia-farc-santos-uribe-paramilitaries-drugs>

Geha, Carmen, 'Understanding Libya's civil society', *Middle East Institute,* 22 November 2016, <http://www.mei.edu/content/map/understanding-libya-s-civil-society> (last accessed 16 March 2020).

Hannay, David, *Cyprus: The Search for a Solution* (London: I.B. Tauris, 2005).

Harari, Yuval Noah, *Homo Deus* (London: Vintage, 2016), p. 307.

Higashi, Daisaku, *Challenges of Constructing Legitimacy in Peacebuilding: Afghanistan, Iraq, Sierra Leone and East Timor* (London: Routledge, 2015).

Hurd, Ian, 'Legitimacy and authority in international politics', *International Organization*, 1999, 53: 2, pp. 379–408.

Inbal, Aliza Belman and Hanna Lerner, 'Constitutional design, identity, and legitimacy in post-conflict reconstruction', in Derick W. Brinkerhoff (ed.), *Governance in Post-Conflict Societies. Rebuilding Fragile States* (London: Routledge, 2007).

Keohane, Robert, *Governance and Legitimacy. SFB-Governance Lecture Series No. 1* (Berlin: SFB, 2007).

Ker-Lindsay, James, *EU Accession and UN Peacemaking in Cyprus* (London: Palgrave Macmillan, 2005).

Ker-Lindsay, James and Spyros Economides, 'Standards before status before accession: Kosovo's EU perspective', *Journal of Balkan and Near Eastern Studies,* 2012, 14.

Lake, David A., *Hierarchy in International Relations* (Ithaca, NY: Cornell University Press, 2009), pp. 8, 10.

Lemay-Hébert, Nicolas, 'Everyday legitimacy and international administration: global governance and local legitimacy in Kosovo', *Journal of Intervention and Statebuilding,* 2013, 7: 1, pp. 87–104.

Lentz, Carola, 'The chief, the mine captain and the politician: legitimating power in Northern Ghana', *Africa,* 1998, 68: 1, pp. 46–67.

Levi, Margaret and Audrey Sachs, 'Legitimating Beliefs: Sources and Indicators', *Regulation and Government,* 2009, 3: 4, pp. 311–33.

Lipset, Seymour M. *Political Man* (New York: Doubleday, 1960).

Mac Ginty, Roger, 'Post-legitimacy and post-legitimisation: A convergence of western and non-western intervention', *Conflict Security and Development* 2019, 19: 3, pp. 251–5.

Menkhaus, Ken, The rise of a mediated state in Northern Kenya: The Wajir story and its implications for state-building, *Africa Focus* 2008, 21: 2.

Nathan, Laurie, *No Ownership, No Peace: The Darfur Peace Agreement.* Working Paper No. 5 (London: Crisis States Research Centre, LSE, 2006).

Nathan, Laurie, *A Clash of Norms and Strategies in Madagascar.* Mediation Arguments No. 4. (Pretoria: Centre for Mediation in Africa, 2013).

Nixon, Rod, 'The crisis of governance in new subsistence states,' *Journal of Contemporary Asia*, 2006, 36: 1.

Odendaal, Andries, *A Crucial Link. Local Peace Committees and National Peacebuilding.* (Washington, DC: USIP, 2013).

OECD, *The State's Legitimacy in Fragile Situations. Unpacking Complexity.* (Paris: OECD, 2010).

OECD-DAC, *Supporting Statebuilding in Situations of Conflict and Fragility: Policy Guidance.* DAC Guidelines and References Series (Paris: OECD, 2011).

Papagianni, K. 'Participation and state legitimation', in Call, Charles T. (ed.) *Building States to Build Peace* (Boulder and London: Lynne Rienner, 2008).

Parish, Matthew, 'Demise of the Dayton Protectorate', *Intervention and Statebuilding*, 2007, pp. 11–23.

Pereira, Martinho and Maria Madalena Lete Koten, 'Dynamics of democracy at the "suku" level', *Local-Global: Identity, Security, Community*, 2012, 11, pp. 222–35.

Pogge, Thomas, 'World poverty and human rights', *Ethics & International Affairs*, 2012, 19: 01, pp. 1–7.

Princen, Thomas, *Intermediaries in International Conflict* (Princeton: Princeton University Press, 1992).

Rawls, John, *A Theory of Justice* (Cambridge, MA: Harvard University Press, 1971).

Richmond, Oliver P., 'Decolonisation and post-independence causes of conflict: the case of Cyprus', *Civil Wars*, 2002, 5: 3.

Richmond, Oliver P., *A Post-Liberal Peace* (London: Routledge, 2011).

Richmond, Oliver P., *Failed Statebuilding* (New Haven: Yale University Press, 2014).

Richmond, Oliver P. and Roger Mac Ginty, 'Mobilities and peace', *Globalizations* 2019, 16: 5, pp. 606–24.

Scharpf, Fritz F., 'Legitimacy in normative and positive theory: comments on Robert O. Keohane', in *SFB-Governance Lecture Series No. 1* (Berlin: SFB, 2007).

Seabrooke, Leonard, *Bringing Legitimacy Back in to Neo-Weberian State Theory and International Relations. Working Paper 2002/6.* (Canberra: RSPAS, Australian National University, 2002).

Schmelzle, Cord, *Effectiveness and Legitimacy in Areas of Limited.*

Statehood SFB-Governance, Working Paper Series 26 (Berlin: DFG Research Center (SFB), 2011).

Stover, Eric and Harvey M. Weinstein (eds), *My Neighbour, My Enemy: Justice and Community in the Aftermath of Mass Atrocity* (Cambridge: Cambridge University Press, 2004).

Thakur, Ramesh, 'R2P after Libya and Syria: engaging emerging powers', *The Washington Quarterly*, 2013, 36: 2, pp. 61–76.

Trindade, Josh, 'Reconciling conflicting paradigms: an East Timorese vision of the ideal state', in Mearns, David (ed.), *Democratic Governance in Timor-Leste* (Darwin: Charles Darwin University Press, 2008).

Turner, Mandy, 'Completing the circle: peacebuilding as colonial practice in the occupied Palestinian Territory', *International Peacekeeping*, 2012, 19: 5, pp. 492–507.

Visoka, Gezim and Grace Bolton, 'The complex nature and implications of international engagement after Kosovo's independence', *Civil Wars*, 2011, 13: 2.

Wallis, Joanne, 'A liberal-local hybrid peace project in action? The increasing engagement between the local and the liberal in Timor-Leste', *Review of International Studies*, 2012, 38: 4, pp. 735–61.

Wallis, Joanne, Renee Jeffery and Lia Kent, 'Political reconciliation in Timor-Leste, Solomon Islands and Bougainville: the dark side of hybridity', *Australian Journal of International Affairs*, 2016, 70: 2, pp. 159–78.

Weber, Max, *On Charisma and Institution Building: Selected Papers*, S. N. Eisendtadt (ed.) (Chicago: The University of Chicago Press, 1968).

Weber, Max, *Economy and Society. An outline of interpretive sociology*. G. Roth and C. Wittich (eds), (Berkeley, Los Angeles and London: University of California Press, 1978).

Weber, Max, *From Max Weber. Essays in Sociology*, H. H. Gerth and C. Wright Mills (eds), (London: Routledge, 1991).

Wellman, Christopher Heath, 'Toward a liberal theory of political obligation', *Ethics* 2001, 111: 4, pp. 735–59.

Wendt, Alexander, *Social Theory of International Politics* (Cambridge: Cambridge University Press, 1999).

The World Bank, 'Conflict, security and development', *World Development Report 2011* (Washington, DC: World Bank, 2011).

Unger, Barbara, Stina Lundström, Katrin Planta and Beatrix Austin (eds), *Peace Infrastructures. Assessing Concept and Practice*, Berghof Handbook Series 10 (Berlin: Berghof Foundation, 2013).

United Nations Development Programme (UNDP), *Building Blocks for a Nation: The Common Country Assessment for East Timor*. (Dili, Timor-Leste: UNDP, 2000).

United Nations Department of Peacekeeping Operations, *Capstone Doctrine: Peacekeeping Operations: Principles and Guidelines* (New York: DPKO, 2008).

United Nations, *UN Peacebuilding: An Orientation* (New York: UN, 2010).

United Nations, *Guidance for Effective Mediation* (New York: UN, 2012).

EU representative:
Easy Access System Europe
Mustamäe tee 50, 10621 Tallinn, Estonia
Gpsr.requests@easproject.com

www.ingramcontent.com/pod-product-compliance
Lightning Source LLC
Chambersburg PA
CBHW051953270326
41929CB00015B/2631